European Yearbook of International Economic Law

EYIEL Monographs - Studies in European and International Economic Law

Volume 36

Series Editor

Marc Bungenberg, Saarbrücken, Germany

Christoph Herrmann, Passau, Germany

Markus Krajewski, Erlangen, Germany

Jörg Philipp Terhechte, Lüneburg, Germany

Andreas R. Ziegler, Lausanne, Switzerland

EYIEL Monographs is a subseries of the European Yearbook of International Economic Law (EYIEL). It contains scholarly works in the fields of European and international economic law, in particular WTO law, international investment law, international monetary law, law of regional economic integration, external trade law of the EU and EU internal market law. The series does not include edited volumes. EYIEL Monographs are peer-reviewed by the series editors and external reviewers.

Kornilia Pipidi-Kalogirou

Regulatory Cooperation Chapters in the new Generation FTAS

Legitimacy Requirements for their Manifestation and Interaction with the EU Legal Order

 Springer

Kornilia Pipidi-Kalogirou
Brussels, Belgium

ISSN 2364-8392 ISSN 2364-8406 (electronic)
European Yearbook of International Economic Law
ISSN 2524-6658 ISSN 2524-6666 (electronic)
EYIEL Monographs - Studies in European and International Economic Law
ISBN 978-3-031-71899-1 ISBN 978-3-031-71900-4 (eBook)
https://doi.org/10.1007/978-3-031-71900-4

Dissertation zur Erlangung des Grades eines Doktors der Rechtswissenschaft (Dr. iur) der Deutschen Universität für Verwaltungswissenschaften Speyer

This Springer imprint is published by the registered company Springer Nature Switzerland AG
The registered company address is: Gewerbestrasse 11, 6330 Cham, Switzerland

If disposing of this product, please recycle the paper.

Contents

Abbreviations

AB	Appellate Body
AG	Advocate General
ASEAN	Association of Southeast Asian Nations
BRICS	Brazil, Russia, India, China, and South Africa
CCP	Common Commercial Policy
CEN	European Committee for Standardization
CENELEC	European Committee for Electrotechnical Standardization
CETA	Comprehensive Economic and Trade Agreement
CJEU	Court of Justice of the European Union
CSF	Civil Society Forum
CSFP	Common Security and Foreign Policy
DAG	Domestic Advisory Group
DDA	Doha Development Agenda
DG JUST	Directorate General for Justice and Consumers
DG SANTE	Directorate General for Health and Food Safety
DSM	Dispute Settlement Mechanism
EC	European Communities
ECJ	European Court of Justice
EESC	European Economic and Social Committee
EMA	European Medicines Agency
EPA	Economic Partnership Agreement
EU	European Union
FTA	Free Trade Agreement
GATS	General Agreement on Trade in Services
GATT	General Agreement on Tariffs and Trade
GDPR	General Data Protection Regulation
GMP	GMPS
GRP	Good Regulatory Practice
HLRCF	High Level Regulatory Cooperation Forum
ICT	Information and Communications Technology
IIA	Inter-institutional Agreement

IoT	Internet of Things
IRC	International Regulatory Cooperation
KOREU FTA	EU-South Korea FTA
LOD	Limit of Detection
MFN	Most Favored Nation
MOU	Memorandum of Understanding
MRA	Mutual Recognition Agreement
MRL	Maximum Residue Level
NAFTA	North Atlantic FTA
NATO	North Atlantic Treaty Organization
NGO	Non-governmental organization
NRA	National Regulatory Authority
NT	National Treatment
OECD	Organization for Economic Cooperation and Development
OIV	Organization for Wine and Vine
PPP	Plant Protection Products
RADAR	Regulatory Action Depot/Dépôt d'Actions Réglementaires
RAPEX	Rapid Alert System for non-food consumer products
RCB	Regulatory Cooperation Body
RCC	Regulatory Cooperation Council
RCF	Regulatory Cooperation Forum
REFIT	Regulatory Fitness and Performance Programme
SINGEU FTA	EU-Singapore FTA
SME	Small Medium Enterprise
SPP	Security and Prosperity Partnership
SPS	Sanitary and Phytosanitary measures
TBT	Technical Barriers to Trade
TEC	Transatlantic Economic Council
TEP	Transatlantic Economic Partnership
TEU	Treaty on the European Union
TFEU	Treaty on the Functioning of the European Union
TRIPS	Trade-Related Aspects of Intellectual Property Rights
TTIP	Transatlantic Trade and Investment Partnership
TTIP	Transatlantic Trade and Investment Partnership
UK	United Kingdom
USA/US	United States of America/United States
USMCA	United States-Mexico-Canada Agreement
VCLT	Vienna Convention on the Law of the Treaties
VCLT-IO	Vienna Convention on the Law of the Treaties-International
WHO	World Health Organization
WTO	World Trade Organization

Chapter 1
Introduction

1.1 Research Context

The last decade marks an important paradigm shift for the trade policy of the European Union (hereinafter EU). During the past decade, after lengthy procedures and year-long negotiations, the EU has emerged as an ever-growing international trade leader. Among its victories, it counts the conclusion of a series of bilateral Free Trade Agreements (hereinafter FTAs) with various global partners, such as Canada,[1] Japan,[2] Singapore,[3] Vietnam,[4] South Korea[5]; the successful termination of

---

[1] Council Decision (EU) 2017/37 of 28 October 2016 on the signing on behalf of the European Union of the Comprehensive Economic and Trade Agreement (CETA) between Canada, of the one part, and the European Union and its Member States, of the other part [2017] OJ L 11/1 (hereinafter CETA).

[2] Council Decision (EU) 2018/966 of 6 July 2018 on the signing, on behalf of the European Union, of the Agreement between the European Union and Japan for an Economic Partnership [2018] OJ L 174/1 (hereinafter EU-Japan EPA).

[3] Council Decision (EU) 2018/1599 of 15 October 2018 on the signing, on behalf of the European Union, of the FTA between the European Union and the Republic of Singapore [2018] OJ L 267/1 (hereinafter EU- Singapore FTA).

[4] Council Decision (EU) 2019/1121 of 25 June 2019 on the signing, on behalf of the European Union, of the FTA between the European Union and the Socialist Republic of Viet Nam [2019] OJ L 177/1 (hereinafter EU-Vietnam FTA).

[5] 2011/265/EU: Council Decision of 16 September 2010 on the signing, on behalf of the European Union, and provisional application of the FTA between the European Union and its Member States, of the one part, and the Republic of Korea, of the other part [2011] OJ L 127/1 (hereinafter EU Korea FTA).

negotiations with Mercosur[6] and partially Mexico[7] and the launch of negotiations with a couple of other strategic trade actors, such as Australia[8] and New Zealand.[9] This proactive trade agenda, inspired by the EU Commission Global Europe Communication of 2006 is a coordinated response to an international trade regime which evolves in directions different to the original ones, which focused on multilateralsim.[10] Through its gradual expansion, it aims to re-affirm the EU's actorness in the global trade arena since the rise of Asia and the BRICS countries challenge the traditional EU-US monopoly in international trade politics. Most importantly, however, it adapts content-wise to the new trade challenges and harnesses the benefits of further trade liberalization through the promotion of forms of deeper integration that guarantee enhanced market access to the concerned markets.

The need for a fresh view on the regulation of international trade stems firstly from the insufficiency of the older disciplines to effectively address contemporary barriers to trade liberalization. Indeed, the international trade regime as introduced with the General Agreement on Trade and Tariffs (hereinafter GATT) 1947 that emerged after the end of the Second World War focused on the reduction of burdensome tariffs and import quotas on the basis of the principle of non-discrimination.[11] In that sense, GATT acted as a catalyst to the sophistication of the global regime. Despite their earlier success, such disciplines nowadays fall short of successfully following the imperatives of contemporary production and business operation. The dependence of production upon internationalised value chains and the ease by which firms can now relocate to seek more favourable environments, thanks to contemporary means of transport and technological developments, has highlighted the need for adjustment and re-assessment of regulatory frameworks so as to reconcile the so-called 'deep disciplines' with liberalizing trade objectives.[12] As 'deep' are characterized the disciplines that focus on the convergence of regulatory areas such as competition, public procurement, intellectual property, investment, financial regulation, health and safety standards, areas that are not directly related to trade, but can severely impact it.[13] The sudden apparition of these barriers however, is not unconnected to the previous disciplines, on

---

[6]Council Decision of 22 March 1999 concerning the conclusion, on behalf of the European Community, of the interregional framework cooperation agreement between the European Community and its Member States, of the one part, and the Southern Common Market and its Party States, of the other part [1999] OJ L 112/65.

[7]EU Commission, 'EU-Mexico Agreement in Principle' <https://trade.ec.europa.eu/doclib/docs/2018/april/tradoc_156791.pdf>.

[8]EU Council, 'Negotiating directives for a FTA with Australia' <https://www.consilium.europa.eu/media/35794/st07663-ad01dc01-en18.pdf>.

[9]EU Council, 'Negotiating directives for a FTA with New Zealand' <https://www.consilium.europa.eu/media/35796/st07661-ad01dc01-en18.pdf>.

[10]EU Commission (2006a).

[11]Araujo (2016), p. 14.

[12]Araujo (2016), p. 14.

[13]EU Commission (2006b), p. 19.

non-discrimination, that are now in need of reassessment. In fact, it would not be a hyperbole to say that the insufficiency of the old rules primarily reflects their earlier success, the fact that they efficiently tackled the trade obstacles for which they were employed. It was indeed the successful elimination of these 'first-line' barriers during the first liberalization rounds that led to the appearance of the next strand of trade barriers to the spotlight, the ones that took the form of internal regulation.[14]

Such regulatory measures, long before falling under the external trade agenda, have been employed by governments to serve as means to the achievement of a legitimate national policy. While this remained their primary function in the domestic agenda of states, they increasingly met considerable increase, this time as trade barriers, to the detriment of other protectionist measures, as are the classic tariffs or the core non-tariff barriers (anti-dumping and countervailing duties, quotas, licences). Their augmenting volume has been attributed by Daniel Kono to the presence of democratic regimes in plenty countries of the contemporary world.[15] His argument lies on the tension between the promises of trade liberalization and domestic regulation. Indeed, politicians are guided in their action from the pressure put upon them by two competing interests groups, the masses that advocate for open, competitive markets and economic growth on the one hand, and on various protectionist interest groups on the other.[16] In an effort to conciliate the two of them, politicians opt for partial trade liberalization through the elimination of tariffs, which can however only take you so far, despite their prima facie liberalizing effect.[17] Due to their simplistic working mode, politicians cannot avoid their elimination, which is actually something they achieved during the various liberalization rounds on the World Trade Organization (hereinafter WTO) level. On the other hand, this is not the case with non-tariff barriers under the form of domestic regulations. The latter, despite the fact that they may serve as protectionist measures, can also be translated as the preference to protect the domestic welfare and serve the competing interests of the electorate.[18] They usually do not discriminate prima facie against imported products or services, thus they remain compatible with the GATT non-discrimination principle. Moreover, their impact on trade flows and prices cannot be easily calculated as tariffs' impact on prices.[19] Consequently, not only can their protectionist nature be easily hidden to trade partners, but their trade distorting effects are also difficult and costly to explain to the voters.[20] Thus, politicians have more incentives to use such non-tariff barriers to trade in order to keep the interest groups satisfied, which leads to their multiplication, a phenomenon

---

[14] WTO (2012), p. 39.
[15] Kono (2006), p. 369.
[16] Kono (2006), p. 369.
[17] Kono (2006), p. 370.
[18] Kono (2006), p. 377.
[19] Kono (2006), p. 370.
[20] Kono (2006), p. 371.

which the author has called "Optimal Obfuscation".[21] Hence, under the contemporary trade jargon regulatory barriers have been described as the new tariffs, as their effect on trade is as significantly disturbing by blocking market access of goods or services that do not comply or do not show conformity with the regulatory standards of the importing market.[22] And even more, their trade disturbing effect becomes more imminent, as the subject of reduction of non-tariff barriers cannot be made as easily a topic in the international negotiations as tariff have become in the past.

Naturally, this situation has not escaped the attention of the multilateral trade agendas. Traditionally, regulatory barriers fell under the GATT general provisions on non-tariff barriers, such as Article III:4 GATT which requires equal regulatory treatment and Article XX GATT, which provides a very small window of opportunity for justification of discriminatory treatment.[23] However, these rules proved insufficient in being able to discern between hidden protectionism and protection of legitimate values.[24] Hence, some of the agreements reached at the multilateral level during the Uruguay round started to gradually move away from the so-called 'negative integration'[25] and began including commitments on 'positive integration'.[26] In other words, the rules' focus shifted from non-discrimination to the exigency of positive rule-making according to the agreed criteria. Examples to this constitute the Agreements on Technical Barriers to Trade[27] (hereinafter TBT), on Sanitary and Phytosanitary Measures[28] (hereinafter SPS). Common characteristic of these Agreements is the introduction of commitments that aim towards regulatory

---

[21] Kono (2006), p. 371.

[22] *See* generally Maskus et al. (2000).

[23] However, due to the very strict requirements posed by the AB for the application of Article XX, only very few cases in the history of the DSM were successful in the end. *See* Weiss (2020), p. 229 ft 1.

[24] Köbele (2007), p. 171.

[25] Negative Integration is understood here as developed by J. Tinbergen in International Economic Integration. According to Tinbergen negative integration is 'the elimination of certain instruments of international economic policy', especially of the discriminatory and trade restricting ones. *See* Tinbergen (1954), p. 122.

[26] *See* Tinbergen (1954), p. 122. Positive Integration, in the words of J. Tinbergen is the 'positive policy of integration is understood as 'supplementary measures in order to remove inconsistencies that may exist between the duties and taxes of different countries'. The positive integration model follows the specific nature of regulatory barriers, the nature that has rendered them immune towards negative integration. As regulatory barriers usually do not discriminate prima facie, and any disguised discrimination can be justified on imperative reasons of public interest, they rarely are caught by the negative integration radar. It is that veil that has facilitated their multiplication as trade barriers. Thus, the general term adopted by Tinbergen on positive integration as the adoption of complementary measures to fight remaining inconsistencies, has been concretized by market imperatives as the total of practices primarily aimed to 'discipline domestic regulation'. Positive integration accomplishes this discipline by demanding regulatory action of the actors, in a positive form.

[27] Agreement on Technical Barriers to Trade [1994] OJ L 336/86 (hereinafter the TBT Agreement).

[28] Agreement on Sanitary and Phytosanitary Measures [1994] OJ L 336/40 (hereinafter SPS Agreement).

harmonization on the basis of international standards. Despite these innovations, the overall nature of the provisions enshrined in these agreements, which will be analysed in detail in the next Chapter, could only support a certain level of positive integration.

The second part of the re-orientation of international trade politics involves the fall of the WTO arena and the rise of other legal environments for trade regulation. The stagnation of multilateralism caused by the hesitance of developing countries during the last negotiation rounds to enrich the multilateral legal environment with further 'deep' disciplines, that touched the so-called 'Singapore issues',[29] was a catalyst to the abandonment of the arena by one of its biggest players, the US, that gradually developed other avenues to satisfy its trade preferences. It thus started following an active trade liberalization agenda via the conclusion of bilateral FTAs.[30] This strategy was standing in the opposite of what the EU had been advocating so far. Indeed, upon the introduction of the Doha Development Agenda (hereinafter DDA) the EU stopped engaging in the negotiation and conclusion of bilateral trade agreements.[31] This situation was about to change. In an effort to overcome the freezing of multilateral negotiations, the EU inaugurates in its Global Europe communication in 2006 a new trade era that includes, as mentioned, not only strategic rapprochement with its major trading partners,[32] but also the elaboration of new rules, that can effectively address regulatory barriers. The realization of the objectives of this strategy relies upon the conclusion of FTAs, to which it also gives the widely recognizable characteristic of 'New Generation'.[33]

Ever since, the new Trade Policy of the European Union has been at the center of attention in political, social and academic environments. So far, driven by a liberal-ization spirit and by a rhetoric that restores the EU leading position as trade leader, the innovations proposed by the New Generation FTAs have been by and large welcomed. One first innovation is of course, sectoral coverage. The New Generation FTAs aim to the highest degree of trade liberalization, objective that justifies their comprehensiveness. Sectors considered as sensitive on the multilateral arena, such as procurement, services, or competition and even sectors that fall under the so-called 'trade and' agenda, such as labour and environment now find their own place in FTAs. Another main characteristic of the new FTAs is institution building. In order

---

[29] According to the WTO Glossary, the term 'Singapore issues' refers to the four issues introduced to the WTO agenda at the December 1996 Ministerial Conference in Singapore: trade and investment, trade and competition policy, transparency in government procurement, and trade facilitation. https://www.wto.org/english/thewto_e/glossary_e/singapore_issues_e.htm.

[30] EU Commission (2006a), p. 14.

[31] Meunier (2007), p. 912.

[32] In comparison to the US, that led an open-door policy for trade negotiations, the EU focused on major trading partners, emerging economies and rather protectionist, towards the EU, markets. *See* Araujo (2014), p. 274.

[33] The New Generation FTAs are opposed to the First and Second Generation FTAs. First Gener-ation FTAs, negotiated before 2006 focus on tariff elimination, while Second Generation FTAs extend to new areas, such as intellectual property rights, services and sustainable development.

to ensure continuous implementation of the undertaken commitments, contemporary FTAs create institutional structures attached to the various treated subject matters, as the ones mentioned above. The existence and functioning of specialised Committees creates primarily a higher level of expectations regarding future implementation. The in-built mechanisms that are to be found, of supervisory, consultative, steering and channelling function on the one hand create pathways for easier communication and provide clear guidance, and on the other hand monitor the progress of the activities.[34]

Yet, the main 'driver' behind the two main changes introduced in trade politics is the development of common regulatory frameworks in the domains that are covered within the FTAs. For example, the *telos* of competition provisions in FTAs does not only aim at ensuring a fair level playing field for all the operating companies, but also envisages to 'promote greater conversion of competition laws and enforcement'.[35] The same understanding applies to IP or procurement, where the EU communicates its wish to promote its own rules abroad.[36] Hence, the comprehensiveness of the domains and the undertaken approach aim to the highest possible liberalization degree in each area. Protagonists and objects of cooperation in this processes become the internal rules seen not only as a barrier but also as vehicles, since they become the object of cooperation themselves.[37]

The pursuance of the regulatory agenda is however more far reaching with regard to trade in goods and services. To this direction, on the one hand, there are some Chapters that play a pivotal role. For example, the Chapters on TBT and SPS introduce WTO plus commitments, meaning that they build upon the multilateral provisions, while reaching beyond them. On the other hand, certain FTAs have also introduced provisions tackling internal regulation. In some FTAs, the parties have agreed on commitments on regulatory transparency. In others, parties have made promises on horizontal cooperation on regulatory matters, launching and maintaining a dialogue between regulators. Such a mechanism, well known now under the name of Regulatory Cooperation, and more specifically the way it appears and functions in Chapters 21 and 18 of CETA and EU-Japan EPA respectively, is the subject of the present thesis.

There are mainly two criteria behind the choice to analyse Regulatory Cooperation only from the angle of these two FTAs. The first reason justifies the focus of the study on FTAs. Indeed, the thesis following the developments of the EU trade policy wishes to introduce Regulatory Cooperation in FTAs as the response to the previous Regulatory Cooperation initiatives, whether in the multilateral arena or as part of political initiatives. It thus chooses deliberatively to focus upon FTAs in general. The second reason of the concentration on these two FTAs is legal certainty, according to which only concluded or finally negotiated Chapters on Regulatory

---

[34] Baccini and Soo Yeon (2012), p. 374.

[35] EU Commission (2006b), p. 18.

[36] EU Commission (2006b), p. 11.

[37] Raustalia (2002), p. 57.

Cooperation will be taken into consideration. Thus, the above criteria exclude not only non-FTA Regulatory Cooperation, but also Regulatory Cooperation in other FTAs, such as Mexico[38] or the US.[39]

It was however on the occasion of the inclusion of Regulatory Cooperation in TTIP as a separate Chapter that the academic and political debate began on the issue. While TTIP as an agreement did not see the light of day, it left a legacy in that it paved the way in many areas for the establishment of New Generation FTAs and their characteristics. And in fact, the form of Regulatory Cooperation as was envisaged in TTIP is now present in the concluded FTAs under examination, namely CETA and EU-Japan EPA.

One must admit that the concept of 'Regulatory Cooperation' is not new in international trade politics. The last years it has been all the more employed in international policy circles as the answer to ever growing regulatory fragmentation, which has been documented as having significant effect on trade. However, the term, wide as it is, has not been given a specific content; rather it has been used mostly as an umbrella term to include a variety of mechanisms that countries implement according to their specific objectives. According to a categorization made by the OECD, the phenomenon of International Regulatory Cooperation (hereinafter IRC) can appear in various fora, as it can be a mechanism attached to an FTA, it can be supervised by a supranational body, or it may also be informal, informed by political initiatives. Most importantly, however, it can take various forms, starting from harmonization and moving to convergence through joint standard setting and adoption of international standards or through regulatory coherence and the initiation of a regulatory dialogue. Nevertheless, despite its pre-existence as a term and range of activities, its inclusion in the FTAs is a novelty, not necessarily content-wise, but also with regard to the decision-making potential that it opens on the international plane.

With regard to the content of the Chapters and introduced activities, these in fact fall under two categories: through regulatory coherence commitments and Regulatory Cooperation mechanisms. As 'regulatory coherence' we refer to the totality of commitments that introduce the so-called good regulatory practices, such as transparency, consultations, and impact assessment procedures within the domestic regulatory environment, aiming to ameliorate the quality of the regulatory process and of the produced regulations and enhance the interoperability of regulatory regimes. As such, they have a strong internal focus. On the contrary, Regulatory

---

[38] The EU is currently negotiating a Chapter on Regulatory Practices with Mexico, hence in the absence of a final text, it would be unwise to include it in this study.

[39] The Regulatory Cooperation Chapter of the negotiated TTIP was the first draft Chapter on Regulatory Cooperation within a European FTA and lied down far reaching commitments both horizontally and vertically. Although it would have constituted a very good case study on its own, had it been concluded, not only the trade agreement as such, didn't see the light of day, but also, the Regulatory Cooperation Chapter, controversial as it was, was subject to constant alterations. Hence, its inclusion is not possible, since we are not in the presence of a concluded FTA, as we are with CETA and EU-Japan EPA.

Cooperation mechanisms have in principle an external view in encompassing specific activities jointly undertaken by two or more parties. While some of these activities have been employed in the past in different fora, it is the first time that they are grouped under a legally binding Chapter, centered on the proceduralisation of horizontal Regulatory Cooperation between regulators.

However, the biggest novelty is represented by the modus operandi of the activities as envisaged in the respective provisions. The new modus operandi is to a big extent based on the operation of institutional structures established by the Chapters. These structures are said to give justice to the character of new generation FTAs as living agreements, as they are placed to steer, guide, help advance, and adapt the cooperation activities according to the arising needs. In the context of Regulatory Cooperation activities, they are referred as Regulatory Cooperation Fora. Novel as they may be, it is their purpose and functioning mechanism that has made them susceptible to criticism as well. Already from the time of TTIP negotiations, the potential and advancement they promised, has been associated with the possible introduction of a layer of international law making within the FTAs, or in general, of a decision-making structure that is susceptible to have considerable influence within EU law-making, without enjoying the proper legitimation.

We could argue that the combination of the two main novelties as described above, gives rise to the following contradiction: On the one hand, the description of these cooperation mechanisms in legally binding terms can play an important role in reaping the benefits of Regulatory Cooperation. On the other hand, their operationalization through the institutional structures, namely the Regulatory Cooperation Fora, intensifies legal constitutional concerns on their interaction with the EU constitutional order. It is upon this controversy that the present thesis is built and around which the research question evolves. How will the—now presumed—legally binding Regulatory Cooperation commitments and their operationalization through the established structures interact with the EU legal order? What effects will they deploy upon it? Will they be subject to sufficient legitimacy guarantees according to the level of interference with the EU legal order?

Indeed, there are many grey areas upon which this thesis focuses, and the clarification of which is necessary in order to be able to reach safe results. Among others the thesis builds the research question along three main axes: a. the exact legal nature of the commitments enshrined within these Chapters and the obligation of the parties to engage in such activities, b. the effects that Regulatory Cooperation results available by the time of the writing deploy in the international and European legal order, and c. the existence or absence of legal or policy guarantees in line with the EU treaties to legitimize those effects in the EU legal order.

Before delving into a concrete discussion on these three axes in the respective thesis Chapters, we shall take a step back and look at the greater image of Regulatory Cooperation as a concept. In that regard, the following parts of the Introduction shall firstly outline with detail and clarity the benefits as well as the potential threats that the functioning of the new Regulatory Cooperation Chapters entail. Moreover, in order to better frame the thesis in the existing legal literature, it will discuss the added value of the research and explain its contribution on the debate in question.

1.2 Regulatory Cooperation in Trade: Friend or Foe?

The debate on the controversy of Regulatory Cooperation has been illustrated with a wide range of arguments. On the one hand, the drivers of the various initiatives on Regulatory Cooperation, attributed mainly to the structure of contemporary trade relations have been extensively studied and concretely identified by differing branches of literature. On the other hand, the reaction that followed the inclusion of Regulatory Cooperation in FTAs expressed the concerns regarding the constitutional challenges such mechanisms pose due to their novel nature. As we shall see later on, Regulatory Cooperation had never been so legalized. Although similar concerns were raised in the past also regarding non-legally binding Regulatory Cooperation commitments, their foundation within political understandings and agreements wasn't enough to justify an imminent constitutional danger. This new understanding of the re-established Regulatory Cooperation marks in essence a clash between these two worlds, one serving economic liberalization and one highlighting the uncomfortable coexistence with the EU legal order. The present section will recall the relevant arguments so far from both sides. In summary, it answers to the following questions: Which are the drivers for Regulatory Cooperation? Can we identify any benefits beyond economic ones, thus rendering it more than just a means to an end? What kind of dangers have been mentioned in the legal literature so far?

1.2.1 Drivers for Regulatory Cooperation

The inclusion of Regulatory Cooperation mechanisms in the new generation EU FTAs associates them primarily with an FTA's main purpose, namely trade liberalization and economic gains. For this reason, we can support that economic considerations are the main driver behind such activities. However, other 'side effects' that Regulatory Cooperation may present to the engaging regulatory orders, as are the enhancement of the internal regulatory structures and the betterment of internal regulatory products are of equal importance and thus find their place in the analysis below.

1.2.1.1 Avoiding Unnecessary Costs Caused by Regulatory Disparity

Regulatory Cooperation efforts in trade relations find their roots in the need to reduce regulatory barriers to trade, whose distorting effect in trade is considerable.[40] By reducing them, economies become more competitive as prices become lower and the variety of products in the markets augments. This comes with economic benefits not only for the producers who have a more significant exporting power but also to the

---

[40] *See* generally Hoekman (2015).

consumers.[41] Still, do these economic gains justify a blind attack to all regulatory barriers? The answer is no. To make the argument clearer, it is necessary to discern between necessary and non-necessary regulatory barriers to trade, illustrating with two short narratives.

Specification and Conformity Assessment costs

Specification costs are the ones that exporters meet when they have to adjust their products to the regulatory specificities of the target market. Conformity assessment costs arise when producers need to demonstrate to the authorities of the importing country compliance of the product they are trying to export with the regulations of the destination and home market. The costs that arise in each category do not necessarily reflect major differences between the two regulatory markets. Specification costs can for example arise because of different labelling requirements. They may as well reflect more substantial differences that demand a change in the production process. The same can be said for conformity assessment costs. These can on the one reflect different testing methods which makes importing products subject to additional conformity assessment in the importing market. They may also be generated because of lack of recognition of conformity assessment bodies of the two regulatory parties. Such requirements duplicate the procedure undertaken at the home market, hence duplicate the costs. According to the type of regulatory obstacle, costs can be discerned into necessary and unnecessary. Obstacles that reflect substantial differences can be necessary. While Regulatory Cooperation might also help in such cases, it can be most beneficial in cases where parity costs can be avoided.

In order to illustrate with an example, we expect an industrialized nation, which accounts high standards for product safety, to reflect this policy choice in its regulations. Another country aiming to increase production will oversee those safety concerns that may render production more expensive. However, when the latter will try to approximate the former's market, it will come across regulatory barriers, and it will not be granted market access, unless it has complied with the higher regulatory requirements, which would implicate usually a change in the production process; this producer, in economic terms, will have to bear the specification costs, the cost required for the actual compliance with different regulations.[42] This case reflects a specification cost, which however is unavoidable, due to the higher standards of the exporting market.

The following example on conformity assessment costs implicates a scenario in which conformity assessment procedures, the ones necessary to *demonstrate* conformity of products with the regulations of the importing (and exporting) markets to the importing authorities represent an unnecessary regulatory barrier, without necessarily reflecting substantial stringency diversification. In such a case, as is for

---

[41] Bull et al. (2015), p. 3.

[42] van Tongeren et al. (2015), p. 2.

example the procedure that certifies safe use of electric equipment, a producer, in order to reach another market, will have to bear the certification cost at the target market, being already susceptible to the certification costs at the exporting market, even though substantially the production has been carried out according to the same safety requirements. Non-substantial regulatory divergence may also implicate the non- recognition of each other's conformity assessment bodies that could in theory demonstrate conformity of the exporting products to the regulations of the target market already before export. In the example of electric equipment, its safe use according to the regulations of the target market could already be guaranteed by the conformity assessment bodies of the exporting country.

The difference between the two examples and the role of Regulatory Cooperation in each one is clear. In the first example, the set regulatory requirements on product safety are neither duplicative nor administrative barriers but reflect substantial legitimate choices. In such a case, gain maximization through market liberalization and reduction of regulatory barriers goes beyond the objective and philosophy of the pursued Regulatory Cooperation in the FTAs, that envisages to tackle only the unnecessary and duplicative barriers to trade. This is not the case for the second example, where Regulatory Cooperation could play a significant role in the coordination of regulatory authorities by means of recognition of the conformity assessment procedures or by recognition of equivalence of the conformity assessment bodies.

Information Costs

The examples mentioned above referred to two categories of costs generated by unnecessary regulatory disparity, namely the specification and conformity assessment costs. Unnecessary regulatory divergence however encloses another category of costs, the so-called information costs. Information costs aim to the acquisition of regulatory information for each regulatory regime, and they multiply when more than one markets are targeted, especially when markets do not share common regulatory traditions.[43] The sums can eventually reach numbers that function as market hurdles, eventually dissuading companies from exporting, and thus influencing the extensive margin, in other words, the number of traders who export to the market.[44] This chain effect affects mostly small and medium enterprises, which face greater difficulties than enterprises who use economies of scale in overpassing the pricey obstacles.[45] Eventually, this will affect the decision whether to export, thus affecting the extensive margin, with hurting effects on consumers' welfare, who face lack of variety.[46] Even in a case where a market actors decide to transcend the costs

---

[43] OECD (2017), p. 16.
[44] *See* generally Andersson (2007).
[45] OECD (2017), p. 14.
[46] OECD (2017), p. 14.

of a particular market with high profitability, it is again the consumers that will finally bear these heterogeneity costs that an exporting firm has to occur as competitive disadvantage against domestic firms.

This short narrative explains how regulatory differences theoretically act as barriers to trade with visible economic consequences not only upon the producers but also upon the consumers. The role of Regulatory Cooperation in addressing such barriers where necessary is self-explanatory. The above claims find their roots in economy theories, however, due to the diversification of regulatory barriers, the inherent difficulty in their identification and the different methods employed in economic science,[47] an exact measurement on the trade liberalization in economic terms is difficult. However, the fact that the impact will be significant is shared among leading trade economists.[48]

1.2.1.2 Betterment of Domestic Regulations

Apart from legitimate reasons causing regulatory disparity, as are the different legal traditions, different risk perceptions, or even fragmentation between regulatory instances across government levels, a great share of trade distortions comes from problems inherent to the regulatory regimes, such as duplication, inaccessibility and ignorance of foreign interests. Regulatory Cooperation along with Regulatory Coherence can address these regulatory barriers not only *ex post* but also *ex ante*, at the moment of their formation.

Regulatory Coherence for example has reasonably been described as a means to rationalize policies.[49] Indeed, as we mentioned before, Regulatory Coherence as a concept includes the presence and utilization by domestic regulators of good regulatory practices, such as the ones published by the OECD, the compliance of regulatory processes with transparency requirements and both internal and external stakeholder engagement in the rule-making procedure.[50] Despite the internal nature of the matter addressed, regulatory coherence has been used both in multilateral and bilateral efforts as a means to achieve less opaque regulatory regimes. In many instances, especially in regional efforts, or between trading partners where coordination would be difficult because of different development paces, regulatory coherence is the only instrument utilized, as for example in the TTP.

To what can serve Regulatory Cooperation then? This question has been answered in a very innovative way with the use of economic theory. Regulatory jurisdictions are parallelized to market actors, as 'producers of legal products. Adopting this analogy, Esty and Geradin, explain how Regulatory Cooperation can overcome the types of market failures from which the exclusively competitive

---

[47] Moser (2017), p. 283.

[48] *See* generally Egger et al. (2015).

[49] Hoekman et Mavroidis (2015), p. 4.

[50] Nakagawa (2016), p. 393.

'market of legal products' suffer, namely information asymmetries, externalities and regulatory opaqueness.[51]

Since one of regulation's primary missions is to address information asymmetries,[52] we can mobilize better regulation techniques arising out of Regulatory Cooperation in order to address more effectively information asymmetries. Such an improvement reflects on the quality of future regulations and provides the national economy with a competitive advantage since national products subject to this regulation become more competitive and their demand rises.[53]

Regulatory Cooperation can also address the externalities of a regulation, which represent unintended costs or effects of a transaction occurring at a third party.[54] As far as the field of regulation is concerned, regulatory externalities may occur when domestic regulators do not take under consideration the possible effects of their action to other jurisdictions, either because they do not have such mandate, or because of protectionism reasons. These externalities can be economic in nature, as are the costs that an international company occurs from ineffective protection from competition in a country, but the most susceptible to externalities are these domains that know no borders, as the environmental, where pollution has broader effects across borders.[55]

If the regulatory jurisdictions are described as legal products, then the regulator-citizen relation can be described as an agent-principal one. In these relations, the less transparent the relation regime is, the more likely is that the agent will stop acting in the best interests of the principal and start satisfying his own or other interests.[56] Same goes for the domestic jurisdictions. Domestic regulatory systems that engage in some kind of cooperation with foreign counterparts, inherently are more transparent than marginalized competitive domestic jurisdictions. Regulation in competitive systems, on the other hand is more susceptible to be oriented towards private interests, than towards the public good, given its opaqueness.

1.2.1.3 Strategic Considerations

The previous parts summarized what has been discussed in the literature from different disciplines regarding the necessity of Regulatory Cooperation in Trade. Guided mostly by economic considerations, Regulatory Cooperation, if wisely pursued, can provide a different playing field for economic actors that are hampered from entering into different markets because of excessive compliance costs. On the other hand, the mechanisms implicated can prove beneficial for the internal

---

[51] Esty and Geradin (2000), p. 235.

[52] Heremans (2014), p. 28.

[53] van Tongeren et al. (2015), p. 3.

[54] Heremans (2014), p. 32.

[55] Esty and Geradin (2000), p. 240.

[56] Heremans (2014), p. 30.

regulatory environment, by enhancing the quality of the regulations through transparency and participation and also avoiding certain market failures that are connected mostly with competitive regulatory systems.

Scholars studying international relations have also referred to the strategic importance of Regulatory Cooperation.[57] Characteristically, TTIP has been alternatively named as 'Economic NATO' because of the promising ability of the envisaged Institutions to promote convergence between two economic and regulatory superpowers.[58] While for the big players this would work as an advantage, for others it is a threat of regulatory imposition.[59] However, this was not the only reason why Regulatory Cooperation is perceived as a threat. The next session will engage in a more sceptic analysis.

1.2.2 Regulatory Cooperation as a Threat

While the uneasiness regarding the democratic fit of the mechanism of Regulatory Cooperation within existing legal structures had been the matter of discussion mostly in stakeholder policy circles,[60] Institutions[61] and domestic political environments,[62] it has been mostly based on factual rather than legal arguments. For example, the most common fear of the 'race to the bottom' has barely been associated with the EU's regulatory sovereignty. The scenario of usurpation of the rule-making capacity from the newly established structures is presented as such and not related to the need to legitimize any decision-making activity that has an impact on the EU legal order. Only more recently have these concerns been treated in more analytical terms by academics.[63] In the next paragraphs, following the categorization of Anne Meuwese's legal constitutional 'translation' carried out in the course of TTIP negotiations on Regulatory Cooperation,[64] we shall present in similar terms the concerns that have been expressed, on the basis of which the thesis is based. While these concerns were raised in the context of TTIP, they apply of course mutatis mutandis to the similar Regulatory Cooperation Chapters of CETA and EU-Japan EPA.

---

[57] *See* generally Hamilton and Blockmans (2015).

[58] Gray (2013), p. 2.

[59] *See* Bull et al. (2015), p. 7.

[60] Trade Justice Movement (2015).

[61] European Commission (2015).

[62] Tweede Kamer (2014).

[63] *See* indicatively Bartl (2016).

[64] Meuwese (2015), p. 153.

1.2.2.1   The Threat to Regulatory Sovereignty

> These officials (of the Regulatory Cooperation Body) would have enormous in-fluence, as they could stop or weaken legislative proposals that would regulate business or, on the other hand, promote legislative proposals that would lower requirements for companies.[65]

Regulatory Sovereignty is a wide concept, which in EU law terms reflects the right of the EU rule makers to regulate as they see fit. The concept of regulatory sovereignty here can be broken down to two strands: the first referring to who makes the rules and the second referring to how the rules are created, against which values and according to which criteria. Regulatory sovereignty reflects thus not only the liberty of the regulator to regulate when it considers necessary but also the regulatory values which must be adhered to. To avoid confusion, the maker of rules is understood not as the democratically elected legislator but as the regulator who proposes them. Under this double understanding of the term are thus to be found various instances of the decision-making procedures of the Union. This also means that the instances in which the regulatory sovereignty may be undermined are plenty and not always visible at first sight.

In the EU legal order, the role of instigator of regulation belongs to the EU Commission, which enjoys the exclusive right of initiative. Whether this prerogative can be compromised depends on the role of the newly introduced actors and their scope of action. Indeed, the role and action of the supervising bodies, namely the Regulatory Cooperation Bodies remains a source for uncertainty, especially in the light of limited results during the first years of its existence.[66] What its exact action will be, whether decisions will be taken on that level, and if yes, what will their legal value be, are crucial questions to be answered in this respect. While EU Institutions tended to reaffirm the absence of legal making capacities of such bodies as early as the commencement of TTIP negotiations, results have to be looked into more detail and with a view to understanding whether the Regulatory Cooperation Bodies introduce another instance of decision-making, different from the ones we are already familiar with.

In the second branch of regulatory sovereignty, which includes the criteria and the values that guide the activity of regulatory making, we can include both the regulatory principles of the EU legal order as well as the methodologies by which regulations are assessed and analysed, such as risk and impact assessment. This second point reflects mainly the wide-spread concern regarding the future of the principle of precaution and the fear of the race to the bottom. Given the importance of the issue, we shall refer to it in more detail in the next Section.

---

[65] Corporate Europe Observatory (2014).

[66] Corporate Europe Observatory (2014).

1.2.2.2   The Threat of the Race to the Bottom

In the literature on Regulatory Cooperation, the threat of the race to the bottom is part of regulatory sovereignty. More specifically, the race to the bottom has been associated with the fear of abandonment of fundamental EU principles that guide EU regulation, for example the precautionary principle. As the main aim of Regulatory Cooperation is regulatory convergence, the Regulatory Cooperation structures have been accused of being able to force it indirectly. And it is suggested that this convergence will not occur upwards; on the contrary it will open the door to the race to the bottom.

In fact, as an argument, the 'race to the bottom' has been used both to defend and oppose Regulatory Cooperation. During the 70s the fear of the race to the bottom was used as an argument to justify regulatory centralization both in the US and the EU.[67] The added value of the centralization was trade facilitation and most importantly the avoidance of individualized regulatory practices, which would attract business and products by means of relaxed regulation. Recently, however, the very same argument is used all the more by the supporters of regulatory competition, who see greater efficiency gains when jurisdictions are in a constant race.[68] Based on the fact that competition among product markets leads to consumer welfare, they argue that competition among jurisdictions leads to better regulation.[69] Thus, they assume that absent this 'race' between jurisdictions, Regulatory Cooperation equals harmonization, which means the abandonment of high quality regulations and the invasion of less protective ones.

With regard to TTIP, Marija Bartl locates 3 different avenues susceptible of causing a negative impact upon the high standards of EU rule-making: (a) the way science is perceived and applied for the development of the regulations, seen under the light of the unification of scientific methods, (b) the risk to alter existing assumptions in the need to find common ones and (c) the deregulatory risk of the requirement to adopt joint positions in international standardisation fora.[70]

The illustration of this argumentation is based on the precautionary principle. Regarding the first two avenues, the use of science in the rule-making cultures of each trading partner and the re-evaluation of regulatory tools, it should be first mentioned that the more advanced Chapters on Regulatory Cooperation like the ones envisaged in the TTIP negotiations and like the ones that are the subject matter of the thesis aim in the long run to dig deeper than substantially reducing regulatory barriers and regard dialogue as the way for avoidance of future parities.[71] Hence, Bartl builds the case study around the incompatibility of the precautionary principle with the normative assumptions present in the US (and hence, also Canadian)

---

[67] Esty and Geradin (2000), p. 236.

[68] Esty and Geradin (2000), p. 236.

[69] Esty and Geradin (2000), p. 236.

[70] Bartl (2017), p. 970.

[71] Bartl and Fahey (2014), p. 11.

regulatory environment. These assumptions are so deeply rooted to the regulatory cultures that any attempt for approximation would need serious compromise. For example, the question whether or not to regulate in cases of scientific uncertainty drives the regulatory parity between the EU and the US.[72] In the same way, the values enshrined in the chosen cost-benefit analysis across the Atlantic match poorly the guiding principles of precautionary principle. Lastly, the author highlights the agreement of the trade partners to speak with one voice in international standardisation fora and warns that the pressure to adopt a common line increases the eventuality of a compromise different from the original lines and how this may eventually lower the already sensible legitimacy of such organisations.

In short, the message that Bartl wants to disseminate boils down to the following statement: Enhancing methodological convergence in order to avoid future divergence is not necessarily wrong but can be harmful when it indirectly increases risk tolerance and therefore reduces the regulatory intervention. To this, I add that it is not only methodological convergence or international standardisation that can offer avenues to invade the EU regulatory system. The real Trojan horse of the new Regulatory Cooperation Chapters is its essential element, the one of the dialogue. Since regulatory dialogue is taking place between bureaucrats and behind the curtains, turning to 'business as usual' with their inclusion in the FTA, without making much noise, its impact can be indirect and gradual, with a potential to shape decisively the content of the regulatory developments.

1.2.2.3 The Threat to Democratic Accountability

The threat to democratic legitimacy reflects both in policy circles and also in academia the fear of decision-making being transposed to structures other than the democratically elected parliaments. It has been illustrated by three strands of arguments, as expressed by the civil society:

The Role of the European Parliament and the Principle of Institutional Balance

> This process will take place outside the regular democratic decision-making processes on both sides of the Atlantic, preventing national parliaments and locally elected bodies from being fully involved and dangerously limiting the public debate.[73]

> It implies an unacceptable power grab by the Commission, strengthens the US impact on EU regulation and weakens the role of the European Parliament.[74]

---

[72] *See* generally van Asselt and Vos (2006).

[73] Corporate Europe Observatory (2014).

[74] Attac Ireland (2016).

Ever since early drafts of the negotiating documents of the Regulatory Cooperation Chapters saw the light of day, the absence of parliaments in the workings of this new mechanism was made clear: this is an affair between regulators.[75] However, the absence of parliamentary participation and oversight was striking and didn't help in appeasing the critics fearing de-regulation and the rise of new actors in the scene. Instead, it was perceived as a 'power grab' by the Commission, a grab that is susceptible of disturbing the institutional balance as set out by the Treaties with regard to decision-making.

Indeed, the absence of parliamentary participation in the process must be seen in the wider context of the EU institutional landscape as well as the constitutional dynamics that are in place with regard to EU decision-making. The Parliament holds the position of co-legislator in the EU legal order and has a decisive say also with regard to the conclusion of international agreements by virtue of 218 TFEU. Should Regulatory Cooperation activities include some regulatory activity on the international level that will have effects internally, the exclusion of the EU Parliament is at first sight not in line with the legitimacy exigencies of EU decision-making. Instead, it constitutes a violation of the institutional balance which inspires the greater idea of democracy enshrined in the EU Treaties. Of course, this statement comes with some caveats. Most importantly, the answer to this question depends on the type and effects of the regulatory activity undertaken on the international level, namely the types of the issued legal acts, any transposition requirement as well as their interaction with existing rules.

The Lack of Transparency and Inclusiveness in Stakeholder Participation

> Institutionalization of lobbying: The proposal provides big business groups with the tools to influence legislation that they have been demanding[76]

Some important transatlantic initiatives to initiate Regulatory Cooperation were essentially based on dialogue. In 1995, the US jointly with the EU introduced a series of bilateral dialogues, such as the Transatlantic Business Dialogue and the Transatlantic Consumers' Dialogue, to bring together stakeholders from both sides of the Atlantic in order to provide them a forum to share and disseminate common ideas and concerns, to influence and steer Regulatory Cooperation discussions at the political level. In principle, and as a concept, stakeholder consultation is nothing new. However, with the rise of the FTAs and the inclusion of Regulatory Cooperation as their integral part, the role that stakeholders may have in the processes has also created much uneasiness, especially between NGOs.

The two contentious issues on to the choice of stakeholders for the consultation procedures and the lack of transparency in the process, have enhanced the worry of

---

[75] Alemanno (2015), p. 635.

[76] Corporate Europe Observatory (2016).

the illegitimate influence that big business may have in the regulatory amendments or initiatives triggered by the Regulatory Cooperation Chapters. Such concerns have been present already from the negotiation phase of the Agreements, which led to criticism on whether the secrecy of the negotiations and the selective consultations carried out by the Commission—notably with representatives of big businesses- are in line with the requirements of a transparent, participatory and deliberative democracy as enshrined in Articles 10 (3), 11 and 15 of the Treaty of Lisbon.[77] Since we value transparency, openness and inclusive participation as part of the democratic identity of the Union, critics are right to question the cohesion of non-inclusive and non-transparent negotiations on the Regulatory Cooperation Chapters as contrary to the requirements of EU democracy.

1.3 Contribution to Existing Literature and Emerging Research Question

While the research discussed has set the constitutional foundations and has rightly located the instances in which legal questions are to be set and answered, it remains incomplete in the absence of final texts and insofar no substantial results can support the assumptions. Thus, while we admit that this research is guided by the same considerations as the present one, it nevertheless takes its own course in the light of the chosen case studies, the Chapters of CETA and EU-Japan FTA and also in the light of the concrete results that have resulted so far from their functioning. Starting from this statement, we shall locate where the added value of this research lies.

The thesis is thus to a certain extent complementary and explanatory, focusing on the one part on shedding light on issues once considered unknown. Academic literature, especially early one that closely followed the negotiations, didn't have the legal texts to engage in a literal interpretation. Regarding TTIP, Alberto Alemanno among others was the one to deal with the Chapter on Regulatory Cooperation, describing the features of the mechanism and especially the possible implementation of the horizontal mechanism in the EU legal order.[78] Still though, while communications from the Commission and negotiating documents informed about the progress made, the exact extent and legal nature of the commitments on paper could only be speculated. In the absence of such information, however, one could not yet tell the difference between the past efforts of Regulatory Cooperation, either multilateral or bilateral ones to the contemporary Chapters, although much had been written about the type of governance, the rules and Institutions on the WTO and bilateral level that target all the more aspects of traditionally domestic mandates.[79] This was also an impediment in commenting with certainty upon the possible impact

---

[77] Pettersmann (2017), p. 48; Delimatsis (2017).

[78] Alemanno (2015); Wiener and Alemanno (2015).

[79] Schaffer (2016); Gerstetter et al. (2014).

of the new Regulatory Cooperation Chapters. And while academic uneasiness on the democratic fit of the Regulatory Cooperation Chapters was evident, one could not provide suitable solutions on the basis of assumptions.[80]

These lacunae are the ones that this research comes to address. Having now an overview of the past initiatives and being in possession of the official texts and having some first implementation results allows us to engage into a legal analysis in order to locate the added value of the Regulatory Cooperation Chapters in legal terms. For this part of the research, I hypothesize that the Regulatory Cooperation commitments enshrined as legally binding commitments go beyond past initiatives. By looking both at the past and present, we are also able to observe the evolution of Regulatory Cooperation in various fora and explain the prevalence of one choice instead of another, taking into consideration not only the narrow path of Regulatory Cooperation but also the greater image arising from the multilateral and bilateral trade universe. For the purpose of the thesis, this analysis will provide the basis for the answering the research question. By itself though, it will complement the existing literature and will provide a comprehensive benchmark for all disciplines conducting further research on Regulatory Cooperation.

Moreover, the thesis concretises part of the legal constitutional questions raised in preceding literature, however, without making the distinction between regulatory sovereignty and democratic accountability, as proposed by Meuwese, but by examining them under the concept of democratic legitimacy in EU decision-making. Indeed, we consider various aspects that we analysed above to fall within the greater sense of the latter. Should we consider Regulatory Cooperation as capable to undermine democratically legitimate EU rule-making in total, this in principle includes the question *who* is regulating (the participating actors and the used tools) and the *how* regulations are made (the values to which they adhere). In this way, aspects such as the influence to EU regulatory values by the counterparts or the role of external actors as are the Regulatory Cooperation Bodies are considered to be threats to the democratic legitimacy of EU rule-making.

Since we understand the process as a whole, we include both stages under the democratically legitimate rule-making procedure. And indeed, should one look more carefully, the lines between the two categories of threats are sometimes blurred. For example regarding institutional balance, as in the who has a say in the rule-making, was identified as aspect of democratic accountability. However, does not the question of who makes the rules concern the inclusiveness and role of external actors as the Regulatory Cooperation Fora and the influence they have on the Commission's right of initiative? Thus, locating the interconnections between the two, the thesis considers all legal points as constituting part of the idea of democratic EU rule-making, as this is mandated by the rules of the Treaties, but also by overarching principles that consolidate the particularities of the EU, as is for example institutional balance.

---

[80] Ahearn and Morelli (2009).

Having this legal constitutional direction, the thesis will examine how the concrete results of Regulatory Cooperation affect this totality of principles underpinning legitimate EU rulemaking. Indirectly, the thesis will fill another gap by deploying in a systematic manner the results of Regulatory Cooperation up until the time of the writing and the effects they have within the EU legal order. The analysis shall begin from the hypothesis that the shift in the legal form of Regulatory Cooperation does matter by producing concrete results, however the results of Regulatory Cooperation are not properly legitimized. Whether they are properly legitimized or not depends on the effects they deploy in the EU legal order and the type of instruments that introduces them in the EU legal order. If the results are not introduced in a manner that guarantees the foundational constitutional requirements of the idea of democracy in the EU, then they suffer from legitimacy problems, which call for appropriate legal solutions.

Based on the above, we can form the emerging research question of the thesis:

How can we address legitimacy gaps emerging from the activities of Regulatory Cooperation as a new form of international rule-making according to the democratic exigencies of the EU legal order?

Each Chapter from now and on is a stepping stone to answering the research question. Each one answers a sub-question, which is a necessary precondition for the Chapters to follow and thus for the complementarity of this research. The exact content of each Chapter, as well as the methodology used for each one and their connection to the other Chapters will be outlined in Sect. 1.5. Before that, we shall dedicate a few pages on crystallizing the subject of the thesis and explaining why certain aspects are left outside its scope.

1.4   The Difference of Regulatory Cooperation Chapters from Other Regulation Related Chapters

This Section elaborates on how the research focus relates to other Regulatory Cooperation activities enshrined in other FTA Chapters. This exercise, while heavily based on the main standpoints of the thesis as presented above, explains the unique character of the activity under consideration, which is so characteristic, that cannot be combined with other similar research areas. The present Section seeks to address possible contestations and objections to the present focus on Regulatory Cooperation Chapters. One could possibly question the limited focus of the thesis on the specific two Regulatory Cooperation Chapters of the FTAs under analysis, namely of CETA and EU-Japan, and argue for a wider reading of Regulatory Cooperation that includes also more targeted Regulatory Cooperation and regulatory coherence activities, that are part of different Chapters. Indeed, joint Regulatory Cooperation activities take place with respect to certain sectors in the TBT and SPS Chapters while more targeted focus on regulatory coherence takes place in the case of most New Generation FTAs in separate Chapters on Transparency. The former refer to specific categories of measures, technical barriers to trade and sanitary and phytosanitary measures respectively. The latter outline commitments that introduce rationalization practices of domestic regulatory systems. Both CETA and EU- Japan EPA include separate Chapters on these issues.[81] Transparency Chapters are also included in other New Generation FTAs, such as the KOREU FTA, the SINGEU FTA, the EU-Vietnam FTA and also the draft EU-Mexico FTA.[82] The question that naturally follows is to what extent are these Chapters different to the Regulatory Cooperation ones, so as to be left outside the scope of analysis of the present thesis? Answering this question is important, as the choice not to include them in the scope of the thesis inherently limits the number of FTAs that are to be examined. This will be done in the following parts following a positive explanation of the thesis' main standpoints.

1.4.1 Its Focus on External Regulatory Cooperation Activities and Its Incompatibility to Transparency Chapters

The research question of the thesis refers to the proper legitimization of the Regulatory Cooperation results in the EU legal order. It is hence based on the assumption, which is later confirmed by the findings, that the Regulatory Cooperation results in their current form and with the current effects they deploy on the EU legal order are not properly legitimized. In order to reach this conclusion, the thesis proceeds to an ex-ante analysis of these results. These results stem to a large extent from the working of the Regulatory Cooperation Fora that until today take the form of agreements and dialogue, as we will see in detail in Chap. 4. Working on the one hand with the agreements reached within CETA, the thesis analyzes them from a legal point of view with regard to their substance and form. In other words it looks into their legal nature but also the instrument with which they are introduced. In this way, it comments upon their legal positioning in the international arena as well as in the EU one. It does the same with regard to regulatory dialogue. Based on an examination of certain legislative areas before and after the regulatory dialogue, the analysis locates the impact of these activities upon them.

From the above, it becomes clear that certain agreements and regulatory dialogue figure as part of the workings of the Regulatory Cooperation Fora, and for this reason are included in the analysis of this thesis. Hence, to understand if Transparency Chapters are to be included in the analysis as well, we need to understand if they could be examined as part of the activities of the Regulatory Cooperation Fora. As a

---

[81] Chapter 17 EU-Japan EPA, Chapter 27 CETA.

[82] Chapter 12 of EU-Korea FTA, Chapter 13 of EU-Singapore FTA, Chapter 14 of the EU-Vietnam FTA, draft Chapter of EU-Mercosur FTA.

first step towards this direction, we need to get familiar with the content of these Chapters.

Given the almost identical structure and wording of most of these Chapters, I will refer only to the provisions of the KOREU FTA.[83] The relevant Chapter in the FTA with South Korea, Chapter 12, lays down provisions which target in general the 'transparency, consultation and better administration of measures of general application, in so far as these may have an impact on any matter covered by the agreements', justifying this action on the importance of the smooth functioning of regulatory environments for both parties.[84] These disciplines do not establish regulator to regulator relations, as in the most advanced Regulatory Cooperation Chapters, but administrative and procedural aspects of domestic regulation. More specifically, the provisions seem to concern not only regulators, but seem to afford certain rights to interested persons in general. While regulators can benefit from the provisions on timely publication and mechanisms for facilitation of subsequent comment and review, the rest of the provisions neither initiate a regulatory dialogue nor indicate other regulatory coherence practices. Furthermore, provisions that promote regulatory quality through exchanges on regulatory tools, are very brief and of declaratory nature, a language which renders rather difficult the identification of a concrete legal obligation.[85] The rest of the provisions, instead, govern procedures for the fair, just and transparent review and appeal of regulatory measures.[86]

It hence becomes clear that the nature of the obligations applies only internally to the regulatory environment of each party concerned, obligations that do not acquire an external dimension. It is safe to say that they largely aim to the betterment, opening and inclusiveness of the regulatory environment towards third parties. It is true that this friendly regulatory environment, that the Transparency Chapters promote, is a pre-condition for and facilitator of a successful Regulatory Cooperation as in the way that it is examined in the present thesis. However, it is not part of its content, as these activities could not be held jointly as part of the workings of the Regulatory Cooperation Fora. For this reason it is deliberately not part of the analysis that follows in the next Chapters. A study of the influence of such commitments on the regulatory environments of contracting parties is a substantially different question that could form part of a very interesting, yet separate thesis. Indeed, to examine the effects of these Chapters on the evolution of regulatory systems would not add particular value to our research question that focuses on the decision-making part of joint cooperation initiatives.

---

[83] It has been argued that the structure of that particular Chapter follows the paradigm of the US Korea FTA whose negotiations were parallel to the European one.

[84] Article 12.2 EU-Korea FTA.

[85] Article 12.7 EU-Korea FTA.

[86] Especially Article 12.6 EU-Korea FTA.

1.4.2   The Incompatibility of the Thesis's Horizontal Focus to TBT and SPS Chapters

In order to be able to capture the incompatibility of the thesis's focus to the TBT and SPS Chapters, a more in depth explanation of the thesis's purpose and potential is necessary. I shall begin from where Sect. 1.3 stopped. Section 1.3 presented the lacunae that the thesis comes to address and explained their relevance in the existing legal literature and beyond. While thus explaining what will be the added value in the literature, it didn't explain how the findings aspire to have a societal impact, and inspire future decision-making around those issues. Indeed, what the thesis aspires to do and the impact it aspires to make on the development of the phenomenon are two crucial aspects that guide the research question. Is this research aiming to examine the Regulatory Cooperation results up until the time of the writing and confine the criticism on insufficient legitimacy only with regard to them? No. Does it use these first examples as a basis in order to deliberate on future possibilities offered by the functioning of Regulatory Cooperation Chapters, in order to examine their potential as a whole and advise on their proper legitimization in advance? Yes. And that is where its originality lies. This research relies upon the few results implemented at the time of the writing and uses them as a guide to shed some light in the unknown decision-making avenues of Regulatory Cooperation. Its purpose is not to measure the impact of Regulatory Cooperation on sectors and legislative areas. While it does engage in such an exercise, it does so only to reach conclusions on the intrusiveness of such activities in the EU legal order and reach more general conclusions about legitimization requirements.

One could rightly point out that TBT/SPS Chapters, could certainly serve as good case studies for the purposes of the research. While we do need to distinguish between the Chapters on Regulatory Cooperation and the ones on TBT/SPS measures, as they co-exist separately in the New Generation FTAs, we should nevertheless affirm that both of them introduce commitments aiming to facilitate regulatory approximation. Indeed, these Chapters, especially on TBT share some characteristics with the Regulatory Cooperation ones. On the one hand, the TBT Chapters of CETA and EU-Japan spell out general obligations for cooperation between private and public actors[87] while also outlining more concrete activities with regard to technical regulations, standards and conformity assessments, which are tailored-made to the needs of the specific regulatory tools.[88] For example, TBT Chapters commit the parties to engage in an intense dialogue in order to facilitate the development and the mutual recognition of compatible and equivalent technical regulations.[89] On the other hand, also SPS Chapters do include some horizontal dialogue[90] and

---

[87] Article 4.3 CETA, Articles 7.6, 7.12 EU- Japan EPA.

[88] Articles 4.4, 4.5 CETA, Articles 7.7, 7.8 EU-Japan EPA.

[89] Article 4.4 CETA, Article 7.5 EU-Japan EPA.

[90] Articles 5.11, 5.12 CETA, Articles 6.11, 6.12 EU-Japan EPA.

commitments on recognition of equivalence,[91] however, we should admit that most of the content is heavily oriented towards specific obligations that apply only to SPS measures. This means that the majority of the commitments is hardly comparable to the Regulatory Cooperation activities. Still, it could be seen as inconsistent to leave them outside the scope of the thesis, all the more because these Chapters have an institutional structures on FTA level[92] which plays an important role in the implementation of the commitments, as does the Regulatory Cooperation one, and could similarly raise legitimacy issues. However, and despite of the common points that the TBT and SPS Chapters share with Regulatory Cooperation ones[93] there are a number of reasons that argue against their inclusion in the project, which are not only related to its extent, that would, in such scenario, be considerably widened.

Firstly, it is the characteristics of these measures and the purpose of their regulation within FTAs that renders their inclusion non-compatible to the research question. In fact, TBT/SPS Chapters build upon the WTO provisions on TBT and SPS measures and within FTAs they have a more sector specific focus. Liberalization in terms of TBT and SPS measures is hence expressed with reference to specific sectors, upon which the parties have agreed to cooperate. This sector specific liberalization argues against a systematic analysis of the TBT/SPS Chapters within the thesis, as in the end, this sector specific liberalization is something that the Regulatory Cooperation Chapters do not do. Instead, through general commitments of varying nature and intensity and with a large scope of application, they provide a first analysis of the practice's potential generally, which is the mission upon which the present thesis embarks. Secondly, this feature of the TBT/SPS Chapters shifts the focus of their possible research potential. Since the Chapters themselves are not purely repeating WTO provisions, but building upon them, their interrelation, namely the question whether they are conflicting or complementary, becomes inherently a focus point for separate research project.[94] Last but not least, the question of legitimacy of TBT and SPS provisions has been well researched in the legal literature.[95] While we do agree that the institutional structures open a different

---

[91] Article 5.6 CETA, Article 6.14 EU-Japan EPA.

[92] Articles 4.7, 5.14 CETA, Article 7.13, 6.15 EU-Japan EPA.

[93] Both categories, TBT and SPS measures refer to specific categories of regulatory measures, technical barriers to trade and sanitary and phytosanitary measures respectively. As such they can constitute unnecessary barriers to trade, hence their further regulation under EU FTAs. That is also why the Regulatory Cooperation Chapters do catch TBT and SPS measures under their ambit. It is indeed true, that part of the tangible results of Regulatory Cooperation examined in Chap. 4 of the thesis fall under multiple agendas, of the Regulatory Cooperation Chapter, and of the TBT/SPS Chapters as well. In more simple terms, there exists a cross-fertilisation between the subjects of the several Committees. However, the scope of the Regulatory Cooperation Chapters goes beyond TBT and SPS measures. Under their scope falls every regulatory measure that can pose an unnecessary trade barrier.

[94] Romanchysyna (2023).

[95] *See* generally Weiss (2020).

page of the same book, the results of this thesis could easily apply mutatis mutandis to legitimise the functioning of the joint structures in the TBT/SPS Chapters as well.

1.5   Research Methodology and Thesis Outline

This thesis undertakes a legal analysis of the Regulatory Cooperation Chapters included in the two FTAs that are the focus of the thesis, CETA and EU-Japan EPA. The objective of the thesis is informed by the gaps in the literature it aspires to fill, as these were outlined in Sect. 1.3, namely a systematic categorization of the legal commitments, a legal analysis of the results these commitments have brought so far and their impact on the EU legal order, and finally a deliberation on their proper legitimization as novel ways of international decision-making.

As an exercise, it is based primarily upon different primary sources; upon the final versions of CETA and EU-Japan EPA, and of other FTAs that are included as case studies within the thesis, upon various WTO Agreements, such as GATT, GATS, TBT, SPS, and corresponding jurisprudence of the Appellate Body (hereinafter AB), upon the EU Treaties and jurisprudence of the European Court of Justice, and upon public international law agreements, such as the Vienna Convention on the Law of the Treaties (hereinafter VCLT). The legal analysis is supported by secondary EU legislation as well as by soft law sources, such as communications issued by the EU Commission. The arguments are further illustrated with references to legal literature that touch upon international trade law, EU constitutional and institutional law, EU external relations law and public international law. While this methodology summary refers to the thesis as a whole, each Chapter is developed methodologically different, in a way that is informed every time by the research question that is to be answered.

The rest of the thesis, as well as a more precise reference to the methodology used, can be summarized below:

Chapter 2: Which are the characteristics of the re-established Regulatory Cooperation and how can these be explained?

Chapter 2 delves more thoroughly into the reasons underlying the inclusion of Regulatory Cooperation Chapters and explains their appearance. This introduction already mentioned the limited reach of multilateral rules as well as the absence of progress in the multilateral arena as reasons behind the appearance of alternative ways to combat regulatory barriers to trade, such as the inclusion of Regulatory Cooperation Chapters in EU FTAs. Chapter 2 develops these arguments more in detail. By examining past experiences and shortcoming, it explains the characteristics of the re-established Regulatory Cooperation. In order to do so holistically and systematically, the Chapter is divided in two Sections that represent the characteristics of the re-established Regulatory Cooperation.

Its first characteristic, which is its bilateral nature is examined and justified against the shortcomings in the multilateral arena. To explain the prevalence of bilateralism over multilateralism in EU Trade relations in general, the Chapter relies upon literature of international relations and political science that explain how the scene setting evolved. On the other hand, to explain the preference to treat Regulatory Cooperation bilaterally rather than multilaterally, the Chapter undergoes a legal analysis of the TBT and SPS agreements, and the corresponding jurisprudence of the AB, explaining their legal shortcomings in fostering Regulatory Cooperation.

Its second characteristic, the choice to include it in a legally binding Treaty is attributed to previous failed attempts undertaken in the political sphere. For this argument, the Chapter relies once more upon political science and international relations literature. The extensive use of literature from other disciplines renders Chap. 2 quite interdisciplinary.

Chapter 3: Which is the level of Legalization of the re-established Regulatory Cooperation?

Chapter 3 reflects upon the move towards law in the international arrangement that is FTA included Regulatory Cooperation. It constitutes the continuation of Chap. 2 in that it describes the significance of the inclusion of Regulatory Cooperation in a legally binding treaty. For this, it employs the well-known conceptual framework of Legalization, (developed by International Relations literature) and its components, obligation, precision and delegation. Each of these elements contribute differently to the move towards law with their differing functions.

Based on each one of them, the aim of the Chapter is threefold: As a priority, the Chapter discusses the legal nature of the commitments of the Regulatory Cooperation Chapters, as the element of obligation dictates. The stronger the nature of the commitments, the greater the move towards law. In order to discover the real legal nature of the commitments, the element of obligation is developed with the use of primary legal sources, such as the FTAs, the VCLT and corresponding legal literature.

After this legal deliberation, the Chapter introduces the element of precision to make a descriptive analysis of the outlined procedures and the implicated subjects and objects and comment upon the precision of those provisions. The more precise the provisions are, the less margin of discretion is left to the parties to interpret according to will and the more is the content of the obligation consolidated. For this part, the Chapter relies exclusively upon the legal text of the FTAs to engage into a descriptive analysis.

Lastly, the element of delegation serves in locating the existence of a dynamic element within the Chapter's structure, which triggers at the international level either the surveillance of the existing law or the production of secondary rules. Again, for this part, the Chapter relies upon the wording of the Regulatory Cooperation Chapters in the FTAs, which it interprets with the help of other FTA provisions.

Chapter 4: What effects do Regulatory Cooperation results have in the EU legal order?

Chapter 4 is devoted to the study of the effects of Regulatory Cooperation results in the EU legal order. At the time of the writing, only the structures of the Regulatory Cooperation Chapter of the CETA have been actively engaging in cooperation activities with concrete results. The thesis considers as Regulatory Cooperation results both the agreements that are reached under the Regulatory Cooperation Chapters and the ongoing regulatory dialogue.

Regarding the agreements that have been reached under the Regulatory Cooperation Chapter of CETA, the Chapter refers to the content of each agreement and places each one within the corresponding EU policy area through a legal analysis. For this, it relies upon the text of the agreements as such, and on EU documents and legislation referring to the corresponding policy area. Furthermore, it deliberates upon the legal value of the agreements and on the legal effects they have on the existing regime, relying upon literature on soft law and legal effects.

For the purposes of Chapter 4, the ongoing regulatory dialogue which is achieved within the structures of the Regulatory Cooperation, is also considered as a result. Chapter 4 thus looks also into the ways that regulatory dialogue impacts EU decision- making. To reach results, the Chapter relies upon communication documents of the Commission and developments in legislative areas that are in close connection to the ongoing regulatory dialogues. From a comparative reading of the two, it examines whether the legislative developments have been impacted somehow by the regulatory dialogue taking place on the international level.

Chapter 5: Are the results properly legitimized ?

On the basis of the findings of the previous Chapter, Chap. 5 will focus on two questions.

Firstly, it will rely upon the impact of the results as outlined in Chap. 4 in order to deliberate on the existence or the absence of legitimacy guarantees in accordance with the idea of democracy in the EU. It is hence primarily against the Treaties that it will assess whether the Regulatory Cooperation results are properly legitimized. For the purposes of this argument, and for analysing where exactly the legitimacy problem lies, I will be using the classic distinction of legitimacy made in the literature of governance that is input legitimacy, throughput legitimacy and output legitimacy.

Input legitimacy corresponds to who makes the rules and who takes the decisions transferring the results in the EU legal order. The EU treaties set in advance a certain institutional balance in EU external relations that should not be overlooked. Output legitimacy refers to the qualitative aspect of the results. In principle, it looks into the question whether the results abide by constitutional values and basic principles. Throughput legitimacy is employed to describe the presence or absence of legitimacy ensuring procedural rules and practices that are enshrined within the decision-making process. In the EU legal order, as such we consider rules on transparency and openness.

Secondly, the Chapter will assess the legitimacy score of Regulatory Cooperation activities on the basis of this constitutional analysis. Hence, it aspires also to propose solutions to practices whose regime does not correspond to EU constitutional exigencies.

Chapter 6: Conclusion

Chapter 6 makes a final assessment of the findings of the previous Chapters and places them into the greater image of global governance through supranational rulemaking.

References

Ahearn R, Morelli V (2009) Transatlantic regulatory cooperation: a possible role for congress. CRS Report for Congress. Available via DIALOG: https://fas.org/sgp/crs/row/RL34735.pdf.

Alemanno A (2015) The regulatory cooperation chapter of the transatlantic trade and investment partnership: institutional structures and democratic consequences. J Int Econ Law 18:625–640

Andersson M (2007) Entry costs and adjustments on the extensive margin - an analysis of how familiarity breeds exports. In: Working Paper Series in Economics and Institutions of Innovation no 81, Royal Institute of Technology, CESIS - Centre of Excellence for Science and Innovation Studies. Available via DIALOG: https://econpapers.repec.org/paper/hhscesisp/0081.htm

Araujo B (2014) The EU Deep Trade Agenda: stepping stone or stumbling block towards multilateral liberalization. In: Herrmann C, Krajewski M, Terhechte J (eds) European yearbook of international economic law 2014. Springer, Heidelberg, pp 263–284

Araujo B (2016) The EU Deep Trade Agenda. Oxford University Press, Oxford

Attac Ireland (2016). TTIP: Civil Society statement on the new EU proposal on Regulatory Cooperation. http://www.attac.ie/ttip-civil-society-statement-on-the-new-eu-proposal-on-regulatory-cooperation/

Baccini L, Soo Yeon K (2012) Preventing protectionism: international institutions and trade policy. Rev Int Organ 7:369–398

Bartl M (2016) TTIP's regulatory cooperation and the future of precaution in Europe In: Postnational Rulemaking Working Paper No. 2016-02. Amsterdam Law School Research Paper No. 2016-07. Centre for the Study of European Contract Law Working Paper Series No. 2016-01. Available via DIALOG: https://papers.ssrn.com/sol3/papers.cfm?abstract_id=2727118#

Bartl M (2017) Regulatory convergence through the backdoor: TTIP's regulatory cooperation and the future of precaution in Europe. Germ Law J 18:969–992

Bartl M, Fahey E (2014) A postnational marketplace: negotiating the transatlantic trade and investment partnership (TTIP). In: Fahey E, Curtin D (eds) A transatlantic community of law: legal perspectives on the relationship between the EU and US legal orders. Cambridge University Press, Cambridge, pp 210–235

Bull R, Mahboubi N, Stewart R, Wiener J (2015) New approaches to international regulatory cooperation: the challenge of TTIP, TPP, and mega-regional trade agreements. Law Contemp Probl 78:1–29

Corporate Europe Observatory (2014) TTIP: Covert Attacks on Democracy and Regulation https://corporateeurope.org/sites/default/files/ttip_covert_attacks.pdf

Corporate Europe Observatory (2016) TTIP: "Regulatory Cooperation" a threat to democracy https://corporateeurope.org/en/international-trade/2016/03/ttip-regulatory-cooperation-threat-democracy?page=0%2C1,1

Delimatsis P (2017) TTIP, CETA, TiSA behind closed doors: transparency in the EU Trade Policy. In: Griller S, Obwexer W, Vranes E (eds) Mega-regional trade agreements: CETA, TTIP, and TiSA: new orientations for EU external economic relations. Oxford University Press, Oxford, pp 216–246

Egger P, Francois J, Manchin M, Nelson D (2015) Non-tariff barriers, integration and the transatlantic economy. Econ Policy 30:539–584

Esty D, Geradin D (2000) Regulatory Co-opetition. J Int Econ Law 3:235–255

EU Commission (2006a) Communication from the Commission to the Council, the European Parliament, the European Economic and Social Committee and the Committee of the Regions: Global Europe: Competing in the World: A Contribution to the EU's Growth and Jobs Strategy, COM(2006) 567 final https://eur-lex.europa.eu/LexUriServ/LexUriServ.do?uri=COM:2006:0567:FIN:en:PDF

EU Commission (2006b) EU Commission Staff Working Document, Annex to the Communication from the Commission to the Council: Global Europe: Competing in the World, A Contribution to the EU's Growth and Jobs Strategy, Brussels 4 October 2006, COM(2006) final SEC (2006) 1230

European Commission (2015) Regulatory Cooperation in TTIP https://circabc.europa.eu/ui/group/09242a36-a438-40fd-a7af-fe32e36cbd0e/library/4b5a32ec-cb40-48af-bd65-84024 ff86b8b/details

Gerstetter C, Donat L, Klaas K, Weingartner K, Weingartner K (2014) Regulatory cooperation under TTIP – a risk for democracy and national regulation?. Heinrich Böll Stiftung TTIP Series. Available via DIALOG: https://ssrn.com/abstract=2540639

Gray B (2013) An economic NATO: a new alliance for a new global order. In: Issue Brief for Atlantic Council's Global Business and Economic Program. Atlantic Council. Available via DIALOG: https://www.atlanticcouncil.org/wp-content/uploads/2013/02/tar130221 economicnato.pdf

Hamilton D, Blockmans S. (2015) The geostrategic implications of TTIP. In: Paper No. 5 in the CEPS-CTR project "TTIP in the Balance" and CEPS Special Report No. 105. Centre for European Policy Studies. Available via DIALOG:https://www.ceps.eu/ceps-publications/geostrategic-implications-ttip/

Heremans T (2014) Why regulate? An overview of the rationale and purpose behind regulation. In: Lim AH, de Meester B (eds) WTO domestic regulation and services: trade putting principles into practice. Cambridge University Press, Cambridge, pp 25–46

Hoekman B (2015) Trade Agreements and International Regulatory Cooperation in a Supply Chain World In: RSCAS 2015/04, EUI Working Papers. Available via DIALOG https://cadmus.eui.eu/bitstream/handle/1814/34207/RSCASper%20cent202015_04.pdf?sequence=1

Hoekman B, Mavroidis P (2015) Regulatory spillovers and the trading system: from coherence to cooperation. In: International Centre for Trade and Sustainable Development (ICTSD), World Economic Forum. Available via DIALOG: http://e15initiative.org/wp-content/uploads/201 5/04/E15-Regulatory-OP-Hoekman-and-Mavroidis-FINAL.pdf

Köbele M (2007) Preamble TBT. In: Wolfrum R, Stoll P, Seibert-Fohr A (eds) WTO – technical barrier and SPS measures. Brill, Leiden-Boston, pp 167–177

Kono D (2006) Optimal obfuscation: democracy and trade policy transparency. Am Polit Sci Rev 100:369–384

Maskus K, Wilson J, Otsuki T (2000) Quantifying the impact of technical barriers to trade a framework for analysis. In: World Bank Policy Research Working Paper. Available via DIA-LOG.https://openknowledge.worldbank.org/bitstream/handle/10986/19754/multi_page.pdf?sequence=1

Meunier S (2007) Managing globalization? The EU in international trade negotiations. J Common Mark Stud 45:905–926

Meuwese A (2015) Constitutional aspects of regulatory cooperation in TTIP: an EU perspective. Law Contemp Probl 78:153–174

Moser C (2017) On the expected economic effects of trade liberalization and the transatlantic trade and investment partnership. In: Griller S, Obwexer W, Vranes E (eds) Mega-regional trade agreements: CETA, TTIP, and TiSA: new orientations for EU external economic relations. Oxford University Press, Oxford, pp 281–285

Nakagawa J (2016) Regulatory co-operation and regulatory coherence through mega-FTAs. In: Chaisse J, Tsai-yu L (eds) International economic law and governance: essays in Honour of Mitsuo Matsushita. Oxford University Press, Oxford, pp 392–410

OECD (2017) International regulatory co-operation and trade: understanding the trade costs of regulatory divergence and the remedies. OECD Publishing, Paris

Pettersmann EU (2017) Democratic legitimacy in CETA and TTIP? In: Rensmann T (ed) Mega-regional trade agreements. Springer, Cham, pp 37–60

Raustalia K (2002) The architecture of international cooperation: trans governmental networks and the future of international law. Va J Int Law 43:1–93

Romanchysyna I (2023) Technical barriers to trade in "New Generation" RTAs and in the WTO agreements: conflict or complementarity? Springer, Cham

Schaffer G (2016) Alternatives for regulatory governance under TTIP: building from the past. Columbia J Eur Law 22:407–430

Tinbergen J (1954) International economic integration. Elsevier, Amsterdam

Tweede Kamer (2014) 21501-02, no 1438 https://zoek.officielebekendmakingen.nl/kst-21501-02-1438.html. Accessed 19 March 2020

van Asselt M, Vos E (2006) The precautionary principle and the uncertainty paradox. J Risk Res 9: 313–336

Tongeren, F van, Bastien V, Lampe M von (2015) International regulatory cooperation, a trade-facilitating mechanism. In: International Centre for Trade and Sustainable Investment and World Economic Forum. Available via DIALOG: http://e15initiative.org/publications/international-regulatory-cooperation-a-trade-facilitating-mechanism/

Weiss W (2020) WTO law and domestic regulation. Nomos, Baden-Baden

Wiener J, Alemanno A (2015) The future of international regulatory cooperation: TTIP as a learning process toward a global policy laboratory. Law Contemp Probl 78:103–136

WTO (2012) Trade and public policies: a closer look at non-tariff measures in the 21st century. https://www.wto.org/english/res_e/booksp_e/anrep_e/world_trade_report12_e.pdf

Chapter 2
Characteristics of the Re-established Regulatory Cooperation

2.1 Introduction

In the Introductory Chapter, we referred to Regulatory Cooperation as a complex, multifarious concept. In fact, its multimodality does not apply only to the forms it can take, but also to the fora where it may appear. Although Regulatory Cooperation does not constitute a new trend in EU trade, under the present state it represents an original swift. Figuring until recently mainly under the TBT and SPS Chapters under the aegis of WTO, or as the subject matter of various international standardizing organizations, bilateral Regulatory Cooperation in the EU trade relations has not known the development it met in other bilateral trade schemes. This has come to change with the New Generation FTAs that, more or less, introduce advanced Chapters on Regulatory Cooperation, separate from the ones on TBT and SPS, which figure as well. Which is the significance of this turn though? How does bilateralism as an external relations tool fits into a concept that partially falls under trade and partially under rule-making? Since Regulatory Cooperation is viewed as a trade related concept that sets domestic regulation under the prism of a beyond-the-borders dialogue, is bilateralism the best venue considering the nature and sensitivities of the regulatory activity itself? What is the status of Regulatory Cooperation activities under the multilateral chart, that de facto projects bilateralism further?

This Chapter will give answers to the said questions through the concept of 'characteristics' of contemporary Regulatory Cooperation, as the latter is envisaged in the New Generation European FTAs. I am referring explicitly to 'characteristics' since, to my view, the elements under analysis give a particular meaning to Regulatory Cooperation and distinguish it from previous forms. These features, that underpin the totality of the Chapters, provide with a basis that contributes to the better comprehension of the legislator's choices that are analyzed in the present thesis. The strong interdependence of past experiences and present choices, which constitutes the main source of the identified characteristics, provides a solid ground

K. Pipidi-Kalogirou, *Regulatory Cooperation Chapters in the new Generation FTAS*, EYIEL Monographs - Studies in European and International Economic Law 36, https://doi.org/10.1007/978-3-031-71900-4_2

to explore the historical background, how political circumstances and market imperatives contributed to Regulatory Cooperation as it is to be found today in European FTAs.

Overall, the Chapter identifies and analyses as characteristics two main features that place Regulatory Cooperation on a different playing field, and dedicates a separate section for each one, despite their circumstantial and historical interconnection. The first characteristic, a bilateral Regulatory Cooperation is to be found under Sect. 2.2. The preference of bilateralism to the detriment of multilateralsim is firstly explained as a general preference of EU Trade Regulation and secondly regarding Regulatory Cooperation as such. Moving onwards, Sect. 2.3 chooses to reflect upon the inclusion of Regulatory Cooperation in an FTA as the second characteristic. Positioned within a legally binding treaty, Regulatory Cooperation acquires a different meaning from a legal point of view. This Section draws upon this legal significance, looking at past initiatives of Regulatory Cooperation, the most prominent example being the transatlantic paradigm, examining their pitfalls and the reasons behind them and juxtaposing them next to the Chapters present in the FTAs.

The Chapters on Regulatory Cooperation chosen to be analyzed for the purposes of this Chapter are the ones of CETA and EU Japan EPA. The choice of these case studies is conscious and, even though its narrow focus may be questioned, it rests upon two criteria, the presence of a concluded or finally negotiated FTA, and the similarity of commitments. These two criteria are in direct relevance with the economy of the thesis. Firstly, since this research undertakes the study of a new phenomenon in EU FTAs and wishes to do so in a systematic manner, it cannot depend on early versions of Agreements, which are susceptible to change; instead it needs to be based upon finalized texts. Secondly, as mentioned in the two previous Sections, Regulatory Cooperation in the way that it forms the subject matter of the thesis, as a horizontal and external procedure is discerned from other neighboring concepts, such as regulatory coherence or sectoral cooperation. It is upon that criterion, namely the similarity of commitments and of the chosen approach that the selection will be made.

2.2 Bilateralism as the First Characteristic of Regulatory Cooperation

The turn to Bilateralism has marked a new era on EU trade relations. The new environment stands wider and ready to accommodate trade-related issues, strongly or marginally connected, re-discuss them and re-regulate them on the basis of a wider bilateral trade relation. Issues like investment, traditionally negotiated on a separate basis and Regulatory Cooperation, the most viable international form of which coincides with the multilateral framework, are now seen as an integral part of the new comprehensive bilateral FTAs.

Apart from previous experiences, the institutional choice of bilateralism on Regulatory Cooperation can be primarily and in abstract to explained by the International Relations and Political Economy literature. Specifically, cooperation theory shall be used in order to put Regulatory Cooperation under the bilateralism-multilateralism microscope, absent a systematic analysis of the criteria that determine the institutional choice between bilateralism and multilateralism.

Cooperation theory literature discerns cooperation process usually in two stages, bargaining and enforcement.[1] The dynamics created during these stages are determining for the institutional building of the cooperation. Bargaining, the first factor that influences the institutional setting, is informed by each party's high concerns about distribution.[2] Distribution balance refers the concessions that have to be made by each party in order for the benefits to be equally balanced. In multilateral cases where the concessions of a party that reflect the corresponding benefits of the other parties are significantly smaller in comparison to the concessions made by the other signatories, the distribution balance is disturbed, and the road to the multilateral agreement is hindered.[3] In such cases, there is usually a party (or more) that has to sacrifice more than the others do. Regulatory Cooperation's nature fits under this theoretical background. The aim of Regulatory Cooperation is to approximate regulatory systems through dialogue and coherence mechanisms. The unique characteristics and functionalities of each regulatory system render the agreement upon common rules on a multilateral system a hard task. The conclusion of the TBT Agreement was of such difficulty. And confirming the above theory, since such disciplines were hard to be implemented by countries which didn't possess the necessary administrative capacity, some players had to make more concessions than others. Given the nature of Regulatory Cooperation and its fundamental dependence upon each regulatory system, it is safer for states to engage into deeper Regulatory Cooperation on a bilateral base, where required concessions by each party are of similar size and importance.[4] This happens to be the case between industrialized nations that share similar societal and regulatory traditions; however, the same cannot be told about nations of different economic development.[5] The incremental nature of bilateralism has been argued to not only facilitate the negotiation process by smoothening the reach of an agreement on the basis of equally significant concessions. Its nature also provides for a flexible implementation environment, whose fine-tuning may require negotiation, especially in such sensitive areas as is Regulatory Cooperation, whose legal and political consequences are unclear.[6]

---

[1] Koremenos et al. (2001), pp. 764ff.

[2] Rixen and Rohlfing (2007), p. 402.

[3] Rixen and Rohlfing (2007), p. 402.

[4] *See* Rixen and Rohlfing (2007).

[5] Kauffmann and Malyshev (2015), p. 4.

[6] Morin and Gagne (2007), p. 67.

The second factor upon which the preference between bilateralism and multilateralism depends are concerns about enforcement issues. Regarding enforcement, it has been found that the danger to deviate from undertaken commitments and the danger to engage in free-riding activities can be brought easier under control under a multilateral setting. This particularly applies on enforcement in the realm of trade and tariffs, where it has been argued that a multilateral setting enhances enforcement by enabling retaliatory measures in case of disobeyance and monitoring free-riding behaviors taking advantage of the MFN principle.[7] In other areas of cooperation, such as double taxation, which is traditionally regulated bilaterally, enforcement is not of fundamental importance, since states are deliberately willing, for a number of reasons to voluntarily grant double taxation relief.[8] This seems to be the case also for Regulatory Cooperation. Aiming to further liberalize trade and battle against non-tariff barriers to trade, effective Regulatory Cooperation cannot be achieved only through enforcement, but primarily needs to be the result of a conscious dialogue. As will be shown, in the realm of trade and Regulatory Cooperation, enforcement has known limited success.

Bilateralism as an institutional choice is thus found to better serve Regulatory Cooperation, a complex activity with strong societal extensions that touch upon sensitive legislative, restricted-to-state activities. However, a holistic comprehension of bilateralism as a characteristic of FTA Regulatory Cooperation cannot be achieved in isolation with reality. It additionally must be viewed in parallel with progress in other fora, in concreto. The rise of bilateralism in EU trade relations has been examined extensively by political theorists and international relations experts. Bilateralism in Regulatory Cooperation should follow the same pattern. It is upon this mission, that this Section embarks. After a short reminder of the re-orientation of EU's trade policy in general, the rest of the Section will address the multilateral developments of Regulatory Cooperation.

2.2.1   EU Trade Policy and Its Way to Bilateralism

The choice of venue for trade negotiations reflects and guides an actor's Trade Policy. The EU's stance on the issue has not been always stable, rather it has been fluctuating over the years. Apart from the commercial interests that usually drive the conclusion of FTAs,[9] the EU's passage to bilateralism was particularly determined by a mixture of internal and external factors, as the creation, progress and completion of its own internal market, the preferences of main trade opponents—mainly the US—and the lack of progress in the multilateral environment. All these reasons were deeply connected to the fundamental shift in international trade relations and the

---

[7]Rixen and Rohlfing (2007), pp. 399 and 407.

[8]Rixen and Rohlfing (2007), pp. 399 and 407.

[9]Woolcock (2014).

pressing need to adapt to the new reality.[10] The latter occurred at the first place with the gradual elimination of border measures, an achievement of previous liberalization rounds, which brought non-tariff barriers to trade to the playing field. Simultaneously, other technological advancements resulting to transport facilitation and the internationalization of Global Value Chains via Trade in Services, targeted non-tariff barriers as their main opponent. The change of the playing field highlighted the need to move past the negative integration[11] paradigm of the GATT 1947 and put greater emphasis on the development of positive integration[12] via what has been described as the 'deep trade agenda'.[13]

2.2.1.1 EU's Own Experiences

The steps through which the EU had to go through in order to establish its internal market influenced significantly its external behavior as a trade actor. Several examples can confirm this. Firstly, the initially limited scope of the EU's exclusive competence in trade (which was further built by the jurisdiction of the Court of Justice) posed a significant obstacle to the construction and promotion of a coherent and comprehensive trade agenda. In the same vain, the subsequent route to its internal market integration constituted a pillar of the EU's open promotion of rule-based deep disciplines in its trade relations. Particular mention merits the Single European Act and the enrichment of the *acquis communautaire* that played

---

[10] During the Tokyo and Uruguay Rounds America failed to regulate its areas of interest multilaterally. Even though matters such as IP, Services or TBT were -although not completely- present, a number of priorities such as Public Procurement and Investment were not agreed upon. *See* Young and Peterson (2006), p. 797.

[11] Negative Integration is understood here as developed by J. Tinbergen in International Economic Integration. According to Tinbergen negative integration is 'the elimination of certain instruments of international economic policy', especially of the discriminatory and trade restricting ones. *See* Tinbergen (1954), p. 122.

[12] Positive Integration, in the words of J. Tinbergen is the 'positive policy of integration is understood as 'supplementary measures in order to remove inconsistencies that may exist between the duties and taxes of different countries'. The positive integration model follows the specific nature of regulatory barriers, the nature that has rendered them immune towards negative integration. As regulatory barriers usually do not discriminate prima facie, and any disguised discrimination can be justified on imperative reasons of public interest, they rarely are caught by the negative integration radar. It is that veil that has facilitated their multiplication as trade barriers. Thus, the general term adopted by Tinbergen on positive integration as the adoption of complementary measures to fight remaining inconsistencies, has been concretized by market imperatives as the total of practices primarily aimed to 'discipline domestic regulation'. Positive integration accomplishes this discipline by demanding regulatory action of the actors, in a positive form. *See* Tinbergen (1954), p. 122.

[13] According to Young and Peterson, the term borrows from the notion of 'deeper integration' introduced by Lawrence to describe the attempts made at the regional and international level to combat the obstacles posed to economic exchange by domestic rules. *See* Young and Peterson (2006), p. 798.

unwillingly a major role to this direction.[14] Other partners however did not equally share this enthusiasm.

2.2.1.2 Hesitance and Lack of Progress in the Multilateral Setting

The expansion of trade rules to disciplines of positive integration was one of the newly added questions that the creation of WTO had to answer. However, already from the Tokyo and later during the Uruguay Round, the emerging coalition of India and Brazil, considering themselves as the representatives of the South blocked consistently the inclusion of deep-trade disciplines in the multilateral arena, as they were seen as annulling the competitive advantage, which they and other developing countries enjoyed in areas such as environment and labor.[15] The consistent lack of development due to the redistribution of bargaining power, a significant loss for the US hemi-hegemony was also, what paved the latter's way to bilateralism. The Union's efforts to re-introduce deep trade instances through the so-called 'Singapore Issues' in the subsequent Singapore, Doha and Cancun meetings were equally unsuccessful,[16] given also US's gradual lack of interest and support.[17]

2.2.1.3 Proliferation of FTAs Globally

The end to EU efforts to revive an ambitious multilateralism slowly came in 2006, where the then Director General of the WTO, Pascal Lamy, announced the suspension of negotiations due to minimum progress being observed, with discussions dominated by old-fashioned issues, mainly tariffs in agriculture.[18] By 2006, in an attempt to gain the losing ground to its main competitors, political forces, especially within the Committee of Article 133, started acquiring consensus on the need to follow the international trend of bilateralism and regionalism.[19] Indeed, the EU had already suffered the first trade diversion effects caused by the conclusion of NAFTA, which had a significant impact on EU exports to Mexico.[20]

The nascent EU trade policy was finally confirmed by the inauguration of the 2006 Global Europe Strategy.[21] The latter would follow the example of other major

---

[14] Woolcock (2010), p. 382.

[15] Efstathopoulos (2012), p. 273.

[16] The main mandate of these working groups was to explore ways to discipline domestic rules on areas like investment, competition, government procurement and trade facilitation. *See* Young and Peterson (2006), p. 798.

[17] Woolcock (2003), p. 251.

[18] Young and Peterson (2006), p. 807.

[19] Young and Peterson (2006), p. 807.

[20] Rigod (2012), p. 290.

[21] EU Commission (2006).

trade actors, mainly US and Japan, who had already engaged actively into bilateral commitments.[22] The Agenda refers to bilateralism as an institution used in other instances of European Foreign Policy. In particular, it states its significance for the smooth functioning of the European Neighborhood Policy and its dominance in Economic Partnership Agreements (hereinafter EPAs).[23] It admits though its limited role for trade liberalization ambitions. Hence its extension to trade relations. Throughout the agenda, the EU promotes the excluded from the multilateral club, deep integration issues. Despite this turn of events, the EU commitment to multilateralism remains deep.[24] Even after the reassessment of its trade policy, the then Commission for Trade committed to guide a liberal trade agenda which would complete, not undermine and impede future multilateralism, while welcoming new multilateral discussions, provided that some consensus would be reached.[25] Further, its commitment to multilateralism, and in particular to the rules-based multilateralism in a number of sectors guides the spirit of the New Global Agenda.[26] Even though multilateral trade may not be explicitly stated as a priority, the belief of the suitability of multilateralism as a governance philosophy transpires the whole Agenda.

2.2.2 An Inadequate Multilateral Setting

Already, the history of multilateral trade relations and negotiations highlights the central role of regulatory obstacles in their context. Their reference as a matter by and of themselves at a point where tariff reductions had reached historically low levels, was unavoidable.[27] Thus negotiators felt the need to dedicate separate agreements on the issue, thus leading to the introduction first time by the Tokyo Round Standards Code in the GATT era. Regulatory Cooperation under the GATT regime began with the Standards Code, the ancestor of the TBT and SPS Agreements, to be later concluded under the WTO scheme. While its scope of application remained limited to technical regulations, standards and conformity assessment procedures covering goods, as the contemporary agreements now do, the Standards Code was the first to introduce segments of Regulatory Cooperation and

---

[22] That was the case for Japan with ASEAN countries and the US with Korea. *See* EU Commission (2006).

[23] For a thorough analysis on the subject *see* Heydon and Woolcock (2009).

[24] EU Commission (2006), p. 15.

[25] EU Commission (2006), p. 15.

[26] Multilateralism is mostly referred in the Agenda in the context of bewished rules-based approaches guided by the UN. Multilateral rules should be sought on a number of issues, such as armed conflict, human rights, food and water security, international combat against terrorism, energy and climate. *See* EEAS (2016).

[27] *See* generally Köbele (2007).

coherence.[28] Regulatory Cooperation provisions mainly highlighted on the one hand the importance of international standards as such, which had to be taken into account by national legislatures during the formation of national technical regulations, and on the other hand, the need for Member States to participate actively to international organisations responsible for their formation; as for regulatory coherence, the agreement introduced obligations to notify and tolerate comments on national regulations deviating from international standards, and to allow a reasonable time between their publication and entry into force.[29]

Soon however, a number of birth deficits limited the actual effect of these provisions. First of all, the Agreement was a plurilateral one, mostly a club for developed countries, which resulted to its fragmented application.[30] Furthermore, its effective application was hindered also from the shortcomings of the GATT Dispute Resolution System, namely the requirement for consensus and the non-provision of appellate procedures.[31] Last but not least, the growing number of barriers in food and agriculture revealed the inability of the provisions to cover them sufficiently and underlined the need for a separate agreement only on these issues.[32]

The Uruguay round resulted in two Agreements dedicated to product regulation, the TBT and SPS, and on various provisions of regulatory nature to be found in the sectoral agreements, the GATS and TRIPS Agreements. Although formerly grouped under a sole Agreement, the Uruguay negotiations resulted into a separation between SPS and TBT measures, due to the inherent particularity of the former.[33] These two Agreements which form the evolution of the Standards Code, introduced similar provisions, although a little bit more elaborated, clarified, and with some additions. Their added value can be found to the fact that they were adopted under Annex 1A of the Agreement establishing the WTO, which renders them part of the multilateral system.[34] This comes in contrast with the Standards Code, which was formatted separately from the GATT and thus open for "acceptance by signature".[35] Their exposure to the Dispute Settlement Mechanism (hereinafter DSM) counted as an additional 'plus' in the overall image of potential.

After this short analysis of how these disciplines came to exist, the following section embarks on a double mission: on the one hand, it aims to discuss to which extent is Regulatory Cooperation to be found in the multilateral setting and on the other hand to highlight the shortcomings of its existing elements through a legal analysis. The reasons will be explored in an analysis of the status and the core provisions of the TBT and of the relevant GATS provisions. When necessary,

---

[28] Nakagawa (2016) 395.

[29] Middleton (1980), pp. 205ff.

[30] Marceau and Trachtman (2002), p. 814.

[31] Kudryavtsev (2013), p. 22.

[32] Marceau and Trachtman (2014), p. 355.

[33] Kudryavtsev (2013), p. 25.

[34] World Trade Organisation (2014), p. 11.

[35] Middleton (1980), p. 201.

parallels to the SPS Agreement shall be drawn. Other Agreements, as is the TRIPS will not be analyzed in this instance, as the purpose of the section is not to go deep into the details of each regulatory discipline in the WTO, but to comment on their general nature and philosophy.

2.2.2.1 Core Multilateral Disciplines: Regulatory Coherence or Regulatory Cooperation?

As a term, Regulatory Cooperation in trade has been connected with activities and initiatives undertaken to tackle unnecessary regulatory barriers to trade. These barriers that form a distinct category of their own, as they may reflect societal values, present characteristics of intrinsic nature and have required measured solutions in the environment where they occurred. Also, in the multilateral setting, where they turned from a development into an imperative, they necessitated a special regime, materialized through the TBT and SPS Agreements, which were tailored made to combat such barriers through alternative measures. Each of these measures has a unique impact and denotes different ways through which the heterogeneity of national regulations is addressed, and approximation is achieved. However, this does not necessarily mean that these measures reflect Regulatory Cooperation as the latter is addressed in the present thesis. On the contrary, the core disciplines build upon GATT provisions. The chosen legal tools which are to be found under both Agreements are the disciplines that prohibit discriminatory treatment and the disciplines that develop a rationality test. Using the TBT provisions as first material to interpret their functioning, the section provides a grasp of the main orientation of these Agreements, which in combination with the findings of the next Section uphold the turn to bilateralism in particular regarding this activity.

Non-Discrimination or Something More?

Article 2.1 demands that *"in respect of technical regulations, products imported from the territory of any Member shall be accorded treatment no less favorable than that accorded to like products of national origin and to like products originating in any other country."* This provision brings together the so-called National Treatment (hereinafter NT) and Most Favored Nation (hereinafter MFN). The focus of this Article on non-discrimination provisions can be deducted from the wording of the Agreement, as its aim has been to address discriminatory behaviors that foreign products could face regarding the technical regulations they would have to abide to. The aim of this Article is to extend the already existing non-discriminatory provisions and catch under its ambit measures that otherwise could not be caught by the GATT.[36] Meanwhile GATT's reach on regulatory measures has been confirmed by the AB: In the US-Tuna II case,[37] Article 2.1 TBT comes simply to expand the anti-discriminatory provisions through a specialized legal regime also to voluntary standards and conformity assessment procedures, that concern not only the products themselves but also their production and process methods.[38] Similarly, Article 2.3 SPS adjusts both non-discrimination principles to the particularities of the SPS Agreement, by requiring that SPS measures do not discriminate between areas that are characterized by similar or identical conditions, no matter whether these areas are within their territory or within the territory of other Members.

In general, non-discrimination provisions fall shortly of introducing Regulatory Cooperation. Their impact to normative approximation can at best be through negative integration. To this direction, AB's judicial reading of provision 2.1 TBT confirms that its focus remains purely non-discriminatory and does not acquire a different meaning within the TBT Agreement. As a general acknowledgement, the AB admitted in the US—Clove Cigarettes case that "the TBT and GATT overlap in scope and objectives".[39] Moreover, this being the first case to necessitate the interpretation of the Article, it is worth mentioning and indicative that the AB held as 'instructive' relevant jurisprudence of the GATT.[40] Key concepts as the 'likeness' of the products and the understanding of 'treatment no less favorable' borrowed their essence from the corresponding GATT ones.[41] The Judiciary's reliance upon previous jurisprudence on the neighboring GATT provisions as source for inspiration and argumentation is indicative of the similarity of the legal construction to the GATT anatomy. Taking into account the AB's emphasis on the structural similarities of the

---

[36] This has been further recognized first in the *EC v. Asbestos* case, where the AB concluded that "the TBT Agreement imposes obligations that are different from and additional to, the obligations imposed on the Member States under GATT 1994" AB Report in WT/DS135/AB/R *EC v. Asbestos*, par. 80.

[37] The AB found that in contrast to the SPS Agreement, conformity under the TBT cannot exclude examination under the GATT, which can be found in the end violated. This finding of the AB on the relation between the two Agreements does not follow closely the rule of *lex specialis* principle. According to the latter, the specific rule (here the TBT rules) is considered first, and the general one (the GATT) only second, if this is necessary. The AB seems to suggest that while TBT rules come first, GATT rules must be also taken into consideration, also in the case of non-violation. *See* in this regard Marceau (2014).

[38] Ming Du (2007), p. 279

[39] AB Report in WT/DS406/AB/R, *United States — Measures Affecting the Production and Sale of Clove Cigarettes*, par. 91.

[40] AB Report in WT/DS406/AB/R, *United States — Measures Affecting the Production and Sale of Clove Cigarettes*, par.180.

[41] As far as 'likeness' is concerned, the AB overruled the findings of the Panel that had argued for an understanding of 'likeness' based on the objectives and purposes of the regulations. In fact, it copied/pasted the concept of 'likeness' of products as found in jurisprudence of Article III:4 GATT, based on the nature and extent of the competitive relationship between the products. Moreover, the concept 'treatment no less favorable' was also given a similar meaning as in the GATT, encompassing both de facto and de jure no less favorable treatment. *See* van den Bosche and Zdouc (2017), pp. 902ff.

TBT and SPS, there is no reason to argue that SPS Article 3.2 is to be interpreted differently to TBT 2.1. It is no coincidence that these provisions find their roots in Article 2.1 of the Standards' Code, an agreement born into GATT's Committees, which proved to be a decisive factor that maximized the influence of the latter to the former.[42]

Substantial Control Through Rationality Requirements?

Since regulatory diversity can be pertinent and unnecessary even if non-discriminatory, a first control of the substance of neutral regulatory measures is realized through the so-called rationality requirements. Found under Articles 2.2 TBT and 2.2 SPS in the respective Agreements, these provisions introduce 'necessity tests' that aim to discipline domestic regulation by imposing to the latter a rationality requirement which serves as the thin line between legitimate regulation and protectionism.[43] The rationality test is implemented by the use of certain values, which work as benchmarks, against which the rationality of the measures is assessed during the development stage.

Article 2.2 TBT reads as follows:

> Members shall ensure that technical regulations are not prepared, adopted or applied with a view to or with the effect of creating unnecessary obstacles to international trade. For this purpose, technical regulations shall not be more trade-restrictive than necessary to fulfil a legitimate objective, taking account of the risks non-fulfilment would create. Such legitimate objectives are, inter alia: national security requirements; the prevention of deceptive practices; protection of human health or safety, animal or plant life or health, or the environment. In assessing such risks, relevant elements of consideration are, inter alia: available scientific and technical information, related processing technology or intended end-uses of products.

In this Article, as benchmark serves the value of necessity, enshrined in the first limb of the provision, in the sense that technical regulations shall not 'be prepared, adopted or applied with a view or with the effect to unnecessarily restrict trade.'[44] The second limb has a double significance: On the one hand, it mitigates the effects of the first and adds to it a gloss of legitimacy. A technical regulation is allowed to be trade disrupting, as long as it serves a legitimate objective, but is not allowed to be more trade-restrictive than necessary. On the other hand, the second limb serves as a mechanism to determine which measure qualifies as 'unnecessary': when a measure is more trade restrictive than necessary to fulfil a legitimate objective, it will be found to violate the first limb.[45] With regard to the SPS Agreement, a similar need to weigh the necessity of an SPS measure against the corresponding objectives is to be found

---

[42] For a detailed background on the roots of Articles 2.1 and 2.2 *see* Lester and Sternberg (2014).

[43] Weiss (2020), Chapter 4, sub I.

[44] The same obligation extends to standards and conformity assessment procedures, on the basis of Annex 3.E and Article 5.1.2 of the TBT Agreement.

[45] Tamiotti (2007), p. 218.

under Article 2.2 SPS, that assesses the rationality not only on the basis of a necessity test but also upon scientific principles and evidence.[46] As far as the GATS is concerned, given the even more demanding impetus to rationalize regulation in the services' area (see below B.ii), a comparable rationality requirement is to be extracted from the rudimentary Article VI:5 GATS, read in conjunction with Article VI:4 GATS.[47] According to this joint reading, Member States shall apply licensing and qualification requirements and technical standards that nullify or impair already undertaken commitments in a manner that *inter alia* is based on objective and transparent criteria and is not more burdensome than necessary to ensure the quality of the service.[48] Thus, Member States undertake the responsibility of applying certain objectivity principles, even if those apply only where restrictive regulation comes to play.

The input of these disciplines to the substance of domestic measures extends certainly beyond non-discrimination, but only up to the point of imposing a rational, objective and appropriate criterion to the proposed regulation.[49] Such disciplines could be seen as a primitive form of positive integration by setting *a common standard of rationality* along which all future TBT and SPS measures have to move, if the WTO judiciary chose to interpret the rationality criteria in a particular, restrictive way.[50] In the very end, despite any impact in the form of a requirement that regulations have to meet, these provisions cannot be seen as introducing Regulatory Cooperation, in the form of approximation, as they only indirectly and marginally influence the substance of the regulations. Under these rules, regulations can still remain diverging and rational at the same time.

2.2.2.2   Regulatory Cooperation with Limits

Despite the primary standing of the aforementioned principles, an approach that nevertheless shies away from them and aims towards a substantial approximation of the regulations through Regulatory Cooperation is sought in the realm of WTO. In the TBT and SPS Agreements this approach is implemented by the importance of international standards during the development of the regulations. Through the relevant Articles 2.4 TBT and 3.1 SPS it is demanded that the Member States depart from a common regulatory point -an international standard of relevance[51]

---

[46] Weiss (2020), Chapter 4, sub. 2b.

[47] Delimatsis (2008), p. 390.

[48] The Article spells out two additional requirements: The first limb includes a requirement on licensing procedures, that must not in themselves restrict the supply of services. The second limb requires that the manner by which Members choose to proceed must not come into contrast to the legitimate expectations created to other Members.

[49] Krajewski (2008), p. 415.

[50] Weiss (2020), Chapter 4, sub I.

[51] In both Articles International Standards have to be relevant in order to be considered. In the TBT Agreement relevance is part of the legal text. For the SPS Agreement, it was the Judiciary which

appropriateness and efficiency—when designing their national regulations. In the GATS, the approximation is mandated on the basis of Article VI:4, by the creation of common rules upon which certain regulations will be based. Both types of commitments can fall under the ambit of Regulatory Cooperation activities, in particular the ones that aim to harmonization.[52]

However, this process of Regulatory approximation finds certain limits, and these limits are decisive when it comes to the materialization, implementation and impact of the provisions. Firstly, limitations can be placed by the lack of implementation by the Member States themselves. An illustration of this provides Article VI:4 GATS, where it is the internal incapacity to reach a decision what is that has impeded the harmonizing potential. A different, but equally important source of limitations can be the judicial understanding of the provisions. Based on the degree of deference that the judiciary wishes to give to the Member States, an interpretation can either restrict or expand their harmonizing potential of a provision. In general, the issues that WTO as a single undertaking addresses, are found very often to acrobat between trade liberalization and protection of other values. Given their sensitive nature, this balance is both necessary to achieve and difficult to draw. In the realm of the TBT Agreement, this balance is firstly spelled out at the sixth recital of the Agreement's preamble, which upholds the sovereign right to regulate towards the protection of legitimate interests.[53] TBT's provision on international standards follows this pattern: On the one side, the positive obligation on the Member States to follow for the content of their regulations and conformity assessment procedures international standards, issued by relevant organizations[54] recognizes international standards as vehicles for reconciling regulatory cultures and minimizing unnecessary barriers to trade. On the other side, the affirmation of Members' sovereign right to regulate as they see fit is expressed through the possibility to deviate from the obligation stated above, when international standards do not correspond or correspond partially to the objectives pursued. Similarly, the SPS Preamble begins by mentioning the balance at stake: on the one hand it opens by reaffirming the national right to regulate but right after subjects it in the context of non-discrimination.[55] Both Agreements are touched by this inherent battle between the two competing values, however inconsistencies regarding the interpretation are to be found. It is upon this inherent battle, that the WTO Judiciary interprets the provisions according to the degree of deference it wishes to grant to the Members. The greater the deference is, the less harmonizing is the potential. This Section will try to delineate the limits of the provisions that

---

confirmed that SPS International Standards have to be relevant to the case, since Article 3.1 does not explicitly mention so.

[52] Harmonization is not understood as an absolute and flat process. Harmonization may as well occur partially or to a certain degree.

[53] Recital 6 of the Preamble of the TBT Agreement.

[54] In comparison to the SPS Agreement, the TBT Agreement does not provide with a list of the international organizations, whose standards are to be followed.

[55] Recital 1 of the Preamble of the SPS Agreements.

prescribe harmonization through International Standards, namely Articles 2.4 TBT and 3.1 SPS through a judicial reading. However, the reading and the interpretation of the examined provisions by the AB, through the few relevant decisions has provided neither a complete nor a consolidated view of the balance measurement at stake.

The Limits of Article 2.4 TBT and 3.1 SPS

As mentioned, in the case of Articles 2.4 TBT and 3.1 SPS, the limits of the provisions depend on the judicial understanding of the articles' key concepts. The parts of significance to the assessment of the measurement at stake are visible already from a first reading of the provisions. Before any assessment, it should be reminded that since the provisions go beyond mere encouragement with the use of the word "shall", the Member States are expected to implement it, following a hard law obligation they have undertaken. The judicial understanding of the instrumental terms "international standards" and "basis" is crucial for the estimation of the Members' legal obligation. Moreover, the choice regarding the placement of the burden of proof is indicative of the emerging balance, as is also the amplitude of the objectives that justify deviation from them. Indeed, which standards qualify as international and to what extent do Member States need to comply with them? How easily can one Member State deviate from the obligation? Is the burden of proof positioned for or against the regulating party?

An answer to those and an effort to locate the balance will be sought at the relevant case-law of the provisions under consideration. While an illustration of the emerging balance between the regulatory margin of manoeuvre of the Members and the depth of the Judiciary's assessment could be based on a standard of review of the regulatory measures, this is not an option for the Agreements at stake, since according to the AB in EC-Hormones, a standard of review has only been chosen for the Anti-Dumping Agreement.[56] A clear standard of review has not emerged through a systematic analysis of the Jurisprudence either. On the contrary, a case-to-case assessment has been observed. Given the lack of a standard of review, it is by answering to the questions set above that the following part, based mostly on case law, will try to locate the interests, towards which the scale tends to lean.

The Obligation to Substantially Base Regulations to International Standards

As far as the TBT Agreement is concerned, of importance to the answer of the two first questions set above are the EC-Sardines and the US-Tuna cases. On these occasions where the AB was given the chance to initiate the interpretation of Article 2.4 TBT, a pro-trade, liberalizing interpretation has been chosen. In the EC-Sardines

---

[56] AB Report in WT/DS26/29 *European Communities — Measures Concerning Meat and Meat Products (Hormones)*, par. 114.

case Peru challenged an EU Regulation which delineated which species of sardines could be marketed as such in the European market. Peru's main argument was on the inconsistency of the EU Regulation with a relevant available international standard, issued by Codex Alimentarius Commission on sardines labeling.[57] For the assessment of the case, the AB discussed among others which international standards qualify as such and as relevant ones for the purposes of the Article. Having confirmed the Panel's view on the question of *relevance* of an international standard, as being one that *"bears upon, relates to the matter in hand; is pertinent to"*,[58] the AB rejected the argument raised by the European Communities that standards need to be adopted by consensus within the International Bodies in order to qualify under the terms of Article 2.4 TBT.[59] This conclusion has been characterized as an unfortunate one, as it creates a paradoxical dynamic between the WTO and the standardizing international organizations. With this decision, the WTO seems to grant a high legal value to non-consensual standards, a value higher than the one the standardizing bodies ascribe to their own decisions.[60] Put differently, the WTO upgraded international standards as values against which national choices are assessed, while completely disregarding their initial legal status and per se enforceability.[61]

The US-Tuna case continued the crystallization of the term "international standards" by shedding light on a different angle of the process of their creation: the environment within which they are adopted, namely, the international bodies that issue them. In the EC-Sardines case, the EC never questioned the capacity of Codex Alimentarius to set international standards as an international standard setting body. This question arose in the US-Tuna case, where Mexico challenged a US measure that regulated the use of a private voluntary standard, the "dolphin safe" labelling.[62] Mexico made claims against the measure on the basis of several TBT provisions, including on the basis of 2.4. Specifically, Mexico argued for the inconsistency of the measure with a relevant international standard, issued by AIDCP, a regional intergovernmental regime for dolphin protection.[63] Altering the Panel's analysis on this argument, which accepted the existence of an international standard but denied its application on the basis of its inappropriateness for the legitimate objective that US was pursuing,[64] the AB rejected the Mexican argument in its totality by denying the presence of an international standard in this case. In assessing the definition of "international standards", the AB draw upon the province of a relevant international

---

[57] Trebilcock (2015), p. 160.

[58] The WTO Panel built upon the literal/ dictionary meaning of the word "relevant". See Tamiotti (2007).

[59] Tamiotti (2007).

[60] Horn and Weiler (2005), p. 254.

[61] Zlepting (2010), p. 383.

[62] Howese and Levy (2013), p. 332.

[63] Howese and Levy (2013), p. 332.

[64] Howese and Levy (2013), p. 332.

standard, that is an international standardizing body. It essentially developed two criteria that international standardizing bodies should meet: openness and recognition. Regarding the criterion of openness, the AB insisted on the necessity to include only standards that come from international organizations that do not set criteria on future memberships. Indeed, as the AB argued, membership should be automatic and not subject to time restrictions. It was on those grounds that AIDCP was disqualified as an international standardization body, since new memberships required an invitation, a requirement that was judged substantial and not merely formal. Regarding the criterion of recognition the AB, having already reached its decision based on the openness criterion, did not proceed on its substantial examination. It provided though some guidelines on what recognition under TBT could entail. In short, a standardization body is recognized when its standardizing action is acknowledged by the Member States through reference to them in their national regulatory action.[65] Massive adoption of body's standard is not necessary for it to be recognized, while even bodies with only one developed standard can be recognized,[66] provided that standardization is recognized as part of their activity by the Member States.[67]

The double-limbed test for the determination of the international character of a standardizing body seems to draw a peculiar balance. While many bodies can be recognized for their standardizing action given the width of the set criteria, which are fair but far from stringent, the criterion of openness could pose serious obstacles to the acceptance of the international character of a body, and eventually to the inclusion of its work in the TBT Agreement. For example, several WTO Member States, such as Hong Kong, are not recognized states, and thus, cannot participate on this capacity in standard setting bodies.[68] Interestingly enough, it has been pointed out that this strict requirement is not jurisprudential, but instead is a limitation that the Member States themselves posed in the text. Indeed, Annex provision 1.4 understands an international body as one "whose membership is open to the relevant bodies of at least all Members".[69] Scholarship has tried to mitigate the constraining effects of this provision. It has been argued that the requirement of openness determines only which standards have a binding effect, while all other standards that do not satisfy the openness requirement, are encouraged to be taken under consideration by the Member States, however, without benefiting from the beneficial presumption of Article 2.5 TBT.[70] However, as it stands now, it cannot be denied that the interpretation given in combination with the Annex provision limiting the application of Article 2.4, reveals a cautious approach taken by the AB.

---

[65] Wijkström and McDaniels (2013), p. 13.

[66] AB Report in WT/DS381/AB/R *United States — Measures Concerning the Importation, Marketing and Sale of Tuna and Tuna Products*, par. 392–394.

[67] AB Report in WT/DS381/AB/R *United States — Measures Concerning the Importation, Marketing and Sale of Tuna and Tuna Products*, par. 390.

[68] Marceau (2014), p. 24.

[69] Marceau (2014), p. 24.

[70] Marceau (2014), p. 24.

Qualification of a standard as international becomes a simpler task under the SPS Agreement. According to Annex A:3 of the Agreement, international standards, guidelines and recommendations are defined by explicit reference to three specific standardization bodies.[71] Although this enumeration is not exclusive, the identification and addition of other bodies belongs to the SPS Committee, depriving the WTO Judiciary from enjoying a similar role in the selection process as it does with regard to the TBT Agreement. Nevertheless, it cannot go unnoticed, that both Agreements set clear limits on what is considered as an international standard. These limits should be regarded as mirroring a fair selectivity, but should not be interpreted as overly restrictive, so as to deprive the provision of its *effet utile*.

The width of the term "international standards" is undoubtedly a crucial element for the depth of Article 2.4 TBT. However, it is not exclusive. The final reach of Article 2.4 is to be viewed holistically after taking into consideration the extent of the Member States' obligation to consider international standards during their regulating activities. Article 2.4 provides that Member States need to use the international standards or the relevant parts of them *as a basis* for their technical regulations. Literature has approximated this requirement via a procedural and substantial alternative. Through the procedural lenses, international standards are the initial piece, the *basis,* upon which national legislators are called to work. Horn and Weiler have mirrored this procedural approach to Union's legislative concept, where the Union's legislators, the Council and the Parliament use the Commission's legislative proposal as a basis; in both cases, the final regulation may differ substantially from the original proposal, which *procedurally* served as a basis.[72] On the contrary, the substantial alternative would use the international standard as a yardstick for a post hoc conformity examination of the national measure.[73] The firstly advocated by the Panel and later affirmed by the AB's textual interpretation, based on dictionaries,[74] lean towards the substantial alternative.[75] The AB uses the phrases "principal constituent", "fundamental principle", "main constituent", and "determining principle" to understand the term "basis", noting the necessity of a substantial relationship between the two notions that should not in any case be contradictory.[76]

While it is made clear that international standards have to impact the substance of the regulation, the AB has not ruled on the desired degree of this impact, on the

---

[71] Annex A(3): "international standards, guidelines and recommendations". https://www.wto.org/ english/res_e/publications_e/ai17_e/sps_anna_jur.pdf, p. 24.

[72] Horn and Weiler (2005), p. 256.

[73] Horn and Weiler (2005), p. 256.

[74] Horn and Weil have criticized this textualistic interpretation by the jurisprudence of the WTO as an unfortunate choice aiming to legitimize their authority. Horn and Weiler (2005), p. 267.

[75] The probability of the substantive alternative is supported also by the fact that the TBT provisions apply to both previous and new measures. While a procedural approach could be adopted for new measures, existing measures could only be altered substantially. *See* Horn and Weiler (2005), p. 256ff.

[76] AB Report in WT/DS231/AB/R *European Communities—Trade Description of Sardines* par. 244–248.

extent to which international standards have to be followed. It has been rightly mentioned, that despite acquiring a strong substantial significance, the requirement to "use as a basis" does not equal to a conformity requirement.[77] On the occasion of the EC-Hormones (Canada) case, the AB reversed the Panel's finding and held a different meaning for the two requirements. It based its finding upon a Dictionary citation and upon the use of the terms in different paragraphs in Article 3, a fact that revealed the differing significance of the two.[78] The AB passionately argued against a total harmonizing effect of Article 3.1 by stating that such a scenario would turn international standards to legally binding norms, thus moving over the initial intention of the parties.[79] In the end, to base does not mean to conform, but it also cannot exclude a close relationship between international standards and national regulations. It would be far-reaching to claim that the requirement 'to base' equals just to 'not contradict'; in the end if this were the case, this would also be reflected in the wording of the provision.

Requirements for Deviation and Burden of Proof

Up until to this point, the analysis has revealed a quite consistent approach towards the interpretation of the main points of both provisions under analysis. This does not hold true for the circumstances that allow deviation from the international standards in each case and the corresponding burden of proof in cases of litigation. Article 2.4's TBT conditions allow a much more favorable environment. A deviation from 2.4 TBT is made easier not only because it is not accompanied with extra obligations, as does deviation in the SPS, but also because in the cases of litigation the AB has created a procedurally favorable environment for the deviating party.

In general, the stance followed regarding the requirements for deviation from the harmonizing obligation of the SPS Agreement and the regarding the burden of proof is more consistent and more convincing, although also stricter than the one chosen for the TBT. According to the AB in the EC-Hormones case, Article 3 contains 3 independent cases, and not a rule-exception relationship between them, as the Panel had argued.[80] Provision 3.1 comprises the obligation to harmonize *on the basis of* international standards, while provision 3.2 grants to measures that *conform to* international standards a rebuttable presumption of necessity and conformity. The third given option is to be found under Article 3.3 which makes deviation from international standards possible provided that two conditions are met: firstly it must be established after a scientific justification/risk assessment that the chosen measure

---

[77] This is also based on the fact that regulations enjoy the presumption of WTO conformity, only when they fully conform to international standards, and not when they are just based.

[78] AB Report in WT/DS26/AB/R, WT/DS28/AB/R *European Communities — Measures Concerning Meat and Meat Products (Hormones)* par. 163, 164.

[79] AB Report in WT/DS26/AB/R, WT/DS28/AB/R *European Communities — Measures Concerning Meat and Meat Products (Hormones)* par. 165.

[80] AB Report in WT/DS26/AB/R, WT/DS28/AB/R *European Communities — Measures Concerning Meat and Meat Products (Hormones)* par.169ff.

must grant a higher degree of protection than the international standards do and secondly the international standards must not suffice in order to reach the desirable higher level of protection. In short, Member States can either base to, conform with, or disregard international standards. However, the option to disregard international standards is conveyed with scientific justification/risk assessment, a task argued to be rather demanding under Article 5 of the SPS Agreement. This requirement makes a possible deviation more complicated in the SPS than in the TBT, where Member States are allowed to deviate when international standards are proven ineffective or inappropriate, a claim, which, however, has to be proved.

In the context of the SPS Agreement, the burden of proving the inconsistency of a measure to international standards rests, according to provision 3.3, with the complaining party. The burden of proof is regulated like this, because, as mentioned, the three provisions are not connected with a rule-exception relationship. According to the AB, Article 3.1 is not the rule, and hence Article 3.3 is not its exception.[81] All three provisions, 3.1, 3.2. and 3.3 are self-standing, disconnected to the others, as each covers a different situation. Thus, the burden of proof rests with the party invoking the violation of Article 3.3, and not with the party that has made use of it.

However, things are more complicated when allocating the burden of proof in the second recital of Article 2.4 TBT. Article 2.4 is a complex construction, that combines under the same provision both the obligation to base national TBT regulations on international standards, and the conditions under which a deviation is allowed. Accordingly, there is a corresponding burden of proof for these two situations, which was dealt on the occasion of the EC-Sardines case. Beginning with the obligation to use international regulations as a basis, it is the complaining party that has to prove the inconsistency of a national regulation with the relevant international standard, just like in the SPS Agreement, which is procedurally sound, since according to standard procedural theory it is the complaining party that has to prove the truth of its allegations. Surprisingly though, the AB also ruled that the complaining party not only had to prove the disregard of the international standard, but also its appropriateness and effectiveness for the public policy concern, which the regulating party wishes to address. Thus, ruling certainly favored the Member State against which proceedings are running, since after having proven the inconsistency of the measure with international standards, the complaining party also needs to provide reasons supporting the correspondence of the international standard to the legitimate objectives that the other state tries to pursue. This mirrors the burden of the defending party to demonstrate the inappropriate fit of the international standard for its legitimate objectives, as found by the WTO Panel. It is the different side of the same argument. And this is the point which draws the balance.

One of the reasons that guided the AB's decision towards this direction was that, as in the EC-Hormones case, where the same rule-exception question arised in the

---

[81] AB Report in WT/DS26/AB/R, WT/DS28/AB/R *European Communities — Measures Concerning Meat and Meat Products (Hormones)* par.172.

SPS framework (see above), we are not in the presence of a rule-exception relationship, which would indeed reverse the burden of proof to the EU. In particular, it argued that the obligation to use international standards and the margin of manoeuvre to disobey as expressed in the last sentence, are not under a rule-exception case, but *"the circumstances envisaged in the second part of Article 2.4 are excluded from the scope of application of the first part of Article 2.4."*[82] The AB justified further its opinion by recalling the existence of transparency provisions within the TBT, namely the obligation to justify national choices under 2.5 and the requirement of Article 10.1 to set up "enquiry points" that would facilitate the exchange of information.[83] According to the Panel's view, these provisions enable the complaining party to acquire information on the legitimate reasons behind a certain regulation, and actually argue for the suitability of an international standard against them. The AB rested upon the facilitating character of these provisions, taking as a fact, that according to the principle "pacta sunt servanda" and the Members States' good faith, one should depart from the point that Member States will actually abide by their international obligations.[84]

The reasoning of the AB seems partially unpersuasive, and, to my view, the AB is cleverly escaping basic procedural principles through the creation of legal plasmas. Regarding the first argument, the AB contended that the relationship between the first and second part of Article 2.4 TBT is not a rule-exception case, but *"the circumstances envisaged in the second part of Article 2.4 are excluded from the scope of application of the first part of Article 2.4."* Following the WTO Judiciary's favorite practice, I rely on a dictionary definition for the purposes of the following argument. Cambridge dictionary defines exception as the situation where "someone or something that is not included in a rule, group, or list or that does not behave in the expected way".[85] If the second part is *excluded* from the scope application of the first, does not this mean that it is supposed not to "behave", to "fit" in a particular way? Is this not a clear exception? Apart from that, the reasoning of the AB comes in contrast with its ruling in the EC-Hormones case. There, in order to exclude any kind of relation between provisions 3.1 and 3.2 SPS, the AB raised the argument that they constitute different provisions, implying that if they were to be somehow connected, they would be positioned in the same paragraph. This is exactly the case of Article 2.4, where requirement and deviation are united under the same provision, which the AB completely disregards. If this relation is not a rule-exception one, why is it then included in the same Article, the second part being the

---

[82] AB Report in WT/DS231/AB/R *European Communities – Trade Description of Sardines*, par. 275.

[83] AB Report in WT/DS231/AB/R *European Communities – Trade Description of Sardines*, par. 277–280.

[84] AB Report in WT/DS231/AB/R *European Communities – Trade Description of Sardines*, par. 278.

[85] Cambridge Online Dictionary (n.d.). Definition of 'exception'. https://dictionary.cambridge.org/dictionary/english/exception.

continuation of the first? If this were to be the intention of the parties, a principle that the AB clearly ignored, shouldn't it be positioned in a different Article?

Regarding the second argument, the reasoning of the AB is safe, and rightly it builds upon fundamental international law principles, as is "pacta sunt servanda". However, it is also safe to argue that, despite the transparency provisions, the complaining party might not always possess the necessary information about the background that led to a particular regulation, since according the EU Report of 2012 many countries are not diligent with their obligations, in the sense that they either report their regulations at an advanced stage, or they avoid answering the questions posed to them by other Members.[86] Lastly, let us not pretend that the regulating Member State can handle the available information in such a way so as to conceal a protectionist measure under a legitimate objective.

Behind this flawed argumentation of the AB stands its effort to grant a greater degree of deference to Members States' choices and provide them with legal advantages that aim to secure part of their regulatory sovereignty and freedom, at least as far as Article 2.4 is concerned. The same could be argued for all the interpretative points towards which the AB chose to take a more restricted stand. However, the inconsistencies that are to be found between the SPS and TBT Agreements are quite remarkable, not only because of the similarity of their provisions on harmonization, but also because of the difference between the level of deference opted for each Agreement. Apart from the term "international standards", which is to be understood differently in each Agreement, their substantial importance that has to be used "as a basis for" remains the same for both Agreements and widens their potential. However, the exigencies for deviation and the litigation terms are decisive regarding the divergence of the two Agreements. While stringent conditions must be met for deviation under the SPS Agreement, the TBT Agreement loses in efficacy mainly because of the unfortunate verdict over the burden of proof, a clear illustration of support towards Members States' regulatory sovereignty, an approach to be welcomed that nevertheless should be built upon sound argumentation.

Services: Multilateral Regulatory Cooperation in the Making or in the Waiting?

In contrast to the Agreements on Goods, GATS's promises regarding Regulatory Cooperation have been more far reaching, mainly due the saliency of regulatory barriers on the issue. Indeed, regulatory intensity and complexity are inherent to the nature of services. This is not only due to the plurality of objectives that may be sought to be achieved through regulation, but also due to services' peculiar nature. To begin with the latter, it is services' multimodality that makes them susceptible to over-regulation. The very concept of trade in services consists of four different

---

[86]Prevost (2013), p. 160.

modes of supply, according to Article I:2 GATS, hence the number of measures that could potentially touch them and prove trade-disturbing instantly multiplies by four. Moreover, certain modes of supply, mode 3 on commercial presence and mode 4 on movement of natural persons have proven to be easier targets for protectionist regulation that may for example impose restrictions on structural elements, as is capital for commercial supply, and people, for movement of natural persons.[87] Apart from the overregulation that follows services' provision's anatomy, services' provision comes hand in hand with a growing amount of regulatory intervention that is necessary in order to safeguard the controlled, risk-free and efficient offer of the service concerned.[88] Given the inapplicability of border measures to their cross-border trade in services, protectionism in services is rooted in national regulations, that sooner or later, to a greater or lesser extent, are susceptible to unfold an unjustified diverting effect. This particularly holds true for discriminatory measures, which are controlled properly under the non-discrimination GATS provisions.[89]

However, a different solution had to be found for non-discriminatory regulation that have been found to be equally trade disturbing.[90] And here is where Regulatory Cooperation comes to play. Member States felt thus the need to negotiate a provision that would positively control non-discriminatory trade-impeding regulation that wasn't justified on public policy grounds.[91] However, the Uruguay Round failed to provide an agreement on the substance of such provision. Thus, the issue was left upon Article VI:4, a provision that falls under Article VI on Domestic Regulation. Article VI:4 therefore provides a mandate to create disciplines on the matter. Such disciplines should tackle non-discriminatory provisions by ensuring that measures addressing the quality and safety of service provision—qualification requirements and procedures, licensing requirements and procedures, and technical standards—do not constitute unnecessary barriers to trade. In the absence of the successful negotiation of such disciplines, the rather rudimentary and restricted (namely applicable only where commitments are made, rather than horizontally as is the scope of Article VI:4 GATS) provision of Article VI:5 analysed above, addresses the issue. As such, Article VI:4 constitutes the first provision that introduces *segments of positive integration*, by setting minimum standards that these types of regulations have to meet.[92]

The mandate of Provision VI:4 led to a first Working Party on Professional Qualifications, which indeed developed Disciplines specific to the accountancy sector.[93] Currently, negotiations on the basis of the mandate are ongoing in relation

---

[87] Delimatsis (2007), p. 16.

[88] Delimatsis (2007), p. 16.

[89] Krajewski (2010), p. 162.

[90] For a holistic analysis *see* Tans (2017), pp. 24–138.

[91] Delimatsis (2009), p. 3.

[92] Delimatsis (2009), p. 4.

[93] The accountancy Sector was set as a priority from the very beginning. *See* OECD (1994), par. 102.

to horizontally applicable disciplines addressing regulations on qualification requirements and procedures, licensing requirements and procedures, and technical standards. Their potential should not be underestimated. It has been argued that they
could set the stepping stone for the conclusion of MRAs, through the ongoing
approximation of regulations on the basis of the mandates of those disciplines.[94]
Be that as it may, one should also admit that negotiations have been ongoing for
almost a decade, which indeed leads to the conclusion that to the moment, multilateral Regulatory Cooperation in services in not in the making, but rather in the
waiting.

2.3   Inclusion in an FTA Structure as the Second Characteristic of Regulatory Cooperation

The positioning of Regulatory Cooperation within a FTA is regarded at this section
as the second characteristic of Regulatory Cooperation. It is primarily considered as
such, since till recently Regulatory Cooperation, seen as a matter of low-politics, has
been initiated outside a strictly legal environment, based on political agreements and
declarations. The placement of Regulatory Cooperation comes indeed at odds with
past choices of negotiation and commitment, and on a first level, one could see a
better match between those less rigid forms and complex regulatory dialogues, that
require by nature some flexibility. Thus, before proceeding into explaining the
passage from past choices to present ones, one should primarily reflect on the
suitability of the design of an FTA to host Regulatory Cooperation activities.

This question has been recently raised by scholars under the context of the
appearance of meta-regulation. In short, the concept of meta-regulation seeks to
depict and explain the appearance of new, non-traditional actors in the area of
regulation. Following the vertical disintegration of production and the emerging
need to mitigate the appearing risks across the supply chain as soon as possible,
regulators rely all the more on the information they receive from actors of production, that have to control it in advance with rigorous controls. Connecting the
question of the suitability of an FTA to the imperatives of meta-regulation, they
firstly observe that the information chains created between regulators and industry
actors are not visible at first sight in the Regulatory Cooperation Chapters, which
seem to coordinate mainly the dialogue channels between regulators.[95] They further
argue that the commitments enshrined in the Chapters focus on drawing parallels
between the established in each order practices, in essence by mandating the
adoption of common practices within each regulatory procedure, which aim to create
frameworks that are interchangeable and that this aim inevitably places key actors

---

[94]Delimatsis (2007), p. 36.
[95]Hoekman (2018), p. 254.

that are situated on a governmental level on the epicenter.[96] Indeed, it is true that the explicit reference to a 'Regulatory Authority' as addressee of the commitments in the Chapter on Regulatory Cooperation of the EU Japan FTA is indicative of its orientation towards the activities of actors that possess the regulatory mandate.[97] The wording insistently pictures regulators as the main subject of cooperation. However, this does not necessarily mean that the Chapters overlook the complex task of regulation and the plurality of actors implicated therein. This is true for two reasons. First of all, despite the detailed enumeration of the activities to take place, the organizational and mainly institutional part of both Chapters has been outlined with laconism. Indeed, the Chapters provide a *framework* for Regulatory Cooperation. Within this framework regulators are expected to be the de facto protagonists, as it is them who are officially given the much-anticipated legal mandate to initiate dialogue as official representatives. Beyond that, however, the nature of relations and interdependences that is developed within frameworks that handle such sensitive and complex issues is unpredictable, and that is the reason that their implementation cannot be predicted. It should not be forgotten that while regulators are situated within a territorial environment, industry presumably is not.

Secondly, the linkage between regulation and production is highlighted through the various commitments themselves. Representative is the case of CETA, where the instruction of consultation procedures with private entities, which may include, inter alia, business representatives is mandated in a sole Article.[98] On that basis, industry's role varies within the Chapters and can range from substantial input to a regulation under preparation, contacts on an informal basis and participation in the Committee's workings.[99] The participation of production actors is thus spread within the Chapters' workings and can may appear in various important instances, as is the development of a regulation and the orientation of the cooperation activities through invitations to the meetings of the coordinating body. Their presence in the regulatory process and the necessity of their contribution as directly implicated entities is thus not ignored, on the contrary, it is welcomed.

A preliminary outline confirms the compatibility of an FTA structure with the imperatives of Regulatory Cooperation. The anatomy of the Chapters as well as the overarching environment of the FTA allow for intensification without narrowing its scope but allowing its harmonious development within the ever-changing environment of regulation. The following paragraphs seek to enhance this argument even further. In particular, the remaining sections will look within and beyond EU borders at initiatives of Regulatory Cooperation, with a view to link in a coherent manner the incentives to include Regulatory Cooperation in an FTA.

---

[96] Hoekman (2018), p. 254.

[97] Article 18.2a EU-Japan EPA.

[98] Article 21.8 CETA.

[99] Article 21.8 CETA; Article 18.7 EU-Japan EPA.

2.3.1 Transatlantic Regulatory Cooperation in the EU Absent an FTA

The European Union has made various efforts to begin a regulatory dialogue, in particular in the transatlantic realm. The most comprehensive case study when one wishes to focus on Regulatory Cooperation initiatives of the EU would be the EU-US relation. Indeed, Regulatory Cooperation between the EU and the US, not only dates back to the Transatlantic Declaration of the 1990s, but also demonstrates a wide range of Regulatory Cooperation activities, ranging from low profile to highly coordinated ones. It is exactly the plurality of the initiatives themselves and the various successes and failures that accompany them that offer a valuable background from which one can extract several arguments about the effectiveness of Regulatory Cooperation policy of the EU.

Regulatory Cooperation in the context of EU-US relations bloomed after the end of the Cold War, which marked the beginning of a new era of economic collaboration between the two superpowers. Inspired from the determination of the Bush Administration to keep a close eye on the transformation of the European Integration, transatlantic relations, which till then were limited to security matters expanded their horizon to trade issues.[100] Since then, transatlantic economic relations have been shaped by the two political declarations of outmost importance for the design of economic transatlantic relations, namely the Transatlantic Declaration and the New Transatlantic Agenda, and still develop within their context.

Regulatory Cooperation has been ever since a necessary tool of economic integration and was highlighted as a priority of political talks, which later materialized as parts of the various Summits. The commitment and belief that Regulatory Cooperation was the answer to the then emerging non-regulatory tariff barriers was apparent from its positioning as a priority at the various transatlantic declarations. Since then, it has been treated as the central subject matter to many initiatives. It has been the central idea around separate agreements, it has been the subject of various dialogue mechanisms, examined both horizontally and with regard to specific sectors. Regulatory Cooperation was of such importance that constituted the central figure of the Transatlantic Economic Partnership (hereinafter TEP), the agreement that actually shaped transatlantic economic relations. Being part of a compromise, TEP's significance for transatlantic economic relations was enormous, as it carried the weight of the failure to reach an agreement on an FTA.[101] And its concentration on the abolition of non-regulatory barriers to trade is revealing for the importance of Regulatory Cooperation at the time. All subsequent regulatory activities were mostly carried within the framework of TEP.

The initial step to establish a sustained horizontal dialogue began with the introduction of the Early Warning Mechanism, aimed to avoid the transatlantic

---

[100] Peterson (2001), p. 54.

[101] *See* Peterson (2001), p. 53.

adventure over the dispute of hushkits.[102] The subsequent Guidelines on Regulatory Cooperation and Transparency gave a clearer direction to the regulatory authorities, by describing holistically the spirit and methodology of horizontal cooperation that regulators are asked to undertake.[103] The establishment of the High Level Regulatory Cooperation Forum (hereinafter HLRCF) was a more coordinated effort to group existing sectoral and horizontal dialogues. Last but not least, the last effort to revitalize dialogue was the Transatlantic Economic Council (hereinafter TEC), built upon past mistakes provided high political oversight and brought hidden actors such as legislators and stakeholders to the epiphany.[104] As for sector specific dialogues, they were established and enhanced mainly under the Roadmaps of 2004 and 2005.[105]

2.3.2 Breaking the Myth: Need for Tighter Institutionalization Through Inclusion in an FTA

All the more nowadays, scholars that conduct research in the various EU External Relations use the term 'institutionalization' in order describe the intensification of the actions through the creation of entities. Also in the area of trade, with the rise of the 'living' FTAs that the EU is signing with its trade partners this term has been used to signify the sudden appearance and proliferation of Institutions that accompany and frame the actions included therein.[106] Especially in the realm of Regulatory Cooperation the arguments about 'institutionalization' of Regulatory Cooperation through the FTAs have been opposed to the failures of the previous transatlantic efforts.[107] In essence, it is argued that the 'added value' of FTAs is their contribution to better institutionalization of Regulatory Cooperation. However, many cases lack to provide a description of the term, their understanding of institutionalization, and how it fits into their claims about Institutionalization of Regulatory Cooperation. This is partially due to the recent appearance in the particular field of EU External Relations, even though methodologically incorrect.

This Section goes against those arguments and tries to depict the Institutionalization of Regulatory Cooperation even before its inclusion in an FTA. It firstly begins with an analysis of the term of institutionalization in the literature and goes on to present and justify the chosen understanding of the term. Right after, the various understandings of institutionalization are applied to the previous transatlantic

---

[102] Steffenson (2005), pp. 61ff.

[103] USTR (2002).

[104] Takacs (2014), p. 177.

[105] EU Commission (2004).

[106] *See* generally Steger (2012).

[107] Fahey (2018b), pp. 8ff.

developments, in order to make the argument that FTAs actually do not contribute to tighter institutionalization, but to something different.

2.3.2.1   On the Nature of Institutionalization in European Integration and Beyond

The concept of Institutionalization is a curious term. Used mainly as a conceptual tool in social and behavioral sciences,[108] it has been insulated in recent years by legal and political sciences scholars studying European Integration in order to capture and explain in an interdisciplinary manner the constant changes in governance both within and beyond the Nation State.[109] According to its understanding in organization theory, institutionalization is the process by which certain structures are consolidated, and it is a process triggered by persisting normative, mimetic and coercive forces.[110] This process often leads not only to consolidation of practices, but also to their legitimation,[111] and this is also how institutionalization has been described within the Nation State, as the process by which a practice gains general acceptance.[112]

A similar understanding is also present in literature dealing with the Institutionalization of European Integration. In fact, there are two elements on which analyses have focused heavily. The first one is concentration upon European Institutions. Mark Pollack has successfully summarized it in connecting EU's dense institutionalization in comparison to other supranational settings to the proliferation of intergovernmental and supranational Institutions that surround it and the augmenting body of EU legislation, known as *acquis communautaire*.[113] The second and most important one is, as mentioned, the perception of Institutionalization as a process of formalization. The gradual process of Institutionalization coincides with the consolidation of a set of norms and formalities that create particular communication dynamics and shape the routines in the European sphere within structures.[114] Thus, relevant Institutionalization debates tend to concentrate mainly on process of formalization and stabilization of Institutions and procedures, of formal or informal character.[115] Similarly, Institutionalization has been used also regarding implicated actors, in expressing their establishment within a given field. In the realm of the changing landscape of EU Regulation for example, institutionalization and

---

[108] The process of institutionalization lies at the core of neo-institutionalism in organization theory. *See* for example Lawrence et al. (2001).

[109] *See* for example Saurugger and Mérand (2010), Saurugger (2015).

[110] Schreyögg and Sydow (2011), p. 330.

[111] Schreyögg and Sydow (2011), p. 330.

[112] Katz and Crotty (2006), p. 206.

[113] Pollack (2004), p. 137.

[114] Immergut (1998); also *see* generally Green Cowles et al. (2001).

[115] See Saurugger and Mérand (2010), p. 7.

de-institutionalization have been employed to describe the gradual establishment of agencies and networks as regulatory actors.[116]

According to another strand of the literature, institutionalization as a notion in the EU context has been detached from its process-centric character and is seen as the result of consolidation of procedures and structures that are difficult to change.[117] Others have highlighted the constant change that came hand in hand with European Integration with the higher levels of institutionalization.[118] Recently, academics have tried to capture the essence of the notion generally beyond the nation.[119] Their analysis begins from the new European Governance trend of promotion of international Institutions in various instances, and extends accordingly to capture the associated procedures that these Institutions promote. Institutionalization beyond the Nation State is understood as a sign of the times, an 'antidote to concerns about the delegation of authority beyond the Nation State', a factor that establishes a certain practice and legitimizes it.[120] According to Fahey though, institutionalization beyond the Nation State should better be described as the *process* of intense cooperation and interaction, rather than its *outcome,* institution or situation.[121]

As outlined above, there is cross-disciplinary convergence in treating Institutionalization as a process, with a few scholars viewing it rather as a result. Institutionalization however has been also treated independently of process/result debate of institution/procedure building. According to Belanger and Fontaine-Skronski, Institutionalization depicts "the degree to which institutional rules govern more the actions of the actors", in other words "the degree to which state behavior, in a particular area of cooperation, falls within the scope of particular rules".[122] The focus here is not whether institutionalization is to be happening during the development or with the creation of an institution. Institution building, either as a process or a result, does not have any significance. What matters here is the range of activities that is covered by those institutional rules.[123] The richer the range, the greater the institutionalization of this particular area of cooperation.

2.3.2.2   Was Transatlantic Regulatory Cooperation Institutionalized?

Institutionalization, understood by one way or another, was not absent from the transatlantic paradigm of Regulatory Cooperation. Let us start from the end. Institutionalization of Regulatory Cooperation, understood as rule coverage, under the

---

[116]Levi Faur (2012), pp. 34–36.

[117]Petrov (2010), p. 3.

[118]Stone-Sweet et al. (2001).

[119]See generally Fahey (2018a).

[120]Zürn (2016), p. 164.

[121]See Fahey (2018b), p. 4.

[122]Belanger and Fontaine Skronski (2012), p. 240.

[123]Belanger and Fontaine Skronski (2012), p. 240.

theory of Belanger and Fontaine-Skronksi cannot be disputed, since the various initiatives described above ranged from horizontal to sectoral ones, comprising diverse rules and engaging many actors, covering thus a wide range of Regulatory Cooperation activities. For example, the Regulatory Cooperation Guidelines were content wise as comprehensive as are the contemporary FTA Chapters, while the Mutual Recognition Agreements (hereinafter MRAs) were the fruit of a sectoral cooperation. In the context of the Guidelines, the HLRCF did eventually proceed to a joint examination and comparison of their impact assessment procedures.[124] As far as sector specific dialogue is concerned, its highlight until today is the MRA, which concerned mutual recognition of the conformity assessment procedures over six sectors: telecommunications and ICT equipment, sport boats and medical devices, pharmaceuticals, electronics and electromagnetic compatibility.[125] With actual, although limited results, it is difficult to argue that Regulatory Cooperation activities were not regulated. They were indeed regulated, however not under strict legal terms.

Secondly, turning to the literature debate on the process/result of institution building, one will observe the development/appearance of institutional structures through the consecutive agreements. Indeed, the functioning of initiatives such as the Early Warning Mechanism, HLRCF or the TEC came along with institutional development and establishment, despite being disregarded during the formation of two major regulatory acts, the REACH Directive by the EU and the Sarbanes-Oxley act by the US.[126]

Under both scenarios, institutionalization could not bring adequate results, and it's neither rule coverage nor weak Institutions to blame. On the contrary, both adequate rule coverage and institutional structures were unable to perform due to their legally weak method of regulation. This was also the reason behind the inherent difficulty to achieve consolidation of the agreed procedures. The latter can be confirmed by existing literature which has associated these shortcomings with a variety of reasons deeply rooted to the lack of legal bindingness and its implications. Indeed, the lack of legal bindingness is the reason that lies at the root of the problem, meaning that it causes inconsistency between several mandates, it provides no base for additional funding and places no substantial pressure on regulators. Regarding the inconsistency of mandates, Regulatory Cooperation is a task largely left upon regulators, who are called to conciliate their main internal regulatory tasks, as these are mandated by their own constitutional framework with cooperation with foreign counterparts, mandated by executive agreements.[127] These two tasks may be contradictory in nature, and regulators, when called to choose between the fulfilment of their constitutional mandate and cooperation with foreign counterparts, they will choose to proceed with complying with the internal requirements. Furthermore, the

---

[124] Meuwese (2011).

[125] Schaffer (2003), p. 303.

[126] Schaffer (2003), p. 303.

[127] Paul (2001).

lack of a formal mandate means that the internal regulatory environment may not be always structurally ready to accommodate Regulatory Cooperation. That may happen because regulators are not accustomed to taking into account trade interests during the development of regulatory acts, due to the very structure of the regulatory system, which may not provide them with this possibility. This is the case of the US, which unlike the EU regulatory system is not accustomed to reconciling regulatory objectives with an internal market.[128] Regulatory action in the US is divided between the varying agencies, which follow a strict mandate and are quite isolated from trade matters.[129] Furthermore, regulators usually have no further funding for the accomplishment of Regulatory Cooperation, and are called to cover potential costs from their existing funds, which of course are dedicated for internal purposes.[130] Last but not least, apart from these institutional problems, the lack of legal bindingness can also stand behind certain *attitudes*. The example of lack of coordination for the development of the European REACH directive and the Sarbanes Oxley Act in the US despite existing available cooperation mechanisms is indicative of the attitude of regulators towards regulatory dialogue. In the end, it was the particular soft law nature of the experiment that could not provide enough reasons for regulators to cooperate, even though the political willingness at the higher levels to activate and advance a regulatory dialogue was apparent.

2.3.3 Stronger Legalization Through the Inclusion in an FTA?

From the conceptualization of impediments to the successful operation of Regulatory Cooperation till today, of fundamental importance is the inadequate degree of legal obligation. As pointed, this feature does not substantially coincide with the concept of institutionalization as examined above, even though it has been associated in the literature.[131] Interestingly, legal bindingness has been used as one of the measurement units that builds the concept of 'Legalization'.[132] Legalization is a conceptual tool developed by International Relations scholars. Legalization as a concept is associated but not equated to Institutionalization. Legalization is, according to its fathers a particular form of institutionalization, characterized by three components: obligation, precision and delegation.[133] According to this construction, the element of obligation measures how binding the undertaken commitments are, the element of precision refers to how precise the rules are and the element

---

[128] Schaffer (2003), p. 309.

[129] Schaffer (2003), p. 309.

[130] Jensen (2017).

[131] Fahey (2018b), p. 8.

[132] Abott et al. (2000).

[133] Goldstein et al. (2000), p. 396.

of delegation is used to depict whether a third party has a delegated authority, *inter alia* on issues of interpretation implementation, monitoring, dispute settlement.[134] Legalization, composed by those three components is a concept empirically built, inspired from characteristics to be found in Institutions.[135] More specifically, it examines the degree to which these components are to be found in each institutional structure. Legalization of Institutions can take several forms and can range in every point of a scale from low to high; its form and intensity depends on the combination of the degrees that the various components may themselves take.[136]

Based on this concept and taking into account the lack of legal bindingness that characterized the previous efforts on Regulatory Cooperation, the question to be explored is to what extent the inclusion in an FTA strengthens the Legalization of Regulatory Cooperation. In other words, the question to be answered is to what extent the legal obligation is harder positioned under an FTA. This includes not only the 'obligation' part, which measures as said, the legal bindingness of the commitments. To this mission, an extensive analysis on the Legalization of Regulatory Cooperation through FTAs embarks the next Chapter.

Apart from the theoretical question on the Legalization of Regulatory Cooperation, it is worth mentioning that practice has associated the presence of an FTA and the achieved results of Regulatory Cooperation activities. In other words, there seems to exist an empirical connection between the existence of an FTA and the advancement of Regulatory Cooperation activities, the latter taking place either within or outside the FTA structures. These preliminary assumptions can be extracted from Regulatory Cooperation efforts beyond the EU, where Regulatory Cooperation activities were supported by an FTA structure. Certainly, a brilliant example of Regulatory Cooperation based on an FTA is the example of Australia and New Zealand, built within the Australia-New Zealand Closer Economic Relations Trade Agreement. With its final goal being the establishment of a single market, this FTA approached Regulatory Cooperation via joint accreditation based on international standards, harmonization, various MRAs and the creation of a joint regulator, the Australia-New Zealand Food Authority.[137] The second example, although a little bit more complicated, is the one of NAFTA. Regulatory Cooperation between the NAFTA partners, although initiated by the FTA, was only advanced later on. The NAFTA saga begins with the inability of the NAFTA light institutional structures to bring any result. The trilateral Committee on Standard Related Measures and the working groups of which it was comprised, established under the FTA did not advance the works on Regulatory Cooperation, due to lack of

---

[134] *See* generally Abott et al. (2000).

[135] Abott et al. (2000), p. 403.

[136] Goldstein et al. (2000), p. 388.

[137] The joint regulatory authority was the result of the 1995 Agreement on Establishing a System for Development of Joint Food Standards. This Agreement finally led the adoption of a joint Australia-New Zealand Food Standards Code in 1999. *See* Steger (2012), p. 115.

political oversight.[138] The Security and Prosperity Partnership (hereinafter SPP) did manage to incorporate to a certain extent the kind of cooperation envisaged in NAFTA.[139] In a way, it completed it. For this reason, the subject was treated once more under the SPP, an executive-type cooperation, with greater success.[140] Later on, in order to intensify the ongoing success, the parties established an even tighter form of cooperation, bilateral this time, the US-Canada Regulatory Cooperation Council (hereinafter RCC), which also implicated the direct participation of regulatory agencies.

Both cases demonstrated better achievements than the EU regarding Regulatory Cooperation sooner or later. And in both cases Regulatory Cooperation was based on a firm background, a legal instrument that regulated solid trade relations. It is not actually a coincidence, that in the realm of NAFTA, the SPP brought far better results in the branch of Regulatory Cooperation than in the Security one, which was not supported by a previous legal instrument.[141] Hence, should Regulatory Cooperation operate more efficiently under an FTA structure, its inclusion in the EU FTAs is heading towards the right direction.

However, as mentioned, the question of the degree of Legalization that Regulatory Cooperation enjoys under its new clothes, is a more complicated one, where many other factors need to be taken into consideration.

2.4 Conclusion

In this Chapter, the concept of characteristics mirrored how Regulatory Cooperation is now abstractly regulated by connecting it to a chain of events that triggered this change. The initiation of Regulatory Cooperation on a bilateral basis did not follow blindly the general stance of the EU Trade Policy. Indeed, as it had already matured as a phenomenon on its own in other fora, there were more than one reasons that lead to the inclusion in an FTA.

In the multilateral setting, legal commitments of low cooperation depth, that concentrated mainly on non-discrimination (Article 2.1 TBT and 2.3 SPS) and rationality requirements (Article 2.2 TBT and 2.2 SPS), were inadequate as to trigger a substantial regulatory dialogue. Moreover, even to these disciplines, the AB imposed restrictive limits. Apart from that, bilateral efforts made mainly on the political arena were condemned to failure, exactly because of their legal weaknesses.

To cure both weaknesses, the coordination of Regulatory Cooperation activities under the premises of an FTA certainly marks the beginning of a different era for their materialization. And its added value does not seem to be located in

---

[138] Steger (2012), p. 112.

[139] Bélanger (2010), p. 31.

[140] Bélanger (2010), p. 31.

[141] Bélanger (2012), p. 157.

institutionalizing Regulatory Cooperation, since existing bilateral Regulatory Cooperation activities with the US extend substantially in coverage and implicated the creation of supranational Institutions. Instead, these steps were mainly hindered due to the absence of a legality gloss, which is exactly what an inclusion in an FTA offers. However, the exact degree to which Regulatory Cooperation is legalized has to be examined on the basis of all the provisions that form the concept of 'Legalization', not only obligation, but also precision and delegation. This exactly is the subject matter of the next Chapter.

References

Abott K, Keohane R, Moravcsik A, Slaughter A, Snidal D (2000) The concept of legalization. Int Organ 54:401–419

Bélanger L (2010) Governing the north American free trade area: international rule making and delegation in NAFTA, the SPP and beyond. Latin Am Policy 1:22–51

Bélanger L (2012) Le régionalisme "soft" en Amérique du Nord: le cas du Partenariat pour la sécurité et la prospérité. In: Lacroix JM, Mace G (eds) Politique étrangère comparée Canada/États-Unis. Peter Lang, Austra, pp 145–159

Belanger L, Fontaine Skronski K (2012) Legalization in international relations: a conceptual analysis. Soc Sci Inf 51:238–262

Cambridge Online Dictionary (n.d.). Definition of 'exception' https://dictionary.cambridge.org/dictionary/english/exception

Crotty W (2006) Handbook of party politics. SAGE, London

Delimatsis P (2007) Due process and good regulation embedded in the GATS—disciplining regulatory behaviour in services through article VI of the GATS. J Int Econ Law 10:13–50

Delimatsis P (2008) Determining the necessity of domestic regulations in services. Eur J Int Law 19:365–408

Delimatsis P (2009) Concluding the WTO Services Negotiations on Domestic Regulation-Walk Unafraid. In: TILEC Discussion Paper Series. Available via DIALOG: https://papers.ssrn.com/sol3/papers.cfm?abstract_id=1460579

EEAS (2016) A global strategy for the European Union's Foreign and Security Policy. https://eeas.europa.eu/sites/eeas/files/eugs_review_web_0.pdf

Efstathopoulos C (2012) Leadership in the WTO: Brazil, India and the Doha development agenda. Camb Rev Int Aff 25:269–293

EU Commission (2004) Roadmap for EU-US regulatory cooperation and transparency. https://ec.europa.eu/commission/presscorner/detail/en/IP_04_816

EU Commission (2006) Communication from the Commission to the Council, the European Parliament, the European Economic and Social Committee and the Committee of the Regions: Global Europe: Competing In The World: A Contribution to the EU's Growth and Jobs Strategy, COM(2006) 567. final https://eur-lex.europa.eu/LexUriServ/LexUriServ.do?uri=COM:2006:0567:FIN:en:PDF

Fahey E (2018a) Institutionalization beyond the nation state. Springer, Cham

Fahey E (2018b) Introduction: institutionalization beyond the nation state: new paradigms? Transatlantic relations: data, privacy and trade law. In: Fahey E (ed) Institutionalization beyond the nation state. Springer, Cham, pp 1–27

Goldstein J, Kahler M, Keohane R, Slaughter A (2000) Introduction: legalization and world politics. Int Organ 54:385–399

Green Cowles M, Risse T, Caporaso J (2001) Europeanization and domestic change: introduction. In: Green Cowles M, Risse T, Caporaso J (eds) Transforming Europe: Europeanisation and domestic change. Cornell University Press, New York, pp 1–20

Heydon K, Woolcock S (2009) The rise of bilateralism: comparing American, European, and Asian approaches to preferential trade agreements. United Nations University Press, Tokyo

Hoekman B (2018) 'Behind-the-border' regulatory policies and trade agreements. East Asian Econ Rev 22:243–273

Horn H, Weiler J (2005) European Communities—trade description of sardines: textualism and its discontent. World Trade Rev 4:248–275

Howese R, Levy P (2013) The TBT Panels: US-Cloves, US-Tuna, US-COOL. World Trade Rev 12:327–375

Immergut E (1998) The theoretical core of the new institutionalism. Polit Soc 26:5–34

Jensen K (2017) International trade and negotiations in global value chains. Centre for International Governance Innovation. Available via DIALOG: https://www.cigionline.org/sites/default/files/documents/2017_Washingtonweb.pdf

Kauffmann C, Malyshev N (2015) International regulatory co-operation: the menu of approaches. International Centre for Trade and Sustainable Development (ICTSD) and World Economic Forum. Available via DIALOG: www.e15initiative.org/

Köbele M (2007) Preamble TBT. In: Wolfrum R, Stoll P, Seibert-Fohr A (eds) WTO—technical barrier and SPS measures. Brill, Leiden-Boston, pp 167–177

Koremenos B, Lipson C, Snidal D (2001) The rational design of international institutions. Int Org 55:761–799

Krajewski M (2008) Recognition, standardisation and harmonisation: which rules for GATS in times of crisis? In: Panizzon M, Pohl N, Sauvé P (eds) GATS and the regulation of international trade in services. Cambridge University Press, Cambridge, pp 407–433

Krajewski M (2010) Services trade liberalisation and regulation: new developments and old problems. In: Herrmann C, Terhechte J (eds) European yearbook of international economic law 2010. Springer, Berlin, pp 153–178

Kudryavtsev A (2013) The TBT agreement in context. In: Epps T, Trebilcock M (eds) Research handbook on the WTO and technical barriers to trade, research handbook on the WTO. Edward Elgar, Cheltenham-Northampton, pp 17–81

Lawrence T, Winn M, Jennings D (2001) The temporal dynamics of institutionalization. Acad Manag Rev 26:624

Lester S, Stemberg W (2014) The GATT origins of TBT agreement articles 2.1 and 2.2. J Int Econ Law 17:215–232

Levi Faur D (2012) Regulatory networks and regulatory agencification: towards a single European regulatory space. In: Rittberger B (ed) Agency governance in the EU. Routledge, New York, pp 32–52

Marceau G (2014) The new TBT jurisprudence in US-clove cigarettes, WTO US-Tuna II, and US-Cool. Asian J WTO Int Health Law Policy 8:1–39

Marceau G, Trachtman J (2014) A map of the World Trade Organization law of domestic regulation of goods: the technical barriers to trade agreement, the sanitary and phytosanitary measures agreement, and the general agreement on tariffs and trade. J World Trade 48:351–432

Marceau G, Trachtman JP (2002) The technical barriers to trade agreement, the sanitary and phytosanitary measures agreement and the general agreement on tariffs and trade: a map of the World Trade Organisation law of domestic regulation of goods. J World Trade 36:811–881

Meuwese A (2011) EU–US horizontal regulatory cooperation: mutual recognition of impact assessment? In: Vogel D, Swinnen J (eds) Transatlantic regulatory cooperation: the shifting roles of the EU, the US and California. Edward Elgar, Cheltenham, pp 249–273

Middleton R (1980) The GATT standards code. J World Trade 14:201–219

Ming Du M (2007) Domestic regulatory autonomy under the TBT agreement: from non-discrimination to harmonization. Chinese J Int Law 6:269–306

Morin JF, Gagne G (2007) What can best explain the prevalence of bilateralism in the investment regime? Int J Polit Econ 36:53–74

Nakagawa J (2016) Regulatory co-operation and regulatory coherence through mega-FTAs. In: Chaisse J, Tsai-yu L (eds) International economic law and governance: essays in Honour of Mitsuo Matsushita. Oxford University Press, Oxford, pp 392–410

OECD (1994) The general agreement on trade in Services (GATS): an analysis. http://www.oecd.org/officialdocuments/publicdisplaydocumentpdf/?doclanguage=en&cote=ocde/gd(94)123

Paul J (2001) Implementing regulatory cooperation through executive agreements and the problem of democratic accountability. In: Bermann G, Herdegen M, Lindseth P (eds) Transatlantic regulatory cooperation: legal problems and political prospects. Oxford University Press, Oxford, pp 385–403

Peterson J (2001) Get away from me closer, you 're near me too far: Europe and America after the Uruguay round. In: Pollack M, Schaffer G (eds) Transatlantic governance in the global economy. Rowman & Littlefield Publishers, Lanham, pp 45–73

Petrov P (2010) Early Institutionalisation of the ESDP governance arrangements: insights from the operations Concordia and Artemis. In: Vanhoonacker S, Dijkstra H, Maurer H (eds). Understanding the role of bureaucracy in the European security and defence policy. European Integration online Papers (EIoP) 14 Available via DIALOG: https://eiop.or.at/eiop/pdf/2010-008.pdf

Pollack M (2004) New institutionalism. In: Wiener A, Diez T (eds) European integration theory. Oxford University Press, Oxford

Prevost D (2013) Transparency obligations under the TBT agreement. In: Epps T, Trebilcock MJ (eds) Research handbook on the WTO and technical barriers to trade. Edward Elgar, p 160

Rigod B (2012) "Global Europe": the EU's new trade policy in its legal context. J Eur Law 18:277–306

Rixen T, Rohlfing I (2007) The institutional choice of bilateralism and multilateralism in international trade and taxation. Int Negot 12:389–414

Saurugger S (2015) Sociological approaches to the European Union in times of turmoil. J Common Mark Stud 54:70–86

Saurugger S, Mérand F (2010) Does European integration theory need sociology? Comp Eur Polit 8:1–18

Schaffer G (2003) Managing US-EU trade relations through mutual recognition and Safe Harbor agreements: 'new' and 'global' approaches to transatlantic economic governance? In: Petersmann EU, Pollack M (eds) Transatlantic economic disputes: the EU, the US and the WTO. Oxford University Press, Oxford, pp 297–326

Schreyögg G, Sydow J (2011) Organizational path dependence: a process view. Organ Stud 32:321–335

Steffenson R (2005) Managing EU-US relations: actors, institutions and the new transatlantic agenda. Manchester University Press, Manchester

Steger P (2012) Institutions for regulatory cooperation in 'new generation' economic and trade agreements. Legal Iss Econ Integr 39:109–126

Stone-Sweet A, Sandholtz W, Fligstein N (2001) The institutionalization of Europe. Oxford University Press, Oxford

Takacs T (2014) Transatlantic regulatory cooperation in trade. In: Fahey E, Curtin D (eds) A transatlantic community of law: legal perspectives on the relationship between the EU and US legal orders. Cambridge University Press, Cambridge, pp 158–185

Tamiotti L (2007) Article 2 TBT. In: Wolfrum R, Stoll PT, Seibert-Fohr A (eds) WTO - technical barriers and SPS measures. Brill, Leiden-Boston, pp 210–235

Tans S (2017) Service provision and migration: EU and WTO Service trade liberalization and their impact on Dutch and UK immigration rules. Brill, Leiden-Boston

Tinbergen J (1954) International economic integration. Elsevier, Amsterdam

Trebilcock M (2015) Advanced introduction to international trade law. Edward Elgar, Cheltenham

USTR (2002) Guidelines on regulatory cooperation and transparency. https://ustr.gov/archive/
    assets/World_Regions/Europe_Middle_East/Transatlantic_Dialogue/asset_upload_file350_
    5680.pdf
van den Bosche P, Zdouc W (2017) The law and policy of the WTO. Cambridge University Press,
    Cambridge
Weiss W (2020) WTO law and domestic regulation. Nomos, Baden-Baden
Wijkström E, McDaniels D (2013) International standards and the WTO TBT agreement: improv-
    ing governance for regulatory alignment. Available via DIALOG: https://papers.ssrn.com/sol3/
    papers.cfm?abstract_id=2258413
Woolcock S (2003) The Singapore issues in Cancun: a failed negotiation ploy or a litmus test for
    global governance?. Intereconomics: review of European. Econ Policy 38:249–255
Woolcock S (2010) Trade policy: a further shift towards Brussels. In: Wallace H, Pollack M,
    Young A, Alasdair R (eds) Policy-making in the European Union, 6th edn. Oxford University
    Press, Oxford, pp 107–133
Woolcock S (2014) EU policy on preferential trade agreements in the 2000s: a re-orientation
    towards commercial aims. Eur Law J 20:718–732
World Trade Organisation (2014) Technical Barriers to Trade. https://www.wto.org/english/res_e/
    publications_e/tbttotrade_e.pdf
Young AR, Peterson J (2006) The EU and the new trade politics. J Eur Publ Policy 13:795–814
Zlepting S (2010) Non-economic objectives in WTO law. Brill, Leiden-Boston
Zürn M (2016) Opening up Europe: next steps in politicization research. West Eur Polit 39:164–182

Chapter 3
Legalization of Regulatory Cooperation

3.1 Introduction

Referring to the inclusion of Regulatory Cooperation in an FTA structure, the previous Chapter briefly introduced the concept of Legalization, as one that could capture the change of playing field of the phenomenon of Regulatory Cooperation, and thus reveal the added value and the rationale behind this inclusion in an FTA. In particular, it was argued that the inclusion within a legally binding treaty could serve in strengthening the legal value of the commitments and in boosting their effectiveness, as other examples beyond EU borders have already demonstrated. Using this assumption as a basis, this Chapter will analyze concretely to which extent Regulatory Cooperation has been legalized. In order to do so, the Chapter will proceed to an examination of the components of Legalization and their application to the case of Regulatory Cooperation Chapters as the latter are to be found in the FTAs under consideration, namely the CETA and EU—Japan EPA.

Before any *in concreto* assessment of the occurring Legalization with an application of the concept to Regulatory Cooperation, it should be clear for comprehension reasons what Legalization is, which components frame its analytical basis and how these will be perceived and assessed in the present Chapter. The following Section shall embark upon that mission. Without going into details on the ontology of the concept as such, as others have done,[1] like the reasons behind the choice of the particular components for the initial conceptualization, or whether those particular components reflect the majority of international phenomena, the next section will be limited to an introduction to the concept, as the latter has been conceived by its fathers, developed further by literature, and finally how it will be used in this particular Chapter. After that, each of the following Sections will focus upon each particular element of the concept of Legalization, will present how it will be

---

[1] *See* indicatively Reus-Smit (2003).

K. Pipidi-Kalogirou, *Regulatory Cooperation Chapters in the new Generation FTAS*, EYIEL Monographs - Studies in European and International Economic Law 36, https://doi.org/10.1007/978-3-031-71900-4_3

understood, and shall apply it to Regulatory Cooperation as seen in the relevant FTA Chapters.

3.2   Understanding Legalization

The concept of Legalization was initially developed to capture the increasing use of law in international relations phenomena. Law in Legalization is not understood as necessarily enforceable by a coercive sovereign, something that classic legal litera-ture would suggest, since international law rarely passes this threshold.[2] On the contrary, the measurement of compliance through law in international phenomena was firstly proposed on a more spherical basis, together with the presence of other elements, that all together form the concept under analysis, namely precision and delegation. These three constructive dimensions, legal obligation, precision and delegation are empiricist in nature and try to encompass characteristics that vary across international Institutions and between international actors.[3]

In essence, what is sought through the construction of this concept, is the "overall constraining nature of an international arrangement", and how this influences state compliance.[4] This is extracted by a combination of the variation of the three dimensions, which can differ across Institutions and actors. Obligation measures the legal quality of the commitments, the extent to which participants are bound by the commitments they have undertaken.[5] Precision relates to the letter of the rules themselves depicting not only how unambiguously or vaguely these rules have been drafted and agreed, but also their coherence with each other.[6] Delegation is a quality that informs on whether the rules have a dynamic effect, by prescribing delegated power to other Institutions to either interpret them and issue rulings on the basis of the interpretation, or to create secondary rules on their basis.[7]

3.2.1   On its Variability and Substitutability of Dimensions

According to the fathers, an important characteristic of the concept of Legalization is its variability, which informs its typology. Although the present Chapter does not examine all elements as capable of presenting variation (particularly obligation is understood mostly as a binary value), it is still interesting to see the various shades

---

[2] Abott et al. (2000), p. 402.

[3] Abott et al. (2000), p. 403.

[4] Belanger and Fontaine-Skronski (2012), p. 241.

[5] Abott et al. (2000), p. 401.

[6] Abott et al. (2000), p. 401.

[7] Abott et al. (2000), p. 401.

Table 3.1 Overview of the variations of legalization according to the intensity of each element

Type	Obligation	Precision	Delegation
Ideal type: Hard law			
I	High	High	High
II	High	Low	High
III	Low	High	High
IV	Low	High	High (moderate)
V	High	Low	Low
VI	Low	Low	High (moderate)
VII	Low	High	Low
VIII	Low	Low	Low
Ideal type: Anarchy			

Source: Abott et al. (2000, p. 406)

Legalization can take, depending on combinations of intensity of the various elements.[8]

In this Table 3.1, the degrees of Legalization are exposed in a descending order. The aim of this categorization is to demonstrate that the combination of dimensions at a differing intensity creates Legalization of differing degrees, with all dimensions playing an equal role. Indeed, according to the original conception, each variable -regardless of its intensity—exists and functions independently from the others.[9] The manifestation of a dimension does not depend on the value of the other ones. And the overall Legalization of an international arrangement cannot be judged solely upon the value of only one dimension, no matter how high the latter may be. In simpler words the authors suggest that each dimension functions and contributes independently to the overall Legalization; however Legalization needs all 3 dimensions to be built. The authors also suggest this is the case, by distinguishing between law and Legalization.[10] Law, the measurement of the 'obligation' dimension, does not coincide with Legalization, as a legalized institution is perceived to be characterized not only of strong legal obligations, but also, of high levels of precision and delegation. A high level of obligation cannot fully compensate for low levels of delegation and precision, no matter how tempting and rational that might be to a lawyer's mindset.

Can it *partially* compensate though? Belanger and Fontaine-Skronski answer this question affirmatively in their contribution, based on a very careful reading of the

---

[8] The variation and differentiation of Legalization across actors, geographical areas and issue-areas can be grounded largely upon internal private influences and domestic political views about sovereignty but also upon globalization imperatives that lead to economic interdependence. *See* generally Kahler (2000).

[9] See Goldstein et al. (2000), p. 388.

[10] The difference between law and Legalization can be best described under the phrase: "Law at a point in time and Law over time". While law has a static nature, as it depicts the body of legal elements existing at a certain point in time, Legalization is a dynamic process, that describes how this legal mass changes and evolves over time. *See* Abbott and Snidal (2012), p. 34.

concept. In their contribution, they argue that, contrary to the authors' claims, the concept of Legalization does not consist of independent variables of equal value, but in essence the dimension of obligation carries significant weight, not only by itself, but also with regard to the other two dimensions.[11] Not only does it set a limit to the amount of overall Legalization that can be attained without it, but also to the degree of the other dimensions as well, especially of delegation. In that way, the 'obligation' dimension becomes of a semi—necessary nature. Quite astonishingly, the authors themselves seem to admit that,[12] while there is also significant convergence in the literature.[13] The creators of the original project implicitly concede to that through the arrangement of rows IV and VI–VIII, where low obligation is accompanied with either low or moderate levels of delegation, but never with high.

This particular understanding of obligation as a semi-necessary condition will be adopted for the purposes of the Chapter as well, as it is methodologically sounder for the legal analysis to follow. As mentioned, Legalization depicts the various nuances of the turn towards law in international relations, although it is not exclusively measured by the presence of law. And since Institutions are understood, as they do, broadly, including not only the structural elements of organization as units, but also encompassing the processes to be carried out through norms and procedures, it is eventually a legal analysis that can inform us about the legal significance that the institution as a whole acquires.

3.2.2 On the Necessity of All Three Dimensions

Apart from the criticism by Belanger and Fontaine-Skronski, who questioned the independent functioning of the three dimensions, the original concept was further challenged by subsequent literature. After the initial enthusiasm caused as a result of the legacy that the conceptualization of Legalization created, warmly welcomed by various branches of literature, the concept eventually opened a rich and continuous academic dialogue. A strand of this literature expressed doubts on the suitability of certain elements to measure Legalization and commented upon missing elements.[14]

---

[11] Belanger and Fontaine-Skronski (2012), p. 242.

[12] One of the authors. Kenneth Abbott actually admits in later work, that the element of obligation was treated as the most important in the original Legalization concept. *See* Abbott and Snidal (2012), p. 38.

[13] For example, Guzman and Meyer implicitly acknowledge that obligation is a necessary precondition for delegation, since, according to them, only highly obligatory rules can become the object of interpretation and adjudication by international tribunals, *See* Guzman and Meyer (2008), pp. 516–517; McGee and Taplin seem to find the same dynamics in the realm of climate change regimes. *See* McGee and Taplin (2008).

[14] For example, in their analysis on the impact of Legalization of Trade on Domestic Policies, Goldstein and Martin add the element of 'increased transparency', which is examined as a self-standing dimension. *See* generally Goldstein and Martin (2000).

Others redefined some (or all) of the constitutive elements,[15] and even proposed different conceptualizations of Legalization.[16] Particularly marginalized among the literature that has been using the concept of Legalization in different phenomena remains the element of precision. While some have just expressed their doubts on the necessity for Legalization, given the relevant imprecision that characterizes other legal regimes, as is the demarcation of sea boundaries or the legal regime of state responsibility,[17] other scholars have gone as far as arguing that precision lessens the Legalization potential of a regime,[18] even though it is the exact opposite that is mostly argued. Regarding delegation, criticism has mostly centered around its binary conception, and whether these two different types of delegation -delegated decision-making and third party dispute settlement—contribute equally to the overall Legalization.[19]

While acknowledging the scientific significance of those variations to further the dialogue and contribute to framing properly an interdisciplinary idea, this Chapter will proceed by using all three dimensions as originally proposed, and this for the following reasons. To begin with, the significance and added value of precise commitments to the overall Legalization of an arrangement is not a novelty firstly advocated by the creators of the Legalization concept. While it is true that imprecision may sometimes be the best solution for agreement on a controversial issue to be reached, it definitely hinders subsequent implementation. The potential effect that precision may have in enhancing or impeding the legal significance of a provision was noted years ago by the late Judge Baxter in his seminal Article 'International law in her infinite variety', where he mentioned that an imprecise, vague provision may deprive a formally binding obligation of its legal force.[20] Moreover, the managerial model on compliance presented by Chayes and Chayes connects the degree of preciseness of a rule with the level of compliance to the rule.[21] Secondly, regarding delegation, the paradigm of delegation in Regulatory Cooperation shows that the far-reaching decision-making capacity which secondary international bodies may enjoy can be considered to advance Legalization as would be the presence of a third-party judicial body.

---

[15] *See* among others Simons (2001); In her analysis on the Legalization of the International Monetary Affairs, Beth Simmons treats only the element of obligation, renaming it into 'credible commitment'. In addition, Michael Gilligan, Leslie Johns, and B. Peter Rosendorff, although being inspired from the original concept of Legalization, slightly differentiate from it and adopt different terminology when referring to the strength of a judicial institution. They mirror the element of obligation to the strength of a court's enforcement regime and match the element of Delegation to their Jurisdiction. *See* Gilligan et al. (2010), p. 23.

[16] Kirton et al. (2011).

[17] Finnemore and Toope (2001), p. 747.

[18] *See* generally Percy (2007).

[19] Belanger and Fontaine-Skronski (2012), p. 253.

[20] Baxter (1980).

[21] Chayes and Handler Chayes (1998), p. 10.

Indeed, the various proposed alternatives do not take full account of the totality of the aspects that the originally envisaged concept does. While they do measure obligation, no matter how they name it, the one thing they present in common is that they set aside either one or both of the remaining dimensions. And a Legalization analysis deprived of the dimensions of delegation and precision ignores largely the International Relations background of Legalization. And while such an omission could be permissible in other institutional arrangements, it would not be for the discussion of Legalization of Regulatory Cooperation. Regulatory Cooperation in the New Generation FTAs falls largely under the combined International Law/International Relations discourse. Legalization, as an interdisciplinary concept is based upon the idea that the content of law is predominantly political, making it a political concept itself. As far as Regulatory Cooperation is concerned, the actors -both public and private—that engage in such activities, act towards a clearly political direction by treating matters that involve active politics, as is the approximation of regulatory traditions, the agreement upon compatible regulations or the setting of common standards respectively. However, these political discourses do not develop in anarchy, but materialize within a legal system, where the implicated parties have to follow certain legal procedures and act within an institutional framework. That institutional framework is set by the Chapters of Regulatory Cooperation. The treatment of politically sensitive matters within a legally set institutional framework is what calls for an interdisciplinary approach in the analysis of Regulatory Cooperation. In the words of Abbott and Snidal: "Law provides boundaries for politics, politics changes those boundaries, yet it is itself bound by law...Because law, Legalization and politics are intertwined in complex ways, neither law nor politics can be said to come first-they come together and coevolve over time".[22] Aiming to draw some conclusions on the Legalization process of Regulatory Cooperation through their presence in FTAs, the following Section will begin a discussion of each separate dimension *in concreto*.

3.3 Measuring Obligation in Regulatory Cooperation

The obligation dimension of Regulatory Cooperation presents a particular interest in the current form and formulation of the corresponding Chapters in the FTAs. To begin with, and in an effort to provide guidance and set the stage for the main points that will be dealt, it is considered necessary to exhibit the particularities of these particular Chapters, on the basis of which obligation is blurred, highlighting the existing margin for discussion. Obligation can be firstly established by the inclusion of the Chapters within the FTAs, which are legally binding international Treaties. Despite this qualification, inbuilt mechanisms question on a first basis the presence of the obligation and on a second basis its strength, presenting it as being

---

[22] Abbott and Snidal (2012), p. 36.

'softened'.[23] Room for such claims is created by the existence of provisions that resemble a "reserve clause"[24] on the voluntary character of the activities in the Chapters on Regulatory Cooperation of CETA and EU-Japan EPA,[25] the non-submission of the commitments to the Agreements' DSMs in the EU—Japan FTA,[26] along with the careful formulation of other provisions, that highlight the non-limiting character of Regulatory Cooperation to internal regulatory processes. An example for this is Article 21.2.4 CETA, which begins in the following way: 'Without limiting the ability of each Party to carry out its regulatory, legislative and policy…'.[27] These protective clauses,[28] mainly the result of heavy criticism and consequent stigma for the nature and scope of the introduced activities have given rise to misconceptions regarding the legal nature and value of the provisions at stake. While they do are indicators about the ability of the provisions to generate compliance, they cannot be decisive on absolute terms, and of course cannot be used as factors to deprive legality from the commitments. Instead, they offer an opportunity

---

[23] De Bievre and Poletti talk about "regulatory exports in FTAs (that) are quite inconsequential, written in legal inflation language with no rights and obligations specified, while enforceability of EU preferences is weak or mostly entirely absent" *See* De Bièvre and Poletti (2013); also on the same argument generally for WTO-X provisions (for FTA provisions not regulated on the multilateral level) Horn et al. (2010), p. 1579.

[24] The term 'reserve clause' is used somehow arbitrarily/abusively. It is questionable whether we can actually call this provision a 'reservation'. According to Article 2 (1) (d) of the VCLT, reservation is defined as "a unilateral statement, however phrased or named, made by a State, when signing, ratifying, accepting, approving or acceding to a treaty, whereby it purports to exclude or to modify the legal effect of certain provisions of the treaty in their application to that State". Such types of reservations as defined in the present Article cannot exist in a bilateral treaty, due to the nature of the latter. *See* Aust (2013), p. 119.

[25] Article 21.2.6 CETA reads as follows: 'The Parties may undertake Regulatory Cooperation activities on a voluntary basis. For greater certainty, a Party is not required to enter into any particular Regulatory Cooperation activity and may refuse to cooperate or may withdraw from cooperation. However, if a Party refuses to initiate Regulatory Cooperation or withdraws from cooperation, it should be prepared to explain the reasons for its decision to the other Party', while Article 18.6.2 EU-Japan EPA states in a similar fashion that: 'The Parties may engage in Regulatory Cooperation activities on a voluntary basis. A Party may refuse to engage in or withdraw from Regulatory Cooperation activities. A Party that refuses to engage in or withdraws from Regulatory Cooperation activities should explain the reasons for its decision to the other Party.'

[26] Article 18.19 EU-Japan EPA; This exclusion was also foreseen at an earlier stage for CETA's Regulatory Cooperation, but it was later abandoned.

[27] In general, the wording of the Regulatory Cooperation Chapter is very carefully chosen as not to create stringent and enforceable obligations. The way by which the content is set out is along with the rest of the elements of importance to the overall binding character of an arrangement, as the French Republic argued in case C-233/02. *See* C-233/02, *France v Commission of the European Communities* [2004], 2004 I-02759, Opinion of AG Alber par. 21.

[28] Clauses of this type belong to the wider category of 'flexibility devices' used by the drafters of a treaty in order to better manage its risks. Other types of such clauses include exit/escape clauses, additional declarations, phase-in provisions and amendment provisions. *See* Helfer (2006), p. 368, 375; For an overview of such 'exceptions' in CETA and comment upon this practice *see* generally de Mestral (2015).

for a legal dialogue, starting point of which is the debate on the dichotomy between hard and soft law and the various nuances with which they can dress an international obligation, either within or outside a legally binding treaty.

This Section follows an analogous pattern to the description made above. Section 3.3.1 presents two frameworks that work as a basis for the analysis to follow: the first framework discusses the presence of a legal obligation. The establishment of a legal obligation subject to the international law regime is a precondition for the discussion to follow. Indeed, the assessment of the stringency of a legal obligation preconditions the presence of one. Once the latter is established, then arises the need to reflect upon the addition of the so-called reserve clauses that create room for uncertainty as mentioned above. That being a big discussion on its own, it calls for the arrangement of an analytical framework, referring to the parameters that will be used to assess the quality of the obligation.

3.3.1 An Obligation Under International Law: Legal Base and Consequences

The EU has grown to become a powerful actor in the international arena. Two indicators are of outmost importance. Firstly, its power in the international arena is to a great extent material, derived by the expanding scope of competences that frame its ability to design its position in the world. A wide scope of competences allows not only for more action, but also for more coordinated action between disciplines, which in the end creates a coherent external action regime, as also Article 21 (3) TEU mandates.[29] Secondly and most importantly, the affirmation of its legal personality, as a consequence of its unification with the previous Community and pillar regime under a single construct, by virtue of Article 47 TEU, on the one hand sets an end to the endless debates on the issue, and on the other hand solidifies the EU's position as an actor in the international arena.[30]

It is on that quality, that its actions need to be consistent with the rules of the international arena, both of written and unwritten nature. In the case of FTAs, their bilateral conclusion under the legal form of an international treaty implies the application of the relevant public international law framework, cornerstone of which is the Vienna Convention on the Law of the Treaties.[31] Despite its hybrid nature, the EU qualifies as an International Organization under international law, and could fit under the VCLT-IO, had it been in force. Moreover, the application of the VCLT is placed in a grey zone for two reasons. Firstly, the EU falls de jure out of the

---

[29] On the importance of coherence as a value of an actor's external action, as well on how the Lisbon Treaty rendered the EU's external action more coherent *see* Koehler (2010).

[30] Koehler (2010), p. 63.

[31] Vienna Convention on the Law of Treaties (Vienna, 23 May 1969) 1155U.N.T.S. 331, entered into force 27 Jan. 1980.

scope of the Treaty, since it is not a state, while possessing though legal personality. Secondly, according to Article 3 of the VCLT, the latter could not be applicable to an agreement between a state and a different international actor, as are the FTAs that the EU is signing with third states. Still, this 'legal gap' can be filled and the extension of their application to mixed situations is legally sound on their concomitant virtue as customary law.[32] It is upon that quality that they apply directly to the totality of both the CETA and EU Japan EPA, and consequently to the Chapters of Regulatory Cooperation that form the center of the thesis. To many, especially lawyers, this assumption might seem superfluous, since it forms part of the bedrock of a lawyer's education. However, the following paragraph does not aim to reproduce what is widely known across disciplines. The following paragraph aims to refer to the legal bases in international law that constrain the parties from not engaging in Regulatory Cooperation. In other words, to frame it simply, to what extent are the parties expected to cooperate, and what would happen if they do not?

Starting point forms Article 26 of VCLT which restates the principle *pacta sunt servanda*, the pillar of treaty law.[33] Its significance is not limited to the proclamation of binding force in international law but also to the requirement of internal performance in good faith.[34] Unlike the plethora of theories on which the normative superiority of the rule *pacta sunt servanda* has been founded,[35] there is cross-disciplinary unanimity with regard to its pivotal position in the international legal order. Once ranked as international obligations, Regulatory Cooperation commitments are bestowed legal bindingness due to the effect of Article 26, a normative value that the parties have to uphold. With Regulatory Cooperation requiring input from both sides, the heart of the Chapters entails both the right of the parties to ask for initiation of Regulatory Cooperation along the agreed lines but also their duty to comply should the appropriate circumstances arise, those being for example the identification of cases of mutual interest, or of emerging areas in need of regulation.[36]

The consequences of Article 26 are however not confined in the creation of a relation formed by rights and obligations; on the contrary this fundamental rule forms the basis for the creation of subsequent legal consequences. Another legal consequence to the rule *pacta sunt servanda* of Article 26 is its corollary, Article

---

[32] Indeed, the law of the treaties, before its codification in 1969 by the International Law Commission constituted a major source of international law, existing only as custom. *See* Aust (2006).

[33] Article 26 reads as follows: 'Every Treaty in force is binding upon the parties to it and must be performed by them in good faith'.

[34] Schmalenbach (2018a), p. 468.

[35] Its existence has been founded among others on naturalism and cognitive thoughts and on the good faith principle. According to some it is elevated to custom status, general principle of law, while for Kelsenians it constitutes a basic norm (Grundnorm). Schmalenbach (2018a), pp. 472ff.

[36] Of such nature is the area of Artificial Intelligence, on the regulatory approach of which the EU has a constant dialogue with the regulators from Canada and especially Japan. EU Digital Day 2019, Brussels.

27,[37] which prohibits a state from invoking its own internal provisions to justify its non-performance with its treaty obligations.[38] Article 27, the content of which has been confirmed in various instances also by jurisprudence already of the Permanent Court of International Justice, and later of the International Court of Justice,[39] deprives internal law[40] from having a say in the international arena.[41] The relationship between the two lies in the fact that Article 27 enhances the *pacta sunt servanda* principle by excluding interference of domestic law with the performance of international obligations.

Both articles, representing guiding principles of the interpretation of the Treaties, find their origin at the general principle of good faith.[42] Good faith, widely met with its latin name *bona fide*, not only forms the bedrock of those two provisions on which obligation to comply can be based, but also helps overcome the lack of enforcement, thus covering possible 'gaps' that the structural choices of the parties created.[43] A cooperation based on the imperatives of good faith in a case such as the one of Regulatory Cooperation, deprived of recourse to a DSM, might prove equally effective to the functioning of the Chapters and the initiation of cooperation. This might be particularly true in the case of Regulatory Cooperation Chapters given also the established preference for a voluntary initiation of such activities. Such a clause that leaves considerable margin of discretion to the parties blurs the lines between conformity and non-conformity. Of course, the parties are required to justify their choice to not engage into Regulatory Cooperation activities, and as mentioned, should not rely on internal law particularities (but see Article 21.2.4 CETA under which the unwillingness to engage in Regulatory Cooperation can be justified by domestic policy reasons...). Such reasons on which cooperation could be denied will likely be tightly tied to public policy considerations, a sphere where an FTA partner has restricted access.

This makes the distinction between performance and non-performance a difficult exercise. Hence, it unavoidably hinders the establishment of International Responsibility. International Responsibility forms vital part of the international legal community since it lies at the heart of the international system, and serves as the corollary and proof of obligations in international law.[44] Its constitutional importance is

---

[37] Article 27 states: A party may not invoke the provisions of its internal law as justification for its failure to perform a treaty, Vienna Convention on the Law of the Treaties.

[38] Aust (2007).

[39] Examples include: Permanent Court of International Justice, 'Treatment of Polish Nationals and Other Persons of Polish Origin or Speech in the Danzig Territory' PCIJ Ser A/B No 44, 24 (1932); International Court of Justice, 'Fisheries Case (UK v Norway)' ICJ Rep 116, 132 (1952).

[40] Absent a definition in Article 2, the term 'internal law' is interpreted broadly as covering written and unwritten laws, regulations, decrees, orders and decisions adopted by all types of authorities and levels of government. It also includes judicial decisions.

[41] Schmalenbach (2018b), p. 496.

[42] Kotzur (2009).

[43] Kotzur (2009).

[44] Pellet (2010), p. 4.

proven on two instances: firstly, International Responsibility can be based on any type of obligation, either an obligation of conduct, as is the one in Regulatory Cooperation Chapters or an obligation of result;[45] and secondly, in direct relation to the first, its establishment is disconnected from the presence of material damage; International Responsibility is of course closely related to it, but not conditioned upon it.[46] According to Articles 1 and 2 of the International Law Commission's Articles on the Responsibility of States for Internationally Wrongful Acts, International Responsibility is founded upon the presence of an internationally wrongful act,[47] which is a breach of an international obligation attributable to a State (or any other International legal actor).[48,49] This conception of responsibility introduces an objective approach and signals that the condition under which a state or any other actor is held internationally responsible marks a red flag about the breach of an international obligation. International Responsibility is thus intrinsically linked to the norm *pacta sunt servanda*, since it derives from its violation, and this justifies the seriousness and heavy significance this characterization to be held internationally responsible bears. In the case of Regulatory Cooperation, as mentioned, inbuilt preference of a voluntary cooperation hinders the prima facie recognition of breach of a commitment, given the wide margin of discretion left to the parties, and the sensitive reasons that the parties can in theory bring up in order to abstain from such activities. However, no matter how hard it might in principle be to ground and prove International Responsibility, its appearance due to non-performance remains as possible as the fulfilment of the obligations. And of course, what would principally matter in such a case would not be the reparation of a caused damage, an unlikely scenario under a hypothetical failure to engage in Regulatory Cooperation, but the reputational damage caused by being held internationally responsible.

This paragraph referred to the norms that constitute the cornerstones of the international legal system and tried to stress the importance of the consequences that derive from the nature of the obligations undertaken by the Regulatory Cooperation Chapters. The fundamental principle of *pacta sunt servanda*, codified in Article 26 of the VCLT, along with its sister provision Article 27, both extracted from the imperatives of *bona fide*, ask for compliance in good faith and invite the parties to honor the terms upon which they have agreed to initiate Regulatory Cooperation. The exact content of the obligations, their existence and duration, are defined by the rest of the provisions of the Law of the Treaties[50] and of course by the

---

[45] Ruka (2017), p. 37.

[46] Ruka (2017), p. 9.

[47] Article 1: Responsibility of a State for its internationally wrongful acts; International Law Commission on the Responsibility of States for an Internationally Wrongful Acts.

[48] Article 2: Elements of an Internationally wrongful act of a State; International Law Commission on the Responsibility of States for an Internationally Wrongful Acts.

[49] Crawford (2010), p. 18; On the International Responsibility of the EU *see* Delgado Casteleiro (2016), pp. 12ff.

[50] Verhoeven (2010), p. 107.

content of the Chapters themselves. A failure to respect them triggers the International Responsibility of the parties, a status which can be independent from material damage, which however entails serious reputational damage in any case.

3.3.2   What Kind of Obligation Under International Law?

This Section continues the analysis from the point the previous one left it: The previous Section, while having clearly defined the obligation under international law and having specified fundamental consequences of the resulting application of public international law framework, did not engage with the kind of obligation at stake. The reference to the 'kind' of obligation at stake reflects the debate whether Regulatory Cooperation obligations, given the reserve clauses are mostly of hard or soft nature, and more fundamentally, whether this hard/soft law approach is most appropriate. Before proceeding to the discussion, a clarification on the used terminology has to be made. This Section relies upon the distinction made by Pauwelyn of legal normativity and legal imperativity. According to Pauwelyn, legal normativity does not necessarily imply legal imperativity.[51] In other words, the fact that all norms that qualify as 'law' carry legal normativity, does not mean that they constitute a source of hard rights and obligations in a way that can influence behaviour. The value of this distinction lies in the fact that it justifies how, within the universe of law, there might be legal norms that are legally binding, but only entail hortatory provisions.[52]

Very often such provisions are described with the term 'soft law'. Soft law is a curious term in legal scholarship and the proliferation of hybrid legal phenomena in the international order has generated interesting discussions about its nature and main functioning, while different strands of literature take different stands on its relation to hard law, placed by some on an antagonistic relation,[53] and perceived by others as alternatives[54] or complements viewed under the prism of the specific governance arrangement. However, the qualification of some international arrangements as soft law has further perplexed the scenery, should one take into account that the entire quality of international law as law is set under question by some

---

[51] Pauwelyn (2012), p. 126.

[52] Pauwelyn (2012), p. 126.

[53] Especially for legal positivists, that very often employ this binary approach, and mostly on non reconciliating terms, the identifying 'soft' before law and its frequently positioning next to 'hard' law fits oddly with the classic doctrinal understanding of law as a mechanism that inherently generates compliance. *See* Klabbers (1996), p. 168.

[54] This view is supported in International Relations literature by rationalists, who unlike legal positivists, do not place hard and soft law on an antithetical relationship, but instead talk about different tools that serve different circumstances, in which the use of hard law as such signals an actor's intention to demonstrate the degree to which it intends to commit. *See* Guzman (2008), pp.71–111.

commentators, given the absence of a centralized coercive authority.[55] The original concept of Legalization seems to accept soft law as part of international law. As the concept itself, so its components are placed on a continuum. Thus, the element of obligation in the original concept of Legalization, does not necessarily imply a legally binding obligation and is not a binary one. Returning to the terminology set by Pauwelyn, by the term 'soft law' it is the legal normativity of a norm that is set on a scale.[56] By giving ab initio such a wide range to soft law, as encompassing norms that do not pass the 'law' threshold to norms whose normativity is said to be 'compromised' due to their soft enforcement or vague wording, it does not seem surprising that there is not unanimity on the very concept of soft law. On the contrary, it is often perceived as a self-conflicting notion.[57]

The opposing to soft law part of the literature rejects the founding element of soft law, the 'relative normativity' of norms and instead insists on a clear separation between law and non-law. This school swears, in other words, by a binary distinction of legality.[58] According to this view, the concept of soft law is redundant, and a threshold of legal normativity does and should exist. However, this school does puts legal imperativity under perspective. As Prosper Weil has placed it "whether a rule is hard or soft does not, of course, affect its normative character. A rule of treaty or customary law may be vague, 'soft', but as the above examples show, it does not thereby cease to be a legal norm."[59] Softness in their perception can characterize the content of the legal norm but not its quality as such.

This approach, accepting that "one cannot be bound softly, yet a binding norm can be soft"[60] avoids the paradox that the very concept of 'soft law' entails. Indeed, in the soft law literature, the 'softness' of a norm—its legal normativity—is assessed on criteria other than the legal form of the agreement—which is self-evident here, as Regulatory Cooperation Chapters are part of CETA and EU-Japan EPA. After all, there is no state practice that can support a distinct category of law: states negotiate and conclude either binding or non-binding agreements.[61] To fill in this gap scholars rather focus on the substance of a commitment instead, as is for example the consequential and influential nature of a rule based, its preciseness[62] or the structure of an agreement, as is its ability to be enforced.[63] Upon such criteria pro-soft law

---

[55] See generally D'Amato (1985); On the criticism of Reus-Smit on existing theories that try to ground acceptance of international obligations by States see Reus-Smit (2003).

[56] Pauwelyn (2012), p. 128.

[57] Chinkin (1989), p. 850.

[58] Raustalia (2005); Weil (1983); Klabbers (1996).

[59] Weil (1983).

[60] Pauwelyn (2012), p. 128.

[61] Raustalia (2005), p. 587.

[62] Baxter (1980).

[63] Baxter (1980), p. 562.

commentators declassify binding legally binding norms to ones of sub-legal, and even non-legal nature.[64]

However, making a judgement on the legality of each separate provision based on its substance and its ability to influence behavior[65] and on its ability to be enforced conflates three distinct notions.[66] Substance and Structure along with Legality of course constitute three components on the basis of which the design of International agreements is examined, however, they represent different aspects of each Agreement and thus should not be muddled.[67] In other words, the status of a rule as law, represented by the dimension of 'Legality' is by no means dependent on how effective a rule is.[68] Of course, some rules may bring better results than others, but this does not deprive them of their status as law. That said, when it comes to the type of obligation in the case of Regulatory Cooperation commitments, particular attention should be given to whether these 'reserve clauses' belong to the Legality or form part of the Substance or Structure of the Agreement. The following parts of this Section will demonstrate that in fact, those elements 'soften' the legal imperativity of the commitments, and not their legal normativity. In fact, they have nothing to do with the nature of the legality of the obligation, but with the substance and structure, not impacting thus the status of the commitments as legally binding ones.

3.3.2.1 Legality and Substance

As far as the examination of the design of an international agreement is concerned, 'Substance' reflects the extent to which states have agreed to change their behaviour.[69] It partially coincides with the 'Precision' element of the Legalization concept,

---

[64] *See* generally Boyle (1999), p. 906; Also Brown Weiss admits that provisions included in International agreements that are hortatory are referred as 'soft law'. However, she seems to recognize the complications that come with the use of the term 'soft law' by referring to either legally binding or non-legally binding agreements. *See* Brown Weiss (1997), p. 3; Shelton (2003); Baxter (1980), p. 554; Chinkin (1989).

[65] Brunnee and Toope (2000).

[66] For those who understand soft law as the type of commitment that is not subject to a DSM, treaties can include both hard and soft law commitments, the hard being the ones that are enforceable through an adjudication mechanism and the soft being the ones that range from non-adjudication to milder forms of reconciliation procedures. However, this vision of soft law is only acknowledged, not shared. *See* Boyle (1999), p. 902.

[67] Also in the Legalization concept, obligation, precision and delegation are three distinct elements, which, although seen together as an overall concept, each one taken separately is viewed and assessed on its own.

[68] Effectiveness should also not be muddled with compliance. As explained by Kal Raustalia, compliance and effectiveness should be viewed separately, because it is effectiveness that provides the causal linkage between a rule and a behaviour, with compliance only demonstrating the conformity between the two. As he has mentioned, the two concepts must be viewed separately. *See* Raustalia (2000), p. 398.

[69] Raustalia (2005), p. 584.

however, it is not identical. 'Substance' does encompass of course how vaguely or precisely the rules are defined; however, its scope reaches beyond that. Its best proxy would be the description of the 'Depth'[70] of the Agreement, signaling "the extent to which an arrangement requires states to depart from what they would have done in its absence".[71] Such an indicator constitutes the provisions that outline the voluntary character of Regulatory Cooperation in FTAs. By giving a voluntary character to the initiation of cooperation, these provisions are an indication of how much the parties are called upon to alter their behavior.

On the voluntary character of the activities, Article 21.2.6 CETA reads as follows:

> The Parties may undertake Regulatory Cooperation activities on a voluntary basis. For greater certainty, a Party is not required to enter into any particular Regulatory Cooperation activity and may refuse to cooperate or may withdraw from cooperation. However, if a Party refuses to initiate Regulatory Cooperation or withdraws from cooperation, it should be prepared to explain the reasons for its decision to the other Party.'

while Article 18.6.2 JEEPA states in a similar fashion that:

> The Parties may engage in Regulatory Cooperation activities on a voluntary basis. A Party may refuse to engage in or withdraw from Regulatory Cooperation activities. A Party that refuses to engage in or withdraws from Regulatory Cooperation activities should explain the reasons for its decision to the other Party.

In this case, parties are called to voluntarily change their behavior, in the sense that they will not be obliged to initiate cooperation.

The relation, and most importantly, the distinction between Substance (voluntary initiation) and Legality has also been part of the thoughts of Advocate General (hereinafter AG) Alber in case France v. Commission, C-233/02. Interestingly enough, the case under consideration, C-233/02, dealt with another Regulatory Cooperation initiative, namely the EU-US Guidelines which were agreed as a political declaration during one of the various bilateral summits. These Guidelines outlined in a quite detailed and coherent manner a series of activities that regulators were encouraged to undertake in order to initiate a sustainable dialogue. Quite alarmed by the content of the Guidelines and the impact they could have on the Commission's right of initiative, France brought an action for annulment against the Commission before the Court of Justice arguing that in fact the Guidelines were concluded as an International agreement, not falling under the Union's competences, the binding character of which could have a serious impact on the Commission's

---

[70] Interestingly, it is through the practice of reserving, as is the case here with a clause on voluntary initiation, that parties manage the depth of the Agreement. Depth can also be a relative unit, with the same obligation being deep for the one party but shallow for the other. One example is the TRIPS Agreement, that on the one hand required substantive changes to the IP regime of most states, which was not the case for the US or Europe for example. *See* generally Otten (2015), p. 56. Be it as it may, in any case 'depth' does not impinge upon the legality of the commitments.

[71] Downs et al. (1996), p. 383.

right of initiative.[72] Before deciding on the compatibility of the Guidelines with the legislative prerogatives of the Commission, the central question that had to be answered was whether the Guidelines were in fact an international agreement, concluded outside the scope of the Commission's competences, and could as such be challenged as a legal act of the Commission under Article 230 EC.

To answer this question, AG Alber went beyond the form of the agreement, and looked into its content, developing an analytical framework which included various dimensions upon which it based its opinion. AG Alber commented on the following elements in order to assess the legal nature of the Guidelines: (a) the context that placed the Guidelines (b) the intention of the parties (c) the use of language (d) the objectives pursued.

Before referring to each parameter separately and seeing how it would apply in our case of Regulatory Cooperation, it is necessary that we locate why this choice of criteria is enlightening for our argument on the distinction between Substance and Legality: The Opinion, while acknowledging on the one hand that a clause on the intention of the parties to engage voluntary can serve as a criterion upon which the legal value of an agreement might depend in cases of uncertainty, on the other hand, it also recognizes that the intention of the parties to engage voluntarily does not always go hand in hand with non-legality. In that sense, the AG distinguishes legality from voluntary engagement.

The intention of the parties is, according to AG, an important factor that guides us about the legal nature that the parties intended to ascribe to an international arrangement in cases of uncertainty; however, it is not decisive. Thus, even if we were in uncertainty about the legal nature of Regulatory Cooperation in CETA and EU-Japan, we could not solely depend on the intention of the parties to give voluntary character, which should be read in conjunction with the other elements as well, such as context, use of language and objectives.

The AG's 'context' criterion confirms that the choice of venue is indicative of the intention of the parties to dress their commitment in more formal clothes. Indeed, by arguing for the weak character of the cooperation activities as introduced in the Guidelines, due to the fact that they were founded in the context of a political arrangement, namely the TEP (par. 59), one can expect some added value through the inclusion in a legally binding agreement, which changes the negotiating and decision-making environment, and thus influences the character of the Agreement as a whole. This 'upgrade' carries the history of countless efforts to promote the regulatory dialogue through the soft, legally fragile 'political treaties', to quote Judge Baxter[73] and signals the intention to commit further along more legalistic lines. This venue also instructs that cooperation is not taking place in a legal vacuum.

---

[72] C-233/02, *France v Commission of the European Communities* [2004], 2004 I-02759, Opinion of AG Alber, par.54.

[73] Judge Baxter uses the term 'international agreements' in order to expand his analysis also to agreements other than binding treaties (as understood for the purposes of Vienna Convention on the Law of Treaties). One of the categories of international agreements that he discerns are the 'political treaties'. These political treaties, examples of which are joint communications and joint

FTAs create a whole new structure of trade relations between the parties—which is of course juxtaposed to the multilateral one, but which also functions independently on some issues—and constitute a new source of authority themselves.[74]

Another important criterion that should be taken into consideration is the use of language.[75] "Legalization implies a discourse primarily in terms of the text purpose and history of the rules, their interpretation, admissible exceptions..." note the instigators of Legalization while unfolding the different dimensions and content of the obligation criterion. Applying this framework to the Regulatory Cooperation Chapters, and beginning from the discourse in terms of language, it can be inferred that the vocabulary according to which the main provisions are formulated, the use of the obligatory 'shall', is indicative of the mandatory nature of the terms, and the hard type of obligation. Such vocabulary is used for example in CETA with regard to Article 21.5 dealing with the Compatibility of regulatory measures: "...each Party shall, when appropriate, consider the regulatory measures or initiatives of the other party on the same or related topics" and with regard to Article 21.7 on Further Cooperation dealing with Information Exchange: "... the Parties shall periodically exchange information of ongoing or planned regulatory projects in their areas of responsibility". Similar language is used repeatedly in outlining the procedure of Regulatory Cooperation to be undertaken in Article 18.12 of the EU-Japan FTA.

Furthermore, the AG took into consideration the objectives pursued. He argued that the objectives as described in the Guidelines, also militated in favour of the non-binding nature of the commitments. However, one can see that the objectives, as described in the Regulatory Cooperation Chapters of modern FTAs, go much further than the objectives pursued with the Guidelines. While the objectives of the Guidelines qualify more as process-orientated, the objects of the Regulatory Cooperation Chapter of the CETA are more result-orientated. The main objective of the Guidelines was to facilitate the dialogue between regulators: This objective is of course present in the new Chapters on Regulatory Cooperation in the FTAs, which however, go even further, by actually setting an objective to the process of Regulatory Cooperation, that being the elimination of unnecessary regulatory barriers, the advancement of the quality of the regulation and the concomitant invigoration of the business sector. Thus, the aim is not solely to initiate a dialogue and to build trust between the regulators, but goes further, to the actual elimination of duplicative, unnecessary trade barriers.

---

declarations, are, according to his analysis, a category of soft law, as opposed to treaties that introduce hard law. *See* Baxter (1980), p. 551.

[74]Martha Finnemore and Stephen J. Toope make the same argument with regard to Legalization of monetary affairs and the impact of the element of obligation to the decisions taken under Article VIII of the IMF Agreement in order to argue that authority and normativity do not derive exclusively from the obligation imposed by a single provision, but also from the wider legal environment that frames these actions, which encompasses the activities and supports them with a firm legal background and relevant expertise. See Finnemore and Toope (2001), p. 752.

[75]C-233/02, *France v Commission of the European Communities* [2004], 2004 I-02759, Opinion of AG Alber, par. 80.

Once having applied this framework to our case of Regulatory Cooperation, it becomes clear that the legal value of the commitments does not depend on the intention of the parties on voluntary initiation. Here we are not in the presence of uncertainty; we are clearly in the presence of an international agreement where the use of language is also binding and the objectives are result-driven. The true significance of the clause on voluntary initiation can be better understood when seen under the dichotomy illustrated by Ruiter and Wessel who have introduced a distinction between the 'legally obligatory' and 'legally committing' nature of norms.[76] According to their theoretical framework, the term 'legally committing' is larger than, but also includes the term 'legally obligatory'.[77] According to its characteristics a norm can be legally committing without being legally obligatory. In the same spirit the presence of this clause on voluntary initiation argues for the non-legally obligating nature of the commitments but does not impinge upon the legality of the undertaken commitment; at least no such intention arises from the legal text.

3.3.2.2 Legality and Structure

The same framework, the need to distinguish between legality and the various design elements, in this case, Structure, applies to the exclusion of the Regulatory Cooperation Chapter in EU—Japan from the DSM.[78] Leading scholars apart from Raustalia, who distinguished between Legality, Substance and Structure, and upon whose framework the present analysis relies, also separate the designation of an adjudication mechanism from legality, agreeing that it remains a design element, which is different and independent from the legal form of a commitment.[79] Even commentators that accept the dichotomy between soft and hard law and equate it to binding and non-binding commitments, understand and present adjudication on a separate basis.[80] Adjudication is thus not associated with legality, but with an enhancement of credibility instead, where also the design element of 'hard law' aims as well.[81]

The irrelevance of this element for the presence of an international obligation has been also confirmed by jurisprudence of the Court of Justice, more specifically by the Opinion of AG Alber in case C-233/02, which was introduced in the previous

---

[76]Ruiter and Wessel (2012), p. 165.

[77]Ruiter and Wessel (2012), p. 165.

[78]Article 18.19 EU-Japan EPA.

[79]Also Guzman is presenting the design elements of 'hard law, dispute resolution and monitoring' as three self-standing design elements. *See* Guzman (2005).

[80]For example Guzman who uses hard/soft law as synonyms for binding/non-binding agreements respectively, admits that one cannot distinguish these two categories of commitment, the kind of legality in other words (hard/soft—binding/non-binding) neither on the basis of an adjudication clause nor on the effects on the behaviour. *See* Guzman (2005), p. 583.

[81]Guzman (2002).

Section. In particular, it is the starting point of AG thoughts that confirms our argument. Indeed, AG Alber commenced his assessment by stating what is irrelevant for the characterisation of a commitment as a legally binding one. According to his analysis, the presence or absence of dispute settlement and liability provisions is irrelevant to the qualification of the Guidelines as an International agreement.[82] Indeed, it is interesting that the same argument raised at the time by the Commission to argue against the legal value is raised also today for the same reason. The choice to subject a commitment to dispute settlement may instead influence the level of effectiveness, but not its qualification as an obligation as such.

3.3.3 Inference on Obligation

Based on the argumentation provided in the previous two Sections, one may safely reach some conclusions on the normative significance of Regulatory Cooperation in the international sphere. As outlined above, the insistence of a voluntary cooperation and the choice in EU—Japan to exclude the provisions from dispute settlement refers to the substance and structure of the Chapters, not to their legality. Thus, they should not be perceived as factors that compromise or deny legal normativity. The choice for a voluntary cooperation mostly impacts the margin of degree that parties enjoy with regard to initiation of the obligation, while the exclusion of a DSM on the enforcement, not on the existence of the obligation as such. Of course, initiation of Regulatory Cooperation will not be forced, one way or another, but will eventually depend on the regulatory priorities of each legal order and the degree of their compatibility. After all, there seems to exist convergence on the suitability of the application of Dispute Settlement to Regulatory Cooperation provisions. Also in the USMCA, the newly signed FTA between the US, Mexico and Canada, recourse to Dispute Settlement is discouraged with regard to Regulatory Cooperation, however not completely excluded. It is only reserved to "address a sustained or recurring course of action or inaction that is inconsistent with a provision of the Chapter".[83]

After all, such regulatory choices are not chosen arbitrarily, but they reflect some kind of uncertainty regarding internal implementation and the need to maintain some kind of flexibility.[84] This of course does not mean that the parties have not undertaken the obligation to pursue it, whenever possible. One must distinguish between the obligation to cooperate given a fertile ground and the obligation to cooperate in any case. The Chapters under analysis create the former type of obligation, respectful of the sensitive nature of cooperation in regulatory matters. The protective clauses

---

[82] C-233/02, *France v Commission of the European Communities* [2004], 2004 I-02759, Opinion of AG Alber, par. 19.

[83] Article 28.20 USMCA, to be found under: https://ustr.gov/sites/default/files/files/agreements/FTA/USMCA/Text/28_Good_Regulatory_Practices.pdf.

[84] Rosendorff and Milner (2001), pp. 832ff; *See* Koremenos et al. (2001).

aim exactly to protect the regulatory orders from a flooding alien invasion that might not always be welcome and guarantee some freedom and discretion to the regulators. Nevertheless, the parties do undertake the obligation on behalf of the implicated regulators and moreover, they undertake a serious commitment to prepare their regulatory environments, legally, ethically, financially in order to accommodate their new mandates as smooth as possible. As an international obligation created through its inclusion in an FTA, certainly the conditions under which Regulatory Cooperation activities are conducted are altered. Indeed, such an obligation carries a heavier legal significance, one that has the power to oversee, prevent and give solutions to internal implementation problems, as the one faced in earlier efforts, exactly because of the weight it carries as an international commitment.

3.4 Precision of Commitments

The second dimension that will be considered here, in order to fill in the Legalization puzzle will be the one of precision. Precision as a term is commonly defined as 'the quality, condition, or fact of being exact and accurate'.[85] According to this definition, precision of rules tantamount to their level of elaboration, in other words, how precisely they are formulated. Precision evaluates among others this quality of the rules, and is a necessary measurement for Regulatory Cooperation. In initiatives of Regulatory Cooperation that implicate sophisticated, multi-level legal orders, with complex regulatory interactions derived either from supranational or a national structure, precision is a valuable tool on the correct implementation and operation of the mechanisms. After all, precision offers a good opportunity to get acquinted with the commitments enshrined in the Chapters, something that is necessary for the comprehension of the subject-matter.

However, in this case precision does not serve as a measurement of rules' elaboration exclusively Instead, the following Section will offer a simultaneous deliberation of both content and the degree of precision of the Regulatory Cooperation Chapters, more specifically it will examine the degree of precision through the content. This will serve the next objective of this Section, the attempt to discover the level of ambition of each Chapter through the presentation that will be undertaken.

The presentation of the commitments and the comment upon their degree of precision shall be attempted on a tripartite basis. The analysis shall commence from the foreseen procedures, since Regulatory Cooperation is about procedural aspects of varying nature, intensity and reach. Procedures in Regulatory Cooperation are the necessary tools that connect the various actors with their working material, thus the analysis to follow will be *ratione personae* and *ratione materiae*, a categorization

---

[85] Definition of Precision, Oxford Living Dictionary, https://en.oxforddictionaries.com/definition/precision.

popular in other social disciplines as the 'subjects/objects' model.[86] Simple as it may seem, it is exactly its inherent simplicity that renders it a unique 'type' that fits most new and complex notions, transforming them into comprehensible figures and contributing to their analytical accessibility. Viewing the Regulatory Cooperation Chapters through this presentation mode allows for their categorization, a clear understanding of the additions and omissions within the Treaties but also of the consequences of the latter.

3.4.1 Precision Regarding Substance and Reach of Regulatory Cooperation Activities

Discovering the substance and reach of the Regulatory Cooperation activities is the first step towards the understanding of the anticipations created by the commitments. Precision in this case is indispensable in order to understand which instances of the regulatory processes will be impacted, and to assess at a later stage, what effects are to be expected upon them due to the undertaken commitments. Taken together, these questions form the essence of the Chapters. For that reason, the analysis shall begin from that category.

On a first basis, the delimitation of commitments and comment upon their precision regarding substance and reach shall take place through the joint examination and interpretation of two different parts of the Agreement, firstly of their objectives and later of the Regulatory Cooperation activities themselves. As with every agreement, also the Chapters under analysis on Regulatory Cooperation serve some objectives. The particular mention of those objectives and their incorporation as self-standing provisions in the legislative texts reflects a long-standing practice which reveals their direct connection with the undertaken commitments. Indeed, the relationship between objectives and commitments is a two-way street. Negotiation of objectives preceeds the negotiation of the actual commitments, which are later formulated in a way as to facilitate the achievement of the objectives. In that sense, objectives frame the contours of the Chapters. Still though, after the agreement upon concrete commitments, the latter are implemented with a view of serving the set-in-advance objectives.

Both Chapters on Regulatory Cooperation follow this pattern, setting already the scene from a difference in focus of their respective objectives, a difference which corresponds to the distinction between Regulatory Coherence and Regulatory Cooperation, as the latter was made in the Introduction Chapter. As we shall see, in both Chapters the undertaken commitments and their reach are later outlined in harmony with the set objectives.

---

[86] Initial inspiration for the categorization on the basis of this model has been the work of Fahey, Bardutzky (2017).

3.4.1.1 Focus on Regulatory Coherence in EU-Japan EPA

Article 18.1 of the EU-Japan EPA is rather laconic when it comes to the objectives of the undertaken cooperation. From the initial provisions however it becomes clear that what is particularly sought is the attainment of a regulatory environment that is characterized by efficiency, transparency, predictability and flexibility, which will render compatibility of the regulatory regimes easier, and which will eventually contribute to the reduction of unnecessary requirements (Articles 18.1.1.a and b). Still though, the reduction of divergences is expected to be the result of compatible regimes rather than cooperation activities, as is for example the conclusion of an MRA. The parties further aim to sustain a bilateral dialogue on regulatory issues and to develop closer cooperation in international fora (Articles 18.1.1.c and d). The focus on Regulatory Coherence is also established through its inclusion in the title of the Chapter and of its first Section.

The content of Sub Section 2 of the Chapter, entitled 'Good Regulatory practices', comes indeed in line with the set objectives. It introduces, as its name suggests, various provisions on the subject and forms the biggest part of the Chapter itself. Key provisions guarantee the transparency and openness of the regulatory mechanism by setting up vehicles that either provide early information on new regulatory proposals (Article 18.6) or give access to public comment procedures (Article 18.7). Further provisions aim at the betterment and affirmation of regulations' compatibility with ongoing developments through impact assessments (Article 18.8) and periodic reviews (Article 18.9). General improvement of regulatory governance is abstractly encouraged through the promotion of horizontal discussions on regulatory tools (Article 18.11).

Contrary to one's expectations after an elaborate framework on regulatory quality, Sub-Section 3 on Regulatory Cooperation that comprises only Article 18.12 outlines mostly the procedure to be followed in order to formally initiate Regulatory Cooperation and spells out in paragraph 5 some necessary preparatory steps, limited to exchange of information on new or existing regulatory measures (18.12.5 a and b). Only paragraph c of the said Article introduces concretely a cooperation activity, the mutual consideration of regulatory approaches adopted by the other party in cases when relevant subject matters of the regulatory activity arise.

Although mainly focused on Regulatory Coherence, the reach of these activities in the regulatory process is expected to be substantial, although a general provision on the impacted instances is lacking in the Agreement. This is firstly understood by context, since the nature of some undertaken commitments render them applicable to specific stages of the regulatory process, something that is usually reflected in the text itself as well; for example, while transparency is required at all stages,[87] public consultations and impact assessment refers to the preparatory phase of a

---

[87] For example, on the basis of Article 18.5 EU-Japan EPA, each party is required to make public any material that describes the processes and mechanisms that are used for the preparation, evaluation and review of its regulatory measures.

regulation,[88] and retrospective evaluation coincides with a later review of regulatory measures. Since the enhancement of the regulatory regime should be as comprehensive as possible, this extensive intervention to the regulatory circle is also met in approaches towards regulatory coherence of other major trading actors. In TPP for example, that contained a promising Chapter on Regulatory Coherence, the good regulatory practices enshrined therein were meant to apply "in the process of planning, designing, issuing, implementing and reviewing regulatory measures".[89]

3.4.1.2   Focus on Regulatory Cooperation in CETA

In contrast to Article 18.1 of the EU-Japan, that merely mentions the advancement of Regulatory Coherence and promotes bilateral dialogue in vague terms, Article 21.3 of CETA lists extensively apt results of Regulatory Cooperation as objectives. Of course, progress on the advancement of Regulatory Coherence figures as part of the set objectives also under Article 21.3. The parties set the mutual understanding of the other party's regulatory governance as a priority, aiming at the improvement of their own respective regimes, which shall be reflected on the overall quality of the regulations (Article 21.3.b). In mentioning Regulatory Coherence as an objective in the aforementioned Article for example, the parties aspire to improve holistically the whole regulatory process, starting with the planning and development of the regulations, passing on to their quality, by rendering them more transparent, predictable and efficient, even if that would mean avoiding regulating and using alternatives, and finally reaching the implementation and compliance stage (Article 21.3.b i-vii). Apart from that, the rest of the Article's provisions spell out concrete Regulatory Cooperation activities to be held as the medium to facilitate trade and investment and boost industry's competitiveness (Articles 21.3.c and d). The parties are primarily called to build upon existing agreements and search new avenues of cooperation (Article 21.3.c.i and ii) in order to minimize unnecessary or duplicative requirements that are burdensome to industry. Parties are particularly encouraged to pursue the application of compatible approaches, either by using compatible frameworks, opting for convergence or recognizing the equivalence of respective regulations (Article 21.3.d.iii. A and B).

In order to attain the described objectives, Article 21.4, entitled 'Regulatory Cooperation activities', comprises a long, elaborated list that groups together under its auspices activities on Regulatory Coherence and Regulatory Cooperation. Unlike Article 18.12 of the EU-Japan on Regulatory Cooperation, in this Article it is the content of the obligations that is precisely outlined and not the procedure to be

---

[88] Article 18.7 EU-Japan EPA on Public Consultations is to be respected 'when preparing major regulatory measures' while Article 18.8 EU-Japan EPA on Impact Assessment obliges the parties to undertake this procedure for 'major regulatory measures under preparation'.

[89] Article 25.2.1 of the Final Text of The Trans-Pacific Partnership Agreement, <https://ustr.gov/sites/default/files/TPP-Final-Text-Regulatory-Coherence.pdf>.

followed for their initiation. Apart from the precise reference to content, another characteristic that renders the obligation more robust is the formulation of the provisions in such a way, as to not only provide the activity, but also to describe the rationale and the expected result. A first idea on the undertaken commitments of Article 21.4 is given with Article 21.1, according to which the reach of the commitments is extensive, expected to apply throughout the whole life circle of regulations, from their elaboration to their evaluation and revision, covering also methodological aspects of their creation. Obligations are thus expected to be diverse, in order to catch the whole regulatory process. Indeed, should one attempt a categorization of the established obligations, one should define five main categories, of differing content:

(a) The first established obligation that burdens the parties is to engage into a sustainable discourse on Regulatory Coherence, mainly in order to exchange experiences on regulatory tools and benefit from each other's know-how (Article 21.4.a. (i) to (iv)).

(b) The second one can be generally defined as the obligation to proceed to consultations and exchange of information on various instances. Exchange of information may concern generally the regulatory process, as part of the regulatory reform dialogue (Article 21.4.b), it shall include early information of the upcoming regulatory activities (Article 21.4.f) and can also extend to non-public information (Article 21.4.c). The reason behind this constant communication throughout all of the stages of the regulatory process, including the implementation, enforcement and review phase (Article 21.4.m) is double; on the one hand the trade partners need to be aware of upcoming regulatory measures that could stand as barrier to trade, and on the other hand, they need to be given the opportunity to understand the regulatory choices of their partner in concreto (Article 21.4.f.i).

(c) Furthermore, parties undertake the obligation to seek and enable foreign input through commenting as soon as possible in the regulatory process. Either on their own initiative, or upon request of the other party, parties are expected to allow sufficient time for comments on regulatory initiatives or on measures expected to have an impact on trade, as are for example TBT or SPS measures (Article 21.4.d, e).

(d) Of outmost importance in the Chapter is the next obligation, which mandates the parties to examine convergence one way or another. Either by jointly running steps of the regulatory process, agreeing on a harmonized or equivalent solution, or through the conclusion of MRAs, parties have to place their efforts on diminishing existing unnecessary regulatory barriers (Article 21.4.r) and impeding the appearance of new ones (Article 21.4.g). To that end, they can also draw inspiration from the regulatory measures of the other party (Article 21.5).

(e) The last obligation concerns the methodological aspects of the regulatory process. With an ultimate view to promote similarity of results, parties agree to examine the possibility of working on the basis of the same or similar data on the nature and frequency of the arising problems (Article 21.4.i) while using the same methodological assumptions (Article 21.4.k). Towards that end, engaging into joint research initiatives on pressing issues in order to gather common data and gain by reducing duplicative research will serve to the creation of a common scientific basis on which the parties can base their future regulations (Article 21.4.n).

The several types of obligation outlined above line up harmoniously and serve to the realization of the Chapter's objectives. Overall this part of the Chapter gains not only in precision, as in detailed provisions but also in coherence. The precise enumeration of the activities along with the rationale for their incorporation among the envisaged ones and the expected results provide the image of a Regulatory Cooperation that has been properly negotiated and agreed upon, where the described activities have a particular aim to serve, and where each provision complements one another.

Broadly speaking, the general image of the objectives of the two Chapters and the general principles that will guide both bilateral efforts, such as the common will to uphold the protection of societal values and safeguard the regulatory prerogatives, largely coincide (Article 21.2 CETA and Article 18.1.2 and 3 EU-Japan EPA). However, a closer look reveals that the difference in the precision and content creates different expectations for the actual substantive commitments. In EU-Japan for example, the Chapter gains in precision only as far as regulatory coherence is concerned despite its strong procedural focus and substantial reach. As far as Regulatory Cooperation is concerned, it fails to enumerate both Regulatory Cooperation activities and the expected results thereof. On the contrary, Regulatory Cooperation in CETA is described with detail, and the typology of the obligations that is created out of the long provisions is informative of its diversity. This diversity concerns in the end not only the activities themselves but also their reach on the regulatory procedures. Overall, however, they are both rather precise on the type of the activities that form their respective core.

3.4.2 Precision Ratione Personae

In the present instance, the use of the terms 'subjects' shall be used to signify to whom the Regulatory Cooperation commitments are addressed. Who is 'subject' to Regulatory Cooperation activities? How precise are the Chapters in outlining the subjects as the main actors? One would wonder why precision matters. The obvious answer to the question of subjects, the regulators, would not suffice in our case. It would suffice in the case of a single state where regulatory action is centralized and flows from top to the bottom, while no regulatory discretion is left to state sub-divisions. Such approach though does not fit either to the regulatory division of complex unions, a federal state, like Canada or to a supranational legal order with regulatory competences accorded on the basis of explicit Treaty provisions such as the European Union. Regarding Canada, one can locate multiple candidates as "subjects" of Regulatory Cooperation. Indeed, Canada's regulatory structure can best be described as a "top-down", where provincial regulators in various instances regulate in parallel with the federal one.[90] This autonomy provided to Canadian provincial regulators, which has been found to be substantial regarding TBT measures, has already marked a flag during negotiations, indicating the inability of the central government to guarantee provincial compliance.[91] The same regulatory complexity takes place on the European side, where the European Union can regulate with respect to its competences, which, even though vast, do not cover the entirety of regulation of the respective Member States.[92] Hence, in such situations, where one can locate multiple "subjects", there is thus a need to clarify which regulators qualify as such.

Regarding subjects, a rather precise answer for both is provided only in the Chapter on Regulatory Cooperation of the EU Japan EPA. Article 2 (a) of the Chapter 18 on Regulatory Cooperation referring to the necessary definitions, clarifies which regulatory authorities are concerned for the purposes of the Chapter. For Japan, the authority concerned is the Government of Japan. For the European Union, it is only the European Commission that is bound by the provisions of the Chapter, excluding national regulators from the workings of Regulatory Cooperation.[93] This of course comes as no surprise, since the EU-Japan EPA is an EU-only agreement.

While the clarification in the EU-Japan EPA is welcomed, the same issue counts as an omission in CETA. In CETA, neither the substantive Chapter provisions, nor Article 1 on definitions provide with an answer. Therefore, arises a plethora of questions, especially when considering the complexity of the two regulatory systems, but also the implications of the choice between centralized and de-centralized regulators. Despite the omission, an answer can nevertheless be extracted by context. CETA seems to adopt a broader perspective on the matter of subjects, since many signs lead to the inclusion of the national/provincial regulators. First of all, unlike EU-Japan EPA, CETA is a mixed agreement and the inclusion of national levels is at least possible. Secondly, the non-specification of the concerned regulators as in the EU-Japan EPA points towards this direction. Should the negotiations have wanted to exclude national/provincial regulators, they could have specified so, as they did with their Japanese counterparts, and as they had done also during the negotiations for the Chapter on Regulatory Cooperation of TTIP.[94] Given also the anatomy of the Canadian regulatory system, and the independence that provincial regulators enjoy, it is very often provincial legislatures the ones that have to translate many international commitments into domestic law and action.[95] Thus, the inclusion of provincial regulators within the workings of Regulatory Cooperation is logical and

---

[90] Stanko (2012), p. 14.

[91] Stanko (2012), p. 13.

[92] Craig (2012).

[93] Article 18.2 EU-Japan EPA.

[94] See Article x2 of the TTIP- EU proposal for Chapter: Regulatory Cooperation, as submitted for discussion by the EU (2016) <http://trade.ec.europa.eu/doclib/docs/2016/march/tradoc_154377. pdf>.

[95] Finnemore and Toope (2001), p. 754.

necessary. Secondly, Article 21.1 of the CETA on the scope of Application mentions that the Chapter applies to the:

> development, review and methodological aspects of regulatory measures of the Parties' regulatory authorities that are covered by, among others, the TBT Agreement, the SPS Agreement, the GATT 1994, the GATS, and Chapters Four (Technical Barriers to Trade), Five (Sanitary and Phytosanitary Measures), Nine (Cross-Border Trade in Services), Twenty-Two (Trade and Sustainable Development), Twenty-Three (Trade and Labour) and Twenty-Four (Trade and Environment).

By encompassing 'regulatory measures of the Parties' regulatory authorities', the Article suggests that also national authorities fall under its scope, since they do constitute 'parties of the Agreement'. Last but not least, from the contributions submitted by the public during the first call for proposals for Regulatory Cooperation activities in the Regulatory Cooperation Forum (RCF) under CETA, one can find out that the interested stakeholders regard Regulatory Cooperation as a process addressed both to European and national regulators.[96]

3.4.3 Precision Ratione Materiae

The question of the subjects is in direct relevance with the question of objects, what are the respective regulators called to work together. However, how precise are the Chapters regarding the object of the cooperation and why does it matter? To understand the necessity of clarity, one must understand how the term 'object' is perceived. Here, the 'object' of the cooperation is a twofold concept. On the one hand, it signifies the scope, the material limits of the cooperation. The object of the cooperation is subject to the material limitations of each regulator's competence and can at best match the entirety of it. But this is not necessarily always the case. By ways of giving an answer as to who is subject to Regulatory Cooperation, one may not provide an answer as to what they are called to cooperate upon, as the scope of the objects under cooperation might be smaller than the actual capacities of each regulator. The answer might also vary from FTA to FTA. On the other hand, the term object must be understood as extending also to the legal acts that are subject to Regulatory Cooperation, of either legislative nature or not, which each regulator can use for the accomplishment of his mandate. Together, the limits imposed by the two create the widest notion of the 'object': the objects could at best correspond to the covered legal acts used for the covered areas of competence. As mentioned though, the agreed terms might be such as to not match the entirety of a regulator's area of competence, both regarding scope and legal tools. For that reason, precision is again, essential.

---

[96] Indicatively, the Trade Union Confederation for Professionals of the Netherlands (VCP) refers to both natoinal and the EU regulators in its letter of reaction to the European Commission's call of proposals.

3.4.3.1 Scope of Application

Although the identification of the scope-object of cooperation is on a first level defined by the identification of the regulator-subject, since the former will always fall within the substantive limits of the latter's competence, these two remain two different issues. Thus, for the example, for the EU, the first limb of the composite 'object' of Regulatory Cooperation finds itself limited firstly by the competences of the EU regulator and secondly by the Chapters on Regulatory Cooperation.

The first limitation, the one of competences follows the constitutional nature of the European Union. In the multilevel EU legal order, the geography of the enumerated in the TFEU competences corresponds to a primary match in the regulation.[97] Consequently, it is the geography of these competences that primarily designs the space of Regulatory Cooperation as well. That means that in the EU-Japan EPA, an Agreement of exclusive EU competence the primary material scope of Regulatory Cooperation is limited to the competence scope of the Union. On the other hand, in the CETA agreement, which includes national regulators as well, the scope of Regulatory Cooperation potentially knows no limitation.

The final contour comes from the second and last limitation, the scope of Regulatory Cooperation, as agreed by the parties. The broadness of the scope of application as stated in the relevant Chapters gives justice to the identity of the new Generation FTAs as going beyond traditional trade matters but also embracing behind-the-border issues of domestic regulation. As expected, both Chapters in EU-Japan EPA and CETA adopt a wide perspective. In CETA, Article 21.1 enumerates some Chapters whose subjects fall within the material scope of Regulatory Cooperation. These include the TBT and SPS WTO Agreements and the corresponding Chapters in the FTAs, the GATT and the GATS, and several Chapters of the Agreement such as Chapter 9 on Services, Chapter 22 on Sustainable Development, Chapter 23 on Trade and Labor and Chapter 24 on Trade and Environment. This enumeration is however non-exhaustive, as Article 21.1 clearly refers to the applicability of the Chapter to those Chapters, *among others*. On that basis, a concrete mapping of the subjects-candidates of Regulatory Cooperation is not possible. A similar wide approach is adopted with regard to the scope of application of Regulatory Cooperation in the EU-Japan EPA. Absent a specific provision, the scope is defined abstractly as catching 'every measure susceptible to affect trade and investment'.[98]

Placing this discussion under the perspective of precision, it could well be argued that the provisions are lacking in it. This is not true. The scope of Regulatory Cooperation seems even broader, should one taken into consideration the *telos* of

---

[97] From Articles 2 to 6 of the TFEU the division of competences is the following: the Union can have exclusive competences, shared ones and competences to coordinate, support and supplement member state action. From those categories of competence, the Union derives a direct right to regulate from the pool of exclusive competences and from the one of shared competences, provided that it respects the requirements of subsidiarity and proportionality.

[98] Article 18.3 EU-Japan EPA.

Regulatory Cooperation, which is the elimination of unnecessary, duplicative behind-the-borders barriers to trade. Due to their unpredictable character and their complexity, it would be foolish to believe that they can fit into pre-fixed categories according to their subject-matter. Hence, the broadness of the scope through the 'open list' approach is to be expected and should not be confused with imprecision.

3.4.3.2 Legal Tools

Article 18.2 (b) of the EU-Japan EPA clarifies further the 'objects' of the Chapter. The provision begins by declaring the applicability of the Chapter to measures of general application. It goes further to clarify which regulatory measures qualify as such at each legal order for the purposes of the Chapter. For Japan, Regulatory Cooperation provisions will cover (a) laws, (b) cabinet orders and (c) ministerial ordinances. For the EU, the regulatory measures concerned are regulations and directives as provided in Article 288 TFEU and delegated and implementing acts of Articles 290 and 291 respectively.[99]

A question that arises from a first textual interpretation is whether legislative acts of the EU, meaning the legal acts of 288 TFEU adopted according to the one of the procedures of 289 TFEU fall under the reach of the Chapter. This question follows the non-reference in Article 18.2 (b) of Article 289 TFEU. In the EU legal system, legislative acts or legislation can be only the instruments of Article 288 (Regulations, Directives and Decisions) adopted under a legislative procedure in accordance with Article 289 TFEU.[100] Delegated and implementing acts can take the form of one of the legal acts prescribed under Article 288, but do not qualify as legislation/legislative acts because they are not adopted according to a legislative procedure.[101]

This feature of EU legislation was made clear during the TTIP negotiations. Indeed, in the negotiating document on Regulatory Cooperation of the TTIP Agreement, it was defined that for the purposes of the Chapter, regulatory acts at central level include "Regulations and Directives within the meaning of Article 288 of the Treaty on the Functioning of the European Union, including: i. Regulations and Directives adopted under a legislative procedure in accordance with the Treaty; ii. Delegated and Implementing acts adopted pursuant to Articles 290 and 291 of that Treaty. At the time, legislative acts were clearly intended to fall under Regulatory Cooperation activities.

The same omission in the EU-Japan EPA Chapter would rather point to the exclusion of legislative acts both from the Regulatory Coherence and Regulatory Cooperation activities. In that sense, the use of the generic 'regulatory measures of general application' along with the specific reference to Articles 288, 290 and 291 TFEU, in combination with the omission of Article 289 TFEU on legislative

---

[99] Article 18.2b EU-Japan EPA.

[100] Türk (2012), pp. 67ff.

[101] Curtin, Manucharyan (2015), pp. 111ff.

acts could create further confusion on whether the legislative acts of the EU fall or not under the ambit of Regulatory Cooperation.

If this were so, then the term 'regulatory measures of general application' would have the same meaning with the term 'regulatory act' of Article 263 § 4 TFEU, as this was crystallized by the Court of Justice on the occasion of case C- 583/11 Inuit Tapiriit Kanatami and other vs Parliament and Council. Indeed, the Court of Justice, upholding the Decision of the General Court and lining up with the AG's Opinion restricted the ambit of 'regulatory acts' to 'acts of general application other than legislative acts'.[102] Thus, as such qualify the legal acts of Article 288 TFEU, Regulations, Directives, Decisions, Recommendations and Opinions, but not if adopted under the legislative procedures set out in Article 289 TFEU. The use of the term 'regulatory measures of general application' would be probably used to avoid any confusion that could arise due to the current hierarchy of norms under the Lisbon Treaty.[103] Indeed, were the term 'legislative acts', or 'legislation' to be used, that would include legislative acts, and exclude the non-legislative acts of Article 290 and 291 which are in fact subject to Regulatory Cooperation.[104]

However, reasons of reciprocity suggest that, despite the omission of Article 289 TFEU, which was present in the TTIP negotiating documents, EU legislative texts are also part of Regulatory Cooperation activities, since Japanese laws fall under its ambit according to Article 18.2g. Still, for reasons of legal certainty, and since the inclusion of legislative instruments is crucial in defining the ambition of Regulatory Cooperation, a clarification would be welcome.

Another category of legal tools added next to legislative and non-legislative acts by virtue of Article 18.3 par. 2 are 'other regulatory measures of general application which are relevant to Regulatory Cooperation activities' such as guidelines, policy documents or recommendations. This non-exhaustive category of non-binding instruments is included as part of Regulatory Cooperation since such documents do carry some degree of influence for the regulatory process. This category of instruments is treated separately since it shall be subject only to Regulatory Cooperation, but not Regulatory Coherence activities, as will the other legal tools be.

As for CETA's Chapter on Regulatory Cooperation, the inclusion of both national and EU regulators, and the Chapter's silence on the legal tools involved contribute towards the creation of a long list, should one consider the totality of the legal acts available to centralised and de-centralised regulators. From a first view, opportunities for Regulatory Cooperation could potentially extend to every legal act, which at least for the EU level, seem to catch also legislative acts in the sense of Article 289 TFEU. Some preliminary conclusions on the legal acts that would stand as potential candidates can be drawn indirectly from the scope of the Chapter. Indeed,

---

[102] According to the ECJ, the use of this term in this particular provision aims to distinguish the acts that fall under the first limb from the ones falling under the second and third limb of the provision. See Case C- 583/11 *Inuit Tapiriit Kanatami and other vs Parliament and Council,* par.58.

[103] For a detailed discussion over the matter *see* Craig (2010), pp. 253ff.

[104] Craig (2010), pp. 253ff.

by examining which legal acts are frequently employed to dress the regulatory measures of the covered scope as stated in Article 21.1, one can reach some indicative assumptions. As with EU-Japan Regulatory Cooperation, delegated and implementing acts, that treat more technical and/or non-essential aspects of a regulation stand as good potential candidates. However, the inclusion of legislative acts at this instance is indicative of the ambition of the particular Chapter, which endeavours to extend Regulatory Cooperation to substantial elements, as are the ones treated with legislation.

3.4.4 Inference on Precision

An obligation of the same character, as is the one in both Chapters of Regulatory Cooperation, is not necessarily escorted by the same degree of precision. Indeed, what becomes clear after the description of the Chapters on the basis of this taxonomy is their differing precision degree. Where Regulatory Cooperation in the EU-Japan EPA gains in precision as far as Subjects are concerned, it loses partially by omitting to enumerate the Regulatory Cooperation activities. Not all imprecise provisions impinge upon the overall Legalization though. An example that proves that is CETA's imprecise reference to the implicated Subjects, which however can be deducted. Problems arise when further imprecision results from already imprecise provisions. Such an example would be the scope of Regulatory Cooperation that is in direct relation to the material limits of an implicated regulator. Still though, the scope is properly addressed separately in both Chapters. A loss in overall Legalization comes mostly from the non-reference of specific Regulatory Cooperation activities, an element that is completely missing from EU-Japan's Regulatory Cooperation. Indeed, when Regulatory Cooperation is to some degree envisaged, as in both Chapters, a holistic depiction of the said activities equals to less uncertainty and functions as a starting point. In this way regulators are given orientation about the desired result and the tools that are to be used towards this direction. Moreover, better precision reduces the discretionary margins left upon the parties to determine the nature, frequency and stringency of cooperation.

Given the above, it becomes apparent that between the two Chapters, it is the CETA one that is overall more precise and more ambitious. This conclusion is attempted not only on the basis of preciseness of the provisions but also from the ambition of the envisaged cooperation. The participation of national regulators due to the Agreement's mixed character renders the procedure more intrusive, which is not the case for EU-Japan Regulatory Cooperation, which remains confined within certain limits.[105] This lower profile Regulatory Cooperation however refers to its

---

[105] However, according to a Report of the National Trade Service of Sweden, the Commission has pointed out that Regulatory Cooperation activities in CETA are intended to cover only EU legislation, and not, at least for the moment national one. See "Analysis of the FTA between the

ambition and has little to do with the overall Legalization of Regulatory Cooperation in the EU-Japan, which could only be impacted from a failure to describe the Regulatory Cooperation activities. Even that though does not necessarily mean that the Legalization degree of this less ambitious arrangement is seriously compromised. The element of Delegation has to be examined too, for a safer overview of the existing Legalization degree.

3.5   Delegation: An Open Question

In the introductory part of this Chapter delegation was presented as the dimension that informs about the dynamic quality of an international arrangement. It was introduced as a two-faced dimension, that could take the form of either delegated power given to third parties to interpret rules and issue rulings on the basis of that interpretation (referred also as Type A delegation) or of a body set up under international law, created to facilitate the implementation of the agreed rules and vested with rule-making authority (Type B delegation). Its two-faced dimension is neatly summarized and formally defined by its authors as:

> (the) authority (that) has been granted to third parties for the implementation of rules, including their interpretation and application, dispute settlement, and (possibly) further rule making.[106]

Although quite a large part of the literature has organically rejected its second guise, and continues to understand it only as the process of development of international tribunals, in reality both of its faces offer a dynamic element to the international arrangement.[107] On the one hand, having been granted the authority to interpret rules by applying them to particular situations, judicial third-parties end up in essentially formulating new rules, as every judicial body does.[108] On the other hand, according to the will of the contracting parties, the power of specialized bodies may go as far as the elaboration upon existing imprecise norms or the creation of new ones. Another difference lies to the form of the produced effects within the legal order. While the first type of delegation commits the parties to abide by a certain ruling, decision-making procedure by international bodies commits the parties to implement secondary international rules accordingly within their respective legal orders and subject to their own procedures. It is exactly because of their differing nature that it would be methodologically incorrect to put them under comparison, as it has been attempted, and make assumptions on that basis regarding their capacity to contribute to

---

EU, its Member States and Canada (CETA)—an assignment by the Swedish government" <https://www.kommers.se/Documents/dokumentarkiv/publikationer/2017/publ-CETA_english%20summary.pdf>.

[106] See Abbott (2000), p. 401.

[107] See Belanger and Fontaine-Skronski (2012), p. 253.

[108] See Abott et al. (2000), p. 415.

Legalization. Still, in order to reach safe results on the significance of each type to the overall Legalization, one has to concretely assess the type, (or types) of delegation conferred and their intensity. It is upon that mission that this Section embarks.

3.5.1 Type A Delegation

In the context of an international agreement, and especially in the context of an FTA treaty, Type A delegation, understood as the authority to interpret and apply rules presupposes the creation of international tribunals which are granted judicial authority with regard to the agreed rules, widely known as the DSMs that each FTA creates. In CETA, third party dispute settlement is regulated under Chapter 29, and in the EU-Japan EPA in Chapter 21. The judicial mechanisms foreseen in those Chapters are separate entities created for the special purposes of the Agreements, to resolve disputes that turn around the correct interpretation and application of the rules whenever these may arise, with an ultimate aim to foster compliance. Regulatory Cooperation is excluded from the relevant procedure in the EU-Japan EPA by virtue of 18.19 EU-Japan EPA.[109] On the contrary, although initially excluded from Dispute Settlement procedures,[110] CETA's Regulatory Cooperation falls under Chapter 29, although the exact circumstances under which a relevant case may arise before the DSM remain unclear, given the precise preference of the parties to initiate a voluntary cooperation.

From a quick glance, the choice to leave Regulatory Cooperation outside the competence of the DSM could mean to some total absence of Type A delegation. After a more thorough reading of the definition provided by the authors, it becomes clear that this choice is not ultimate for the complete exclusion of Type A delegation, for DSM forms only one side of its coin. Indeed, the definition of 'delegation' as cited above, separates the authority to interpret and apply rules from the authority granted to a third-party DSM. In reality, these two constitute two separate kind of authorities, both however granted to judicial entities. While interpretation and application of international rules is of course task of a DSM, it can take place also domestically, thus implicating directly the respective courts of each legal order. As far as the EU legal order is concerned, this phenomenon is widely known as the 'direct effect' of international agreements.[111] Direct effect of international rules, in

---

[109] Even though this excludes this kind of delegation, which could cost to the overall degree of Legalization, what is interesting to observe is that dispute settlement is a parameter that falls under delegation and not obligation, confirming the argumentation exposed above on the irrelevance of the dispute settlement for the assessment of obligation.

[110] *See* for example Vidigal and Schill (2018).

[111] The judicial phenomenon of direct effect as part of the 'delegation' branch of Legalization has been confirmed in relevant literature. *See* Keohane et al. (2000) and Abbott (2000).

offering individuals rights on the basis of which they can litigate, inevitably implicates the interpretation and application of the rules at stake.[112]

However, as mentioned briefly also above, Regulatory Cooperation Chapters, as
part of the respective FTAs, are deprived from having direct effect. Indeed, Article
30.6 of the CETA and Article 23.5 of the EU Japan EPA exclude in advance any
possible direct effect in order to prevent relevant questions from arriving at the
Chambers of the Courts. Consequently, the parties remain the owners of the agreements and clearly define the results they wish to have, so that the latter do not fall
within the jurisdiction of the judges. By excluding both possibilities of recourse to a
judicial body, whether set up internationally or domestically, Type A of delegation is
definitely absent from EU-Japan's Regulatory Cooperation Chapter and is partially
present in CETA's Chapter. Still, the process of its Legalization is not over, once
delegation Type B is to be found.

3.5.2   Type B Delegation

New Generation FTAs as is the CETA and the EU-Japan EPA are discerned from
previous ones due to their quality as 'living agreements'.[113] The Agreements owe
this characterization to a provision of structures that allows constant development of
the bilateral relationship according to the needs that may arise. These structures,
forming an elaborate institutional framework correspond to Type B Delegation. Both
CETA and EU-Japan EPA follow the same pattern: in both Agreements the institutional architecture consists of a central body, with a general mandate to overview the
functioning of the Agreement and of various specialized bodies, whose focus centers
upon the particular Chapter under which they are created. In CETA, the centralized
Joint Committee is created by Article 26.1.1. and it is rest of the Article's provisions
that paint the contours of its action.[114] In EU-Japan EPA, the relevant with the Joint
Committee issues are regulated in Article 22.1.[115] Although constituting separate
entities as they are founded by different Chapters of the respective Agreements, the
Joint Committees are interconnected and on various instances supplement the
activity of the specialized Committees, created collectively in Article 26.2 CETA
and 22.3 EU-Japan EPA. In the category of specialized bodies are included the ones
foreseen under the Regulatory Cooperation Chapters, the RCF in the CETA and the
RCB in the EU-Japan EPA (hereinafter referred as Regulatory Cooperation Fora).[116]
A joint reading of the mandates of both, is for this reason, necessary in the first place,

---

[112]Keohane et al. (2000), p. 467.

[113]Many stakeholders have adopted this lexicon to describe the FTAs under question. *See* for
example Meyer-Ohlendorf et al. (2016); Wagner and Huber (2016).

[114]*See* generally Article 26.1 CETA.

[115]Chapter 22 EU-Japan EPA.

[116]Article 21.6 CETA, Article 18.14 EU-Japan EPA.

in order to examine the range, depth and nature of Type B delegation in Regulatory Cooperation. Furthermore, the possibility to use the avenue of other specialized committees in order to take binding decisions on issues discussed within the context of Regulatory Cooperation Chapters, will further be examined.

3.5.2.1 Absence of a Decision-Making Mandate of the Regulatory Cooperation Fora

From a first textual analysis of the mandate of the Regulatory Cooperation Fora enshrined in Articles 21.6 CETA and 18.14 EU-Japan EPA, it is easily deductible that this remains confined to implementation and support activities. Regarding implementation, in the main corpus of the mandate belongs the promotion of the operation of sustainable dialogues, either sector-specific or horizontal. To that end, they are expected to generally promote cross-sector dialogues on regulatory governance (Articles 21.6.2.a CETA, 18.14.3.d and 18.14.3.e EU- Japan EPA), identify areas of common interest (Article 18.14.3.g EU-Japan EPA) and provide a forum for the development of those bilateral dialogues (Articles 21.6.2.a, 21.6.d CETA and 18.14.3.a EU-Japan EPA). As far as their policing role is concerned, they are generally vested with the power to overview the progress, the outcome, and the implementation of the Regulatory Cooperation undertaken by the regulators, independently of their regulatory stage in which they might take place (Article 21.6.2.c CETA and 18.14.3.i in combination with 18.16.8 EU-Japan EPA). Their role is further generalized to encompass assisting functions to the ones already mentioned. Apart from assistance in terms of encouragement and identification of priority areas, the Regulatory Cooperation Fora shall be responsible to support regulators in practical terms, for example by seeking appropriate partners or providing them with the necessary tools and by delegating certain activities to sub-Committees (Article 21.6.2.b CETA and Article 18.14.3.j EU-Japan EPA).

Interestingly, decision-making does not seem to be listed among the powers vested to either of those Regulatory Cooperation Fora. This absence of delegation seems however inconsistent when considered along certain elements of the Chapters. For example, one of the main aims of the Regulatory Cooperation Chapters is the promotion of regulatory convergence. In CETA this figures both as objective (Article 21.3.d) and is further reflected under the envisaged activities (Article 21.4. g), while in the EU-Japan EPA, one of the main competences of the specialized committee is to suggest any kind of Regulatory Cooperation activity, fostering thus rule convergence (Article 18.14.3.d). Of course, not all instances of Regulatory Cooperation will necessitate a decision to be taken. Especially when it comes to new regulatory areas, regulatory convergence could take place in parallel and along the same substantial basis. However, this will not be the case in areas where elaborate regulation already exists from both sides. In that case, regulatory convergence will need to be mandated in an instrument. Such an instrument can take the form of mutual recognition, or harmonization, on the basis of a relevant decision. It is surprising though that its formal adoption falls out of the scope of the Regulatory Cooperation Foras' competence.

3.5.2.2 Absence of Binding Decision-Making of the Joint Committees on Regulatory Cooperation Issues

Given the absence of decision-making capacity of the Regulatory Cooperation Bodies but also the telos of Regulatory Cooperation, as this is promulgated by the two Chapters, one should expect that gap to be filled by the Joint Committees. Such a complementary activity comes naturally given the nature of the relationship that binds the respective structures in the Agreements. Indeed, various provisions confirm a principal-agent structure. First and foremost, all specialized Committees, the Regulatory Cooperation bodies included, are founded under the Chapter and after the Joint Committees as specialized Committees.[117] Secondly, the action of the specialized Committees is under the constant supervision of the Joint Committees (Articles 21.1.4.b CETA and 22.1.4.b, 22.3.8 EU-Japan EPA), which also enjoys the right to re-arrange their operation, structure and content (Articles 26.1.5.a, 26.1.5.g, 26.1.5.h CETA and 22.1.5.a and 22.5.1.b EU-Japan EPA). This hierarchical relationship is not only spelled out through general provisions on the functioning of those Joint Committees, but sometimes it is further confirmed under the scope of action of the specialized bodies in the respective Chapters. An example constitutes Article 21.6.4.c of CETA, which states the responsibility of the RCF to further report to the CETA Joint Committee the progress made on Regulatory Cooperation activities. Last but not least, the specialized Committees share the scope of their material mandate with the Joint Committees of the relevant Agreements. Generally speaking, the material scope of the Joint Committees is vast and extends to the totality of issues regulated under each Agreement (Article 26.1.3 CETA and Article 22.1.4.a EU-Japan EPA). Consequently, and without prejudice to the mandates of the specialized Committees, it is further clarified in Articles 22.3.5 and 22.3.7 EU-Japan EPA that the Joint Committees can treat directly any specialized matter or resolve any issue not properly addressed at the specialized level Article.

Given the hierarchical relationship and the material concurrence, it would not come as a surprise if the centralized Joint Committees had the capacity to adopt decisions on Regulatory Cooperation issues.

Generally speaking, according to Article 22.5 EU-Japan EPA and 26.2.4 CETA, the specialized Committees can have decision-making power of their own, when the Agreements clearly states so, and they can also submit proposals to the respective centralized Joint Committees, in order for the decision to be adopted on the basis of the proposal at the upper level. From the wording of the respective provisions, it

---

[117] Indeed, the specialized Committees are not founded under the respective Chapter, but under the main Chapter on Institutional Provisions in each Agreement. It is only their mandate that is outlined in the respective specialized Chapter. *See* Article 22.3.2 EU-Japan EPA and 26.2.1 CETA.

becomes clear that specific reference has to be made only for their decision-making part, but not for the submission of proposals. The discretion to submit a proposal exists independently of whether this is explicitly mentioned in each separate specialized committee. This reading is supported in CETA by the positioning of the comma: 'The specialised Committees may propose draft decisions for adoption by the CETA Joint Committee, or take decisions when this Agreement so provides'. The same comma appears in other language versions,[118] a fact that confirms the intention of the drafters to differentiate the two. In EU-Japan, no such comma exists, however, there is no evidence that supports a different intention of the drafters.

As it was outlined before, in both Agreements the Regulatory Cooperation bodies are deprived of this decision-making capacity of their own, as the latter is not clearly stated in the relevant provisions. Still however, one could assume that they can make use of the aforementioned provisions on their capacity as specialized Committees and submit for adoption any substantive outcome reached after a successful Regulatory Cooperation activity. However, this is not the case either. And that is for the following reason.

According to Articles 26.3.1, 26.3.2 CETA and 22.2.1 EU-Japan EPA, each centralized Joint Committee is vested with a general power to adopt decisions *when the Agreement so provides*, which shall have binding force upon the parties.[119] The phrase in italics, found in EU-Japan EPA slightly differently—*where provided for in this Agreement*—makes clear that the decision-making capacity of each Joint Committee has to be grounded in the Agreement, in a provision other than Articles 22.5 EU-Japan EPA and 26.2.4 CETA. And indeed, there are such provisions to be found in both Agreements. In most cases, there is a specific mandate in a specialized Chapter, on the basis of which the specialized Committee under consideration can submit a proposal to the centralized Joint Committee for decision. Indicatively, such is the case of Articles 10.16.2.a, 2.35 c, 14.53.3 in EU-Japan EPA, 2.13.2, 6.14.4 CETA. Absent such a provision in both Regulatory Cooperation Chapters, it seems that decisions are, at least for the time being, excluded.

3.5.2.3 Absence of Binding Decision-Making on Regulatory Issues in the Context of the Specialized Committees of the TBT and SPS Chapters

While the above Sections demonstrated effectively an absence of binding decision-making within the context of the Regulatory Cooperation Fora and each Joint Committee on the basis of proposals from the former, it should still be considered

---

[118]To my understanding Greek, French, Italian, Spanish, German.

[119]The use of the term 'decision' is also indicative of the binding effect with which the parties wish to dress this type of action. Indeed, the term 'decision' in the relevant legislative texts is discerned from 'recommendations' that the centralized Joint Committees can also take (Article 26.3 CETA and 22.2.2 EU-Japan EPA) and it moreover corresponds to general practice under public international law when it comes to describing legally binding acts. *See* Weiss (2018).

whether issues discussed within the Regulatory Cooperation Chapters could form the object of binding decision-making of another specialized committee, such as the ones of the TBT and SPS Chapters of the FTAs. This cross-fertilisation is indeed possible given the broad scope of application of the Regulatory Cooperation Chapters as examined in Sect. 3.4.3 above.

As far as the SPS specialised committees are concerned, we shall begin by examining whether any actions of the Joint Management Committee for SPS measures established under Article 5.14 CETA and the Committee of Sanitary and Phytosanitary measures established under Article 6.15 of EU-Japan EPA could, in a legally binding (according to international law) way decide on regulatory cooperation issues that touch upon SPS measures and policies.

As regards CETA, the Joint Management Committee for SPS measures enjoys decision-making powers only insofar amendments to Annexes 5A–5J are concerned, on the basis of Article 5.14.2 (d) CETA. Thus, it cannot in principle decide on horizontal policy issues that alter a regulatory practice, or decide on the recognition of equivalence of measures of the parties, which is a possibility under Article 5.6 CETA. Moreover, according to the treaty rules the CETA Joint Committee is also prevented from issuing decisions for subject matters falling under Chapter 5 CETA. As per Article 26.3.1 CETA: *"The CETA Joint Committee shall, for the purpose of attaining the objectives of this Agreement, have the power to make decisions in respect of all matters when this Agreement so provides"*; however, such a power is not granted for Chapter 5 on SPS measures. For the same reason, as established previously, the RCF does not have this power either, neither by itself nor via the submission of a draft decision to the Joint CETA Committee. The same is the case for the Committee of Sanitary and Phytosanitary measures, whose tasks do not entail at all a decision-making element. Similarly, a mandate for decision-making capacity of the Joint Committee regarding SPS measures it is not provided in the Chapter either.

As far as the TBT specialised committees are concerned, it is important to underline that both Chapters on TBT measures of CETA and EU-Japan EPA recognise and state by means of an Article the importance of cooperation in TBT measures, mentioning also the role that the Chapters on Regulatory Cooperation play therein[120]; hence some cross-fertilisation is certainly possible between the two committees. As regards the decision-making capacity of these committees, Article 4.7 CETA does not seem to allow CETA's Committee on Trade in Goods to take decisions with regard to the management of the Chapter. What it does provide them under Article 4.7.1 f is the possibility to review the Chapter on the basis of developments on the WTO level and develop recommendations to amend it for consideration by the CETA Joint Committee. Any other decision-making capacity of the CETA Joint Committee on TBT matters is not envisaged in the Chapter. Similarly, the power to propose amendments to the Joint Committee is bestowed by virtue of Article 7.13.2.c EU-Japan EPA also to the EU-Japan EPA's Committee

---

[120] Article 4.3 CETA.

on TBT. The latter shall also, by virtue of Article 7.13.2. and upon delegation by the EU-Japan EPA Joint Committee carry out other functions. Of course, in order for that Joint Committee to delegate decision-making powers to the Committee on TBT, it implies it possesses the power to decide upon TBT issues, which is not the case. Indeed, Chapter 7 EU-Japan EPA on TBT does not mandate any decision-making capacity of the Joint Committee regarding TBT measures, hence no decision could be taken by the Joint Committee or delegated to the Committee on TBT.

Despite the absence of decision-making capacity, Regulatory Cooperation by means of recognition of equivalence is however envisaged in those Chapters. Indeed, as mentioned above, both SPS Chapters envisage the possibility of recognition of equivalence of their respective SPS measures, under certain circumstances (Article 6.14 EU-Japan EPA and Article 5.6 CETA), while CETA's TBT Chapter provides for this possibility under Article 4.4.2. In such cases, any recognition of equivalence takes place by the parties by means of their respective internal processes, but not from the committees, centralised or specialised.

3.5.3 Inference on Delegation

Both Chapters on Regulatory Cooperation follow a similar approach to Delegation. Should one consider the two types of delegation as distinct values/substitutes, then in both cases Delegation as a component of Legalization is absent from Regulatory Cooperation Chapters, as secondary rulemaking is excluded at both the centralized and specialized level. On the other hand, if seen as complementary measures, then CETA's inclusion of Regulatory Cooperation under the DSM, that corresponds to Type A Delegation, raises the overall delegation of CETA's Chapter, as the two types form a single unit together.

Irrespectively of the chosen approach, it is undeniable that the absence of Type B Delegation deprives from Regulatory Cooperation the characteristic 'living' element. The innovation of this web of institutional structures in both Agreements, which renders them 'living' ones is exactly both their general capacity to issue decisions on various issues and to escort them with binding force. As far as the centralized Joint Committees are concerned, apart from the fundamental influence they exercise on the specialized Committees and the binding effect of the decisions they can take on the basis of their recommendations, they also enjoy rulemaking powers, insofar they can amend parts of the respective Agreements, (Article 26.1.5.c CETA and 22.1.5.d EU-Japan EPA), interpretative powers, since they provide binding interpretations to the Agreements' provisions (Article 26.1.5.e CETA and 22.1.5.e EU-Japan EPA) and adjudicative ones. Moreover, there are specialized Committees, like the Joint Committee on Mutual Recognition of Professional Qualifications (MRA Committee) of Chapter 11 in CETA that have binding decision-making powers of their own.

Given this ambitious authority bestowed upon the various Committees on several instances, the absence of decision-making in Regulatory Cooperation, both within the RCF and the specialized committees stands out. Most probably, the absence of decision-making is provisioned due to the severe legitimacy issues it could give rise to. Indeed, such decision-making could go as far reaching as bindingly establishing equivalence between two regulatory regimes, setting common understandings on the cornerstones of future regulation or concluding MRAs. Its normative pull would be strong, since the parties would be under the obligation to implement any decision taken at the centralized Joint Committee level, following of course, their own internal procedures (Article 26.3.2 CETA and 22.2.1 EU-Japan EPA). Under the present circumstances, should any result be reached under the Regulatory Cooperation Chapters, it will be to be adopted in the respective legal orders one way or another. Still, this will happen externally, outside either Agreement's structure.

3.6 Conclusion

This Chapter borrowed the concept of Legalization from International Relations literature to depict the change that was initiated through the inclusion of Regulatory Cooperation in the FTAs under analysis. The assumption that lied at the heart of the analysis argued for a higher level of the overall bindingness of Regulatory Cooperation as the main reason that guided this approach. And the concept of Legalization offered a valuable platform upon which that argument could be made, since it introduced overall bindingness not on a purely legal basis, but it also considered other elements, the precision of the commitments and the presence of a 'living' element as factors upon which the judgement was founded.

And in fact, after an in concreto examination of all the components of 'Legalization', obligation, precision and delegation, the hypothesis is confirmed, as Regulatory Cooperation is more 'legalized', mostly thanks to its qualification as a legal obligation. Of course, some differences between the level of Legalization of the two is to be observed, since the two FTAs do not necessarily view Regulatory Cooperation with equal ambition. Most importantly though, the fact that Regulatory Cooperation in both CETA and EU-Japan EPA qualifies as a legal international obligation, in comparison to previous Regulatory Cooperation commitments that were undertaken only on a political level, already informs us about a rather powerful type of obligation, the status of which cannot be set under doubt because of a clause on voluntary initiation or simply as a result of its exclusion from Dispute Settlement. It thus carries a normative weight in the international arena and is accompanied by a set of fundamental rules to which actors must abide. The main differentiation on their achieved level of Legalization comes mostly by the difference in which the substance of the obligations is generally outlined, with CETA's Regulatory Cooperation being rather precise, in comparison to the case of EU-Japan, a fact that renders it more 'legalized'.

Still though, the concept of 'Legalization' revealed a shortcoming of Regulatory Cooperation in the FTAs under analysis. This shortcoming lies exactly in the absence of secondary rulemaking in Regulatory Cooperation, when seen next to the set objectives of the Chapters and the provision of secondary rulemaking in other instances. Indeed, on the one hand, negotiators seek concrete progress on regulatory coherence, for example via the avenues of regulatory harmonization or mutual recognition. On the other hand, however, they lack to provide with the relevant instruments (within the agreement) on which the concrete results that further regulatory coherence will be imprinted. The frustration becomes striking should one consider that both CETA and EU-Japan EPA include secondary rulemaking mandates as a task of various bodies of their institutional framework. This reality, not only deprives the overall arrangement of its full Legalization potential, but also creates questions on how Regulatory Cooperation activities will be introduced and implemented in the EU legal order.

This question is of direct relevance to the influence Regulatory Cooperation outcomes are expected to exert in each separate implicated legal order. What form will Regulatory Cooperation outcomes take within the EU Legal Order? Are there any limits to the forms that these outcomes may take and how will they interact with the EU constitutional order? Especially, what impact will they have upon the EU decision making? Giving an answer to these questions is the mission upon which the next Chapter embarks.

References

Abbott F (2000) NAFTA and the legalization of world politics: a case study. Int Organ 54:519–547

Abbott K, Snidal D (2012) Law, legalization and politics: an agenda for the next generation of IL/IR scholars. In: Dunoff J, Pollack M (eds) Interdisciplinary perspectives on international law and international relations: the state of the art. Cambridge University Press, Cambridge, pp 33–56

Abott K, Keohane R, Moravcsik A, Slaughter A, Snidal D (2000) The concept of legalization. Int Organ 54:401–419

Aust A (2006) Vienna Convention of the law of the treaties (1969). In: Wolfrum R (ed) Max Planck Encyclopedia of Public International Law. https://spacelaw.univie.ac.at/fileadmin/user_upload/p_spacelaw/EPIL_Vienna_Convention_on_the_Law_of_Treaties_1969.pdf

Aust A (2007) Pacta Sunt Servanda In: Max Planck Encyclopedia of Public International Law https://opil.ouplaw.com/view/10.1093/law:epil/9780199231690/law-9780199231690-e1449,

Aust A (2013) Modern treaty law and practice. Cambridge University Press, Cambridge

Baxter R (1980) International law in her infinite variety. Int Comp Law Q 24:549–566

Belanger L, Fontaine-Skronski K (2012) Legalization in international relations: a conceptual analysis. Soc Sci Inf 51:238–262

Boyle A (1999) Some reflections on the relationship of treaties and soft law. Int Comp Law Q 48:901–913

Brown Weiss E (1997) Introduction. In: Brown Weiss E (ed) International compliance with non-binding accords. Oxford University Press, Oxford, pp 1–21

Brunnee J, Toope S (2000) International law and constructivism: elements of an interactional theory of international law. Columb J Transnatl Law 39:19–74

Chayes A, Handler Chayes A (1998) The new sovereignty: compliance with international regulatory agreements. Harvard University Press, Massachussets

Chinkin C (1989) The challenge of soft law: development and change in international law. Int Comp Law Q 38:850–866

Craig P (2010) The Lisbon treaty: law, politics and treaty reform. Oxford University Press, Oxford

Craig P (2012) EU administrative law. Oxford University Press, Oxford

Crawford J (2010) The system of international responsibility. In: Crawford J, Pellet A, Olleson S (eds) The law of international responsibility. Oxford University Press, Oxford, pp 17–27

Curtin D, Manucharyan T (2015) Legal acts and hierarchy of norms in the EU. In: Arnull A, Chalmers D (eds) The Oxford handbook on EU law. Oxford University Press, Oxford, pp 103–125

D'Amato A (1985) Is international law really 'law'? New York Law Rev 79:1293–1314

De Bièvre D, Poletti A (2013) The EU in trade policy: from regime shaper to status quo power. In: Gerda F, Patrick M (eds) EU policies in a global perspective: shaping or taking international regimes? Routledge, Oxon-New York

De Mestral A (2015) When does the exception become the rule? Conserving regulatory space under CETA. J Int Econ Law 18:1–13

Delgado Casteleiro A (2016) The international responsibility of the European Union: from competence to normative control. Cambridge University Press, Cambridge

Downs G, Rocke D, Barsoom P (1996) Is the good news about compliance good news about cooperation? Int Organ 50:379–406

Fahey E, Bardutzky S (2017) Framing the subjects and objects of contemporary EU law. Edward Elgar, Cheltenham-Northampton

Finnemore M, Toope S (2001) Alternatives to legalization: richer views of law and politics. Int Organ 55:743–758

Gilligan M, Johns L, Rosendorff P (2010) Strengthening international courts and the early settlement of disputes. J Confl Resolut 54:5–38

Goldstein J, Martin L (2000) Legalization, trade liberalization, and domestic politics: a cautionary note. Int Organ 54:603–632

Goldstein J, Kahler M, Keohane R, Slaughter A (2000) Introduction: legalization and world politics. Int Organ 54:385–399

Guzman A (2002) The cost of credibility: explaining resistance to interstate DSMs. J Leg Stud 31: 303–326

Guzman A (2005) The design of international agreements. Eur J Int Law 16:581–612

Guzman A (2008) How international law works: a rational choice theory. Oxford University Press, Oxford

Guzman A, Meyer T (2008) International common law: the soft law of international tribunals. Chinese J Int Law 9:515–535

Helfer L (2006) Response: not fully committed? Reservations, risk and treaty design. Yale J Int Law 31:367–382

Horn H, Mavroidis P, Sapir A (2010) Beyond the WTO? An anatomy of EU and US preferential trade agreements. World Econ 33:1565–1588. https://www.greenpeace.de/sites/www. greenpeace.de/files/publications/20161104_greenpeace_studie_ regulatorycooperationunderceta.pdf

Kahler M (2000) Conclusion: the causes and consequences of legalization. Int Organ 54:661–683

Keohane R, Moravcsik A, Slaughter A (2000) Legalized dispute resolution: interstate and transnational. Int Organ 54:457–488

Kirton J, Marina L, Savona P (2011) Making global economic governance effective: hard and soft law institutions in a crowded world. Routledge, Oxon-New York

Klabbers J (1996) The redundancy of soft law. Nordic J Int Law 65:167–182

Koehler (2010) European foreign policy after Lisbon: strengthening the EU as an international actor. Caucasian Rev Int Aff 4:57–72

Koremenos B, Lipson C, Snidal D (2001) The rational design of international institutions. Int Organ 55:761–799

Kotzur M (2009) Good Faith (Bona Fide) in Max Planck Encyclopedia of Public International Law. https://opil.ouplaw.com/view/10.1093/law:epil/9780199231690/law-9780199231690-e1412? prd=EPIL

McGee J, Taplin R (2008) The Asia–Pacific partnership and the United States international climate change policy. Colorado J Int Environ Law Policy 19:179–218

Meyer-Ohlendorf N, Gerstetter C, Bach I (2016) Regulatory Cooperation under CETA: Implications for Environmental Policies. In: Ecologic Institute. Available via DIALOG:

Otten A (2015) The TRIPS negotiations: an overview. In: Watal J, Taubman A (eds) The making of the TRIPS agreement: personal insights from the Uruguay round negotiations. World Trade Organization Publications, Geneva, pp 55–79

Oxford Living Dictionary. Definition of Precision. https://en.oxforddictionaries.com/definition/precision

Pauwelyn J (2012) Is it international law or not, and does it even matter? In: Pawuelyn J, Wessel R, Wouters J (eds) Informal international law making. Oxford University Press, Oxford, pp 125–161

Pellet A (2010) The definition of responsibility in international law. In: Crawford J, Pellet A, Olleson S (eds) The law of international responsibility. Oxford University Press, Oxford, pp 3–16

Percy S (2007) Mercenaries: strong norm, weak law. Int Organ 61:367–397

Raustalia K (2000) Compliance and effectiveness in international regulatory cooperation. Case Western Reserv J Int Law 32:387–440

Raustalia K (2005) Form and substance in international agreements. Am J Int Law 99:581–614

Reus-Smit C (2003) Politics and international legal obligation. Eur J Int Rel 9:591–625

Rosendorff P, Milner H (2001) The optimal Design of International Trade Institutions: uncertainty and escape. Int Organ 55:829–857

Ruiter D, Wessel R (2012) The legal nature of informal international law: a legal theoretical exercise. In: Pawuelyn J, Wessel R, Wouters J (eds) Informal international law making. Oxford University Press, Oxford, pp 162–184

Ruka P (2017) The international legal responsibility of the European Union in the context of the World Trade Organization in areas of non-conferred competences. Springer, Cham

Schmalenbach K (2018a) Article 26. In: Dörr O, Schmalenbach K (eds) Vienna convention of the law of the treaties. Springer, Berlin, pp 467–492

Schmalenbach K (2018b) Article 27. In: Dörr O, Schmalenbach K (eds) Vienna convention of the law of the treaties. Springer, Berlin, pp 493–507

Shelton D (2003) Law, non-law and the problem of soft law. In: Shelton D (ed) Commitment and compliance: the role of non-binding norms in the international legal system. Oxford University Press, Oxford, pp 1–21

Simons B (2001) The legalization of international monetary affairs. Int Organ 54:573–602

Stanko S (2012) Regulatory cooperation to remove non-tariff barriers to trade in products: key challenges and opportunities for the Canada-EU Comprehensive trade agreement. Legal Iss Econ Integr 39:3–28

Türk A (2012) Law-making after Lisbon. In: Biondi A, Eeckhout P, Ripley S (eds) EU Law after Lisbon. Oxford University Press, Oxford, pp 62–84

Verhoeven J (2010) The law of responsibility and the law of treaties. In: Crawford J, Pellet A, Olleson S (eds) The law of international responsibility. Oxford University Press, Oxford, pp 105–114

Vidigal G, Schill S (2018) Addressing interstate dispute settlement concerns in mega-regional agreements. In: International Centre for Trade and Sustainable Investment and World Economic Forum. Available via DIALOG: https://pure.uva.nl/ws/files/42471702/addressing_interstate_dispute_se.pdf

Wagner N, Huber R (2016) Warum ist CETA ein Demokratieproblem? Sieben Gründe, warum die Parlamente CETA ablehnen müssen. In: Mehr Demokratie. Available via DIALOG: https://www.mehr-demokratie.de/fileadmin/pdf/2016-07-18__Demokratieproblem_CETA.pdf.

Weil P (1983) Towards relative normativity in international law? Am J Int Law 77:413–442

Weiss W (2018) Delegation to treaty bodies in EU agreements: constitutional constraints and proposals for strengthening the European Parliament. Eur Const Law Rev 14:532–566

Chapter 4
Regulatory Cooperation Results and Their Effects in the EU Legal Order

4.1 Introduction

The findings of the previous chapter established the general move towards Legalization. This move is mainly observed due to the appearance of the obligation element at an increased degree, as commitments figure as legally binding international obligations and the highly precise and detailed provisions of the chapters under consideration.

Their status as such in the international arena reflects and influences their position in the EU as well. Based on the jurisprudence of the CJEU on EU Treaties and acts adopted under them, starting with the *Haegeman II* jurisprudence, one can derive the conclusion that, from the moment of their adoption, Regulatory Cooperation commitments integrated in FTA treaties concluded by the EU form an 'integral part of EU law'.[1] This initial finding was complemented with following jurisprudence, which crystallized further their position in EU Law (and hence also in domestic law) and the obligation of the Community and domestic actors (on the basis of Article 216 (2) TFEU) to comply. According to the Court in *Hauptzollamt Mainz v. CA Kupferberg,* International Agreements are to be considered an integral part of the Community legal order and therefrom derives the requirement for the Institutions and the Member States to comply with the undertaken commitments (derived from 228 par. 2 EEC, now Article 216 (2) TFEU), which is first and foremost an obligation towards the Community,[2] a statement which it repeated in *Demirel v*

---

[1] In this case, the Court asserted its preliminary rulings jurisdiction over the interpretation of the Association Agreement with Greece, by characterizing it as an 'act of the Institutions', in order to fulfill the requirement of Article 177 EEC Treaty. *See* C-181/73 *Haegeman v. Belgium (Haegeman II)* [1974] ECR I-449, par. 3 and 4.

[2] Case C-104/81 *Hauptzollamt Mainz vs CA Kupferberg* [1982] ECR I-3641 par. 13.

K. Pipidi-Kalogirou, *Regulatory Cooperation Chapters in the new Generation FTAS*, EYIEL Monographs - Studies in European and International Economic Law 36, https://doi.org/10.1007/978-3-031-71900-4_4

Stadt Schwäbisch Gmünd.[3] This constitutional anchor[4] spells out the binding effect of the Agreements on the Institutions and the EU Member States.[5] The applicability of the cornerstone principle of *'pacta sunt servanda'* to the Union's obligations is a common assumption to be found in abundant jurisprudence.[6] Its corollary, Article 27 VCLT, is also a provision with which the Court has engaged, also in recent jurisprudence.[7] Moreover, the performance of those international obligations in good faith has been admitted by the Court as a general principle that guides Union's external action.[8]

Despite their elevated legal status in the EU legal order and the resulting obligation of compliance with the commitments, the absence of the delegation element revealed a shortcoming. Indeed, for the moment and based on the analysis in the previous chapter of the relevant legal rules in Regulatory Cooperation Chapters, it can be excluded that there will be secondary rulemaking on issues that fall under the ambit of those chapters, neither within the centralized joint Committees of the agreements, nor by the specialized bodies established under the Regulatory Cooperation Chapters, despite the fact that the language used in the Regulatory Cooperation processes is clearly result-orientated and sets concrete results as milestones. So, how, meaning in which legal form and with which legal consequences will the results following from the implementation of the Regulatory Cooperation Chapters be expressed?

The questions that naturally follow are what instruments will be used in the implementation of Regulatory Cooperation activities, which legal forms will the activities themselves have under international law and then in the EU legal order and how they will react with it? Given the novelty of the practice, Regulatory Cooperation has not revealed its full potential yet and may evolve in the future towards different directions. Yet, the contributions in this part will be based on the existing legislative framework and the current practice of the Commission. Guidance on the current practice of the Commission is mostly offered by the official documents that describe the meetings of the joint Committees founded in the Agreements, both

---

[3] In Demirel, in order to defend its jurisdiction to interpret a mixed Agreement under the preliminary reference procedure, the Court stated that: 'in ensuring respect for commitments arising from an agreement concluded by the Community Institutions the Member States fulfil, within the Community system, an obligation in relation to the Community, which has assumed responsibility for the due performance of the agreement'. Case C-12/86 *Demirel v Stadt Schwäbisch Gmünd* [1987] ECR I-3719 par. 11.

[4] Referred in C-87/75 *Bresciani* [1976] ECR I-129 and in C-270/80 *Polydor v. Harlequin* [1982] ECR I-329.

[5] This provision has been interpreted by some commentators as confirming the hierarchical supremacy of International law over secondary EU Law. See Ágoston Mohay (2017), p. 157.

[6] See indicatively Case C-537/11 Mattia Manzi and Compagnia Naviera Orchestra v. Capitaneria di Porto di Genova [2014] ECLI:EU:C:2014:19, par. 38 and Case C-162/96 *Racke GmbH & Co. v. Hauptzollamt Mainz* [1998] ECR I-3655, par. 49.

[7] See indicatively joined Cases C-317/04 and C-318/04 *European Parliament v. Council of the EU and EU Commission* [2006] ECR I-4721.

[8] Case C-104/81 *Hauptzollamt Mainz vs CA Kupferberg* [1982] ECR I-3641, par. 18.

specialized and centralized ones.[9] Those Agendas, Reports and Work Plans offer a starting point of the dialogue that is taking place, indicate the progress that has been made so far on the bilateral level and also mention the future initiatives that are proposed on the Committees' level. Thus, they constitute a legitimate source of information in offering a background for a preliminary assessment of the limits of the current practice. At the time of the writing (March 2020), regarding Regulatory Cooperation, one may find at the Commission's website the minutes from the first two meeting of CETA's RCF in December 2018 and February 2020 and a more detailed working plan, published during the summer of 2019 in preparation of the last meeting in February.[10] Its counterpart from the EU-Japan EPA has not held such meetings till today. Hence, while the analysis shall begin from the two CETA documents, the assumptions and considerations may equally extend to Regulatory Cooperation in EU-Japan EPA, that also aims at ambitious outcomes.

The primary aim of the present chapter will be to explore the legal effects that Regulatory Cooperation results introduce in the EU legal order in order to analyze the resulting subsequent constitutional legal issues raised by them at a later stage. Through this analysis of these first examples, it also wishes to offer a preliminary analysis on the typology of instruments that will be used in Regulatory Cooperation activities in order to map their constitutional limits later. Deriving information from the available documents, in Sect. 4.2 we shall briefly identify in which legal forms and informal ways Regulatory Cooperation results are taking place in the RCF level. In Sects. 4.3 and 4.4 we will engage into a separate analysis for each method of cooperation, analyse the findings of Sect. 4.2 more in detail, examine for each case study whether these have been implemented somehow in the EU level or not and comment upon the issuing legal effects in the EU acquis. Section 4.5 will conclude.

4.2 Looking for Legal Effects of Informal Instruments and Regulatory Dialogue

Should one study the official documents furnished by the Commission, one shall notice the following pattern in terms of results: proclaimed to be informal instruments taking the form of a series of administrative arrangements and of course, regulatory dialogue.

Regarding the first, frequent use of informal instruments chosen to outline the procedure and details of the cooperation activities is characteristic. For example, bilateral exchange of information on safety of non-food products is regulated by the recently concluded administrative arrangement between the European Commission's Directorate-General for Justice and Consumers and the Department of Health

---

[9]EU Commission 'CETA - Meetings and documents'. <https://circabc.europa.eu/ui/group/09242 a36-a438-40fd-a7af-fe32e36cbd0e/library/205dba99-7521-44fc-82bb-789155c58138>.
[10]EU Commission (2019a).

of Canada, and which finds its legal basis on Article 21.7 CETA.[11] Moreover, the same category of informal instruments dominate the undertaken cooperation on pharmaceutical inspections. A series of administrative arrangements were concluded, as per the Commission website, in order to *support* Article 15.3 of the CETA Protocol on Pharmaceuticals, or, as per the Article per se, to *implement* it.[12] The CETA Protocol on Pharmaceuticals sets out the conditions for the mutual recognition on Good Manufacturing Practice (GMP) on certain pharmaceutical products and is one of the two areas where convergence commitments were agreed on the treaty level, along with the motor vehicle industry.[13] The implementation activities of the Protocol are supervised by the Joint Sectoral Group on Pharmaceuticals,[14] which formally adopted the administrative arrangements. Cooperation on Pharmaceuticals forms part of the agenda of the RCF, hence, it is interesting and relevant to study the implementation tools of the cooperation in this area. Their detailed formulation is delegated in Article 15.3 of the CETA Protocol of Pharmaceuticals, which itself describes generally the steps to be taken. Article 15.3 reads as follows: *"The Joint Sectoral Group shall conclude a GMP Administrative Arrangement to facilitate the effective implementation of this Protocol. The GMP Administrative Arrangement shall include: a. the terms of references of the Joint Sectoral Group; b. the two-way alert programme; c. the list of contact points responsible for matters arising under this Protocol; d. the components of the information sharing process; e. the components of a GMP compliance programme; f. the procedure for evaluating new regulatory authorities; and g. the equivalence maintenance programme."*[15] It is thus upon this basis that the implementation of the Protocol relies.

The other areas of Regulatory Cooperation have been dominated by regulatory dialogue of varying ambition. Much promising seems to be the case of Regulatory Cooperation in Cybersecurity and Internet of Things (hereinafter IoT), where Regulatory Cooperation activities are carried out with a view to 'align Canadian and EU regulations and standards, as necessary'.[16] Impetus for the cooperation is the joint recognition of the security challenges that connected devices in digital and connected economy presents for citizens and the realization of the need to place

---

[11] Administrative Arrangement (AA) between the European Commission's Directorate-General for Justice and Consumers and the Department of Health of Canada on the exchange of information on the safety of non-food consumer products <https://ec.europa.eu/info/sites/info/files/aa_final_en-eu_version.pdf>.

[12] Article 15.3, Text of the Comprehensive Economic and Trade Agreement—Protocol on the mutual recognition of the compliance and enforcement programme regarding GMPS for pharmaceutical products.

[13] Sieber Gasser (2016), p. 561.

[14] EU Commission (2018).

[15] Even though the provision speaks about one Administrative Arrangement, in fact every point mentioned above is published separately. For this reason, we shall refer to each one separately as well in this chapter.

[16] EU Commission (2019a), p. 7.

those activities within a predictable regulatory regime.[17] Regulatory dialogue in the case of Animal Welfare concerns the exchange of best practices, without indication of alignment efforts.[18] In that case, however, the desired outcomes as set in the Work Plan are limited to information sharing and technical cooperation on practical aspects of long-distance transport of animals. Although Animal Welfare has been the subject matter of cooperation between the parties in the past,[19] no mention of a more ambitious goal is made and the undertaken activities reflect the intention of the parties.

These results come naturally given the inability of the RCF to produce its own rules. Now it all boils down to study the effects of these informal structures. Before proceeding to the effects of each structure it is worth taking a moment to have a clearer view on what kind of effects to expect from each category. At this point we should clarify that for the purposes of the present chapter, i.e. to analyse the legal effects of Regulatory Cooperation activities with the EU legal order, it is only the legal effects as developed by the Court of Justice or comparable effects by soft, informal instruments that are the ones of relevance and not the practical ones. Since we need to analyse legal questions, we do not abide by Snyder's often cited definition of soft law that includes practical effects to greater category of the effects of soft law. By practical effects, we refer to the technical implementation of the commitments, to the infrastructure that is meant to support them and not to their legal consequences. This research rather abides to the definition of soft law provided by Senden, which also includes certain indirect legal effects to this group of law.[20]

With regard to the status of non-binding international agreements in the EU, it must first be stated that as generally non-binding agreements do, they form part of the *acquis communautaire*.[21] There is broad institutional consensus on this. The General Court has early encompassed Commission's 'soft-law' in the notion of the acquis, on the occasion of case T-115/94 Opel Austria v. Council, and the rest of the Institutions adopt a wide definition of the term.[22] With regard to the category of administrative arrangements, it is difficult to assess with certainty whether belonging to the *acquis communautaire* has the same meaning with being "an integral part of EU law" as international Treaties do. It surely means though that soft instruments even not falling under the realm of law in the strict sense of the term, still find their place within the wider EU legal environment, as part of its essential elements.[23] For

---

[17] EU Commission (2019a), p. 7.

[18] EU Commission (2019a), p. 9.

[19] EU Commission (2019b), p. 3.

[20] According to Senden, soft law is a body of 'rules of conduct that are laid down in instruments which have not been attributed legally binding force as such, but nevertheless may have certain (indirect) legal effects, and that are aimed at and may produce practical effects' *See* Senden (2004), p. 112.

[21] Judgement in Case T-115/94 *Opel Austria v. Council* [1997] ECR II-39, par. 117.

[22] Peters and Pagotto (2006).

[23] Stefan (2013), p. 119.

this, there is broad consensus among academics and judiciary on the existence of indirect legal effects, generated by informal instruments.[24] A particular category of soft international agreements, the so-called Administrative Agreements have been steadily proliferating as tools in the Union's external action, however their practice as instruments is still not consolidated, in a way that does not allow for a systematization of the legal effects they can produce in the EU legal order.[25] Consequently, for our category of administrative instruments, the administrative arrangements, the search for effects in Sects. 4.3 and 4.4 will not be focused on a certain category but will extend to the totality of effects informal agreements can give. For the purposes of this chapter, the terms "soft law", "informal agreements" and "non-binding agreements" shall be used interchangeably. Passing on to the possible effects of dialogue, due to the nature of the activity which targets the rule-making we will demonstrate through concrete examples the ways Regulatory Cooperation dialogue can impact EU decision-making. With the term decision-making priorities we include both the decision of the Commission to regulate as such and the content of the regulations, either in the legislative process or in EU executive rulemaking. In order to base our argument, we will present a series of regulatory developments that are one way or another, connected to the Regulatory Cooperation activities.

4.3   Administrative Arrangements

This section analyses the first Administrative Arrangements signed as part of the Regulatory Cooperation activities in order to discover their content, legal nature and the produced legal effects. As described above, implementation of Regulatory Cooperation in the areas of pharmaceuticals and product safety rests upon the conclusion of administrative arrangements, a rather unused instrument by the EU Commission, which reminds of the neighbouring category of Administrative Agreements. Before proceeding to the examination of each separate case-study, the first part will outline the resemblance of this novel category of Administrative Arrangements with the one of Administrative Agreements. To which extent do they resemble and which aspects, if any, differentiate the two? The question is important, since, given the scarcity of literature resources for administrative arrangements, we could apply by analogy the limited analyses carried out for Administrative Agreements in order to deliberate on their nature and their ability to produce legal effects, which shall be examined in due course.

---

[24] See also Opinion of AG Sharpston at Case C-660/13 *Council of the European Union v. European Commission* [2016] ECLI:EU:C:2016:616, par. 69; Pauwelyn (2012), p. 152; Sloan (1987), p. 45.
[25] Wessel (2018).

4.3.1 General Considerations on Administrative Agreements as a Benchmark for Administrative Arrangements

This section refers to an application par analogy of general characteristics of Administrative Agreements to the category of administrative arrangements. As a comparative view of the two categories of agreements reveals, the difference, if any, between the two, could only be semantic, rather than legal/structural which in fact allows us to rely upon the literature of Administrative Agreements in order to deliberate on the legal nature of administrative arrangements. It is important to draw the analogy between the two for the following reason: we mentioned in Sect. 4.1 that the purpose of this chapter will be to explore the legal effects that Regulatory Cooperation results introduce in the EU legal order in order to analyze the resulting subsequent constitutional legal issues raised by them at a later stage. At this stage, by establishing the resemblance between administrative arrangements and Administrative Agreements we can safely presume that the former can present the same legal implications as the latter did. One such implication can be the conclusion of the instrument by an incompetent body, which was found to be the case in two cases implicating an administrative agreement with third parties, when they were brought before the Court of Justice.[26] Indeed, mainly based on the content of these Administrative Agreements, the Court found them to have been illegally adopted by the EU Commission, which lacked competence.

Proceeding to the examination of the analogy, we locate mostly similarities, rather than differences between the two. A first indicator is that the Commission is not consistent with the use of the two terms in order to allow a clear distinction. One example for this is the case of the "Administrative arrangement for activities to be developed by the European Union National Institutes for Culture (EUNIC) in partnership with the European Commission Services and the European External Action Service".[27] While the text is signed as an arrangement, the link guiding to it refers to it as an agreement.[28] And indeed, methodologically speaking, administrative arrangements do constitute agreements, in the sense that they have been agreed between the two parties.

Moreover, both Administrative Agreements and administrative arrangements were born out of institutional practice of the Commission.[29] Similar agreements in other legal orders as their name suggests, are signed by the administration, and exist

---

[26] Case C-327/91 *French Republic v Commission of the European Communities* [1994] ECR I-3641 and Case C-660/13 *Council of the European Union v. European Commission* [2016] ECLI:EU: C:2016:616.

[27] Administrative arrangement for activities to be developed by the European Union National Institutes for Culture (EUNIC) in partnership with the European Commission Services and the European External Action Service, <https://eeas.europa.eu/sites/eeas/files/2017-05-16_admin_arrangement_eunic.pdf>.

[28] EEAS (2017).

[29] Case C-233/02 *France v. Commission* [2004], ECR I-2759 Opinion of AG Alber, par. 65.

as a separate (sub)category of agreements in international state practice, regulated differently in the legal orders where they are found. In most EU Member States, they respectively do not need ratification by the national legislator.[30] Such agreements are either concluded as implementing instruments to commitments made in previous international treaties or by delegation based on a domestic legal instrument, or just in areas traditionally belonging to the executive.[31] Indeed, in the various jurisdictions, Administrative Agreements are met with varying frequency and coverage capacity, but as a general rule most EU Member States draw the balance between formal treaties and Administrative Agreements on the political or technical character of the arrangement.[32] Located at governmental or agency level, these agreements do not treat political question but regulate tasks whose nature requires international coordination at administrative level.[33]

The same balance is in theory drawn regarding both Commission's Administrative Agreements and arrangements, either binding or non-binding ones, founded by a delegating provision or self-standing. As an administration itself, the Commission invented this practice for similar reasons. The difference lies in the fact that while under Member States' practice these agreements are recognized, in the EU legal order they do not. Administrative Agreements and arrangements are not international ones in the sense of Article 218 par. 1 TFEU, they are thus not regulated *stricto sensu* by the Treaties. However, they both qualify as part of the *acquis communautaire*, but under a legal form which is still uncharted. Their unclear legal status in the EU legal order matches their odd placement within the international legal order as well. Indeed, this type of agreements does not exist as a category, distinct from international agreements as far as the international legal order is concerned, as AG Tesauro argued in its Opinion in C-327/91 France v. Commission.[34]

Despite that, the Commission has been using this type of administrative instruments for a variety of instances in its relations with third countries or international organizations. It happens that they are usually mandated by a provision; in this sense, they are delegated instruments. All administrative arrangements signed in the context of Regulatory Cooperation find their basis on provisions of CETA. Also beyond

---

[30] Ott (2018), p. 210.

[31] Morrison (2007), p. 1.

[32] Ott (2018), p. 210.

[33] Ott (2016), p. 1029.

[34] Case C-327/91 *French Republic v Commission of the European Communities* [1994] ECR I-3641, Opinion of AG Tesauro, par. 22.

our case-study, based on either primary[35] secondary law,[36] or international agreements,[37] the EU has signed various legally binding and non-binding Administrative Agreements as delegated instruments. These can cover a range of subjects, from financial cooperation to neighboring policy and so on. Their existence is not prima facie problematic, provided that the delegation requirements are respected and they remain confined to regulating issues that fall outside the political realm, although it has been rightly argued that such type of delegation should be accompanied by political and legal safeguards similar to the ones of Articles 290 and 291 TFEU.[38] Nevertheless, the Commission has also introduced binding and non-binding Administrative Agreements and arrangements in its practice also without a specific mandate. Examples to this constitute the "Agreement between the Commission and the United States on the application of their competition laws"[39] and the "EU-US Guidelines on Regulatory Cooperation and Transparency",[40] "Administrative arrangement for activities to be developed by the European Union National Institutes for Culture (EUNIC) in partnership with the European Commission Services and the European External Action Service"[41] and more recently the "Commission Decision C(2013) 6355 final of 3 October 2013 on the signature of the Addendum to the Memorandum of Understanding (hereinafter MoU) on a Swiss financial contribution." Even though these Administrative Agreements, apart from the last two, were found to have been illegally concluded by the Commission, because of its lack of

---

[35] One example is Article 6 of Protocol No. 7 on the Privileges and Immunities of the European Union, on the basis of which the Commission can conclude agreements with third countries, in order for the latter to recognize the 'laisser-passer' as valid travel documents of EU staff within their territory. See Consolidated version of the Treaty on the Functioning of the European Union Protocol (No 7) on the privileges and immunities of the European Union [2012] OJ C 326/266.

[36] Such an example are the agreements on financial cooperation with third countries, by which Commission's power to act accordingly is given the power by secondary legislation. See Articles 58, 60 (5), 184 (2)b and 58 of Financial Regulation No. 966/2012/EU of the European Parliament and of the Council of 25 October 2012 on the financial rules applicable to the general budget of the Union and repealing Council Regulation (EC, Euratom) No 1605/2002, [2012] OJ L 298/11; Articles 5, 8 of Regulation No 231/2014/EU of 11 March 2014 establishing an Instrument for Pre-accession Assistance (IPA II), [2014] OJ L 77/11.

[37] Article 5 of Protocol 1 of the Association Agreement with Moldova mentions that the conditions under which Moldova participates in Union programs shall be agreed by the Commission and Moldova by means of a binding administrative agreement.

[38] See generally Ott (2018).

[39] Agreement between the Government of the United States of America and the Commission of the European Communities regarding the application of their competition laws [1995] OJ L 95/47.

[40] USTR, TEP Guidelines on Regulatory Cooperation and Transparency (2020) <https://ustr.gov/archive/World_Regions/Europe_Middle_East/Europe/US_EU_Regulatory_Cooperation/TEP_Guidelines_on_Regulatory_Cooperation_Transparency_Implementation_Roadmap.html>.

[41] Administrative arrangement for activities to be developed by the European Union National Institutes for Culture (EUNIC) in partnership with the European Commission Services and the European External Action Service, <https://eeas.europa.eu/sites/eeas/files/2017-05-16_admin_arrangement_eunic.pdf>.

competence (see supra), they are nevertheless mentioned as examples of the practice, irrespectively of whether this practice is legal or not.

Another similarity they share is the fact that both Administrative Agreements and arrangements are rarely published as such. Sometimes they are published under a Commission decision, as was the Administrative Agreement of the Swiss MoU, implemented by Commission Decision C(2013) 6355 final of 3 October 2013. However, the Administrative Agreement on the "EU-US Guidelines on Regulatory Cooperation and Transparency" was not officially published as such, but only online. Neither was the "Agreement between the Commission and the United States on the application of their competition laws" at the time of its signing, as an administrative agreement, published. Only after its annulment by the Court, which found it illegal based on Commission's lack of competence, was the latter published as an international treaty, endorsed by the Council.[42] Here too, all of the administrative arrangements under analysis have not been implemented by a Commission decision or any other internal measure, they only have been implemented by the parties' practice. Moreover, there is also no indication regarding their categorization on the official document to be found online and also neither the "Administrative Arrangement on the exchange of information on safety of non-food products" nor the GMP Administrative Arrangements have been published under any form on eur-lex. This has been also confirmed by two officials of the EU Commission via exchange of email.

From the analysis above it is made clear that the two categories of instruments share their constitutive elements. Moreover, there is no difference between the two patterns of conclusion between Administrative Agreements and Administrative Arrangements. Indeed, when looking at the mode of conclusion of the Administrative Agreement on EU-US Guidelines on Regulatory Cooperation and Transparency, we see that it was expressly approved by the College of Commissioners as a whole,[43] in contrast to the Administrative Arrangements that have been concluded by separate departments of each administration. However, this is not the case as the Administrative Agreement between the Commission and the United States on the application of their competition laws was agreed between the then Commissioner for Competition for the EU and by the Attorney General and the President of the Federal Trade Commission, on behalf of the Government of the United States.[44] In short, they both are informal international agreements and any further difference between them could only be semantic, in that the Commission maybe wants to give a gloss of informality when referring to administrative arrangements instead of Administrative Agreements. Indeed, should we take a horizontal look to the thematic of cooperation, we observe that it has been treated both with Administrative Agreements and

---

[42] Agreement between the Government of the United States of America and the Commission of the European Communities regarding the application of their competition laws [1995] OJ L 95/47.

[43] Case C-233/02 *France v. Commission* [2004] ECR I-2759 Opinion of AG Alber, par. 47–49.

[44] Case C-327/91 *French Republic v Commission of the European Communities* [1994] ECR I-3641, par. 2.

arrangements, with two examples being the EU-US Administrative Agreement on Regulatory Cooperation Guidelines or the Administrative Arrangement on the exchange of information through RAPEX (Rapid Alert System for non-food consumer products) and RADAR (Regulatory Action Depot/Dépôt d'Actions Réglementaires). One could rightly wonder whether the Commission tries to redress the category of Administrative Agreements under the term administrative arrangements, in order to avoid litigation which it had to face with regard to other Administrative Agreements.

From these similarities, we can extract that administrative arrangements can have legal effects. One first legal effect can be extracted already by existing jurisprudence, in that they can constitute the object of an action for annulment, in the same way the unpublished Administrative Agreements did.[45] Despite the lack of publicity of such agreements and arrangements, they nevertheless take the form of institutional acts and have been treated as such also at the few decisions that arrived before the Court.[46] In fact, central point in determining their position and status in the EU legal order have been the inherent legal effects flowing from such agreements.[47] In both cases C-233/02 and C-327/91 the AGs insisted in determining whether the alleged informal Administrative Agreements did produce legal effects. Of course, in those cases, this assessment was carried out in order to answer whether the Court could assume jurisdiction, which it enjoys only as far as acts of the Institutions having legal effect are concerned. However, the significance of legal effects reaches beyond admissibility questions. The existence or absence of legal effects of the administrative arrangements can also determine whether they were legally binding ones in disguise.[48]

Here, we present another reason for mapping legal effects of such instruments: to see whether despite their proclaimed non-binding nature they introduce binding obligations or far-reaching legal effects, whether we have a hardened obligation under a soft cloth.[49] Indeed, according to the text of all administrative arrangements, they are signed as not legally binding ones.[50] In the parts that follow we shall discuss the two Regulatory Cooperation areas that were implemented by administrative arrangements separately, in order to map whether they present any legal effects in

---

[45] Stefan et al. (2019).

[46] Case C-327/91 *French Republic v Commission of the European Communities* [1994] ECR I-3641 Opinion of AG Tesauro, par. 28.

[47] Senden (2004), p. 235.

[48] Case C-233/02 *France v. Commission* [2004] ECR I-2759 Opinion of AG Alber, par. 67.

[49] Term borrowed from Lancos (2018).

[50] All Administrative Arrangements on Pharmaceuticals begin by the following statement: "This administrative arrangement is not intended to create rights or obligations under international or domestic law and, in line with Article 15(7) of the Protocol, is not subject of the provision of Chapter 29 of the CETA Agreement." Article 12, Administrative Arrangement (AA) between the European Commission's Directorate-General for Justice and Consumers and the Department of Health of Canada on the exchange of information on the safety of non-food consumer products <https://ec.europa.eu/info/sites/info/files/aa_final_en-eu_version.pdf>.

the EU legal order. The challenge to this analysis is posed by the scarce jurisprudence on non-binding instruments in EU's external relations, which adds an extra layer of complexity. While scholarly analysis has been augmenting on the study of soft law before the courts, this remains largely concentrated to internal "soft" instruments on different areas and their perception by the Court of Justice and the national courts.[51] Still, apart from the few cases that are placed within the external action, part of the jurisprudence and literature on internal "soft" instruments can be applied by analogy to the external action when necessary, in order to de-mystify their effects on a content-based analysis.

4.3.2   Administrative Arrangements on the Mutual Recognition of the Compliance and Enforcement Programme Regarding GMP for Pharmaceutical Products

The Administrative Arrangements that we shall analyze in this part have been signed to implement the 'CETA Protocol on the mutual recognition of the compliance and enforcement programme regarding GMP for pharmaceutical products'.[52] Within its context, parties will be recognizing on an ongoing basis each other's certificates of compliance with GMP, with the ultimate goal being the extension of the recognition regime to certificates of one party that confirm compliance of a manufacturing facility located outside the respective geographical territories of the parties.[53] While referring to the scope, procedure and goal of the different Administrative Arrangements, we shall demonstrate the importance of the produced legal consequences for pharmaceutical manufacturers and exporters. This importance can only be understood when viewed under the relevant EU context, and the place that GMP have within it. For this reason, the first part will explain the background as well as the prominent role of in the EU. The second part will outline the relation of the Administrative Arrangements to the EU procedure, the relevance of the produced legal consequences, and the legal issues that arise from the choice of the specific instrument.

---

[51] *See* for example Lancos (2018) and Stefan (2012, 2013).

[52] CETA Protocol on the mutual recognition of the compliance and enforcement programme regarding GMP for pharmaceutical products [2017] OJ L 11/581.

[53] EU Commission (2019a).

4.3.2.1   Background and Importance of Good Manufacturing Practice in the EU

In the EU, the quality and risk control of pharmaceutical products is a complex multilevel process, implicating various actors at different levels. The main legislative documents that regulate the activity are: (a) Commission Directive 2003/94/EC of 8 October 2003 laying down the principles and guidelines of Good Manufacturing Practice (hereinafter GMP) in respect of medicinal products for human use and investigational medicinal products for human use,[54] (b) Regulation (EC) No 765/2008 of the European Parliament and of the Council of 9 July 2008 setting out the requirements for accreditation and market surveillance relating to the marketing of products and repealing Regulation (EEC) No 339/93,[55] (c) Commission Delegated Regulation (EU) No 1252/2014 of 28 May 2014 supplementing Directive 2001/83/EC of the European Parliament and of the Council with regard to principles and guidelines of GMP for active substances for medicinal products for human use[56] and (d) Commission Directive of 23 July 1991 laying down the principles and guidelines of GMP for veterinary medicinal products.[57]

Central mechanism of this legislative environment are market authorizations granted to the manufacturing facilities, which certify the adherence of each facility to safety and quality requirements. The authorization is granted following regular inspections of each time competent regulatory authority. This system of marketing authorization is key for all EU manufacturers, regardless of whether their products are intended for the internal market or for external trade.[58] Such inspections and the subsequent market authorizations are carried out by the national regulatory

---

[54] Commission Directive 2003/94/EC of 8 October 2003 laying down the principles and guidelines of GMP in respect of medicinal products for human use and investigational medicinal products for human use [2003] OJ L 262/22.

[55] Regulation (EC) No 765/2008 of the European Parliament and of the Council of 9 July 2008 setting out the requirements for accreditation and market surveillance relating to the marketing of products and repealing Regulation (EEC) No 339/93 (Text with EEA relevance) [2008] OJ L 218/30.

[56] Commission Delegated Regulation (EU) No 1252/2014 of 28 May 2014 supplementing Directive 2001/83/EC of the European Parliament and of the Council with regard to principles and guidelines of GMP for active substances for medicinal products for human use [2014] OJ L 337/1.

[57] Commission Directive 91/412/EEC of 23 July 1991 laying down the principles and guidelines of GMP for veterinary medicinal products [1991] OJ L 228/70.

[58] Article 4, Commission Directive 2003/94/EC of 8 October 2003 laying down the principles and guidelines of GMP in respect of medicinal products for human use and investigational medicinal products for human use [2003] OJ L 262/22.

authorities (hereinafter NRAs) in each member state for the facilities that are located within its territory.[59] This activity is further coordinated by the European Medicines Agency (hereinafter EMA).

The assessment of the quality of the manufacturing activity is made against the requirements of the GMP as the latter are outlined by the main legislative documents mentioned above. In order to ensure the uniform interpretation and implementation of the requirements, which are harmonized Union-wide, manufacturers and NRAs may consult the GMP Guidelines, which constitute an interpretative document of this legislation, issued by the Commission and EMA.[60] In the pharmaceutical jargon GMPs represent the minimum standards that a manufacturing facility has to meet in the production process.[61] They were first introduced by the World Health Organization (hereinafter WHO) in 1968 as part of the WHO certification scheme on the quality of the pharmaceutical products intended to circulate globally.[62] These criteria touch every step of the production activity, starting from the materials and extending to the hygiene of the premises to the training of the personnel. Their primary aim is thus to ensure that at proper quality assurance standards are followed throughout all steps of the production of every product the so that the final product is risk-free.

GMP, along with Quality Risk Management[63] form the Pharmaceutical Quality System, which according to Article 6 of Directive 2003/94/EC of 8 October 2003 has to effectively be set up by each manufacturer, according to the size and the complexity of the activities, and which has to be in line with the marketing authorization, thus the legal requirements.[64] Thus, at the EU level, the respect of GMP is a condition sine qua non in order for a manufacturer to obtain a marketing authorization.[65]

Key actors thus to this procedure are first and foremost the NRAs whose mandate is to inspect the manufacturing facilities according to the exigencies listed in the legislation and issue the marketing authorizations and certify the GMP followed, thus allowing for the marketing of the products.[66] Equally bound by the same legal criteria are the manufacturers who have to ensure the respect for GMP as part of the market approval procedure of their products. After having outlined the protagonists of the procedures, in the following section we shall examine the content of the Protocol and the implementing Administrative Agreements in order to understand

---

[59] Article 3, Commission Directive 2003/94/EC of 8 October 2003 laying down the principles and guidelines of GMP in respect of medicinal products for human use and investigational medicinal products for human use [2003] OJ L 262/22.

[60] EU Commission (2011).

[61] European Medicines Agency (2023).

[62] WHO (2018).

[63] Quality risk management is described in broad terms, as the totality of factors that determine the quality of a product. It comprises GMP and Quality Risk management.

[64] EU Commission (2011), Chapter 1, p. 2.

[65] EU Commission (2011), Introduction, p. 2.

[66] Article 6, Directive 2001/83/EC of the European Parliament and of the Council of 6 November 2001 on the Community code relating to medicinal products for human use [2001] OJ L 311/28.

how they relate to the procedure described above and whether they impose new obligations upon them.

4.3.2.2 Legal Obligations Arising from the Administrative Arrangements as the First Legal Consequence

For our case study, we will focus on four out of the six Administrative Agreements signed between DG Sante and Health Canada to implement Article 15.3 'Protocol on the Mutual Recognition of the Compliance and Enforcement Programme regarding GMP for Pharmaceutical Products'.

The objective of the Protocol, according to Article 2 is *'to strengthen the cooperation between the authorities of the Parties in ensuring that medicinal products and drugs (as mentioned in Annex 1) meet appropriate quality standards through the mutual recognition of certificates of GMP compliance'*.[67] To this end, a multilevel process has to be followed. First, the national regulatory authorities of the parties (hereinafter NRAs) must be found to be equivalent to the ones of the other Party according to Articles 4 and 12 of the Protocol. For the purpose of the Protocol, a regulatory authority is 'an entity in a Party that has the legal right, under the law of the Party, to supervise and control medicinal products or drugs within that party'.[68] In other words, the regulatory authorities for the EU are the national ones, indicated in Annex 2 of the Protocol. After the recognition of equivalence, the equivalent authorities can issue certificates with which they certify that a manufacturing facility in their territory and under their control follows the GMP stated in the certificate.[69] According to Article 5.1 of the Protocol the other party has to accept the certificates issued.

It is interesting to observe that the NRAs are the main protagonists of these procedures even though the Administrative Arrangements were signed by the administrations, DG SANTE and Health Canada respectively. This is also stated on paper since a closer look on the content of the provisions proves that they extend to and bind, at least in the EU territory, further parties as well, namely the national regulatory authorities, which are different administrative entities. This consideration concerns of course all the Administrative Agreements of the Protocol alike, but it is also made clear in Article 3 of the Administrative Agreement under 15.3 (f) on the Procedure for Evaluating New Regulatory Authorities, which states as participants to the agreement the regulatory authorities of the EU and of Canada. Based on the

---

[67] Article 2, CETA Protocol on the Mutual Recognition of the Compliance and Enforcement Programme regarding GMPS for Pharmaceutical Products [2017] L 11/581.

[68] Definition of 'regulatory authority' Article 1, CETA Protocol on the Mutual Recognition of the Compliance and Enforcement Programme regarding GMPS for Pharmaceutical Products [2017] L 11/581.

[69] Article 5.1, CETA Protocol on the Mutual Recognition of the Compliance and Enforcement Programme regarding GMPS for Pharmaceutical Products [2017] L 11/581.

above, we identify the addressees of the procedures to be followed for the equivalency to take place.

These procedures, vaguely described in the Protocol, are implemented by the Administrative Arrangements under question. Various components of the procedure are addressed with these Administrative Agreements. Some serve merely informative purposes. For example, Administrative Arrangement under Article 15.3 (c) just lists the Contact Points. Another example is the Administrative Arrangement under Article 15.3 (f) on the Procedure for evaluating new Regulatory Authorities, which just outlines the procedural steps of the process, the actions that have to be taken by the administrations in order to proceed to the evaluation of equivalence of the regulatory authorities. The effects of the Administrative Arrangements of organizational or informative nature are thus merely practical. However, other Administrative Agreements go beyond merely informative purposes and contain concrete information that concretize the duties of the parties.

To begin with, since key to our analysis is the equivalence of regulatory authorities, it is necessary to understand the role of the arrangements in the equivalency process. Relevant for this exercise are the Administrative Arrangement under Article 15.3 (e) entitled 'Components of GMP Compliance Programme' and the Administrative Arrangement under Article 15.3 (g) entitled 'Equivalence Maintenance Programme', which outline the criteria against which the equivalency of a regulatory authority will be assessed and maintained respectively. Once the procedures laid down in the Administrative Arrangement regarding the Components of GMP Compliance Programme are applied, and equivalence of the third party NRAs is granted, this gives them the right to the production of GMP certificates which the EU has the obligation to accept. From the opposite direction, a negative finding on the compliance to the exigencies of the Administrative Agreement comes with the legal consequence of non-equivalence, and thus the inability to produce GMP certificates. The same opportunity is offered for new NRAs, as per the Administrative Arrangement regarding the Procedure for Evaluating New Regulatory Authorities. Moreover, by virtue of Article 13 par. 3, 4 and 5 of the Protocol, the NRAs are in a constant obligation to report any internal change they may undergo on elements that were controlled as part of the equivalence assessment, which may give rise to a re-evaluation of the equivalence regime.

After having introduced the role of the most relevant Administrative Arrangements and the type of procedures they outline, now the question turns to the legal way in which they bind the parties. On what basis do the parties have to execute and abide by the procedures?

Regarding the legal value, one logically may rely upon the repeating introductory provision of the arrangements, which state their non-legally binding nature: "This administrative arrangement is not intended to create rights or obligations under international or domestic law and, in line with Article 15(7) of the Protocol, is not subject of the provision of Chapter 29 of the CETA Agreement". This does not mean though that the EU could just disregard the procedure as a certain complying effect could be grounded on the basis of good faith and legitimate expectations.[70] However, it is not on the basis of these principles that any legal effects shall be observed. In fact, should one read the administrative arrangements and the Protocol as a whole, one shall observe that the administrative arrangements are given legally binding force by virtue of Articles 12.2 and 13.1 of the Protocol, which state that a Party *shall* apply the components of the said administrative arrangements in order to determine or maintain the equivalence of a regulatory authority.[71] This comes in contrast to the non-legally binding character of the arrangements as promulgated by the text of the arrangements' provisions, and is the first direct legal effect created by these Administrative Agreements.

In fact, the aforementioned regime set out by the Administrative Arrangements is in fact a legal regime, which entails rights and obligations for the participating actors. Despite the soft *instrumentum*, there is no soft *negotium*, instead, the parties have undertaken a legally binding commitment by virtue of Articles 12.2 and 13.1 of the CETA Protocol on Pharmaceuticals to follow the procedures as set out in the Administrative Agreements, in order to be able to obtain and maintain formal equivalency of the regulatory authorities. Compliance by the implicated parties is now grounded in the rule of 216 par. 2 TFEU, which stipulates the "objective effect of bindingness" of international commitments for the Institutions and the Member States.[72] Therefrom, a number of legal effects arises.

4.3.2.3 Legal Effects Within the EU Legal Order

The fulfilment of the legal obligations mentioned above is not only mandated by the imperatives of international law. The functioning of the mechanism has the capacity to alter the legal situation of the actors located in the authorization/export process of

---

[70] Peters (2011), p. 2. It could be argued that compliance is grounded also on the constitutional duty of sincere cooperation, by virtue of Article 4 (3) TEU. The latter encompasses a principle of general application in the EU legal order which applies also the totality of the EU's external action. Clarifying further the scope of the obligation, the Court of Justice has not made any distinction between the legal acts that could give rise to the duty of sincere cooperation. According to its jurisprudence, this principle obliges the Member States and their authorities to *"take any appropriate measure, general or particular, to ensure fulfilment of the obligations arising out of the Treaties or resulting from the acts of the Institutions of the European Union and refrain from any measure which could jeopardise the attainment of the European Union's objectives."*

[71] On the recognition of equivalence Article 12.2 reads as follows: "The evaluating Party *shall* evaluate the new regulator authority by applying the components of a GMP compliance programme under the Administrative Arrangement referred to in Article 15.3." CETA Protocol on the Mutual Recognition of the Compliance and Enforcement Programme regarding GMPS for Pharmaceutical Products [2017] L 11/581.

[72] Steinbach (2017), p. 39.

pharmaceuticals, without the implication, however, of a legal mechanism. Indeed, the regulation of the equivalence is neither supervised nor enforced by a judicial authority.[73] Instead, the only ramification of non-compliance remains constrained to a denial of equivalency of the NRA. However, this denial of formal equivalency deprives the concerned authority from certifying bindingly through the means of a certificate that a manufacturing facility in its territory follows certain GMP that guarantee the quality of the products. This means that the facilities that fall under its territory will not benefit from this advantage and will have to be tested by the counterparts with regard to their GMP compliance during the export procedure.

The importance of this exchange of certificates is thus double and is not to be disregarded. First and most important, it removes a considerable obstacle for future imports and exports, when considering the importance of abidance to GMP for pharmaceutical companies. Moreover, this reciprocal exchange of certificates operationalizes the equivalency of GMP between Canada and the EU, which was designed to develop progressively in the 1998 MRA between the two parties, an agreement triggered by the discrepancies that developed over time, mostly because of EU's decision to develop its own system of GMP, thus diverging from the once common regime.[74] Indeed, the Administrative Arrangements have no impact on the content, on the meaning ascribed to the term of GMP by the GMP Guidelines in the EU legal order. The equivalency of the understanding of the GMP can in fact be traced back to the MRA. To this MRA, the Administrative Agreements have a complementary role, in that they give the power to the administrative bodies to operationalize it. After the conclusion of CETA and its provisional application, the 1998 MRA was suspended and incorporated within the latter. The ratification of CETA by the Member States and its entry into force will mean the termination of the MRA.[75]

Given the key role bestowed upon the recognition of equivalence of NRAs, a precondition for the issuing of binding GMP certificates, we need to examine whether some aspects of the Arrangements will need to be implemented internally by the Member States. On the one hand, NRAs will at a later stage need to issue GMP certificates, these, being administrative acts with the legal consequences described above. For this an internal legal basis to ground this capacity is probably already provided for in domestic law. Now, the question turns to whether the Administrative Arrangements create the obligation for domestic acceptance of a GMP certificate issued by a Canadian NRA as a precondition for the marketing authorization. Should we take a closer look to the marketing authorization procedure in the EU, we understand that this is not the case, as the procedure is centralized and

---

[73] According to Article 15.7 of the Protocol: The Parties shall establish the GMP Administrative Arrangement upon entry into force of the Agreement. This Arrangement is not subject to the provisions of Chapter Twenty-Nine (Dispute Settlement), CETA Protocol on the Mutual Recognition of the Compliance and Enforcement Programme regarding GMPS for Pharmaceutical Products [2017] L 11/581.

[74] Kalomeni (2020), p. 182.

[75] European Medicines Agency (2023).

the final decision on the authorization is taken by the Commission, upon proposal of the EMA.[76] EMA, on the other hand, is bound itself by the equivalency of the GMP certificates, which are necessary documents in the authorization file of a medicine seeking EU-wide authorization, and which are evaluated by the agency in order to form an opinion on the issue.

On the basis of the preceding analysis, we understand that these Administrative Arrangements cannot be presented as non-binding instruments with no legal effects in the EU legal order. Not only are they legally binding international agreements in disguise, but also their implementation entails a series of obligations for several actors and creates a chain effect that has considerable impact on the trade relations of the two, which is anyway, the main object of these activities. To the observed mismatch between instruments on the one hand, with its legal nature and consequences on the other, we will refer extensively later on.

4.3.3 Administrative Arrangement Between the European Commission's Directorate-General for Justice and Consumers and the Department of Health of Canada on the Exchange of Information on the Safety of Non-food Consumer Products

The practice of Administrative Arrangement started as early as few months after the provisional application of the CETA Agreement, with the first one being the Administrative Agreement between the European Commission's Directorate-General for Justice and Consumers and the Department of Health of Canada on the exchange of information on the safety of non-food consumer products.[77] The Arrangement finds its legal basis on Articles 21.7.4 and 21.7.5 CETA, which provide that the parties may engage in cooperation activities in the area of non-food product safety through the extension of their information networks, RAPEX and RADAR respectively. Even though not acquiring a legally binding character as such, the Administrative Arrangement imposes concrete obligations upon the parties, which can have a certain say on the free circulation of goods in the internal market. Of course, this is not necessarily not welcome in an interconnected economy but certainly demonstrates the effects that this type of cooperation may entail. To illustrate the case and make the argument clear, we shall firstly refer to the positioning of RAPEX in the area of product safety in the EU, and at a later stage we

---

[76] European Medicines Agency (2019), p. 22.

[77] Administrative Agreement between the European Commission's Directorate-General for Justice and Consumers and the Department of Health of Canada on the exchange of information on the safety of non-food consumer products, <https://ec.europa.eu/info/sites/info/files/aa_final_en-eu_version.pdf>.

will outline the obligations that arise from the Arrangement and the legal effects in the EU legal order.

4.3.3.1   EU Background and Mechanisms on Product Safety

Product Safety is a pillar of the internal market, the cornerstone of the EU. To this end the EU has developed a sophisticated system through an elaborate framework of legislation, enforcement and other cooperation mechanisms of administrative nature, as is the Safety Gate Rapid Alert System formerly established as Community Rapid Information System, or RAPEX.

Product safety within the EU is guaranteed primarily by means of legislative texts that outline the regulatory requirements applicable for each non-food product. In that regard, the General Product Safety Regulation, which was published in the Official Journal on 23 May 2023 and will replace the current General Product Safety Directive 2001/95/EC of the European Parliament and of the Council of 3 December 2001 on general product safety as of 13 December 2024,[78] moves along horizontal lines and provides general safety requirements for non-food products that has a complementary function to sector specific, or relevant national legislation.[79] This horizontal focus is imposed due to the inability to provide legislation for every single product on the market, not only because of the variety but also because of the continuous development of market products. Other regulatory requirements can also be set the so called European Standards[80] that are product-specific and agreed upon by the Commission, the Member States and the relevant Committees by the EU standardisation bodies, CEN and CENELEC. In the absence of the above, other instruments such as national and international standards, guidelines or business practices and the current state of art might as well be used as substantive criteria.[81]

Product safety is further enhanced via the functioning of mechanisms that guarantee the conformity of the products with the regulatory requirements (by means of

---

[78] Article 52, Regulation (EU) 2023/988 of the European Parliament and of the Council of 10 May 2023 on general product safety, amending Regulation (EU) No 1025/2012 of the European Parliament and of the Council and Directive (EU) 2020/1828 of the European Parliament and the Council, and repealing Directive 2001/95/EC of the European Parliament and of the Council and Council Directive 87/357/EEC [2023], OJ L 135/1.

[79] Article 1, Directive 2001/95/EC of the European Parliament and of the Council of 3 December 2001 on general product safety [2002] OJ L 11/4.

[80] According to Article 10 §6 of Regulation 1025/2012 a standard becomes European when it gets published in the OJ, Regulation (EU) No 1025/2012 of the European Parliament and of the Council of 25 October 2012 on European standardisation, amending Council Directives 89/686/EEC and 93/15/EEC and Directives 94/9/EC, 94/25/EC, 95/16/EC, 97/23/EC, 98/34/EC, 2004/22/EC, 2007/23/EC, 2009/23/EC and 2009/105/EC of the European Parliament and of the Council and repealing Council Decision 87/95/EEC and Decision No 1673/2006/EC of the European Parliament and of the Council Text with EEA relevance [2012] OJ L 316/12.

[81] Article 3, Directive 2001/95/EC of the European Parliament and of the Council of 3 December 2001 on general product safety [2002] OJ L 11/4.

certificates issued by conformity assessment bodies). This coordinated enforcement system is set up under Regulation (EC) No 765/2008 on the requirements for accreditation and market surveillance relating to the marketing of products. This system, comprising a web of actors at various levels, ensures that, despite the decentralized conformity assessment, uniform application of the legislation is nevertheless guaranteed. The task of ensuring compliance with regulatory requirements belongs to the conformity assessment bodies. Once accredited by the relevant national authorities, on the basis of Articles 3–14 of Regulation no 765/2008, conformity assessment bodies can issue conformity certificates for products when the EU legislation so provides. The added value of these certificates lies in the validity of their statement, which is supported by their previous accreditation, demonstrating their technical competence to carry out these tasks.[82] They thus constitute important proof in the hands of the manufacturers that wish to authoritatively demonstrate the conformity of their products within the EU.

Additionally, EU legislation provides for other cooperation mechanisms of administrative nature, as is the Safety Gate Rapid Alert System, known as RAPEX, first established by the General Product Safety Directive 2001/95/EC and now designed under the new name Safety Gate Rapid Alert System and complemented by the new General Product Safety Regulation. The RAPEX mechanism facilitates the quick exchange of information when national authorities are confronted with a dangerous product, which takes place through notifications sent to a centralized system by a Member State and the subsequent reactions by other ones. In particular, according to the procedure outlined in Article 26 of General Product Safety Regulation, (and Article 12 of Directive 2001/95/EC) a Member State's primary task is to notify the Commission through the system of any measure taken by the national authorities or economic operators that affects the placing of the products on the market, which can range from a simple warning to withdrawal from the market.

Focusing on that cooperation mechanism, it is important to observe a chain effect after an initial entry in the system by a Member State. Indeed, according to Article 26 par. 5 of the General Product Safety Regulation (Article 12 par. 2 of the previous Directive) the Commission examines the legality of the measure upon reception and informs accordingly the other Member States, which may also react accordingly by notifying their own measures. Such a notification may concern as mentioned either a harmonized or non-harmonized product, as long as it falls under the said Regulation. Still, a reaction in line with the notifying member state, which may also impose withdrawal of a product is supported by the principles of mutual recognition and mutual trust between the EU authorities, developed in the context of the internal market.

---

[82] Preamble Point 9, Regulation (EC) No 765/2008 of the European Parliament and of the Council of 9 July 2008 setting out the requirements for accreditation and market surveillance relating to the marketing of products and repealing Regulation (EEC) No 339/93 [2008] OJ L 218/30.

The system extends also beyond EU borders. Indeed, the possibility for third countries to have access to the RAPEX is provided for in Article 12 par. 4 of Directive 2001/95/EC and is conditioned upon the negotiation of framework agreements between the EU and an interested third party that wishes to join. A relevant agreement with China is already in place.[83]

4.3.3.2   Legal Obligations Arising from the Administrative Arrangement

It is this extraterritorial extension towards which the Administrative Arrangement aims. Its scope and ambition are quite straightforward. While falling under the general discussion of non-food product safety, it only extends the regime of the RAPEX mechanism and of RADAR, the Canadian equivalent, by establishing a framework for cooperation between the two administrative entities in charge, Health Canada and DG JUST. The Arrangement is, as mentioned, mainly promulgated by Article 21.7 of CETA itself, but it is also clear that its conclusion is also allowed by existing EU legislation, Article 12 par. 4 of Directive 2001/95/EC (General Product Safety Directive), which indicates that the legal basis for its implementation exists in the EU legislation already.

When it comes to the legal nature of the Administrative Arrangement, in contrast to the Arrangements on Pharmaceuticals, this Administrative Arrangement does not acquire a legally binding character by virtue of its mandating provision. In comparison to the Administrative Arrangements on the cooperation on pharmaceuticals which are given legally binding force by virtue of the CETA Protocol, par. 4 of Article 21.7 of CETA, states that the parties *may* establish exchange of information. Thus, Article 21.7 only provides the possibility of its realisation, delegating the rest to be decided by means of a further instrument. More specifically, Article 21.7.5 of CETA informs us that the implementing measures that are to be concluded, namely what is now the Administrative Arrangement under question, has to be endorsed by the CETA Committee on Trade in Goods, before it becomes operational. And in fact, not long after the Arrangement's signature, during its first meeting, the CETA Committee on Trade in Goods did endorse the instrument.[84] This development makes us wonder whether this endorsement took the form of a Committee decision, and has become, on this capacity, binding on the parties.

In principle, according to Article 2.13, the Committee on Trade in Goods cannot take decisions by itself, it can only recommend to the CETA Joint Committee draft decisions on the acceleration or elimination of a customs duty on a good. However,

---

[83] EU Commission, 'Memorandum of understanding between DG SANCO and AQSIQ regarding the EU-China formal cooperation on product safety'—Last updated in 2010 <https://ec.europa.eu/info/sites/info/files/joint_statement_of_extention_of_mou_on_adm_coop_arrangements_between_sanco_aqsiq_en.pdf>.

[84] EU Commission (2019c).

this represents a specific case under Chapter 2, it does not preclude that the Committee has decision-making capacity on the basis of other CETA provisions. In fact, Article 21.7.5 is one of the occasions of Article 26.2.4 CETA, which suggests that the specialised Committees can take decisions also 'when the agreement so provides'. Although a relevant decision of the CETA Committee on Trade in Goods has not been published online, this does not cancel the nature of Article 21.7.5 CETA as one of instance of the Agreement giving a decision-making mandate, and cannot ground firmly an opposite view. In this regard, it has been demonstrated that the use of instruments of administrative nature can be introduced as substitute of what otherwise would qualify as decision in cases where neither primary nor secondary law provides for the use of a decision.[85]

This reading is supported by a couple of additional arguments. First of all, the immediate implementation of the Arrangement is a development in line with the need to comply with a legally binding commitment. Indeed, the Arrangement was agreed following CETA's provisional entry into force, and now it is fully operational,[86] according to the Commission officials that handle it. Moreover, such coordination is part of a greater market cohesion, hence, it would be odd to regulate such a mechanism of cooperation with third parties by means of an informal instrument, while for intra EU coordination, it is being regulated by a directive, mainly because of the formality that should accompany this activity. Article 12 par. 4 of directive 2001/95/EC provides some guidance. More specifically, this provision requires the possibility to open access to RAPEX to third countries and organisations, to be implemented by means of "agreements". While it is not entirely clear whether the term agreement refers to an international agreement, as in an international treaty, or to any type of agreement, as are the informal agreements, it is more probable that the former is the case, as an informal instrument could be described with different terminology. Other language versions apart from English are not more helpful on this. In principle, given the formality of the intra-EU mechanism, the provision should be understood as requiring a more formal structure, a reading which indeed confirms the legally binding character of the arrangement.

These legal obligations concretize the duty of institutional cooperation sought by the extension of the RAPEX and RADAR regimes. By regulating the framework of exchange of information, the margin of discretion of each administration is minimized. For example, the Arrangement mentions the scope and the type of information that will be shared to the other party. The type of information to be shared from the EU side, which is outlined in Annex II of the Arrangement concern products that are either harmonised at EU level or fall under Directive 2001/95/EC. Moreover, the parties, upon implementation of the technicalities are expected to initiate the exchange of information, as they have agreed to do so, by virtue of Article 5 of the Arrangement. The EU has thus agreed to provide to the Canadian counterparts

---

[85] Hofmann (2011), p. 652.

[86] According to the exchange of mails, the administrative and technical set-up followed shortly after the conclusion of the arrangement, and the arrangement is now fully operational.

the required information by means of an encrypted format, which will be available to a certain number of officials, if possible, on a daily basis.

It should be mentioned that the process of exchange of information in the case of this Administrative Arrangement, unlike the ones on pharmaceutical GMP, is constrained to the Commission. While it is the Member States as described that have the active role in the functioning of RAPEX, in the case of this bilateral cooperation it will be the EU Commission that will allow access to the Canadian administration, after the technical necessities are in place, according to Article 5 of the Arrangement. What effect is this kind of exchange of information likely to have in the free circulation of goods in the internal market? And how does the implementation of this cooperation mechanism fit with other legal and regulatory requirements in the EU legal order?

4.3.3.3   Legal Consequences Within the EU Legal Order

The above described procedures which result in this flow of information from the Canadian authorities to the EU Commission and vice-versa can potentially have tangible effects on the circulation of products in the internal market. For example, the arrival of a warning for a product found dangerous from the Canadian counterparts and the communication of measures taken against a certain product, according to Article 5 (b) of the Arrangement, could trigger also an investigation within the EU, and could lead to similar restrictions taking place in the internal market as well. This piece of information is not thus merely informative; the process follows the logic that RAPEX does internally. This has already been the case with the relevant RAPEX-China mechanism, where, upon receipt of a relevant notification and subsequent investigation, the relevant authorities may issue restrictions. The simple exchange of information certainly does not go hand in hand with the imposition of similar restrictions, but they provide the impetus for a similar reaction from the EU side.

Another issue refers to whether the current Administrative Arrangement as it stands indeed satisfies the EU confidentiality and data protection requirements, given its legally character and the fact that also such information could potentially be the subject of this mandatory cooperation. Of course, according to Article 7 of the Administrative Agreement, parties do not intend to exchange personal data, and if they do, they shall take the appropriate measures and inform immediately the other party. However, such an exchange can take place. Should we have a careful look to Annex II of the Administrative Arrangements that outlines the data fields that can be communicated to the other party, we observe that among other figure certain data of the manufacturer and exporter (Name, Address, City, Country) of a certain product. Since these data fields constitute personal data, the guarantees of the General Data Protection Regulation (hereinafter GDPR) should be upheld.

The Arrangement contains only provisions that inform about the applicability of the privacy and confidentiality laws of each legal order to the received information. Such statements are to be found in Articles 6(a), 6(d), 6(e), 8 (b) and 8(g) of the

Arrangement. From a first look, these assurances could be considered as satisfying the requirement stipulated in Article 12 par. 4 of directive 2001/95/EC, which explicitly mentions the presence of specific provisions. However, what is absent from the Arrangement is a tool that guarantees the adequacy of the level of data protection between the EU and Canada, as a precondition for the legality of the transfer of data to a third country pursuant to Article 44 ff. of Regulation (EU) 2016/679 (hereinafter GDPR).[87]

And even though an adequacy decision of the Commission with regard to the Canadian '*Personal Information and Electronic Documents Act*' already exists,[88] it must be noted that it was rendered pursuant to EU Data Protection Directive 95/46/EC,[89] which was replaced by the GDPR. Given that the GDPR has introduced significant changes in comparison to the previous legal regime,[90] this adequacy decision is, to a certain extent, outdated. Moreover, Article 12 §4 of 2001/95/EC refers to the presence of provisions within the Agreement. This means that such an adequacy guarantee should be part of either CETA or the arrangement itself, by means of an annexed decision to CETA or by means of the so-called model clauses to the Arrangement itself. Absent such an adequacy guarantee until today, any exchange of personal data will take place outside a protective framework, a practice that comes in direct contrast to the internal regime.

4.4   The Effects of Regulatory Dialogue and the Commission's Right of Initiative

This section will discuss the legal effects of regulatory dialogue, based on three areas that have been matter of Regulatory Cooperation at the CETA level, namely cooperation on pesticides in the context of a legislative revision, regulatory dialogue on the safety of non-food products and 'cosmetic-like' drug products. The case studies shall demonstrate that the legal effects go beyond exchange of information and are able to generate concessions from either of the parties, which are in need of legislative activity.

---

[87] Regulation (EU) 2016/679 of the European Parliament and of the Council of 27 April 2016 on the protection of natural persons with regard to the processing of personal data and on the free movement of such data, and repealing Directive 95/46/EC (General Data Protection Regulation) (Text with EEA relevance) [2016] OJ L 119/1.

[88] 2002/2/EC: Commission Decision of 20 December 2001 pursuant to Directive 95/46/EC of the European Parliament and of the Council on the adequate protection of personal data provided by the Canadian Personal Information Protection and Electronic Documents Act (notified under document number C(2001) 4539) [2002] OJ L 2/13.

[89] Directive 95/46/EC of the European Parliament and of the Council of 24 October 1995 on the protection of individuals with regard to the processing of personal data and on the free movement of such data [1995] OJ L 281/31.

[90] *See* generally Tikkinen-Piri et al. (2018).

Others could argue though that, although being a legal commitment, Regulatory Cooperation Chapters have many escape clauses, thus, there is ground to argue that regulatory dialogue can remain just that. Indeed, its degree of influence on future or existing regulatory initiatives remains an uncharted territory, which is difficult to map if not specifically mentioned. This is particularly true for areas of cooperation that still do not present concrete results. For example, cooperation on cybersecurity certification for IoT devices has also been dominated by regulatory dialogue, mainly because both jurisdictions have recently introduced relevant regulatory measures, the EU cybersecurity act[91] and Canada's Digital Charter, still in progress.[92] In this case, cooperation was restricted to only informing the counterpart on the progress made internally.

Strictly looking into the EU universe, these discussions narrow down to the degree of commitment this regulatory dialogue entails and how it might interfere with the Commission's right of initiative and more generally, with the EU's regulatory freedom. The following paragraphs delve into the description of the ongoing dialogue and current development in order to guide the discussion more generally to the interaction of Regulatory Cooperation with Commission's right of initiative.

4.4.1 Changes in EU Legislation: Market Surveillance Regulation

This example builds upon the analysis made in Sect. 4.3.3 and the Administrative Arrangement on the exchange of information on the safety of non-food consumer products. While the obligation to report in the RAPEX system under Directive 2001/95/EC covers products irrespectively of their status of harmonization and thus extends to every competent member state authority, it is further concretized by being addressed particularly to market surveillance authorities, which may use the platform to communicate the specific measures they are entitled to take themselves regarding harmonized dangerous products. This extension takes place by virtue of Article 20 of Regulation (EC) No 765/2008, and more recently by virtue of Article

---

[91] Regulation (EU) 2019/881 of the European Parliament and of the Council of 17 April 2019 on ENISA (the European Union Agency for Cybersecurity) and on information and communications technology cybersecurity certification and repealing Regulation (EU) No 526/2013 (Cybersecurity Act) [2019] *OJ L 151/15*.

[92] Government of Canada, 'Canada's Digital Charter in Action: A plan for Canadians by Canadians' (2019) <https://www.ic.gc.ca/eic/site/062.nsf/vwapj/Digitalcharter_Report_EN.pdf/$file/Digitalcharter_Report_EN.pdf>.

20 of Regulation (EU) 2019/1020, the new market surveillance Regulation, which entered into force in 2021.[93]

Indeed, the revision of the market surveillance regulation, which is, as mentioned one of the main legislative texts in the EU legal environment for product safety followed only a few months after the signed administrative agreement. The more pertinent addition was Article 35 on International Cooperation, a provision which did not exist in the previous version of the Regulation. This is merely a coincidence. To begin with, trade as a driver behind the rationale for the revision is mentioned in the relevant Commission preparatory document: "Regarding global trade, the Commission reaffirmed its policy based on openness and cooperation".[94] Moreover, a Commission official presented this development as the implementation of the commitments undertaken under the Regulatory Cooperation Chapters.[95] Last but not least, the content of Article 35 par. 1 and 2 comes to support this interpretation. The first two paragraphs of Article 35 of the Regulation provide for the possibility for the Commission to exchange market surveillance information with regulatory authorities of third parties regarding: (a) risk assessment methods used and the results of product-testing; (b) coordinated product recalls or other similar actions; (c) the measures taken by market surveillance authorities under Article 16.

It could thus be argued that the provision of the possibility to establish cooperation and information exchange mechanisms similar to the one for RAPEX also for market surveillance authorities follows to a great extent the cooperation regime of the administrative arrangement. This generally comes in line with the EU reality, which foresees the extension of the RAPEX mechanism to information shared between market surveillance authorities. The inclusion of this possibility in the Regulation will probably work as a legal basis for a future bilateral regime, which will concern the market surveillance authorities in particular. Such a regime could neither be based on Article 21.7 CETA whose content was very specific to the primary function of RAPEX, nor on the previous market surveillance regulation. Given however that market surveillance is equally crucial for ensuring product safety, it is logical that exchange of information could be useful also with regard to these activities.

---

[93] Article 44, Regulation (EU) 2019/1020 of the European Parliament and of the Council of 20 June 2019 on market surveillance and compliance of products and amending Directive 2004/42/EC and Regulations (EC) No 765/2008 and (EU) No 305/2011 [2019] OJ L 169/1.

[94] Proposal for a Regulation of the European Parliament and of the Council laying down rules and procedures for compliance with and enforcement of Union harmonisation legislation on products and amending Regulations (EU) No 305/2011, (EU) No 528/2012, (EU) 2016/424, (EU) 2016/425, (EU) 2016/426 and (EU) 2017/1369 of the European Parliament and of the Council, and Directives 2004/42/EC, 2009/48/EC, 2010/35/EU, 2013/29/EU, 2013/53/EU, 2014/28/EU, 2014/29/EU, 2014/30/EU, 2014/31/EU, 2014/32/EU, 2014/33/EU, 2014/34/EU, 2014/35/EU, 2014/53/EU, 2014/68/EU and 2014/90/EU of the European Parliament and of the Council, Brussels, 19.12.2017 COM(2017) 795 final 2017/0353 (COD).

[95] Commission Official, Internal meeting with third party counterparts.

4.4.2   Cooperation on Pesticides: Undermining the Precautionary Principle

Another European example on the possible influence regulatory dialogue can have on the Commission's decision-making, and especially on the application of precautionary principle to the latter, is the case of cooperation on pesticides, more specifically on the presence of maximum residue level (hereinafter MRLs) of particular dangerous pesticides at or on imported food, under the premises of Chapter 5 of CETA on SPS measures an area which is also subject of the Regulatory Cooperation Chapter, according to Article 21.1 CETA. The EU ban on such particular pesticides has always been a matter of criticism not only from trading partners but also from big lobbying corporations, with the saga dating back to 2017.[96] More recently, a greater incentive by big industry players and Canada to put even more pressure on the revision of particular aspects of the regime was given during the course of revision of two key Regulations under the Regulatory Fitness and Performance Programme (hereinafter REFIT) of the EU aiming to keep EU legislation under constant evaluation in order to make sure that it keeps fulfilling its original goal in view of new developments and constant evaluations.

The Regulations under question are Regulation 1107/2009[97] concerning the placing of plant protection products (hereinafter PPP) on the market and Regulation 396/2005[98] on MRLs of pesticides in or on food and feed of plant and animal origin. The two regulations are complementary: on the one hand, Regulation 1107/2009 sets out the procedure for the authorization of active substances in the EU and the procedure for the authorization of PPP in the Member States, covering in other words, the risk assessment part. This Regulation relies upon the precautionary principle and sets as the main criterion for non-approval the identification of hazard properties of substances classified as carcinogenic, endocrine disruptors, mutagenic, or reproductive toxins, regulating on the basis of hazard-based approach. If a substance does not meet the cut-off criteria, then its authorization depends on the usual risk-assessment. Similarly, the discussion on MRLs concerns the tolerance of residue levels of such active substances on and in food. Regulation 396/2005 operationalizes the risk management part of the authorization procedure regulated

---

[96]Holland (2020).

[97]Regulation (EC) No 1107/2009 of the European Parliament and of the Council of 21 October 2009 concerning the placing of plant protection products on the market and repealing Council Directives 79/117/EEC and 91/414/EEC [2009] OJ L 309/1.

[98]Regulation (EC) No 396/2005 of the European Parliament and of the Council of 23 February 2005 on maximum residue levels of pesticides in or on food and feed of plant and animal origin and amending Council Directive 91/414/EEC Text with EEA relevance [2005] OJ L 70/1.

by 1107/2009.[99] Once an active substance is judged as hazardous, the tolerance for maximum level of residue is automatically brought to the Limit of Detection (hereinafter LOD).[100]

It is particularly this complication and how it would reflect to imported goods that was at the epicentre of the consultations of big industries and trade partners with the EU Commission. Essentially, the question boiled down to whether imported goods containing residues of toxic pesticides would be allowed in the EU market, or would be completely banned. Normally, the letter of the law, which dictates a LOD residue level to all substances meeting the cut-off criteria, should apply to all goods alike, independently of their origin. This was originally the stance of the EU Commission. However, according to leaked documents provided by the NGO Corporate Europe, it was demonstrated that this option found great resistance from big industry players as well as Canada, the moment CETA came into force, as such a choice would restrict significantly international trade, being in direct opposition to WTO commitments as well.[101]

Leaked documents provided by another civil society actor, the Council of Canadians suggest that Canada has expressed its concerns about this pesticide regime more than once and in a more general context. In fact, Regulation 1107/2009 has been one of the long-term targets of the Canadian side. Indeed, according to one of them: *"The long term goal for the EU is to move away from a hazard-based cut-off criteria as a basis for regulatory decisions"* and that *"The European Union's implementation of a hazard-based regulatory decision making requirements under Regulation 1107/2009 (concerning the placing on the market of PPP), threatens the continued market access of Canadian exports of agricultural commodities valued at over $2.7 million dollars CAD annually"*.[102]

By exposing the magnitude of the pressure exerted to the Commission during its bilateral meetings and general discussion since the entry into force of CETA, and also from external actors, the same source arrived to confirm that in this context it has started to abandon the original plan and move towards a more risk-based rather than a hazard abased approach. Concretely, it referred to a statement by Commissioner Andriukaitis, with which he opted to allow a risk assessment for the purposes of setting MRLs and import tolerances for products containing hazardous pesticides. Hence, while according to a hazard-based approach, the Commission regulates on the basis of the intrinsic properties of the substances, without taking account of the data on the exposure to the substance, this is not the case of the risk-based approach,

---

[99] Stoll et al. (2016), p. 9.

[100] When one substance is authorised under the PPP Regulation, then an MRL value can be set and added in the Annexes of the Regulation. This means that the active substances that are not included in the Annexes of the MRL Regulation, are not authorised, for example because they meet the cut-off criteria. For all substances not included in those Annexes, the LOD is set to 0.01 mg/kg.

[101] Holland (2020).

[102] Foodwatch (2020), p. 4.

where the inherent danger of a substance will be judged also upon the effects of a potential exposure.[103]

And indeed, the REFIT evaluation does in fact indicate the fact that the Commission allows for a risk assessment for the purposes of setting MRLs and import tolerances for products containing hazardous pesticides, while it does not allow so internally.

The REFIT evaluation is indicative of the regulatory pressure exerted by the specific interest group and Canada on the issue of import tolerances of hazardous substances according to risk assessment criteria. It essentially abandons the initial stance of the Commission that supported the complete deletion of MRLs for substances considered hazardous. Instead, the evaluation explicitly mentions repeatedly that third country interested parties can submit an import tolerance for substances for which no MRL exists, because there is no use in the EU. One reason why there is no use of a substance in the EU is that it can be judged as hazardous, and hence discontinued. Nevertheless, also in those cases, external operators are allowed to ask for an import tolerance. The REFIT evaluation reads in that regard:

> There was a need to recognise that different agricultural practices outside the EU led to different residue levels on imported products. This meant there was a need to set import tolerances for imported products provided they were safe for consumers.[104]

> Provided they are judged safe for EU consumers, MRLs corresponding to CXLs based on uses in non-EU countries are not deleted, nor are MRLs that had been specifically set as import tolerances.[105]

> There is criticism from stakeholders, farmers and the public that farmers in the EU face unfair competition compared to non-EU countries, because import tolerances can be set for active substances that are not approved in the EU. Farmers in non-EU countries can then use plant protection products (hereinafter PPPs) that are not available to EU farmers while still exporting to the EU, decreasing the competitiveness of EU agriculture and exporting the risks associated with the use of those PPPs to other countries.[106]

---

[103] European Commission (2016).

[104] EU Commission, 'COMMISSION STAFF WORKING DOCUMENT Accompanying the document REPORT FROM THE COMMISSION TO THE EUROPEAN PARLIAMENT AND THE COUNCIL Evaluation of Regulation (EC) No 1107/2009 on the placing of plant protection products on the market and of Regulation (EC) No 396/2005 on maximum residue levels of pesticides' {COM(2020) 208 final}, Brussels, 20.5.2020 SWD(2020) 87 final, p. 14.

[105] EU Commission, 'COMMISSION STAFF WORKING DOCUMENT Accompanying the document REPORT FROM THE COMMISSION TO THE EUROPEAN PARLIAMENT AND THE COUNCIL Evaluation of Regulation (EC) No 1107/2009 on the placing of plant protection products on the market and of Regulation (EC) No 396/2005 on maximum residue levels of pesticides' {COM(2020) 208 final}, Brussels, 20.5.2020 SWD(2020) 87 final, p. 20.

[106] EU Commission, 'COMMISSION STAFF WORKING DOCUMENT Accompanying the document REPORT FROM THE COMMISSION TO THE EUROPEAN PARLIAMENT AND THE COUNCIL Evaluation of Regulation (EC) No 1107/2009 on the placing of plant protection products on the market and of Regulation (EC) No 396/2005 on maximum residue levels of pesticides' {COM(2020) 208 final}, Brussels, 20.5.2020 SWD(2020) 87 final, p. 49.

The trade friendly stance of the evaluation does not end there. It goes on to recognize problems faced by the third parties when asking for import tolerances and proposes solutions. More concretely, once a substance is found to be hazardous, and its authorization is revoked under the PPP Regulation, the Commission prepares a measure to revoke any existing MRL.[107] When this is done, WTO members are informed via the SPS procedure. In that regard, trade partners complained that "*the time in which they can react is insufficient to prepare an import tolerance application to prevent the lowering of the MRL.*"[108] The Commission, instead of preventing this from happening on the basis of the precautionary principle, decided instead to help trade partners in their task to challenge MRL revisions, by preparing a Communication[109] outlining the overall MRL review process and listing the active substances for which an MRL review is planned.

The trade friendly stance is further reflected in the REFIT evaluation. Apart from constantly reminding how the lowering of MRLs is burdensome procedurally to trade partners and susceptible to creating trade barriers, the evaluation also pointed to the bigger problem at stake, the cut-off criteria. It recalled how the compatibility of the cut-off criteria with the EU's international obligations is raised all the more frequently and in various fora.[110] It also made a connection between the lowering of MRLs due to non-approval decisions and the creation of barriers to trade. This statement implicitly points to the precautionary principle as the reason behind the creation of these trade barriers.[111]

As it now stands, this approach has the following consequences. On the one hand, from a legal perspective, it equals to an abandonment of the precautionary principle for imported products containing residues of hazardous pesticides, as the LOD does not automatically apply, but rather a risk assessment takes place, as if the cut-off criteria are not met (except that they are). On the other hand, it implies an unequal treatment of imported and EU originated products, with different, more stringent standards imposed for the latter.

---

[107] EU Commission, 'COMMISSION STAFF WORKING DOCUMENT Accompanying the document REPORT FROM THE COMMISSION TO THE EUROPEAN PARLIAMENT AND THE COUNCIL Evaluation of Regulation (EC) No 1107/2009 on the placing of plant protection products on the market and of Regulation (EC) No 396/2005 on maximum residue levels of pesticides' {COM(2020) 208 final}, Brussels, 20.5.2020 SWD(2020) 87 final, p. 18.

[108] EU Commission, 'COMMISSION STAFF WORKING DOCUMENT Accompanying the document REPORT FROM THE COMMISSION TO THE EUROPEAN PARLIAMENT AND THE COUNCIL Evaluation of Regulation (EC) No 1107/2009 on the placing of plant protection products on the market and of Regulation (EC) No 396/2005 on maximum residue levels of pesticides' {COM(2020) 208 final}, Brussels, 20.5.2020 SWD(2020) 87 final, p. 55.

[109] Committee on Sanitary and Phytosanitary Measures, Communication from the European Union, On-going review of maximum residue levels of pesticides in the European Union (G/SPS/GEN/1494/Rev.1).

[110] EU Commission (2020), p. 17.

[111] EU Commission (2020), p. 26.

4.4.3   Changes in Canadian Legislation: 'Cosmetic-Like' Drug Products

Among the first regulatory discussions were the ones on 'cosmetic-like' drug products, a specific category of products whose particularity lies in their double character: their primary function is to serve a medical purpose, to protect or treat, while also their marketing resembles products of pure cosmetic nature. Due to their primary function however, they must meet additional criteria of health and safety. Throughout the regulatory dialogue, Canada aims to "increase regulatory harmonisation with the EU" regarding some of the products of this type, which are mainly of low risk and for which medical prescription is not necessary.[112]

Regulatory discussion has already been narrowed down to certain categories of products, namely sunscreen products, antidandruff products and toothpastes and already since February 2019 Canada has exempted imported EU sunscreen products from retesting and quarantine before entering the Canadian market.[113] In fact, by exempting EU products from these requirements, Canada extended its Expanded Sunscreen Pilot Project. Canada had initiated this project in order to except from these requirements of sunscreen products imported from countries which had in place similar GMP, and with which relevant MRAs were in place.[114] Some legislative amendments were for this purpose necessary.

What is more interesting though is the fact that apart from the Exemption Pilot Project, Canada prepares a greater category of regulatory amendments targeting the Food and Drug Regulations. The latter are currently undergoing amendments in order to include clauses on exemptions for certain low risk 'cosmetic-like' drug products, in order to relieve importers and manufacturers from what has always been considered as an irritant.[115] According to the updated workplan of the CETA RCF, these amendments will further exempt from re-testing and quarantine other EU low risk drug products. The regime will also concern countries that have comparable GMP programmes to Canada. We thus observe internal regulatory activity, which according to the Canadian Ministry, builds upon the commitments made by Health Canada under the Canada-US RCC to decrease regulatory barriers regarding non-prescription drugs. The same commitment was also made in the CETA RCF, as we mentioned above. Thus, we can now with certainty state that regulatory dialogue can and does trigger internal regulatory amendments.

On the basis of this and of the previous analysis on Regulatory Cooperation on GMP (see Sect. 4.3.2), we can extract the complementarity of the cooperation activities. Indeed, the CETA Protocol on Pharmaceuticals as well as the implementing Administrative Agreements aim to establish recognition of

---

[112] EU Commission (2019a), p. 5.

[113] EU Commission (2019a), p. 5.

[114] Government of Canada (2019).

[115] Government of Canada (2019).

equivalence of GMP between the two orders. The main facilitation of this initiative concerned the import of pharmaceutical products from certified manufacturers. However, it seems that, since it implicates a recognition of equivalence of GMP in general, it will also provide the ground for the planned exemptions to apply.

4.5 Conclusion

The examination of the Regulatory Cooperation results on the basis of the available documents and corresponding internal legislation demonstrated their ability to produce concrete legal effects in the EU legal order.

With regard to Regulatory Cooperation on GMP on Pharmaceuticals, we can primarily ground the observed legal consequences to the binding character that the implementing Administrative Arrangements acquire by virtue of the CETA Protocol on Pharmaceuticals, which regulate in binding terms the determination of equivalence of the NRAs, a procedure which creates several rights and obligations for the implicated parties. However, since the latter do not figure as signatories of the Agreement, but the regime nevertheless extends to them, some implementing regulatory action will be needed on each national level. Member States are further called to abide, not only on the basis of their constitutional mandate for sincere cooperation and for implementation of international commitments but also because of the importance of the equivalence procedure, which aims to provide a trade advantage for pharmaceutical manufacturers at a later stage.

With regard to the Administrative Arrangement on the exchange of information on non-food product safety, its main legal effect is the concretization of obligations that will enable the initiation of an external cooperation activity through the extension of the RAPEX regime to the Canadian counterparts. This activity, apart from the procedure, shares also the aim of the original RAPEX mechanism, which extends to the quicker identification of dangerous products and the faster response through appropriate measures. This however means that the exchange of information through this mechanism can in theory provide the basis for measures that impact the circulation of products within the internal market, a legal effect that is not produced from the arrangement as such, but rather as a consequence of its functioning and implementation.

As for the regulatory dialogue, concrete effects can be traced to substantial regulatory additions or regulatory revisions. The effects refer to amendments and additions to the regulatory plans of each side. In the EU, each regulatory amendment or addition can be traced back to the Commission's right of initiative. Thus, the overarching question refers mostly to the compatibility of the regulatory dialogue with the Commission's right of initiative. The findings of the chapter suggest that, while input from the Regulatory Cooperation dialogues falls under the broader requirement of Stakeholders' Consultation during the regulatory process, this compatibility cannot be absolute. Rather, it has to respect in procedural and substantive terms, the Commission's independence. However, the influence exerted upon the

Commission in order to abandon the precautionary principle from the pesticide regulation does not seem to respect this boundary.

The issues that follow after the study of concrete effects relate to constitutional considerations. Are the produced legal effects in line with legitimacy exigencies of instruments that usually produce such kind of effects in the EU legal order? Does the conclusion of the bilateral agreements in the form of Administrative Arrangement respect the constitutional guarantees that external decision-making demands according to EU treaties standards? And more generally, what are the limits to the use of Administrative Arrangements in light of their content and the competences of the Commission? Which constitutional issues arise from the illegal disregard of the Commission's independence from its trading partners through regulatory dialogue? And which rules set the limits to the interaction between regulatory initiatives and third country input? Based on the findings of this chapter, the next one will focus on answering all these questions, and more, following a constitutional approach.

References

EEAS (2017) National Institutes for Culture and EU to further enhance cooperation. https://eeas.europa.eu/headquarters/headquarters-homepage/26249/national-institutes-culture-and-eu-further-enhance-cooperation_en

EU Commission (2011) EudraLex - volume 4 - GMP (GMP) guidelines. https://ec.europa.eu/health/documents/eudralex/vol-4_en

EU Commission (2018) Meeting of The Joint Sectoral Group (JSG) of the protocol to the CETA between the European Union (EU) and Canada on the mutual recognition of the compliance and enforcement programs regarding GMPS (GMP) for pharmaceutical products. https://trade.ec.europa.eu/doclib/docs/2018/december/tradoc_157566.pdf

EU Commission (2019a) Comprehensive economic and trade agreement RCF work plan. https://trade.ec.europa.eu/doclib/docs/2019/june/tradoc_157952.pdf

EU Commission (2019b) Report of the 1st Meeting of the CERA RCF December 14, 2018. https://trade.ec.europa.eu/doclib/docs/2019/february/tradoc_157679.pdf. Accessed 19 Mar 2020

EU Commission (2019c) Report of the Meeting of the Trade in Goods Committee, 29 November 2018 (by videoconference). https://trade.ec.europa.eu/doclib/docs/2019/april/tradoc_157818.pdf

EU Commission (2020) REPORT FROM THE COMMISSION TO THE EUROPEAN PARLIAMENT AND THE COUNCIL: evaluation of Regulation (EC) No 1107/2009 on the placing of plant protection products on the market and of Regulation (EC) No 396/2005 on maximum residue levels of pesticides. https://eur-lex.europa.eu/legal-content/EN/TXT/PDF/?uri=CELEX:52020DC0208&from=EN

European Commission (2016) Frequently asked questions: endocrine disruptors. https://ec.europa.eu/commission/presscorner/detail/en/MEMO_16_2151

European Medicines Agency (2019) From laboratory to patient: the journey of a medicine assessed by EMA. https://www.ema.europa.eu/en/documents/other/laboratory-patient-journey-centrally-authorised-medicine_en.pdf

European Medicines Agency (2023) Mutual recognition agreements. https://www.ema.europa.eu/en/human-regulatory/research-development/compliance/good-manufacturing-practice/mutual-recognition-agreements-mra

Foodwatch (2020) Leaked documents of the CETA SPS Committee. https://www.foodwatch.org/fileadmin/-NL/Toelichting_documenten.pdf

Government of Canada (2019) Forward Regulatory Plan 2019-2021: regulations amending the food and drug regulations (finished product testing). https://www.canada.ca/en/health-canada/corporate/about-health-canada/legislation-guidelines/acts-regulations/forward-regulatory-plan/plan/food-drug-regulations-testing-requirements-certain-categories-imported-finished-prod ucts.html

Hofmann H (2011) Administrative agreements. In: Hofmann H, Rowe G, Türk A (eds) Administrative law and policy of the European Union. Oxford University Press, Oxford, pp 651–666

Holland N (2020) Toxic residues through the back door: pesticide corporations and trade partners pressured EU to allow banned substances in imported crops. Corporate Europe 2020. https://corporateeurope.org/en/2020/02/toxic-residues-through-back-door

Kalomeni K (2020) Proliferation of PTAs and EU trade policy: a functionalist approach to regulatory cooperation design variation, lessons drawn from CETA. Unpublished PhD thesis, Thesis in co-supervision Universite Laval, Canada and University LUISS Guido Carli, Italy, p 182

Lancos P (2018) A hard core under the soft shell: how binding is union soft law for Member States. Eur Public Law 24:755–784

Mohay A (2017) The status of international agreements concluded by the European Union in the EU legal order. Pravni Vjesnik 33:151–164

Morrison F (2007) Executive agreements. In: Wolfrum R (ed) Max Planck Encyclopedia of Public International Law. https://opil.ouplaw.com/view/10.1093/law:epil/9780199231690/law-97801 99231690-e1403

Ott A (2016) The European Parliament's role in EU Treaty-making. Maastricht J Eur Int Law 23: 1009–1039

Ott A (2018) The EU Commission's administrative agreements: "Delegated treaty-making" in between delegated and implementing rule-making. In: Weiss W, Tauschinsky E (eds) The legislative choice between delegated and implementing acts in EU law: walking a Labyrinth. Edward Elgar, Cheltenham, pp 200–232

Pauwelyn J (2012) Is it international law or not, and does it even matter? In: Pawuelyn J, Wessel R, Wouters J (eds) Informal international law making. Oxford University Press, Oxford, pp 125–161

Peters A (2011) Soft law as a new mode of governance. In: Diedrichs U, Reiners W, Wessels W (eds) The dynamics of change in EU governance. Edward Elgar, Cheltenham, pp 21–52

Peters A, Pagotto I (2006) Soft law as a new mode of governance: a legal perspective. NEWGOV: New Modes of Governance. https://ssrn.com/abstract=1668531

Senden L (2004) Soft law in European community law. Hart Publishing, London

Sieber Gasser C (2016) TTIP and Swiss democracy. In Bungenberg M, Herrmann C, Krajewski M, Terhechte JP (esd) European yearbook of international economic law 2016. Springer, Cham, pp. 557-571

Sloan B (1987) General assembly resolutions revisited (forty years later). Br Yearb Int Law 58:39–150

Stefan O (2012) European Union soft law: new developments concerning the divide between legally binding force and legal effects. Mod Law Rev 75:879–893

Stefan O (2013) Soft law in court: competition law, state aid and the Court of Justice of the European Union. Kluwer, the Hague

Stefan O, Avbelj M, Eliantonio M, Hartlapp M, Korkea-aho E, Rubio N (2019) EU soft law in the EU legal order: a literature review. https://papers.ssrn.com/sol3/papers.cfm?abstract_id=334 6629

Steinbach A (2017) EU liability and international economic law. Hart Publishing, Oxford

Stoll P, Douma W, de Sadeleer N, Abel P (2016) CETA, TTIP and the EU precautionary principle: legal analysis of selected parts of the draft CETA agreement and the EU TTIP proposals. Foodwatch International. https://www.foodwatch.org/fileadmin/Themen/TTIP_Freihandel/Dokumente/2016-06-21_foodwatch-study_precautionary-principle.pdf

Tikkinen-Piri C, Rohunen A, Markkula J (2018) EU General Data Protection Regulation: changes and implications for personal data collecting companies. Comput Law Secur Rev 34:134–153

Wessel R (2018) 'Soft' international agreements in EU external relations: pragmatism over principles? Draft paper, presented at the ECPR SGEU conference, Panel Hard and Soft Law in the European Union, Paris 13–15 June 2018. https://ecpr.eu/Filestore/PaperProposal/f1f2a338-11 f1-44b8-81d8-034f29099c28.pdf

WHO (2018) GMP. https://www.who.int/biologicals/vaccines/good_manufacturing_practice/en/.a

Chapter 5
Legitimacy of Regulatory Cooperation Activities

5.1 Introduction

The results analysed in the previous chapter are not to be considered as a surprise, given the Legalization of the Regulatory Cooperation that took place, as described in Chap. 3. Indeed, the trade partners put their commitments into practice early on, demonstrating varying results in different areas. However, this procedure, and more particularly its operationalization throughout the Regulatory Cooperation Fora and the interaction of the latter with the EU legal order is certainly something novel that merits attention from a constitutional point of view.

Certainly, these results are only the first of the many to come, which means, that we cannot have a crystal clear view of their potential. However, they provide a good basis for the dialogue to open. This chapter opens indeed this discussion. Under these circumstances, it focuses its questions of constitutionality on the existing *modus operandi* of contemporary Regulatory Cooperation, more specifically on the issuing results, as described in Chap. 4. Indeed, the first section of the previous chapter, based on the provided Commission reports and agendas analysed in detail the substance and form of the activities of the RCF and the two administrations so far. We observed that, the administrative arrangements, although deprived on paper from any legally binding force, are in fact legally binding agreements, either by virtue of their delegating provision or by means of a Committee decision. Also, it was shown that the regulatory dialogue and the commitments made on that occasion may in fact have a far reaching effect on the content of existing or future legislative developments.

This chapter will thus zoom into these developments and will examine their legitimacy from a constitutional law point of view, having the EU Treaties as a benchmark. On the basis of the findings it will made suggestions that are in line with EU exigencies of democracy. Section 5.2 explains how legitimacy shall be treated in the chapter and sketches the conceptual framework. The choice of conceptual

© The Author(s), under exclusive license to Springer Nature Switzerland AG 2024
K. Pipidi-Kalogirou, *Regulatory Cooperation Chapters in the new Generation FTAS*, EYIEL Monographs - Studies in European and International Economic Law 36, https://doi.org/10.1007/978-3-031-71900-4_5

framework is as comprehensive as to allow for the examination of legitimacy gaps during all the stages of this decision-making, before, during and after the adoption of the Regulatory Cooperation results. It does so by using a tripartite concept of legitimacy that is split into input, output and throughput, each of which is connected to constitutional rules about decision-making. Section 5.3 examines the use of informal administrative arrangements under the lenses of input legitimacy and makes proposals on institutional participation in their conclusion. Section 5.4 puts the results of regulatory dialogue under the microscope of output legitimacy, while Sect. 5.5 highlights the absence of a legal framework regarding guiding values and due-process procedures, referring directly to the added value of throughput legitimacy mechanisms to the improvement of legitimacy of Regulatory Cooperation results. Section 5.6 refers to possible legal tools that could accommodate the proposals made throughout the chapter to enhance legitimacy shortcomings. Section 5.7 concludes.

5.2 A Conceptual Framework

According to public law theory, the legality of an administrative act can be judged upon its external characteristics as well as on substantial matters. To the external characteristics belong issues such as the suitability of the act's form, or the competence of the administrative body to issue it. As far as the substantial matters are concerned, the control moreover extends to internal aspects of the act, namely on the one hand the *interna corporis* of the administrative body to which the process followed each time to issue the act belongs and on the other hand the conformity of the content of the act with substantial norms. A positive finding of the above confirms the total conformity of the acts to the legal regime which foresees them, and their conformity to constitutional requirements, since legality is firstly, a constitutional principle.[1]

By applying this framework, this chapter will thus analyze the compatibility of the Regulatory Cooperation results with the administrative rules that generally govern EU decision-making, in the internal and external action combined, in order to see to what extent they live up to the relevant EU standards. For this, it will employ a tripartite analysis based on the concept of legitimacy as the latter has been developed by Vivien Schmidt. Building upon Fritz Scharpf's classic distinction of legitimacy into input and output,[2] Vivien Schmidt assesses the legitimacy of EU action against an additional normative criterion which she names throughput legitimacy.[3] In the following parts, we shall outline our understanding of the different aspects of legitimacy. We shall also particularly explain the considerations on the

---

[1]Dyzenhaus et al. (2001), p. 6.

[2]Scharpf (1970).

[3]Schmidt (2013).

basis of which we include throughput legitimacy in our study and we choose to abstain from the classic distinction between input and output, as well as why this type of legitimacy applies to Regulatory Cooperation.

5.2.1 Input and Output Legitimacy

Input legitimacy, a widely accepted factor for legitimacy, refers to the question of who takes the decisions and how they represent participation '*by* the people'.[4] In other words, it answers the question to whom have the people given the competence to make which decisions. To frame it under the general public law theory, questions belong to the constitutional control of the external characteristics of the Administrative Agreements. In EU decision-making terms, input legitimacy refers to the type of instrument used as well as the Institutions that are participating in the various decision-making processes and their corresponding capacity.

In Regulatory Cooperation the choice of Administrative Arrangements comes with several consequences that raise questions of input legitimacy, such as whether the choice of the specific legal tool is correct as well as the Commission's competence to employ it. Indeed, is the use of these informal instruments in line with their produced legal effects, as described in the previous chapter, or should they better be part of a formal agreement? If so, on what legal basis? To what extent differ informal over formal international agreements and what consequences does the choice of the former over the latter entail for democratic legitimacy? In order to map the legal character of the agreements in normative terms, we shall be based upon the findings of the previous chapter and legal constitutional literature on Article 218 TFEU. The answer to this question is necessary to answer the next question, which concentrates upon the competence of the Commission to sign this category of agreements on its own according to the powers it has by virtue of the Lisbon Treaties without violating the institutional balance and separation of powers, structural principles of EU external relations law.[5] We are thus treating two separate questions, one referring to the legality of the instrument, and the other being the competence of the Commission, which, when seen together can give a comprehensive response on whether these informal agreements are in line with EU's input legitimacy requirements for the content they introduce.

Output legitimacy focuses instead on what has been agreed, what the outcome is and what its value is "*for* the people".[6] It thus refers among others to the values that are promoted within the results themselves, and whether they correspond to the

---

[4] Scharpf (2003), p. 3.

[5] The term 'structural principles' is borrowed by Marise Cremona's book title. Institutional Balance and Conferral are examined as examples of structural principles in EU External Relations Law at the chapter by Christophe Hillion. *See* Hillion (2018).

[6] Schmidt (2013), pp. 10ff.

law-maker's promises.[7] The search for a normative benchmark for values is interesting when viewed under the lenses of the EU trade plus agenda, meaning the agenda that aims beyond economic liberalization. In theory, since EU decision-making obeys to several overarching principles these ones should also apply with regard to Regulatory Cooperation as a type of regulatory activity. However, viewed in the context of an FTA, one could content that the principal value remains confined to economic liberalization. On the other hand, given the areas that are liberalised through the activities, which span from pharmaceutical products to pesticides and product safety, it is imperative that other values relevant to these areas are also taken into consideration during any decision-making that might take place. Thus, in the case of Regulatory Cooperation, the output legitimacy of the activities should be demonstrated with the existence of elements that guarantee the conformity of the produced results with fundamental EU values to which similar internal regulatory activity obeys. Output legitimacy is thus about performance, but the question to ask is against which criteria performance should be measured.

5.2.2 The Choice to Include Throughput Legitimacy in the Study of Legitimacy of Regulatory Cooperation

The added value of throughput legitimacy has been located by its instigator in the fact that it serves as the 'cordon sanitaire' between the two other types of legitimacy. On the one hand, it serves as a cordon in the sense that it covers the steps between input and output. Its sanitary function is the main difference to the other types of legitimacy, which are perceived as being complementary.[8] Indeed, more throughput legitimacy will not add value to the existing beliefs on input and output legitimacy. On the other hand though, bad throughput processes risk in resulting in an opaque and questionable in many terms decision, which will eventually reflect on both other two types and de-legitimize them.[9] In other words, it guarantees the presence of a fair environment in which decisions are taken. As such, it consists of the various procedures that guarantee interest intermediation with the people.[10] These procedures, having both institutional and constructivist nature, aim to secure among others, accountability, reliability and responsiveness.[11]

Throughput legitimacy consists thus of normative elements, the theorizing of which however has to be made on a case by case basis. In this sense, the concept

---

[7] Schmidt (2013), pp. 10ff.

[8] Jean d'Aspremont and Eric De Brabandere use the terms legitimacy of origin and legitimacy of exercise in order to argue for their complementarity in legitimizing international governance. See d'Aspremont and de Brabandere (2001).

[9] Schmidt (2013), p. 3.

[10] Schmidt (2006), p. 5.

[11] Wolf (2006), p. 214.

shares common elements with two legal-rational legitimacy, one of the types of legitimacy developed by Max Weber, which grounds obeyance to legal rules to the fact that they were adopted according to norms set by each legal system that place constraints upon this authority.[12] In essence, legal-rational legitimacy borrows its legitimizing force from the body of legal norms that regulates the concerned authority.[13] In the same vain, throughput legitimacy ensures that decision-making is based upon but also constrained by a body of rules that are met differently with respect to each legal order. Consequently, both remain 'value-free' concepts.

Irrespectively of the differences met across legal cultures, this body of rules falls largely under public law, in this case more specifically under administrative law. Legal orders use the form of administrative procedures for the formalization and rationalization of their decision-making.[14] Indeed, accountable on a chain of delegation by the legislature on the one hand, administration is bound by rules of public character that ensure the legitimacy and legality of its actions on the other.[15] Such procedures materialize the due process values as enshrined in each administrative tradition. In other words, public law, in this case its composite, administrative law, serves as a purifying instrument to the blunt exercise of public power. And since it acts from within, in-between input and out, it is translated into throughput legitimacy. This is all the more the case for the EU, where the need to legitimize its administration becomes even more pressing, in the light of absence of connection between the administration and a democratically elected government.

Generally in the EU, decision-making is guided by the European perception of democracy, which is composite: according to Article 10 (1) TEU, it is mainly representative, given the representative function of both Parliament and Council, on the hands of which is decision-making within the community. On the other hand, it also contains strong participatory elements, enshrined in Articles 10 (3) TEU and 11 TEU, which although addressed to all Institutions, are nevertheless of high relevance to the action of the administrative branch. Indeed, openness, participation and transparency, form now essential part of the EU's constitution, and according to the Commission's White Paper on European Governance, they are considered necessary mechanisms that serve the enhancement of legitimacy of the EU, since the latter has been greatly questioned.[16]

And while the principles of openness, participation and transparency might be considered by some as overlapping and duplicative, or present difficulties regarding which is considered to be the overarching one, suffice is to say that they all derive from the principle of democracy, as proclaimed in Article 1 (2) TEU, which states that «decisions are taken as openly as possible and as closely as possible to the citizen» and carry the same connotation, the 'opposite of opaqueness, complexity or

---

[12] Dogan (1992), p. 117.

[13] Spencer (1970), p. 125.

[14] von Bernstorff (2010), p. 778.

[15] Röttger-Wirtz (2021), p. 63.

[16] EU Commission (2001), p. 3.

even secretiveness'.[17] A democratic participatory functioning of the administration works as complementary next to the chosen representative model and has the purifying action, in that it guarantees that the results of the process, which will later be adopted by the legislature come out as unbiased and uncorrupted, executing in other words the functioning of throughput legitimacy.[18]

5.3   Input Legitimacy: The Legitimacy Requirements of Administrative Arrangements

This part of the thesis referring to input legitimacy aims to expand on the thoughts expressed and questions posed earlier in Sect. 5.2. Indeed, among others, it aims to answer whether the use of Administrative Agreements in Regulatory Cooperation is properly used to codify the commitments they have introduced so far, and whether the Commission had the competence to adopt them independently. The steps leading up to the answer of that question shall also shed light into what the Commission may or may not adopt independently and where other institutional participation is necessary.

Section 4.2 pinpointed to the legal effects of these Administrative Agreements, as the benchmark to use in order to answer those questions. In other words, it is the legal effects of these agreements that will inform us about the legality of their employment at each specific case and the applicable legitimacy requirements. From an EU law point of view, the constitutionality of the Administrative Arrangements in light of the produced effects refers primarily to the alignment of the practice with EU primary law. Highlighting however the legal constitutional problems arising from the practice of administrative arrangements as used in Regulatory Cooperation Chapters against EU primary law is a complicate issue. This is mostly because, informal international instruments are not as such foreseen in the Treaties.

That is why the examination of their nature will start from existing literature of public international law. Administrative Agreements, otherwise known as agreements in simplified form signed by the executive have also been used in the past by international actors, however, in the EU legal order the codification of other forms of agreements by means of the Treaties to cater for various needs shadowed the presence of this otherwise known practice. Still, legal commentators had discerned between traditional treaties and Administrative Agreements of the executive on the basis of certain criteria, a distinction which is very useful in our case studies that concern agreements signed by the Commission.

Following the example led by previous literature, the next parts will use those criteria to discern between the existing decision-making avenues agreements in the EU legal order as codified by the Treaties and the category of Administrative

---

[17] Prechal and de Leeuw (2008), p. 202.

[18] See Schmidt (2013), p. 8.

Agreements. For that purpose, it will look into the specific role of the Commission in the adoption of the codified agreements of Article 218 TFEU, which informs us about the different decision-making procedures and acts that are regulated by the Treaties. Parts of this category are of course the international treaties of Article 216 TFEU as well as the specific categories of decisions of Article 218 (7) and (9) TFEU that can modify, amend or complement an international agreement. This analysis will help us understand whether the Administrative Agreements of the Commission overlap with the existing arrangements or if they represent a distinct type of autonomous decision-making. Should the latter be the case, the scope of this autonomous decision-making of the Commission will need to be carved out.

The next parts of this section carry out an analysis of these briefly presented thoughts in detail. Section 5.3.1 begins with the presentation of the practice of agreements in simplified form and presents a methodology on how to examine Administrative Agreements signed by the Commission against the requirements of EU law. Section 5.3.2 operationalises the identified methodology and proceeds on a two step basis: it first looks at the role of the Commission in the existing decision-making landscape of Article 218 TFEU and then looks for further competences in existing jurisprudence. Section 5.3.3 clarifies the scope of autonomous decision-making capacity of the Commission and applies the developed framework to the concrete Regulatory Cooperation Administrative Agreements in order to decide on the legality of their adoption by the Commission as such. Section 5.3.4 presents alternative avenues to decision-making for issues that the Commission is not competent for. Section 5.3.5 concludes.

5.3.1   International Administrative Agreements as a Distinct Category of Agreements in International Practice

The present section will not engage with an analysis of the practice of Administrative Agreements/Administrative Arrangements in the EU legal order. Such an analysis has been carried out in Chap. 4 (see Sect. 4.3.1) for the purposes of introduction to the practice of Administrative Agreements in the EU to the reader, before engaging in the examination of each arrangement separately. As mentioned already in the aforementioned section, the purpose of this introductory description of the use of Administrative Agreements/Arrangements was twofold: firstly, the analysis needed to demonstrate that there is no substantial difference between the two categories and, secondly, the Administrative Arrangements can present legal effects exactly as the Administrative Agreements do. This part, however, aimed only to demonstrate the possibility of existence of legal effects, as this was also later concretely established from the case studies themselves. On the basis of these findings, the purpose of this part is to discuss the suitability of the instrument under the prerequisites of EU constitutional law. Hence, that is exactly what we will do here. For this purpose, we will begin by looking into the state practice of such Administrative Agreements and identify the legal theories around their existence. It is upon this basis that we will draw their limits according to EU constitutional law.

The practice of international Administrative Agreements can be traced back in the literature of the beginning of the twentieth century. Even before the adoption of the VCLT legal commentators had identified their existence in international practice and had distinguished them from the traditional treaties signed between Heads of States. It is interesting to observe that the literature of the time does not make a distinction on the basis of the formal designation of the agreement for international Administrative Agreements were still treaties caught by the provisions of public international law to their understanding.[19] Instead, they used to make the distinction on the basis of the implicated parties.[20] While the traditional inter-state treaties are the ones signed between Heads of States, commentators discerned also other types of international treaties, for example signed between governments, governmental departments and decentralised authorities. Such agreements were grouped under the category 'Agreements in simplified form'.[21]

Although modern literature on the subject is scarce, preceding literature has focused mostly on defining the criteria that characterise the international Administrative Agreements. Among the commentators, there was generally consensus on the essential criterion for their distinction from international treaties and their identification as a specific legal category of treaty-related instruments. This criterion rests upon the absence of the state authority (the contracting party) of a general competence to bind the state. As international Administrative Agreements are qualified as the ones *"concluded by an organ in which the municipal constitution did not, expressis verbis, vest treaty-making power"*.[22] At the time, legal scholars referred very often to the presence of diplomatic channels as the norm to treaty-making as well as the absence of parliamentary approval for their ratification.[23] This rule of course should be understood as referring to each legal orders' constitutional regime for the conclusion of international treaties. With regard to "accords en forme simplifiée" the same criterion has been identified also in French literature.[24]

With that in mind, some commentators seem to confuse the category of international Administrative Agreements with what is known in the US as 'executive agreements'. A characteristic of this category of agreements is their atypical mode of conclusion which does not demand approval from the legislator. In US terms, this

---

[19] Seerden (1992), p. 189, footnote 8.

[20] Paul Reuter admits that: "Il arrive que les parties à un accord soient, non pas directement les États, mais des services de l'État, plus ou moins décentralisées, ou même des personnes morales de droit publics (communes, établissements publics, agences, etc.). Dans ce cas-là, il faut rechercher si le service engage l'État; en cas de réponse negative, se posera alors la question de savoir s'il s'agit d'un accord international de forme particulière, mais s'apparentant étroitement aux traités entre États." *See* Reuter (1985), p. 36.

[21] Hamzeh (1968).

[22] Wildhaber (1971), p. 141.

[23] Vierdag (1989), p. 42.

[24] Rousseau (1970), p. 73.

means escaping the procedure of Article I of the Federal Constitution for international treaties.[25] In the US for example, they constitute the major source of international agreements given the demanding process formal treaty making entails and the mounting powers of the President on external relations.[26] Endorsed by the Supreme Court, and acknowledged by Congress, the conclusion of executive agreements is the rule in the treaty making activity, while the procedure entailing Senate involvement is seldom.[27] However, as literature and practice informs us, the importance of this 'institution' in the US is mirrored in the fact that they constitute the primary treaty making avenue, which is not the case for the Administrative Agreements that are the subject of the present analysis.[28] One of the reasons is the fact, that, while in US executive agreements there is a power by the executive to bind the state by means of a delegating provision, in international Administrative Agreements this issue is not always crystal clear.

Indeed, the question that follows the identification of an international administrative agreement is whether the contracting party had the power to bind the state in the matters in which it did. Since the principal subjects of international law are the states (and the IOs) this means that they can establish firstly whether they can be bound by a treaty-making activity of one of their constituents, and if yes, on which issues this treaty-making capacity will be valid. This means that any potential treaty-making capacity of any subdivisions has to be rooted in internal constitutional law. Seerden writes that in the absence of general explicit ('full') powers to act internationally in this respect, some kind of implicit powers will be necessary to enable organs to do so.[29] In this respect, the provisions of internal constitutional law are decisive on the legality and legitimacy of international Administrative Agreements, and any further analysis has to be carried under the said provisions. According to McNair, as a starting point one should examine whether the contracting party is authorized to act in this way, either ex-ante or ex-post. According to him, this requirement translated to whether the contracting party is authorized to act in this way, either ex-ante or ex-post, independently of whether these rules are part of written norms or exist as administrative practice inspired by the greater constitutional environment.[30] In this regard, authorization can be based on an existing treaty[31] or internal provisions on the repartition of powers. Rousseau has also argued for the presumption of legality of international Administrative Agreements where a

---

[25]This of course is not the case of some countries, like the United Kingdom, where all international agreements are concluded solely by the executive with no involvement of the legislative. However, in cases where a treaty requires amendment to a domestic statute or affects private rights, the executive may ratify it only after the Parliament has passed a suitable statute. *See* Templeman (1991).

[26]Paul (2001), p. 389.

[27]See Morrison (2007), p. 3.

[28]Borchardt (1944).

[29]Seerden (1992), p. 193.

[30]McNair (1960), p. 60.

[31]Burdeau (1981), p. 115.

constitutional prescription is missing, provided that the contracting organ acts within the limits of its functional competences.[32] In certain cases, the functional competences reflect an increasing autonomy of the contracting entities on the external sphere, which mirrors their increasing internal competences.[33]

On the basis of the preceding analysis, the central role of internal constitutional law to the identification of international Administrative Agreements and the issuing deliberation on their legality is evident. It is this legal framework that we will apply to the case of Regulatory Cooperation Administrative Arrangements in order to reach conclusions upon their legality in the EU legal order and their compatibility with the Commission's general mandate and functional competences.

5.3.2 A Legal Framework for International Administrative Agreements in EU Law and the Role of the EU Commission Therein

The previous section identified two criteria for the identification of international Administrative Agreements: the absence of a general treaty-making capacity of the contracting body and, at a second stage, its power to bind by means of the agreement it signed. This section has a double mission. On the one hand, it examines the application of the said criteria with regard to the EU legal order and the Administrative Arrangements of Regulatory Cooperation practice. On the other hand, it fuses these questions with the issue of the openness of the EU legal order to new concepts and legal tools. Indeed, in order to see how a distinct category of agreements 'fits' within a legal order, one has to see as well, apart from the agreements themselves, the existing landscape of legal acts and whether the given legal order is open to the introduction of new legal tools. Only then can we have a holistic view on whether and how the category of Administrative Agreements could co-exist with existing rules and acts. The first section will start by outlining the existing decision-making acts in the universe of EU external relations law, as provided by the Treaties. It will thus refer to the first identified criterion. By informing us about the institutional landscape of treaty making in the EU legal order, it shall prove that the EU Commission has no autonomous treaty-making power. The next sections will answer the question whether the Commission, as a contracting party to Administrative Arrangements enjoys a power to bind the Union per agreements it signs itself in a given area.

---

[32]Rousseau (1970).

[33]Lejeune (1984), p. 412. This statement was made on the basis of the Swiss practice but can have a more general application to state subdivisions engaging into autonomous treaty-making.

5.3.2.1 International Treaties and Simplified International Decision-Making

In legal literature, Article 218 TFEU has rightly been described as the 'procedural code' of the EU's treaty making.[34] As Piet Eeckhout argues, although this procedural subject might seem self-referential at first sight, it does present however important constitutional and institutional extensions, which is all the more witnessed by the augmenting jurisprudence in the area.[35] The provision introduces the division of the various tasks to be executed, which in principle reflects the general role of each institution within the European polity according to the legal act concerned. Article 218 TFEU introduces us to three decision-making avenues: the basic procedure for the conclusion of international treaties as well as two simplified decision-making procedures.

The vast majority of the provisions of Article 218 TFEU refer to the constitutional regime of the different phases in the life cycle of International agreements that the EU is capable of signing with third countries or international organisations. These phases include the one of negotiation on the one hand and the ones of signature and conclusion on the other, and the role given to each Institution. Indeed, the multi-level process which serves to the input of each implicated institution, the Commission as the negotiator, and the Council and the Parliament as decision-makers in different capacities according to the material basis of the agreement, legitimises their existence in the legal environment. This holds especially true for international treaties, whose characteristics have far-reaching consequences.[36] Constituting the external legislative activity of the EU in its area of competence,[37] international agreements form part of the EU legal order, according to standing jurisprudence of the Court of Justice. Their legally binding nature upon Institutions and Member States which renders them as point of reference and interpretative instruments but also the direct effect they in principle are capable to demonstrate—but which CETA does not— justifies a clear legal environment with legitimacy safeguards to regulate their conclusion.

As a derogation from the procedure spelled out above on the negotiation and conclusion of international treaties, Article 218 TFEU foresees also two simplified procedures for entering into international commitments that are of secondary importance and auxiliary nature to the commitments undertaken by the international treaties. Such simplified procedures are laid down in Articles 218 (7) and

---

[34]Dashwood et al. (2011), p. 936.

[35]Rosas (2017) and Van der Mei (2016).

[36]This is primarily admitted regarding international treaties by the Masters of the Treaties who allowed for the possibility of a judicial control prior to their conclusion, by virtue of Article 218 (11) TFEU.

[37]It was particularly in the Mauritius and Tanzania cases that the Court of Justice equated international treaties to legislation. *See* Case C-658/11 European Parliament v. Council (Mauritius)- ECLI:EU:C:2014:2025; Case C-263/14 *European Parliament versus Council (Tanzania)*, ECLI: EU:C:2016:435.

(9) TFEU. On the one hand, the provision under par. 9 of Article 218 TFEU refers to the procedure to be followed either in the cases of suspension of an international agreement or in the case where a position has to be taken on the Union's behalf in a body set up by the agreement, when the latter decides upon the adoption of acts having legal effects. This provision generally applies to the augmenting tendency of norm-creation by international organisations.[38] At these instances, the decision to suspend or the position to be taken is determined in advance by a Council decision, which in principle has to consent for the conclusion of any international commitment.[39] On the other hand, the provision under par. 7 of Article 218 is in fact, an exception of par. 9 and outlines the (more) simplified procedure to be followed for the modification of international agreements, according to which the negotiator can approve amendments to the original agreement as participant to a designated committee, by means of a simplified procedure, after securing authorization from the Council and under any requirements the latter may have set. With regard to FTAs and more specifically to CETA, this provision has been used for the adoption of the CETA Joint Committee decision on the amendment of Annex 20-A based on Article 20.22 CETA.[40]

Under the light of the above, the relation between international treaties on the one hand and the decisions of 218 (7) TFEU modifying their Annexes or the category of decisions of 218 (9) TFEU suspending their application on the other hand is quite clear. However, the formulation of Article 218 (9) TFEU regarding the acts to be adopted by an international body, for the formulation of which the EU has to decide upon a certain position is not very clear regarding the nature of the acts concerned. It is thus worth shedding more light on this category and their relation to international treaties.

According to Article 218 (9) TFEU, the procedure enshrined within applies when it comes to establishing the positions to be adopted on behalf of the Union in a body set up by an international agreement, when this body is supposed to adopt acts that will have legal effects. In that case, it is the Council upon proposal by the Commission or the High Representative for External Affairs that will adopt by means of a decision the position to be taken in the international body. First of all, it becomes clear that in that case, the acts are taken by the body which is established by an international agreement, not by the Union itself. This sheds some light on the relationship between these acts and the ones of the international treaties that set up the international bodies. As the Court pointed out in case C-73/14 *Council v. Commission*, the acts foreseen under this procedure are the ones that are *applying or implementing* the (each time concerned) agreement.[41] Despite that, it is

---

[38] Rosas (2017), p. 370.

[39] Rosas (2017), p. 370.

[40] Article 2, Council Decision 2017/38 on the provisional application of CETA, OJ 2017 L 11/1080.

[41] Case C-73/14, *Council v. Commission*, ECLI:EU:C:2015:663, par. 65.

established jurisprudence of the Court, that these acts are part of the EU legal order and that they may also present direct effect.[42]

Also, the 'legal effect' they are supposed to have upon the EU legal order has been in fact broadly interpreted. The issue arose in case C-399/12 Germany v. Council. The case generally concerned an action for annulment brought by Germany against a Council decision establishing the position to be adopted on behalf of the Union regarding some resolutions that were to be voted in the context of the Organisation for Wine and Vine (hereinafter OIV). The German government sought the annulment of the decision on two grounds: firstly, it argued that the procedural basis of Article 218(9) TFEU did not apply, as the EU was not itself member of the organisation which meant that the Member States should have coordinated their action on the basis of mutual cooperation; secondly, it argued that the said provision applies only to acts that are supposed to be legally binding under public international law, an interpretation which excluded the resolutions of the OIV that lacked legally binding force.[43]

Hence, the Court, with the second plea of the German government was called to define the scope of 'legal effects' that such acts are capable to present. The different opinions that were presented on the interpretation of the term is indicative of the ambiguity that accompanied the provision all these years. On the one hand, the AG, guided by the wording, the context and *telos* of the provision, sided with the narrow interpretation suggested by the German government and supported that these acts to be adopted by the international bodies have to be legally binding under public international law.[44] However, the Court decided to adopt a wider interpretation and suggested that the 'legal effects' need not necessarily be legal binding ones. It argued that the fact that the recommendations to be adopted in the OIV were "capable of decisively influencing the content of the legislation adopted by the EU legislature in the area of the common organization of the wine markets" constituted in and by itself a legal effect for the purposes of the provision.[45]

The reading given to the provision by the Court of Justice inherently broadens the scope of potential international decision-making that can fall under Article 218 (9) TFEU. This is principally in line with the *telos* of Article 218 (9) TFEU as providing a legal avenue for the implementation of the international agreement at stake. It is true that legally binding acts present *ab initio* effects in the EU legal order. This does not mean however that non-binding norms are not capable of presenting legal effects as such. The Court of Justice here simply acknowledged the

---

[42] According to the Court of Justice, decisions of bodies set up by agreements concluded by the Community form an "integral part of Community law" in the same way as the international agreements themselves and may have direct effect. *See* Case C-30/88, *Greece v. Commission*, ECLI:EU:C:1989:422; Case C-192/89, *S. Z. Sevince v Staatssecretaris van Justitie*, EU:C:1990:322.

[43] Case C-399/12, Germany v. Council, ECLI:EU:C:2014:2258, par. 36.

[44] Case C-399/12, Germany v. Council, ECLI:EU:C:2014:2258, Opinion of AG Cruz Villalon, par. 88–99.

[45] Case C-399/12, Germany v. Council, ECLI:EU:C:2014:2258, par. 63.

consolidated by legal literature existence of legal effects of soft law instruments, to which the previous chapter briefly pointed (see Sect. 4.2).

To conclude, this part, by outlining the decision-making avenues in EU external relations law, it also made clear that the rules of 218 TFEU do not bestow upon the Commission an autonomous international decision-making capacity. Instead, in the cases where the legal basis of the agreement does not fall under the CFSP, the Article bestows upon the Commission a very prominent role, the one of negotiator. On this capacity, it enjoys the prerogative to submit a negotiations' proposal for adoption to the Council in order to carry them out with the third party concerned. With regard also to simplified decision-making, the Commission proposes the position to be taken to the Council. This decisive capacity of the Commission is generally in line with its general institutional profile as provided by the TEU, and should be read in line with its primary functions. Indeed, the Commission is by virtue of Article 17 TEU entrusted as the competent Institution to promote the general interest of the Union and to represent it externally, and by enjoying the right to initiate a proposal, it is given the power to put these primary responsibilities in practice. Despite its pivotal role in the formation of external rule-making, the Commission is not, nevertheless, the decision-maker. This function rests upon the law-makers of the EU, namely the Council and the Parliament, subject of course to the procedural specificities of Article 218 TFEU and the type of legal act concerned.

5.3.2.2   Jurisprudence on the Clarification of Decision-Making Capacity of the Commission

The analysis above, on the role of the Commission in EU's external relations decision-making satisfies the first criterion set by legal scholars, that the contracting party to an international administrative agreement must not have general treaty-making capacity. The next two sections will now examine whether the Commission derives the power to bind the Union by virtue of other provisions or existing jurisprudence and if so, regarding which issues.

C-327/91: Denying a Separate Treaty-Making Capacity of the Commission in Areas of Its Internal Competence

We should begin by admitting existing practice according to which administrative entities in the past were found to have bound the Union as a whole, even when acting outside the decision-making rules of the Treaties. In case C-327/91, the Administrative Agreement between the US and the EU on the application of their competition laws was found to be binding upon the Union in general despite having been agreed between the then Commissioner for Competition for the EU and the Attorney General and the President of the Federal Trade Commission, on behalf of the Government of the United States.[46] Consequently, this means that the fact that the

---

[46] Case C-327/91 *France v. Commission,* ECLI:EU:C:1994:305, par. 2.

signatories in case are administrative entities did not deprive them from having 'full powers' according to Article 7 of the VCLT and VCLT-IO, hence did not exclude that they are not able to bind their legal orders generally neither under international law nor under EU law. According to Article 7 (1) (b) VCLT and VCLT-IO it is possible that a person or an entity can be considered as representing the State if «it appears from practice or from other circumstances that it was the intention of the States and international organizations concerned to consider that person as representing the State for such purposes without having to produce full powers.» The fact, however, that on the occasion of that case, the administrative entities were found to bind the entities they represent on the international level by means of conclusion of an agreement between them, does not mean this was done in a legally compliant manner on EU level. More concretely, this means that while the agreement was valid under international law, the internal procedure prescribed by the EU Treaties for the conclusion of international agreements was not respected, as the respective Commissioner lacked the capacity to proceed to the conclusion of international agreements.

For the EU, the question whether the Commission has its own treaty making capacity finds its basis on the questionable formulation of former Article 300 par. 2 EC, which subjected the Council's prerogative to sign an international agreement to the Commission's powers in this field. This statement had been, and not illogically, interpreted as bestowing a separate power to the Commission to sign certain types of international agreements in the fields where its powers allow so.[47]

And indeed, the Commission didn't hesitate to use this argument in order to defend its measure that was subject to the action brought against it in the case C-327/91, the first *Commission v. France,* where France contested the validity of agreement between the EU and the United States in the field of competition law, which was only signed by the Commission. The Commission relied upon the slightly different French version of that provision in order to ground its competence to sign the so-called international Administrative Agreements, deriving it from provisions other than within the Treaties, for example from the practice of the Institutions.[48] The Court of Justice however claimed that a mere practice could not override the Treaty provisions and hence, denied an implicit treaty making power of the Commission.[49] In that regard, it followed the opinion of the AG, who, while practically recognizing the existence of the practice, dismissed a general capacity of the Commission to conclude Administrative Agreements, given the absence of the term from the Treaties and the unwillingness of the Court to recognize the legal basis of a mere practice just on the basis of its continuing precedent.[50] According to the Court, this is also the case in areas where the Commission enjoys powers internally, as is the area of competition law, powers that, nevertheless cannot change

---

[47] Eeckhout (2011), p. 205.

[48] Case C-327/91, *France v. Commission, I,* ECLI:EU:C:1994:305, par. 31.

[49] Case C-327/91, *France v. Commission, I,* ECLI:EU:C:1994:305, par. 33–37.

[50] Case C-327/91, *France v. Commission, I,* ECLI:EU:C:1994:305, par. 36.

the allocation of powers between the Institutions regarding the conclusion of inter-national agreements.[51] In dismissing this argument, the Court of Justice ruled clearly on the interpretation given to Article 300 (2) EC. In the EU legal order, the authorization of an agreement which binds the EU under international law and obliges it not to undermine by any act or omission its purpose and object, rests with the Council.

We can infer that the Commission may not generally bind the Union as a whole also from the argumentation that grounded the illegality of its actions by the Court and the AGs, who based their understandings on the role of each Institution in the formation of the external policies of the Union. Indeed, the illegality of the Com-mission's action did not depend only on its own constitutional prerogatives and what it is allowed to do as an administrative entity, but was mainly grounded to the encroachment upon the prerogatives of other Institutions in the sphere of external action. From this, we can keep that binding the Union was not something not allowed only in these circumstances, but applies generally.

C-660/13: Denying the Ability to Sign Informal Instruments of Political Char-acter on Behalf of the EU

With more recent jurisprudence, the Court of Justice was given the chance to further clarify the Commission's capacity to act on its own internationally, this time with the use of informal international instruments. The issue had been firstly addressed in the second France v. Commission where the Court only underlined that the non-binding character of agreements cannot justify an autonomous power of the Commission to conclude them.[52] Complementing this line of jurisprudence, it was on the occasion of the case C-660/13 that it provided a more analytical argumentation on why it deprived from the Commission the power to conclude non-binding agreements of political nature.

The case concerned the "Decision of the European Commission of 3 October 2013 in the signature of an addendum to the MoU on a Swiss financial contribution to the new Member States of 27 February 2006". The 2013 addendum was the second addendum to the original MoU, following the first one in 2008. The cause that sparked the dispute between the Council and the Commission was the fact that the 2013 addendum was singed solely by the Commission, in contrast to previous MoU and 2006 addendum which were signed both by the Presidency of the Council and by the Commission. All agreements, the 2013 addendum included, introduced non-binding commitments between the EU and Switzerland. It was thus on this occasion that the Court was called to answer whether that practice of the Commis-sion violated, along with the principle of sincere cooperation, the separation of powers of Article 13 (2) TFEU and thus the institutional balance, as far as the conclusion of international agreements is concerned. In other words, the Court was called to comment upon the constitutionality of the practice, whether it belongs to

---

[51] Case C-327/91, *France v. Commission, I*, ECLI:EU:C:1994:305, par. 41.

[52] C-233/02 *France v. Commission II*, par. 40.

Article 17 (1) TEU that sketches out the Commission's powers, or it encroaches upon the policy-making powers of the Council according to Article 16 par. 1 TEU.

Central point of the Council's argumentation was the fact that the institutional balance of 218 TFEU (which reflects Articles 16 and 17 TEU) should not be disregarded in the case of non-binding agreements that fall out of the scope of 218 TFEU.[53] This balance has constitutional significance whatever the circumstances. The Commission responded that it does possess the power to conclude non-binding agreements of political nature on behalf of the Union in cases where the Union's position has been established and characterized the alleged capacity as part of its external representation entrusted to it by Article 17 (1) recital 6 TEU. This provocative argument disturbs the core balance of the legal order by relying on a non-binding character of an instrument. However, the argument was rightly dismissed by both the AG and the Court. Indeed, the balance of Articles 16 and 17 TFEU exists independently from 218 TFEU, as it reflects the division of work in external relations in general, irrespectively of the binding character or not of an arrangement. It thus applies mutatis mutandis to non-binding instruments and supports the view that the Commission has only negotiating autonomy in the external relations, which however tends to oversee, with this case not being the first time.[54]

The line of reasoning was followed by the AG, who applied the current regime on the separation of powers to non-binding agreements in order to reach her conclusions by making an assessment of the political character of the agreement at stake.[55] It is still worth mentioning that while the AG upheld the Council's allegation and confirmed the Commission's action beyond its constitutional prerogatives, she still admitted the lack of a generally appropriate legal basis for agreements of this type, and the unsuitability of an analogous application of Article 218 TFEU given their non-legally binding character, without providing a solution.[56] Same omission was present in the Court's judgement.[57]

Surprisingly, the Court did not comment upon the separation of powers reflected in non-binding agreements and jumped to its conclusion. Despite its lack of reasoning, the verdict was the same: they both denied any competence of the Commission to sign on its own non-binding political agreements—even when they are in line with existing EU policy—under the current treaty rules. Such an activity is not an act of representation under Article 17 (1) TEU that can be carried out without the Council's approval.

---

[53] Case C-660/13 *Council of the European Union v. European Commission* [2016] ECLI:EU:C:2016:616, Opinion of AG Sharpston, par. 91.

[54] For similar controversies between the Commission and the Council on the EU's external representation in the field of migration *see* Garcia Anrade (2016).

[55] Case C-660/13 *Council of the European Union v. European Commission* [2016] ECLI:EU:C:2016:616, Opinion of AG Sharpston, par. 99–117.

[56] Case C-660/13 *Council of the European Union v. European Commission* [2016] ECLI:EU:C:2016:616, Opinion of AG Sharpston, par. 108.

[57] Verellen (2016), p. 7.

5.3.3 The Character of Agreements as Technical/Administrative or Political: Drawing the Line for Commission's Decision-Making Capacity

Although in the previously analyzed case-law the AG and the Court did not delve further into the issue of the circumstances that would allow for a conforming adoption of agreements from the part of the Commission only, but only stated the illegality of its actions in the respective cases, they did give us some guidelines about what the Commission cannot do, issues that fall outside its scope of competence. According to C-327/91, the Union does not dispose a separate treaty-making capacity, capable of binding the Union as a whole, not even in its areas of internal competence, such as competition. According to C-660/13, the Commission is not allowed to enter into non-binding political agreements on behalf of the Union, even when the agreement is in line with established Union policy.

Clearly, in its jurisprudence, the Court did not associate this alleged decision-making capacity of the Commission with the type of agreements that the Institution can conclude as an administration.[58] Some commentators, among them also AG Sharpston in her opinion to the case C-660/13, differentiates the category of agreements that the EU Commission has the capacity to sign on its own find their basis in the principle of administrative autonomy enshrined in Article 335 par. 3 TFEU.[59]

From the previous case-law combined, we can make the distinction in order to draw the limits of the Commission's autonomous decision-making capacity on the character of the agreement as political/international or mere administrative/technical: the above decisions leave room for the Commission to enter into the latter category of agreements (be it legally binding or soft), which may still have legal effects on the Commission solely on the basis of Article 335 par. 3 TFEU. Legally binding international agreements binding the Union as a whole or soft law instruments of political character are hence out of the scope of the EU Commission's autonomous decision-making capacity.[60]

Central to this section in drawing further the Commission's decision-making capacities are thus the definitions of what can qualify as political and what is technical or administrative, categories that are outlined below.

---

[58] Opinion of AG Tesauro in case C-321/97 France v. Commission I, par. 17, 23.

[59] Case C-660/13 *Council of the European Union v. European Commission* [2016] ECLI:EU:C:2016:616, Opinion of AG Sharpston, par. 78. In fact apart from establishing the principle of autonomy, Article 335 TFEU crystallizes further the Commission's duty of external representation of the Union of Article 17 (1) rec. 6 TEU.

[60] Chamon and Demedts (2019), p. 18.

5.3.3.1   Agreements of Political Character

As the term 'political character' is quite vague on its own, this section will elaborate more concretely on what can qualify as being of political nature, and hence falling outside the scope of Commission's autonomous decision-making capacity, either by means of an international treaty or a soft law agreement.

Commitments that Relate to Policy-Making
Case C-660/13 illustrates a category of commitments that may not be entered by the EU Commission alone, the ones related to policy-making. Indeed, as described in detail in the section above, the Court did not give justice to the EU Commission's initiative to sign on its own a non-binding international agreement that nevertheless included policy elements, even if these were defined by the Council previously, as this encroached the policy-making prerogatives of the Council. As a result, we infer that any commitment related to policy-making, a function granted to the Council, cannot be the subject matter of the Commission's autonomous decision-making capacity. What can be considered as policy-making though? This section builds on identifying what qualifies as a policy-making function, in order to carve out in more detail what falls outside the EU Commission's autonomous decision-making.

Central role in that regard has Article 16 par. 1 TEU, which enumerates the competences of the Council, which, shall carry out legislative and budgetary functions (in cooperation with the EU Parliament), as well as policy-making and coordinating functions. The fact that the policy-making function of the Council is mentioned in a declaratory term is only a novelty following the Constitutional treaty (Article I-23.1 thereof), which was later kept in the Lisbon Treaty. As such it does not provide prima facie guidance on what falls under it. This has indeed created some confusion, especially with regard to the question how to set the boundaries between the Council's policy-making function on the one hand, and the European Council's competence to define the general political directions and strategies of the Union, and the executive powers of the Commission on the other hand.[61] Lying in-between the two last competencies of the other actors, the European Council's and the Commission's, the policy-making function of the Council could indeed raise concerns on institutional competition.[62]

By answering to this concern, Blumann has also built upon a more concrete description of what this policy-making capacity entails. Indeed, he has argued that the Council finds its place in between the roles of the other Institutions by concretising the general policy directions taken by the European Council, always within the framework of the Treaties but not to such extent to touch upon the Commission's executive role.[63] In practice, what operationalises this competency of the Council are the various conclusions and resolutions that it issues on different

---

[61] Edjaharian (2013), p. 654.

[62] Edjaharian (2013), p. 654.

[63] Blumann (2005), p. 312.

topics. These documents contain the political position to be adopted on different topics by the Council's different ministerial configurations, and can contain political commitments, which are however not binding from a legal point of view.[64]

Regarding the elements that substantiate this competence of the Council, it is also interesting to see how AG Kokott approached the political decision-making capacity of the Council in case C-660/13, on the basis of which it identified the issue at stake as political. According to her findings, of central importance to whether an issue is political or not is the identification of the interests in hand.[65] In the particular case C-660/13 the interests at stake comprised both the decision to proceed to a financial arrangement with Switzerland and the signing of the decision after the end of the negotiations. More specifically:

> the decision that an objective for which the Union is competent can be pursued by obtaining a commitment (whether or not binding) from a third State to pay a financial contribution to a new Member State pursuant to a future bilateral agreement between those two parties (assuming no such decision has been taken earlier) and thus by participating in external action, in the form of negotiations and possibly the subsequent conclusion of an instrument to obtain that commitment.[66]

The AG reached this conclusion based on the fact that the negotiations that follow the political decision to pursue a financial arrangement can leave a margin of discretion to the Commission, which the Council has to later verify and conclude that the content of the commitments agreed, and the form of external action used at the negotiations are still relevant and appropriate, respect any posed constraints and are acceptable to the Union.[67] On this basis, one may infer that the political decision-making capacity of the Council comprises every stage of a process in which interests of the EU have to be defined, validated and agreed.

Commitments that May Interfere with Human Rights
While commitments that may interfere with human rights include policy considerations and hence fall more broadly on the category above, it is worth mentioning them as a separate category, especially in the light of activity that caught the attention of the academia some years ago.

Reference is made in particular to an informal instrument signed on behalf of the EU in order to regulate the increased immigration from Afghanistan to the EU observed during the previous decade, the "EU-Afghanistan Joint Way Forward on migration issues". This instrument, adopted during the Brussels Conference on Afghanistan in October 2016, was closely related to the allocation of development funds to Afghanistan, hence it constituted a continuation of the political cooperation

---

[64]EU Council, 'Council conclusions and resolutions', https://www.consilium.europa.eu/en/council-eu/conclusions-resolutions/ accessed 10 February 2022.

[65]Case C-660/13 *Council of the European Union v. European Commission* [2016] ECLI:EU:C:2016:616, Opinion of AG Sharpston, par. 110.

[66]Case C-660/13 *Council of the European Union v. European Commission* [2016] ECLI:EU:C:2016:616, Opinion of AG Sharpston, par. 111.

[67]Chamon and Demedts (2017), p. 250.

between the two actors, by which, in essence the Afghan government committed to cooperate on the return and readmission of Afghan nationals, in compliance with international law and human rights obligations. It has been argued that this instrument touches upon issues that interfere with fundamental rights through detailed commitments over migration matters, while being concluded as an informal instrument. This instrument was 'rushed' to be concluded as such, in the absence of concrete progress on the conclusion of the relevant international treaty, the EU-Afghanistan Cooperation Agreement on Partnership and Development (CAPD), which was only signed later as a mixed agreement.[68]

Although the text of the Joint Way Forward is not any more available online through the Institutions' websites, academic literature of the time of its adoption judges the fact that it contains detailed provisions on the modalities of return of Afghan nationals, that normally belong to a binding re-admission agreement, as mandated by Article 79 (3) TFEU.[69] Interestingly, the EU Commission admits on its website that a non-binding readmission agreement with Afghanistan exists.[70] In particular, it sets a framework to facilitate the return of individuals residing illegally in the EU, including the ones considered more 'vulnerable' through actions such as the issuance of travel documents, the organisation of flights to Afghanistan. Re-admission agreements spelling out the conditions for cooperation between the EU and a third country on the return of individuals need to offer the guarantees of the Return Directive and other asylum secondary legislation. Such agreements are called to provide the necessary guarantees exactly because fundamental rights are at stake, and a political assessment has to be made in order to reach the conclusion that these guarantees do exist. In particular, EU action on the basis of the provisions of this instrument interfered to a great extent with the status of human rights of the concerned individuals, the respect of which was questionable upon their return to Afghanistan. That is the reason why it is mentioned above that such commitments fall more broadly under the category of commitments of political nature. Essentially, in this case, the guarantees required by the legislation were offered through an informal agreement, which did not benefit neither from the policy input of the EU Council neither from the scrutiny of the EU Parliament. Similar assessments are present every time fundamental rights are at stake, and as such, it is safe to argue that no executive actor has the competence to conclude it on its own.

This is further supported by the interpretation given to Article 220 TFEU, which provides in its first paragraph that the EU shall *"establish all appropriate forms of cooperation with the organs of the United Nations and its specialised agencies, the Council of Europe, the Organisation for Security and Cooperation in Europe and the Organisation for Economic Cooperation and Development"*, as well as with

---

[68] Warin and Zhekova (2017).

[69] Warin and Zhekova (2017), p. 151.

[70] EU Commission, 'A humane and effective return and readmission policy' <https://ec.europa.eu/home-affairs/policies/migration-and-asylum/irregular-migration-and-return/return-and-readmission_en>.

other organisations, while bestowing in the second paragraph the task of implementing this cooperation upon the High Representative of the Union for Foreign Affairs and Security Policy and the Commission. The ambiguity of this legal basis as regards the procedures and tools employed in the implementation of this provision has sparked the debate on whether it constitutes an autonomous decision-making function of the High Representative or the EU Commission in its relations with these organisations, given the fact that the EU Commission has not hesitated to invoke it as a legal basis along with 218 TFEU.[71] Nevertheless, academic literature seems to agree on the issue that this provision refers to administrative cooperation of the EU Commission and the HR with these organisations and in no way extends the Commission's or HR's power to the point where they can bind the Union with political commitments on issues that may impact fundamental rights in deliberations with the organisations named in the provisions (or other policy choices, when relations concern other organisations).[72]

Commitments that May Underpin Legislative Choices
This part refers to commitments that underpin legislative choices as the ones that are in a position to determine the political reasoning associated with each proposed measure.[73] The reasoning behind a certain direction in the legislation or another impacts the content of the legislation as a whole and consequently remains a prerogative of the legislature. While the EU Commission in its right of initiative may opt for a certain direction over another one, the final say belongs to the co-legislators. Hence, any agreement on the part of the Commission that includes commitments capable of binding the legislature to a certain political reasoning is out of the scope of Commission's autonomous decision-making.

One may identify this category of commitments by reference to what was described in the Introduction as one of the risks linked to Regulatory Cooperation, namely the commitments that may challenge the regulatory sovereignty and trigger the race to the bottom. Among others, such commitments may impact (a) the way science is perceived and applied for the development of the regulations, seen under the light of the unification of scientific methods, (b) the risk to alter existing assumptions in the need to find common ones and (c) the deregulatory risk of the requirement to adopt joint positions in international standardisation fora.[74]

Future activities and possible agreements arising therefrom, either of informal or formal nature that directly or indirectly influence the assumptions and tools on which regulations are founded, as described by Bartl above, can arise from the text of Article 21.4 CETA. Although not in binding terms, the parties are encouraged to minimise divergences through the concurrent or joint risk assessments and

---

[71] Gosalbo-Bono and Naert (2016), p. 49.
[72] Gosalbo-Bono and Naert (2016), p. 49; See also Ott (2020), p. 601.
[73] Bartl (2017), p. 970.
[74] Bartl (2017), p. 970.

regulatory impact assessments where possible,[75] to use similar assumptions, to promote the similarity of results, to conduct joint studies on the development of regulations, to use common data in order to avoid duplicative research with a view to establishing, when appropriate, a common scientific basis. These commitments mirror the change which is susceptible to take place on the level of regulatory development, either by fostering scientific convergence under the caveat of economy or by seeking the similarity of results and using every mean towards this direction.

By enumerating the various possibilities of Article 21.4 we can conclude positively to the scenario of such commitments capable of achieving an altering effect upon the regulatory development, which points to the need of their treatment as commitments capable of intruding in the fabric by which legislations are made. Such commitments are as such highly political and hence fall outside the scope of the EU Commission's autonomous rule-making.

Commitments that Involve a Transfer of Regulatory Authority
One example par excellence of a possible future political agreement in the context of Regulatory Cooperation are the MRAs. Such agreements have been concluded in the past by the EU with third countries on a bilateral basis as international treaties, outside the framework of a formal relationship, as are the FTAs. Now, the institutional structures, and particularly the Regulatory Cooperation Fora are here to play a central role in such type of future cooperation. As we have mentioned, such exercises are foreseen directly by the Regulatory Cooperation Chapters. Indeed, Articles 21.4. g. and 21.4.r. CETA list various tools to attain convergence; joint undertaking of the regulatory process, harmonization, equivalence, MRAs. Indeed, Canada has already proposed the conclusion of an MRA on Drug Facility Inspections in third countries, which also lies beyond the scope of the CETA Protocol on Pharmaceuticals, while Japan envisaged the mutual recognition of its privacy laws with the one of the EU as the ultimate political goal of the EU-Japan EPA and the regulatory convergence that would follow.[76] The present part will explain why such instruments include commitments that involve a transfer of regulatory authority and why, as such, they are out of the scope of EU Commission's autonomous decision-making.

The observation that MRAs include a transfer of regulatory authority has been first made by Nicolaides and Schaffer in order to explain the functioning of MRAs in legal terms: *'...governments adopt mutual recognition as a contractual norm whereby they agree to the effective transfer of regulatory authority-or jurisdiction-from the host country where a transaction takes place, to the home country from which a product, a person, a service, or a firm originates, subject to agreed (and managed) conditions.'*[77]

The transfer of regulatory authority or jurisdiction from the host to the home country concerns the recognition of the assessments of the latter as equal to the ones

───────────────

[75] Article 21.4 (g) (i) CETA.

[76] Bartl and Irion (2017).

[77] Nikolaides and Schaffer (2005), p. 264.

of the former with respect to certain subject matters. This by and itself constitutes a political choice that requires the input of the legislator. This is all the more true, considering that integral part of this recognition are also the considerations on which this choice is made. In the absence of fixed criteria on which are these conditions, it is for the contracting parties to decide. They do so by examining the differences between the systems and deciding whether the existing differences are so fundamental as to preclude the equivalence between them.[78] Of course, deciding on the acceptability of third parties' legislation characteristics constitutes a delicate exercise which also entails highly political considerations that tantamount to internal rule-making. It should be recalled here that this might apply not only to regulations outlining technical standards, such as product characteristics (i.e. safety requirements) but may as well cover production processes, hence extending this legitimization exercise to the examination of 'trade and' issues. It is undeniable that the breadth of a possible equivalence may vary from shallower to deeper, which then has an impact on the extent of the political exercise to be carried out.

This structural characteristic of MRAs, namely the inherent political choices they carry is evident also from the legal basis which allows the EU to engage in convergence (and hence Regulatory Cooperation) activities, developing thus its external regulatory policy. Indeed, the external regulatory policy falls in fact under the overarching scheme of the CCP.[79] This was confirmed with the inclusion of the TBT Agreement under the CCP by the Court of Justice in its seminal Opinion 1/94. Central point of the Court's argumentation was the *telos* of the Agreement, the fact that the aim of the provisions of the Agreement is to ensure that the instruments which it concerns (technical regulations, conformity assessment procedures, standards) do not pose unnecessary barriers to trade.[80] This is all the more important, given the fact that CCP does not have an explicit regulatory dimension.[81] One should not oversee though that the progressive abolishment of barriers to trade is one of the aims of the CCP, according to Article 206 TFEU and of course the primary aim of Regulatory Cooperation.[82]

It is well known that the primary legal basis for the EU's external regulatory policy is Article 207 TFEU on CCP according to Article 3 (1) (e) TFEU. However, the use of the trade legal basis for convergence purposes, especially in the context of enhanced MRAs, might not always be enough. The reason is because convergence accomplished through these instruments, apart from abolishing a barrier to trade, may also have a direct impact on the internal market. A mutual recognition decision on the equivalence of a regulation to the one of a third country, or to an international standard, has the same effects as a harmonization exercise.

---

[78] Nikolaides and Schaffer (2005), p. 264.

[79] Regulatory Cooperation form part of an FTA, whose main legal basis is with Article 207 TFEU.

[80] Opinion 1/94 [1994] ECR I-5267, par. 33.

[81] Cremona (2013), p. 162.

[82] Article 206 TFEU.

On this basis, existing case law informs us that as regards measures that concern the 'development, adoption and enforcement' of standards so as 'to avoid unnecessary barriers to trade', measures that in other words, open up a part of the internal market to foreign imports, can be sufficiently adopted only on the basis of 207 TFEU.[83] This is because such measures, like the ones introduced by traditional MRAs that only opt for a mutual recognition of conformity assessment procedures without alignment of the underlying regulations, only concern barriers to trade and they leave existing rules untouched. This is not the case for the category of enhanced MRAs that imply a regulatory convergence, to which this section refers. Indeed, this category of MRAs, which includes some kind of harmonization of standards that touch upon existing rules has to be based on an internal market basis along with the trade one, like Article 114 TFEU.[84]

Either built solely upon 207 TFEU or in combination with 114 TFEU, according to the nomenclature of EU legal instruments, MRAs would qualify to be concluded as international treaties on the basis of the TFEU provisions on international treaty making. With regard to agreements finding their legal basis on Article 207 TFEU, the latter in its paragraph 3 points to the procedure of Article 218 TFEU for the conclusion of international agreements falling within the scope of the provision. Similarly, international instruments that implicate an indirect harmonization and fall equally under 114 TFEU are to be concluded as international treaties as they fulfill the requirement of Article 218 (6) alinea a, case (v) TFEU, since internal legislation on internal market are adopted via the ordinary legislative procedure.[85]

This development has important ramifications with regard to the required institutional participation in case of conclusion of agreements on Regulatory Cooperation via means other than international treaties. Indeed, the material bases indicate that agreements that find their material bases on Articles 207 and 114 TFEU would normally require parliamentary participation should they be concluded as international treaties. Hence, not to include the EU Parliament in a potential decision-making process on such Regulatory Cooperation issues would tantamount to a violation of the rule of law, the democratic principle of Article 10 (3) TEU, as well as the institutional balance of Article 13 (2) TEU, as the systematic reading of EU legitimacy would be bypassed simply by the use of an informal instrument.[86]

5.3.3.2   Agreements of Technical or Administrative Character Under 335 TFEU

Another question is of course whether the power deriving from that provision include Administrative Agreements signed internationally, as the situations covered

---

[83] Opinion 1/94, [1994] ECR I-5267, par. 4.

[84] Cremona (2013), p. 164.

[85] Article 207 (2) TFEU and 114 (1) alinea b TFEU.

[86] Garcia Andrade (2018), p. 122; Verellen (2016), p. 1233.

by that Article are unclear. Primarily, this Article is an expression of the Commission's power to represent the Union externally, before national and international courts, as clarified by the Reynold's jurisprudence.[87] Nevertheless, the third recital of the Article gives to each Institution a greater margin of discretion to act by virtue of their administrative autonomy. It reads that: «the Union shall be represented by each of the Institutions, by virtue of their administrative autonomy, in matters relating to their respective operation».[88] This has been interpreted as bestowing upon the Institutions the power to assume obligations binding only on them internally. On the basis of this provision the power of the Institutions to represent the Union is constrained in matters relating to their respective operation. This has been interpreted as including "matters of concern to it" (e.g. as regards the procurement of goods and services of its own).[89] The term being quite comprehensive, it can be interpreted as including agreements used to facilitate the workings of the administration on every level, agreements that materialize the current needs of each Institution, for which each Institution can best decide. However, this provision has also been used by the Legal Service of the EU Council with regard to the external action of Institutions.[90] Commenting upon the procedural legal basis of Agreements such as MoUs that outline practical aspects of cooperation between an EU Institution and an IO, the Council's Legal Service took the view that in such cases, it is only the Institution that is bound by the MoU, and that Article 335 TFEU applies.[91]

Administrative Agreements Pertaining to the Commission's Operation
This provision has been employed as to include agreements signed on the international sphere, restrained however to matters of each Institution's respective operation, a notion interpreted widely, not only with regard to private matters of the Institutions. Accordingly, we can infer that the Commission is empowered to undertake obligations that bind only the Commission, on the basis of its administrative autonomy, enshrined in Article 335 par. 3 TFEU. Hence, should the Commission wish to establish cooperation procedures that are only of technical character, it is free to do so, using the avenue of administrative arrangements, or any other informal instrument. It should be mentioned here, that as long as the commitments remain purely technical, these instruments may as well be binding on that legal basis.

Andrea Ott has carried out an extensive mapping of such instruments to which she found the common characteristic that they are in fact signed by the respective

---

[87] While the letter of the first and second recitals establishes the right of the Commission to represent the Union in each Member States, the *Reynolds* jurisprudence, commenting upon the nature of the predecessor of Article 335 TFEU, Article 282 EC, extended the representation right also to third countries, finding that it expressed a general principle rather than a specific mandate constrained to European borders.

[88] Article 335 TFEU.

[89] Oliver and Martenczuk (2018), p. 576.

[90] See Chamon and Demedts (2017), p. 250.

[91] Council of the European Union (2013), Brussels, 1 February 2013, 5707/13.

DGs of the EU Commission and bind only the Institution as such.[92] Indeed, as mentioned earlier, the EU Commission has engaged in such technical/administrative cooperation in the past including in the international sphere, even though only sporadically. However, the nature of these agreements give a glimpse of what a technical/administrative aspect can be. Past agreements include the Administrative Arrangement concerning a Framework for Cooperation between the Secretariat of the Central Commission for the Navigation of the Rhine and the Directorate-General for Mobility and Transport of the European Commission,[93] the Administrative Arrangement between the European Commission and the African Union Commission establishing a staff exchange and administrative cooperation programme,[94] or similar arrangements between the Directorate General for Competition (hereinafter DG COMP) and third countries regarding cooperation issues in the field of competition such as the MoU between DG COMP and the Competition Commission of India.[95]

One characteristic of such instruments is their purpose and content. In the Administrative Arrangements mentioned above, the purposes include either the establishment of cooperation frameworks,[96] the facilitation and strengthening of cooperation,[97] and exchange of information.[98] Aiming to facilitate the workings between the two administrations, they constitute agreements that either outline practicalities of cooperation that the implicated administrations must carry out, or design the contours of cross-institutional practices. In that regard they are

---

[92] Ott (2020), pp. 579ff.

[93] EU Commission, 'Administrative Arrangement concerning a Framework for Cooperation between the Secretariat of the Central Commission for the Navigation of the Rhine' <https://ec. europa.eu/transport/sites/default/files/modes/inland/promotion/doc/administrative_arrangement_ en.pdf>.

[94] EU Commission, 'Administrative Arrangement between the European Commission and the African Union Commission establishing a staff exchange and administrative cooperation programme' https://africa-eu-partnership.org/sites/default/files/userfiles/administrative_arrange ment-_staff_exchange.pdf.

[95] EU Commission, 'India-EU MoU on Cooperation' <https://africa-eu-partnership.org/sites/ default/files/userfiles/administrative_arrangement-_staff_exchange.pdf>.

[96] Article I.1, 'Administrative Arrangement between the European Commission and the African Union Commission establishing a staff exchange and administrative cooperation programme', <https://africa-eu-partnership.org/sites/default/files/userfiles/administrative_arrangement-_staff_ exchange.pdf>, and Article 2, 'Administrative Arrangement concerning a Framework for Cooperation between the Secretariat of the Central Commission for the Navigation of the Rhine' <https:// ec.europa.eu/competition-policy/system/files/2021-06/India-EU_memorandum-of-understand ing_2013_en.pdf https://ec.europa.eu/transport/sites/default/files/modes/inland/promotion/doc/ administrative_arrangement_en.pdf.

[97] Article I.1, 'India-EU MoU on Cooperation' <https://ec.europa.eu/competition-policy/system/ files/2021-06/India-EU_memorandum-of-understanding_2013_en.pdf>.

[98] Article 1, 'Administrative Arrangement (AA) between the European Commission's Directorate-General for Justice and Consumers and the Department of Health of Canada on the exchange of information on the safety of non-food consumer products' https://ec.europa.eu/info/sites/default/ files/aa_final_en-eu_version.pdf.

process-related without adding any substance to the existing legal relation of the parties, apart from making it more concrete.

Administrative Agreements that Complement Political Commitments
However, there is also another interesting characteristic that Ott spots as being present at some agreements, which is closely related to the previous category, as they share content and purpose, but nevertheless merits attention. It is often the case that such administrative arrangements are employed to complement political commitments that have been made in other instruments, such as MoUs, instruments that foresee their implementation through such arrangements by specific provisions.[99] One example is the MoU between the European Union and the Republic of Panama on International Cooperation and Development, which foresees the potential use of administrative arrangements to determine the conditions for collaboration between the sides.[100] It thus can be supported that such implementing instruments can be signed by the EU Commission, even when the provision that foresees the use of such an arrangement in the primary instrument does not provide specifically which actor has to act. This observation offers an additional criterion on the characterization of an arrangement as technical/administrative, which is the fact that the process described within them usually finds its legal basis in a different, political instrument. Such an observation provides assurance that the provisions of an administrative arrangement are not undertaken in a legal vacuum but point concretely to the legal bond on which they rely. To frame it briefly, through an administrative arrangement, the implicated parties in a legal relationship decide on its operationalisation, rather than on the presence or absence of the relationship as such, which can be traced elsewhere.

5.3.3.3 The Application of These Criteria to the Administrative Arrangements

Administrative Arrangements on Pharmaceuticals
In the context of Regulatory Cooperation, the Administrative Arrangements on Pharmaceuticals can be considered to fall under the category just described above, namely as an instrument that does not introduce, but rather complement existing political commitments. Indeed, we should mention that the conclusion of these Administrative Arrangements is firmly rooted in delegating provisions of CETA, specifically by Article 15.3 of the CETA Protocol on the mutual recognition of the compliance and enforcement programme regarding GMP for pharmaceutical products, and also more generally by Article 4.5 of the TBT CETA, which called for a firmer coordination on the issue of mutual recognition on pharmaceuticals.

---

[99] Ott (2020), p. 583.

[100] EU Council, 'MoU between the European Union and the Republic of Panama on International Cooperation and Development', p. 6 <https://data.consilium.europa.eu/doc/document/ST-6886-2018-INIT/lt/pdf>.

With regard to the Administrative Arrangements on Pharmaceuticals, suffice it to say that despite their length and detail of the provisions, they do not in fact introduce additional legislative choices next to the ones made in the Protocol. The Protocol, which provides for the initial legal basis, is the one that outlines the main legal commitment, namely the one regarding the mutual recognition of GMP certificates. These Administrative Arrangements on the other hand outlines in detail the modalities of how this mutual recognition will take place. In order to briefly recall what was in detail described in Sect. 4.3.2.2, the mutual recognition of GMP certificates begins from the establishment of equivalency of the regulatory authorities (NRAs) of the two parties, which is provided for in is stated in Articles 4 and 12 of the Protocol. Once established, the equivalency allows the NRAs to issue certificates proving that a manufacturing facility under their scope abides by GMP. The role of the arrangements in the equivalency process is exactly the one described above, as in outlining in detail the criteria against which the equivalency of a regulatory authority will be assessed and maintained respectively.

As demonstrated, these Arrangements do not include for the first time legal commitments and they do not expand the obligations that already exist. What they do is to operationalize the commitments enshrined in the Protocol and offer additional information where necessary. In that regard, they qualify as 'technical' or 'administrative' ones, and in that capacity they can be signed by the Commission autonomously on the basis of Article 335 TFEU, as analysed in the previous section.

Administrative Arrangement on Exchange of Information on Non-food Products

As regards the Administrative Arrangement on the exchange of information on non-food products, it rather falls under the premise of Sect. 5.3.3.1, which stipulated that no autonomous decision-making shall be granted to the executive in cases where an agreement entails an interference with human rights. In the previous chapter, when discussing its possible consequences in the EU legal order we referred to the exchange of information that would take place on the basis of its provisions. Indeed, reference was made to Annex II of the Administrative Arrangement that outlines the data fields that can be communicated to the other party (for example Name, Address, City, Country of the exporter of a certain product).

In the absence of an updated adequacy decision for Canada on the basis of Article 44 ff. GDPR, the Administrative Arrangement by promulgating the exchange of such data as part of the cooperation procedures interferes with the right to privacy, as it could de facto establish an adequacy regime—or disregard the current requirement on adequacy—that would allow for a transfer of personal data between the administrative authorities. While access to RAPEX and exchange of information between the authorities is foreseen under Article 12 par. 4 of Directive 2001/95/EC, this legal basis cannot be interpreted as circumventing the requirement of adequacy, as the latter interferes directly with fundamental rights. Indeed, Article 12 par. 4 of Directive 2001/95/EC only provides the possibility to open RAPEX to third countries but does not provide a waiver to requirements that protect fundamental rights. More specifically, the Article states:

Access to RAPEX shall be open to applicant countries, third countries or international
organisations. within the framework of agreements between the Community and those
countries or international organisations, according to arrangements defined in these agreements. Any such agreements shall be based on reciprocity and include provisions on
confidentiality corresponding to those applicable in the Community.[101]

Hence, while the regime of exchange of information relies upon that Article, it does
not mean that it can act independently of any other legal requirements. This
interpretation is further supported by the second limb of the provision that requires
confidentiality provisions equal of the ones of the EU. And while the cooperation is
foreseen under 21.7 CETA, the adequacy of the privacy regime is not. And at least in
theory, the adequacy requirement could be circumvented if this would be provided in
an international treaty like CETA. On that basis, it can not be concluded that the
Commission possessed the capacity to sign this Administrative Arrangement as an
administration. Rather, the participation of other institutional actors should have
been foreseen.

5.3.4   Considerations on How to Expand International Secondary Decision-Making Beyond the Commission's Own Decision-Making Powers

On the basis of the above findings, according to which the autonomous decision-
making scope of the Commission was found to be quite limited, but also reflecting
on the potential future directions of the Regulatory Cooperation Chapters according
to their purpose, this section reflects upon the circumstances under which the
secondary decision-making power can be further enlarged, jointly with other Institutions. As we will describe below, the limited potential of Administrative Agreements on the basis of Article 335 par. 3 TFEU cannot encompass other Regulatory
Cooperation results which may be present in future bilateral endeavours and of
political character; a different legal solution has to be found in order to expand the
secondary international rule-making beyond the Commission's own decision-
making powers.

5.3.4.1   A Non-binding Political Agreement with the Involvement of the Council and the Parliament

On the occasion of the litigation analysed above, the Court of Justice submitted that
for the conclusion of the Swiss MoU, a non-binding political agreement from the
part of the Commission, the Council should have been consulted in order to confirm

---

[101] Article 12 par. 4 Directive 2001/95/EC.

and agree upon the political direction taken.[102] As supported by the findings of the AG mentioned above, this stems from the repartition of competences between the Institutions, which exists in harmony with Article 218 TFEU, on the basis of which the EU Council enjoys the policy making functions on the basis of Article 16 (1) TEU and the Commission has the power of representation by virtue of Article 17 (1) TEU.[103]

Although implicitly, the Court accepted the possibility of such a commitment to be made under the right participatory circumstances. Hence, one possibility with regard to the possible future agreements on political issues could be their inclusion in a non-binding political agreement signed by the Commission, after the consultation and approval of the Council. Such a scenario would correspond to what has been identified in the legal literature on international soft law as a soft agreement 'preceding' and preparing a binding one to follow.[104]

Indeed, while this kind of arrangement would not equal to a binding commitment itself, it would serve as a means to prepare and smoothen the formal endorsement of their content at a later stage as international treaties. There are several benefits that come along with this option in the realm of Regulatory Cooperation. First of all, the preparations on a technical level take place in the context of the RCFs, which are specialised entities to support this kind of talks. This has as a result that the part of the negotiations takes place in already existing structures, and hence the need to create new ones is not pending. Secondly, the closure of the procedure that requires the agreement and input of the Council and EU Parliament would secure the ex-ante approval of the Institutions that are in charge of the international treaty-making. Last but not least, the leading role of the EU Commission through its services in the RCFs is of course in line with its role as the negotiator according to Article 218 TFEU.

This solution, as any other, presents advantages and disadvantages. On the one hand, the EU is bound on a political level as a whole, as the EU Commission is signing on its behalf, and the institutional participation that an international treaty would require is present, while the procedure is already staged in an existing framework and legal environment. On the other hand, the political character of such an agreement raises questions as regards its future implementation in the EU legal order as well as its enforcement. Indeed, for the commitment to have a legal value the formal procedure for the conclusion of an international treaty would need to follow. For this, it would be of tantamount importance to secure the inclusion of the EU Parliament and the Council, so that no objections would be raised at a later stage.

The above considerations for the need of parliamentary participation do not mean that these agreements should in any case be concluded as international treaties.

---

[102] Case C-660/13 *Council of the European Union v. European Commission* [2016] ECLI:EU: C:2016:616, par. 46.

[103] Case C-660/13 *Council of the European Union v. European Commission* [2016] ECLI:EU: C:2016:616, Opinion of AG Sharpston, par. 91.

[104] Ott (2020), p. 574.

Indeed, on the one hand, from the categorization made above on what the Commission can and cannot sign on its own, as well as why, it became clear from the cited case law that the EU Commission cannot decide autonomously on political issues, even by means of a soft law agreement. On the other hand, however, this does not mean that the conclusion of agreements other than international treaties is excluded, provided of course that the necessary institutional participation is foreseen.

5.3.4.2   The Use of Article 218 par. 9 TFEU

Drawing parallels from that reasoning provided in the Swiss MoU case, which put institutional balance in the epicentre, another solution to combine efficiency along with legitimacy requirements could be the utilisation of Article 218 (9) TFEU along with enhanced parliamentary participation. Even if currently Article 218 (9) cannot be employed, as both the RCF and the Joint Committees lack decision-making powers themselves with regard to Regulatory Cooperation, it might be worth for the parties to revisit the options available, even if this would drastically change the nature of Regulatory Cooperation. In fact, this will not be an innovation under CETA as MRAs on recognition of professional qualifications can already be prepared by the Joint Committee on MRAs on the basis of Article 11.3.6 CETA in order to be ratified by the parties. In a similar manner, the CETA Joint Committee could bestow either a similar drafting capacity or a decision-making capacity similar to the one in 11.3.6 CETA on the RCF on the basis of Article 28.1.5 (a) and (g) CETA. This provision allows the Joint Committee to *'delegate responsibilities to the specialised Committees established pursuant to Article 26.2'* and *'change or undertake the tasks assigned to specialised Committees established pursuant to Article 26.2'*.

Should decisions on Regulatory Cooperation be taken by those bodies, the EU Commission will be able to agree on their content on the basis of Article 218 (9) TFEU. Indeed, it is much more legitimate to use existing decision-making avenues, especially for issues of importance such as MRAs rather than informal instruments such as the Administrative Agreements, even with parliamentary and executive participation. This reading is also supported by Article 296 (1) TFEU. According to the latter, *'Where the Treaties do not specify the type of act to be adopted, the Institutions shall select it on a case-by-case basis, in compliance with the applicable procedures and with the principle of proportionality'*. This provision has been rightly interpreted as an obligation limiting the margin of discretion of the Commission also in the international sphere on the choice of legal instruments, especially regarding fields of action in which democracy considerations would require parliamentary consent for certain decision-making of Article 218 (9), as is for example the case of MRAs.[105] And in any case, the consistent and repetitive regulation of EU's external action with legal tools other than the ones provided in the

---

[105] See Garcia Andrade (2018), p. 121.

Treaty risks creating a parallel universe of EU legal orders susceptible to bypass more easily EU principles and values.[106]

Article 218 (9) is the best match in the EU legal order for this exercise. To begin with, Article 218 (9) TFEU could theoretically apply since it exists to introduce in the EU legal order acts that are taken to implement international agreements and that are decided by an international body established by the international agreement at stake, even if the EU is not directly part of that agreement. With regard to Regulatory Cooperation results, we are indeed in such a case, where the potential results would be decided by an international body established by an international agreement, namely CETA. These bodies could be for example the RCF or the Joint Committees. Moreover, the analysis made in Sect. 5.3.2 on the existing international instruments confirmed that broad scope of candidate acts to fall under this provision, including acts with binding and non-binding legal effects. Undoubtedly, the effects of agreements of political character, such as MRAs, whether of binding or non-binding nature are considerable to the extent they constitute a degree of harmonization as explained above.

Contrary to Administrative Agreements solely signed by the Commission, Article 218 (9) TFEU matches better the institutional balance in rule-making on the international sphere and addresses comprehensively the need of the participation of the executive, namely the EU Council, as the political decision-taker. Indeed behind Article 218 (9) TFEU lies the need to align the simplified procedure with the idea that international commitments are to be concluded by the Council.[107] However, what this provision fails to do is to acknowledge and reflect the parliamentary participation at least to the extent it exists regarding normal treaty-making. That is why constitutional law scholars have proposed some avenues to enhance the democratic legitimacy and include some form of parliamentary participation. According to Weiss, that could be achieved for example both on the international and EU level.[108] Indeed, the participation of the EU Parliament could be guaranteed at the level of those international bodies, by granting a formal status to some of its members, something that could be established under the rules of procedure of the specialised Committees.[109] Another idea is to take full advantage of Article 218 and slightly modify the procedure of Article 218 (9) as to include extra steps to reflect the opinion of the parliament. For example, the Council could directly implicate the EU Parliament during the formation of its opinion, either by receiving directives from it, asking for a consent on the final stage—a reading which is in line with the reasoning made above—or by asking for the institution's opinion on the matter.[110] At the very least, the general Article 218 (10) should be put in good use in any case.

---

[106] Wessel (2021), p. 83.

[107] Rosas (2017), p. 370.

[108] Weiss (2018), p. 564.

[109] Weiss (2018), p. 564.

[110] Weiss (2018), p. 564.

The same repartition of tasks among the Institutions should be proposed independently of the instrument in place, may it be a binding decision-making in the specialised Committees or a non-binding political agreement. One drawback of this option is that, as for the moment the binding decision-making by the specialised Committees on Regulatory Cooperation does not exist. It could be of course possible to organise a procedure similar to the one of Article 218 (9) TFEU which also secures parliamentary participation to support the decision-making process of other non-codified instruments that might occur from practice and that are political in nature. However, it is questionable whether this would be a viable option, should it to be organised independently of Article 218 (9) TFEU.

5.3.5   Inference on Input Legitimacy

This section examined the first leg of legitimacy as chosen to be examined in the thesis, namely input legitimacy, which refers in simple words to the issue of the competent decision-maker, a question which is pertinent to the examination of the Administrative Agreements that have been so far concluded under the CETA Regulatory Cooperation structures. Do the Administrative Arrangements discussed in Chap. 4 actually fall under the EU Commission's autonomous decision-making capacity or do they go beyond it?

In order to answer this question, this section started the analysis by discerning the classic international treaties from this category of executive international agreements. This category of agreements, in the past known as *'accords en forme simplifiee'* has been documented in classic international law literature as having a certain characteristic: the organ who undertakes them, while lacking 'full powers' of treaty-making should have the competence of binding the entity it represents in the subject matters that concern the particular decision-making. Usually, such competence stems from the internal constitutional framework. In the absence of such specific competence, the organ who undertakes the instruments acts beyond the scope of its powers.

Relying upon this premise, the section further assessed the role of the EU Commission in international decision-making, based upon the Treaties and relevant jurisprudence of the Court of Justice and reached a double conclusion: firstly, according to Article 218 TFEU, the Commission lacks full powers to engage in traditional treaty-making, a fact which the Court of Justice further confirmed by denying full powers to issues of its internal competence; and secondly, recent jurisprudence left out of its scope also non-binding agreements of political nature. While these considerations restricted the EU Commission's decision-making capacity, the role of Article 335 TFEU was also considered as a possible legal basis that allows certain decision-making from the part of the EU Commission on matters of administrative nature. Hence, the limits of the Commission's autonomous decision-making capacity were found to rely upon the character of the agreement as political or mere administrative/technical.

The section proceeded to examine what issues qualify as political and which as administrative. The proposed categories while being quite broad, were proposed in a way that would fit the activities that could fall under Regulatory Cooperation. Commitments that relate to or constitute policy-making, commitments that may interfere with human rights, commitments that underpin legislative choices and commitments that include a transfer of regulatory authority were placed under the category of agreements with a political character, and were hence identified as falling out of the autonomous decision-making capacity of the EU Commission. On the other hand, agreements that pertain to the EU Commission's own operation or agreements that implement technically an otherwise made commitment may be concluded by the EU Commission autonomously.

The section relied upon this categorization to comment upon the legality of the already concluded Administrative Agreements. The Administrative Agreement on Pharmaceuticals was found to implement the CETA Protocol on the mutual recognition of the compliance and enforcement programme regarding good manufacturing practices for pharmaceutical products, which explicitly provided for the conclusion of an implementing instrument. As such, it was rightly adopted by the EU Commission on the basis of its own mandate to represent externally the Union and on the basis of Article 335 par. 3 TFEU. The same conclusion could not be reached with certainty regarding the Administrative Arrangement on the exchange of information on non-food products. In particular, this instrument was found to be susceptible to enable data transfers in the context of its operationalisation, in the absence of an updated adequacy regime between the EU and Canada. As such, it could interfere with the fundamental right to privacy and data protection, hence falling out of the EU Commission's scope of autonomous action.

The section concluded by proposing alternatives to international decision-making for the issues of political nature that otherwise fall outside the scope of the capacities of the EU Commission. It considered the more frequent use of non-binding political agreements with the necessary institutional participation as preparatory instruments to possible future treaties or self-standing along with the possibility to further binding decision-making in the specialized CETA Committees.

5.4 Output Legitimacy: Regulatory Cooperation Under CETA as a Threat to Fundamental Regulatory Values?

As the previous parts established, Regulatory Cooperation has been employed early on, while the existing promises on cooperation and future aspirations have triggered some regulatory developments in both jurisdictions. Indeed, we determined the extent of the regulatory dialogue effects and found their variability and appearance at various instances. To recall shortly, the case studies which the previous chapter referred to (see Sect. 4.4), pointed to the presented effects, which translate to direct and indirect changes in EU and Canadian legislation. For example, the introduced amendments to the Canadian Food and Drugs Regulation demonstrate that the internal legislative implementation of the promises made on the RCF level, is a form of Regulatory Cooperation effects. Similarly, the revision of the Market Surveillance Regulation from the EU side suggested that also internal legislative changes related to cooperation activities can be traced back to the relevant regulatory dialogue. And this is to be expected, as commitments that are undertaken on the international level might need also an internal legal basis to be properly implemented.

Apart from these legislative additions triggered in the two jurisdictions by Regulatory Cooperation, in order to facilitate the undertaken commitments, the previous chapter referred to the undertaken Regulatory Cooperation dialogue with regard to pesticides. The presented leaked documents suggested that the Regulatory Cooperation activities can be far more intrusive than the legislative implementation internally of undertaken commitments. They are in fact susceptible of undermining internal regulatory processes and their output legitimacy.

The purpose of this paragraph will be to discuss whether output legitimacy requirements have been met with regard to the Regulatory Cooperation activities that have had an impact so far to the Commission's regulatory initiative. In order to illustrate the argument we will primarily use the example of Regulatory Cooperation dialogue in pesticides, and its impact on the REFIT process, for which we previously suspected that it can undermine the application of the precautionary principle in the EU legal order. Section 5.4.1 will start on a general note by examining the compatibility of the Regulatory Cooperation input with the Commission's regulatory activities. This step is necessary in order to ensure that any regulatory input from Regulatory Cooperation structures is in principle compatible with any initiation or revision of legislation, in short with the Commission's right of initiative. Section 5.4.2 will refer to the case study and will describe the input received through Regulatory Cooperation during the legislative revision of the pesticides legislation through the REFIT process. On the basis of it, Sect. 5.4.3 will turn to analyse how output legitimacy requirements should be measured and if the EU Commission has respected them with regard to Regulatory Cooperation activities, especially in the revision of the pesticides legislation.

5.4.1 The Interaction Between the Input from Regulatory Cooperation and the Commission's Right of Initiative

5.4.1.1 On the Compatibility of Regulatory Cooperation Dialogues with the Commission's Right of Initiative

The general compatibility of the Regulatory Cooperation with the Commission's right of initiative can be inferred primarily from relevant jurisprudence of the Court, the findings of which are supported from other legal sources regulating the state of art of EU decision-making activity.

With regard to previous jurisprudence on the issue, the same question of the compatibility between the EU-US Regulatory Cooperation Guidelines, a political agreement forming part of a chain of several political initiatives, and the Commission's right of initiative was raised in a case mentioned earlier in Chap. 3, case C-233/02 *France v. Commission*. Recalling shortly the facts, in this case France challenged the conclusion of the Guidelines firstly on the basis of the chosen instrument (Administrative Agreement instead of International agreement) and secondly on the basis of their unlawful restriction of Commission's right of initiative.

Since the two types of Regulatory Cooperation share similarities, it is worth revising the main arguments and the justification of the Court and apply it to today's Regulatory Cooperation. Indeed, the content of the provisions of the two agreements is to a large extent similar, and regulatory dialogue plays the most important role in both. Mostly, it is the pattern of commitments in the Chapters of Regulatory Cooperation that is similar to the ones undertaken by the former Guidelines. For example, both documents give particular importance to the timely and continuous exchange of information, address cooperation opportunities in existing and future regulations, express the wish to tackle methodological and systemic problems of regulation, and mention the possibility to achieve convergence through various avenues. The Guidelines also included some segments of regulatory coherence, in the form of transparency requirements. Of course, apart from similarities, there is a fundamental difference between the two cases, which could be determining for the future behaviour of the parties. On the one hand, the Regulatory Cooperation guidelines were a political agreement with no legal value, which is not the case for the Regulatory Cooperation Chapters, as the previous chapter demonstrated. This is important because the absence of the legally binding character was one the main drivers for the parties', the Court's and the AG's reasoning on case C-233/02 that ruled out the possibility of illegal interference with the Commission's right of initiative.

Indeed, should one read the opinion of the AG thoroughly, one will notice that apart from the parties to the dispute, both the AG and the Court connect the ability to impact of the Commission's right of initiative with the legal nature of the Guidelines. This consideration is the core of France's argument that considered the Guidelines as legally binding: since the Commission is bound by the Guidelines and must take them into account, its monopoly to initiate legislation is constrained.[111] The United Kingdom that intervened in support of the Commission also makes this connection in arguing that a non-binding consultation of American authorities is covered by Commission's right of initiative.[112] The same link is present to the AG's assessment and the Court's reasoning as well. In paragraph 63 of his opinion the AG argues that while the Guidelines may create procedural obligations, they definitely do not create substantive ones, and the relevant authorities are completely free to reject and

---

[111]Case C-233/02 *France v. Commission* [2004] ECR I-2759 Opinion of AG Alber, par. 27.

[112]Case C-233/02 *France v. Commission* [2004] ECR I-2759 Opinion of AG Alber, par. 42.

disregard any foreign input they consider inappropriate.[113] The Court makes a similar statement in its decision while responding to the second plea in law in opening by pointing out that the non-binding character of the Guidelines does not impose any obligations on the Commission during the exercise of its part of the legislative process.

In the reasoning outlined above, all of the parties relied upon the soft legal nature of the Guidelines in order to dispute any claim of incompatibility of regulatory dialogue with the Commission's right of initiative. Would that mean that the outcome of the case would differ should the same question had arisen with regard to legally binding Regulatory Cooperation? The answer to this question was given in paragraph 62 of the AG's Opinion in France v. Commission C-233/02, where he considered consultations with foreign governments as an exercise of the right of initiative rather than a restriction.[114] It is upon the same consideration that an incompatibility with Commission's right of initiative could presumably not be founded here, despite the different legal status of the commitments involved. Indeed, the Commission is vested with the exclusive political right to sketch out future legislation.[115] As the instigator of legislation acting for the general interest of the Union, the Commission has to follow an open door policy with regard to its rulemaking activities and collect information from other actors of varying backgrounds.[116] In fact, it has been rightly placed that the Commission has a de jure but not a de facto monopoly.[117] In the area of trade, and given the importance to avoid future trade disputes, consultations with foreign governments, even if regulated in legal terms could still fall within this open-door policy, rendering it as an exercise rather than restriction.

These statements can be confirmed from other sources as well. Most importantly, the requirement to conduct consultations is rooted in primary law. Article 11 TEU itself states that *"the European Commission shall carry out broad consultations with parties concerned in order to ensure that the Union's actions are coherent and transparent."*. Moreover, the annexed to the Treaties Protocol No. 2 on the application of the principles of subsidiarity and proportionality mentions that *"before proposing legislative acts, the Commission shall consult widely"*. The content of this constitutional stipulation is further developed in the Better Regulation Guidelines, a set of documents issued by the Commission, in order to guide its officials implicated in the design of regulation, so that the latter achieve maximum results while having minimum cost.[118] Stakeholder consultation is in that sense a part of the skeleton of

---

[113] Case C-233/02 *France v. Commission* [2004] ECR I-2759 Opinion of AG Alber, par. 63.

[114] Case C-233/02 *France v. Commission* [2004] ECR I-2759 Opinion of AG Alber, par. 62.

[115] This is with no prejudice to the right of the European Parliament to ask the Commission to submit a proposal.

[116] *See* generally Noel (1973).

[117] Rasmussen (2007), p. 248.

[118] EU Commission (2021), p. 23.

the Guidelines, as it is developed in a separate chapter.[119] As a process, it applies to all stages of regulatory activity, the initial design, the evaluation and revision of policy initiatives. Part of the process is also the identification of the relevant stakeholders, and in that respect, third country partners are recognised by the document as a category of stakeholders, whose input must be considered throughout the regulatory process.[120] The dialogues carried out through the implementation of Regulatory Cooperation Chapters provide a platform through which input on trade matters can be provided. Hence, these mechanisms are in principle in line with the Commission's right of initiative, as this is manifested in the various regulatory processes. Nevertheless, this general compatibility does not mean that the Regulatory Cooperation dialogue cannot have far-reaching impact on the deliberations at EU level. The next part will briefly recall the findings of the example of the Regulatory Cooperation dialogue, as it took place with regard to the revision of the pesticides regulation, that precisely proves that point.

5.4.1.2 The Impact of Regulatory Cooperation Dialogue on the REFIT Process on MRLs of Hazardous Substances on Imported Products

Back in Sect. 4.4.2, while outlining the regulatory dialogue taking place regarding cooperation on pesticides, we identified the main thorny issues that were tackled by big industry players as well as the Canadian counterparts. It is worth underlining here that the documents used were leaked, however, that does not deprive them of their informative nature. They remain official documents originating from the respective authorities. As they suggest the abandonment of the precautionary principle and its regulatory ramifications remains the long term victory for the Canadians. Such an option would ground the approval of active substances on the basis of risk-assessment, and not on the basis of the cut-off criteria, which constitute a direct application of the precautionary principle. According to the regulatory regime before the REFIT process, only the active substances that did not meet the hazard cut-off criteria were subject to the usual risk assessment, and if this assessment turned positive, MRLs were set accordingly. Indeed, as analyzed above, the short-term goal of this pressure group was to ensure that importers could nevertheless ask for import tolerances of hazardous pesticides contained in their products on the basis of a risk assessment, even if the substances under question were to be identified as hazardous on the basis of the cut-off criteria. And indeed, in light of the findings described in Sect. 4.4.2, the REFIT evaluation did in fact demonstrate the fact that the Commission allowed for a risk assessment for the purposes of setting MRLs and import tolerances for products containing hazardous pesticides, while it does not

---

[119] EU Commission (2021), pp. 12ff.

[120] Third countries are considered under the Better Regulation Guidelines. *See* EU Commission (2021), p. 5.

allow so internally. The REFIT evaluation did not follow the initial proposal of the Commission that favoured the deletion of MRLs for hazardous substances, i.e. meeting the cut-off criteria. Third-country interested parties are thus not prevented from submitting import tolerance applications for such substances. Furthermore, the REFIT evaluation underlined problems brought up in the various WTO and international fora, allegedly created by the elimination of import tolerances for substances meeting the cut-off criteria.

The input provided by the Regulatory Cooperation, which inspired the report in the way described above falls under the general stakeholder consultation requirement, as discussed in the previous Sect. 5.4.1.1. As such, it is in principle compatible with the revision process. However, in this case the revision of the pesticides legislation raises questions regarding the impact of the input in the process as a whole. Indeed, in the sensitive area of pesticides regulation, where the Commission traditionally opted for a strict regulation based on the precautionary principle, the developments suggest that the dialogue within the relevant CETA Committees was decisive in the observed re-orientation of the Commission's position, towards a less strict, allegedly more WTO-compatible approach. This insinuates that the way in which Commission's independence was undermined was substantial rather than procedural, which is questionable from an output legitimacy point of view. The next part will focus upon this point. It will first provide with a framework on how to 'measure' output legitimacy. On the basis of it, it examines why in this case the EU Commission did not respect the output legitimacy requirements as set by EU law and what the EU Commission should have done instead. It will also refer more generally to the legitimacy requirements that output legitimacy sets for the Regulatory Cooperation activities.

5.4.2 The Status of Output Legitimacy in the REFIT Process for Pesticides Legislation and Beyond

5.4.2.1 Output Legitimacy Requirements in Regulatory Cooperation: How to Define the Regulatory Values and What Do They Instruct?

When explaining the tripartite distinction of legitimacy that is employed in this chapter, we referred to output legitimacy as the presence (or absence) of certain values that are promoted within the results themselves. In the context of an FTA, and in the context of Regulatory Cooperation, it is the prevalence of values that is related to the trade agenda and economic liberalization to the expense of other regulatory values that marks the case for absence of output legitimacy. In other words, in the case of Regulatory Cooperation, the output legitimacy of the activities is guaranteed by the absence of a de-regulatory effect, which would entail the prevalence of economic liberalization objectives to the expense of the level of protection guaranteed in the EU in each domain, for the sake of liberalization.

The search for the regulatory values that will instruct the output legitimacy requirements begins from the EU's 'normative basis. According to Ian Manners, this fundamental normative basis shapes the EU's normative palette and is comprised of the following founding principles: liberty, democracy, respect for fundamental rights and human dignity and the rule of law.[121] This list includes some of the EU values enshrined in Article 2 TEU, which also includes the rights of minorities, pluralism, non-discrimination, tolerance, justice solidarity and equality as common values shared by its Member States as well.[122] This fundamental normative basis has allowed the EU to be properly legitimized in the eyes of the constituents of the participating Member States as something more than manager of economic liberalization in the EU arena, but as a good global actor, with fundamental values that have shaped its internal and external core identity.[123] These founding principles are then found in the core of EU's normative palette that define the values that the EU promotes throughout its regulatory agenda, which are later concretized in the different regulatory areas. To give an example, Article 3 (3) TEU concretizes how these values are translated in the creation of an internal market, which shall: «...*work for the sustainable development of Europe based on balanced economic growth and price stability, a highly competitive social market economy, aiming at full employment and social progress, and a high level of protection and improvement of the quality of the environment. It shall promote scientific and technological advance*».[124]

Hence, as Regulatory Cooperation can expand to a variety of topics, the list of values that the EU Commission has to respect in the context of Regulatory Cooperation cannot be predefined. Instead, the values at stake will need to be determined on the basis of each cooperation topic. The different Titles of Chapter 3 of the TFEU referring to different regulatory areas, for example, Title on Consumer Protection, Title XX on Environment outline the different values that guide objectives that must be achieved respectively. We thus see that the regulatory values are to be extracted to a big extent from the provisions of the EU Treaties that define each regulatory area, and how these have been concretized so far through internal regulatory action.

The starting point in submitting any Regulatory Cooperation activity to an output legitimacy test would be to identify the EU policy area and the values that surround it. Output legitimacy would thus require from the participants of Regulatory Cooperation, the EU Commission in the case of the EU, to uphold these regulatory values throughout the whole procedure, and to not blatantly undermine their application for the benefit of economic liberalization and trade. Hence, output legitimacy requires that the final result of Regulatory Cooperation promotes the identified regulatory values while of course achieving other objectives in the context of trade. Of course, it is understandable that a balancing exercise will always take place and the various

---

[121] Manners (2002), p. 243.

[122] Article 2 TEU.

[123] Manners (2002), p. 244.

[124] Article 3(3) TEU.

interests at stake will need to be measured. However, a complete disregard of a regulatory principle would be characteristic of an output legitimacy gap.

So far, this does not seem to be the case with the majority of the Regulatory Cooperation results, both the Administrative Arrangements and the additions to the legislation that took place. Indeed, the legislative addition of a new Article to the Market Surveillance Regulation has as its principal objective to expand the exchange of information between the relevant authorities. The main regulatory value at stake is product and consumer safety, a regulatory value enshrined in Article 169 TFEU and which is rather furthered than compromised. More specifically, the new Article 35 of the Regulation provides for the possibility for the Commission to exchange market surveillance information with regulatory authorities of third parties regarding: (a) risk assessment methods used and the results of product-testing; (b) coordinated product recalls or other similar actions; (c) the measures taken by market surveillance authorities.[125] This amendment aims to expand the possibility of further coordination in the context of product safety. The same objective is furthered with both Administrative Arrangement on RAPEX and Pharmaceuticals, whose finalities respectively are to enhance coordination and exchange of information between the two alert systems on dangerous products[126] and to ensure that medicinal products and drugs meet appropriate quality standards through the mutual recognition of certificates of GMP compliance.[127]

However, the same cannot be said for the case study of the pesticides legislation revision. The analysis of the leaked documents and the REFIT report following the consultation actually suggest that the EU Commission gave in to regulatory pressure from its trade counterparts and adopted a different view from the one originally envisaged. In that regard, how do these considerations apply to the case study of the pesticides legislation revision? From which parts will we understand whether the output legitimacy requirements have been respected? In the following parts we will carry out this exercise for the precautionary principle, which is at the core of pesticides regulation and is in our example, at stake. After explaining why we identify the precautionary principle as a relevant regulatory value, we will measure the output legitimacy score of the revision process of pesticides legislation.

---

[125] Proposal for a Regulation of the European Parliament and of the Council laying down rules and procedures for compliance with and enforcement of Union harmonisation legislation on products and amending Regulations (EU) No 305/2011, (EU) No 528/2012, (EU) 2016/424, (EU) 2016/425, (EU) 2016/426 and (EU) 2017/1369 of the European Parliament and of the Council, and Directives 2004/42/EC, 2009/48/EC, 2010/35/EU, 2013/29/EU, 2013/53/EU, 2014/28/EU, 2014/29/EU, 2014/30/EU, 2014/31/EU, 2014/32/EU, 2014/33/EU, 2014/34/EU, 2014/35/EU, 2014/53/EU, 2014/68/EU and 2014/90/EU of the European Parliament and of the Council, Brussels, 19.12.2017 COM(2017) 795 final 2017/0353 (COD).

[126] Administrative Agreement between the European Commission's Directorate-General for Justice and Consumers and the Department of Health of Canada on the exchange of information on the safety of non-food consumer products, <https://ec.europa.eu/info/sites/info/files/aa_final_en-eu_version.pdf>.

[127] Article 2, CETA Protocol on the Mutual Recognition of the Compliance and Enforcement Programme regarding GMPS for Pharmaceutical Products [2017] L 11/581.

5.4.2.2   Defining the Regulatory Principle at Stake in the Revision of Pesticides Legislation

Added originally in the EU legal order with the revision of the Maastricht Treaty[128] and developed on the basis of the *Vorsorge* principle of German law, the precautionary principle is currently detailed in Article 191 TFEU as a regulatory principle of environmental law, where a high protection level is mandated, on the basis of preventative regulation. However, the importance of precautionary principle is not studied solely on the basis of this Article, which is of limited scope. In fact, the precautionary principle constitutes a general principle of EU law. Its qualification as such, which renders its disregard unconstitutional, rests upon three main axes, its reference in primary law, its elevation as a general principle by the Court, and its use as such by the administration in other regulatory areas.

Indeed, it is not through its inclusion in the TFEU, to which we referred earlier that the precautionary principle owes its qualification as a general principle. Given its limited scope in the Treaties, it is through its migration to other regulatory areas by the jurisprudence of the Court and also on the administrative practice of the Commission that it has earned an additional value in the EU legal order. Its status as such is largely owned to the broad scope that jurisprudence of the Court of Justice has ascribed to it. According to the Court of Justice, the precautionary principle has as consequence that "where there is uncertainty as to the existence or extent of risks to human health, protective measures may be taken without having to wait until the reality and seriousness of those risks become fully apparent".[129] This broad scope of application was subsequently made more explicit with regard to the areas that it applies when human and public health comes into play.[130] This was confirmed by the Tribunal in the *Artegodan* case, which established the connection between the precautionary principle and its contribution to ensuring not only environmental, but also health and consumer safety.[131] In other words, given that health and consumer safety figure as objectives of the treaties as well, the precautionary principle is a tool that could be used for their attainment. The Tribunal went even further to proclaim the autonomous nature of the precautionary principle that stems from the Treaty provisions aiming to safeguard the environment as well as health and consumers.[132] These findings of the Court have further been confirmed by the Commission itself. Indeed, the precautionary principle has migrated to other areas of risk regulation, such as food, chemicals, plant health and consumer protection, as the EU

---

[128] De Sadeleer (2001), p. 83.

[129] Among others in Case T-13/99 *Pfizer Animal Health SA vs Council of the European Union [2002] ECR* II-3318, par. 139.

[130] De Sadeleer (2006), p. 142.

[131] Cases T-74/00, T-76/00, T-83/00, T-85/00, T-132/00, T-137/00, T-141/00, *Artegodan GmbH vs. Commission of the European Communities*, ECR II-4950, par. 183.

[132] Cases T-74/00, T-76/00, T-83/00, T-85/00, T-132/00, T-137/00, T-141/00, *Artegodan GmbH vs. Commission of the European Communities*, ECR II-4950, par. 184.

Commission itself has confirmed.[133] And for that reason the precautionary principle is relevant as the regulatory value at stake in our case as well. In the next part, we will discuss how the EU Commission disregarded its application during the REFIT process, which will form the basis to determine the 'output legitimacy score' of the particular cooperation.

5.4.2.3   Output Legitimacy Score of the Regulatory Cooperation Dialogue in the REFIT Process for Pesticides Legislation

The revision of the pesticides legislation was a good opportunity for the EU Commission to remedy existing legal gaps and inconsistencies in the regime of approval of active substances as described above. To recall briefly, with the revision the EU Commission would have the chance to submit import tolerances of active substances to the cut-off criteria that are in place in the EU. This would primarily require a change in the MRL legislation, which applies to imports and which does not explicitly mention the cut-off criteria. The original intention of the EU Commission was to align the internal with the external practice. This would remedy the existing breach where EU manufacturers are deprived of the use of active substances caught by the cut-off criteria and thus face a competitive disadvantage by third country competitors, which can apply for an important tolerance for the same substance that is prohibited internally.[134] Instead, the procedure that follows in that case is the approval or rejection of the import tolerance after a risk assessment. In other words, the disadvantage for the EU farmers that are hindered to use crops because of ingredients falling under cut off criteria whereas importers are granted an import tolerance, remained as it used to be, while the original plan envisaged a change in the legislation to remedy this inconsistency.

This change in the MRL legislation, by imposing the cut-off criteria to imports as well would bring the practice in line with the precautionary principle. As we mentioned in Sect. 4.4.2, the cut-off criteria concern intrinsic properties of the substances (i.e. whether they are carcinogenic, endocrine disruptors, mutagenic, or reproductive toxins) and in that context stem directly from the precautionary principle. Should one substance fall under one of these categories, its approval is automatically revoked under the PPP Regulation. With the current regime, as it now stands, substances that are not allowed to be used for EU crops are allowed to be imported from abroad provided they ask for an import tolerance after a risk assessment. However, this goes directly against the precautionary principle, and is what is being demanded in the trade fora by the polemics of EU's stance towards chemicals.

Unfortunately, the EU Commission lost the momentum and did not proceed towards that direction, as described in the REFIT report. Instead, the policy direction described above rather points to the fact that by choosing not to submit the import

---

[133] EU Commission (2000).

[134] EU Commission (2020b), Point 2.9.

tolerances of active substances to the cut-off criteria that are in place in the EU as an application of the precautionary principle, the EU undermined the output legitimacy of the regulatory dialogue. In fact, while it can't be said that the Regulatory Dialogue caused the breach of the precautionary principle in the first place, without doubt it was the reason why it was continued. Hence, it clearly shows that the Regulatory Dialogue has a power over the regulatory decisions of the EU Commission that is so important as to persuade them to depart from their original approach.

In the specific example of Regulatory Cooperation, the requirements set by output legitimacy suggest that the precautionary principle should have been upheld despite the regulatory pressure. This would have led the EU Commission to take a different direction and strengthen its position with regard to the import tolerances of active substances that are anyway prohibited in the EU. In fact, this requirement does not only uphold the precautionary principle, but also avoids the discrimination that the current practice bears against EU producers.

5.4.3 Inference on Output Legitimacy

This section examined the second arm of legitimacy, the output legitimacy of Regulatory Cooperation, which refers to the adhesion of the cooperation activities to certain values for the people, as these are set by the internal legal order. The section first answered in the affirmative that the cooperation activities and the input received in their context are compatible with the regulatory initiative of the EU Commission. The legality of this interaction was important to be clarified for the following reason: should the interactions in the context of Regulatory Cooperation be considered illegal, the question of their input becomes redundant. Hence, the confirmation of compatibility was a necessary step for the subsequent examination of any possible impact of Regulatory Cooperation to the internal regulatory activities.

The section later clarified what it identifies as regulatory principles for the purpose of the argument. This is important as it is on the basis of these regulatory principles that output legitimacy requirements are measured. In general, output legitimacy requires that general regulatory principles found or drawn by constitutional norms in the EU legal order should prevail over a possible regulatory pressure in the context of trade agreements.

On the occasion of the concrete example of cooperation in pesticides, it was argued that the precautionary principle figures as a general regulatory principle of constitutional value in the EU legal order, a statement backed up by the evidence mentioned above, and also supported by thick consensus in academia. Hence, as such, it should set a substantial limit to the impact that a regulatory dialogue could have on the Commission's orientation with regard to a particular subject-matter and should be promoted throughout the different cooperation activities in which the EU engages. The examination of the documents of this particular case study point for the moment to the opposite direction, and indicate that the precautionary principle was not upheld in the recent revision activity of the pesticides legislation; instead it was pushed back due to trade considerations, which originated from the Regulatory Cooperation dialogue. This finding gives certain lessons: first and foremost, it confirms that the Regulatory Cooperation activities are indeed susceptible of driving actors to a 'race to the bottom', which was an important part of the criticism these activities received upon the conclusion of the FTAs; secondly, with regard to our case study, that for the moment, the output legitimacy was compromised.

Undoubtedly, the conclusion that was reached on the basis of this analysis was made possible due to the publication of the REFIT report and of course, of the background leaked documents. In reality, in their absence the identification of the output legitimacy gap would be difficult. The question that is now naturally posed, is whether the Regulatory Cooperation Chapters or internal mechanisms in the EU legal order offer enough control mechanisms that control the adherence of the administration during regulatory making first and foremost to rules ranking on a constitutional level. The next section will refer exactly to the presence or absence thereof.

5.5 The Need for Throughput Legitimacy Mechanisms to Remedy Output Legitimacy Threats

In the previous part, on the occasion of cooperation in pesticides we discussed the limits that fundamental regulatory rules could pose to the compatibility of Regulatory Cooperation dialogue with the Commission's right to initiate or review legislation. However, the case study on pesticides, in the light of the REFIT programme of the EU Commission confirmed the power of regulatory dialogue, and demonstrated how the precautionary principle is intended to continue being left unapplied, amidst the regulatory pressure. Indeed, it became clear that the evaluation of the EU Commission was influenced by the input provided by the trade partners, which were also supported by big industry actors. This was however not reflected directly in the REFIT documents, which simply reproduced the main criticism in general lines. Arguably, the secretive stance of the EU Commission was facilitated by the absence of effective transparency measures and concrete participation mechanisms at the level of the Joint Committees. And indeed, the REFIT process produced an end result, a policy direction which reflects the direction to be taken in the subsequent steps of the revision of the legislation, according to which the Commission will frame its proposal. Hence, the absence of transparency on the content of its legislative proposal will subsequently not become compensated for by the more transparent legislative procedure and the participation mechanisms it entails.

The part ended by posing the question whether the Regulatory Cooperation environment offers enough control mechanisms to monitor the adherence of the administration to these rules when receiving and considering input from such activities. This is the question that this section turns to. Are there or should there be any provisions for transparency and participation in that regard? Transparency and participation under 'openness' have been identified as the throughput legitimacy tools of EU law in Sect. 5.2.2 above. This section, based on the connection between the absence of such mechanisms with the limited transparency of the Commission in its published documents, argues for the inclusion of relevant mechanisms already existing for other chapters to the one of Regulatory Cooperation.

5.5.1 Extension of the Openness Requirements to Regulatory Cooperation

Regarding the components of 'openness' and how they fit in the sphere of EU external relations, the present section will begin by briefly describing the notions as enshrined in primary law. It will then proceed to discuss why these legitimacy yardsticks are to be applied in EU external regulatory activities, especially in the light of the nature of the Regulatory Cooperation activities and under which form the openness requirements are met in those activities.

5.5.1.1 The Requirement of Openness Under EU Law

Resulting from the combination of participation and transparency, openness as a democracy-enhancing tool is about being responsive, ensuring acceptance from and remaining accountable to the people. In the words of the Court, "*It is first necessary to point out that the principle of transparency is intended to secure a more significant role for citizens in the decision-making process and to ensure that the administration acts with greater propriety, efficiency and responsibility vis-à-vis the citizens in a democratic system. It helps to strengthen the principle of democracy and respect for fundamental rights*".[135] The requirement of openness is embodied in Article 298 par. 1 TFEU as applicable to the EU administration as a whole, according to which: «*In carrying out their missions, the Institutions, bodies, offices and agencies of the Union shall have the support of an open, efficient and independent European administration.*» Insofar the EU Commission acts within its administrative tasks, it is expected to apply this principle by ensuring the operationalisation of its two components, transparency and participation.

On the one hand, transparency, as in the totality of the mechanisms that guarantee the absence of secrecy in the institutional business is considered a prerequisite for and thus composite of today's broadened understanding and functioning of openness. Article 15 TFEU comes to confirm both these deliberations. Firstly, the broadened conception of openness is proclaimed in Article 15 TFEU. It begins by declaring its instrumental nature: "*In order to promote good governance and ensure*

---

[135]Case T-211/00, *Kuijer c. Council* [2002] ECR II-485, par. 52.

the participation of civil society, the Union's Institutions, bodies, offices and agencies shall conduct their work as openly as possible."[136] Secondly, the rest of the provisions confirms the dependency of openness on transparency. Article 15 (3) TFEU provides the constitutional ground of the right for access to documents, as the operational composite of the principle of transparency.[137] Described by the Court as a general principle of EU law,[138] transparency is now outlined not only as an obligation to report information but also as an active duty of the Institutions according to Article 15 (3) TFEU to ensure the transparency of their proceedings and make available apart from the final legislation all background documents leading to it, as per Article 15 (3) alinea d TFEU,[139] exposing also the reasons behind each decision.

On the other hand, the second branch of openness is the requirement of participation. Enshrined in Article 11 TEU, it has largely codified prior Commission practices that the latter had initiated after the adoption of the White Paper on EU Governance.[140] Earlier concretized in the jurisprudence as the right to be heard,[141] it was also employed through informal structures by the Commission as a mechanism to have input from interest parties whose contribution would be valuable to the amelioration of regulation.[142] Nowadays, the inclusion of participation in the TEU under the provisions on democracy is argued to be transformative in demanding a new normative reading of Article 11, a reading that signals the passage from participatory governance to participation as a part of democracy, which extends beyond the introduction of a duty incumbent upon the Institutions and turns into a normative standard against which the legitimacy of the administration is assessed.[143]

Both these due process principles that have acquired the status of constitutional rules by the Treaty of Lisbon, provide the basis for the operationalisation of respective procedures to be applicable in the EU legal order. Transparency in the form of access to documents is materialized by Regulation 1049/2001,[144] while more recently transparency in its active form, namely by initiative of the Institutions is all the more demanded in the initial negotiation stage of EU law-making, despite its somewhat sensitive nature which provides various safety valves.[145] Participation,

---

[136] Article 15(1) TFEU.

[137] It is also worth mentioning that access to documents is also a fundamental right of the EU enshrined in Article 42 of the Charter of Fundamental Rights.

[138] Case C-58/94 [1996] *Netherlands v. Council* ECR I-2169, paras 34 and 35.

[139] Case C-345/06 *Heinrich* [2009] E.C.R. I-1659, paras. 41–47 and 64–66.

[140] Such mechanisms were codified in instruments such as the following: *See* EU Commission (1993, 2002).

[141] Mendes (2009), pp. 264ff.

[142] Greven (2007), p. 240.

[143] Mendes (2011), p. 1857.

[144] Regulation (EC) No 1049/2001 of the European Parliament and of the Council of 30 May 2001 regarding public access to European Parliament, Council and Commission documents [2001] OJ L 145/43.

[145] Abazi and Adriaensen (2007), pp. 76ff.

on the other hand, has largely remained outside the realm of law,[146] while unsettled differences on the content of Article 11, on whether it establishes a right or a duty, have further perplexed the issue. Examples from the operationalization of participation in the EU administration one may find to be the Citizen's Initiative or the access (even though constrained) of non-privileged applicants to the Court.[147] Although the Legalization of participation remains a thorny issue in the literature, such requirements in the legislative rule-making can be found in other soft documents, such as the IIA on Better law-making[148] and the Better Regulation guidelines, which were also mentioned above.[149] With the former, the EU Commission commits towards the other Institutions to engage in such consultations, while with the latter, elaborates more detailed guidelines to be used by the relevant Commission services. What is important about the implementing mechanisms in place to operationalise these constitutional requirements, is that despite their highlighted shortcomings and pitfalls, these provisions shape the normative yardstick against which any decision-making should be legitimised and against which existing mechanisms should be revised or new ones should be designed.

5.5.1.2 The Extension of Openness to Regulatory Cooperation

As with every regulatory activity taking place beyond EU borders, Regulatory Cooperation activities need to obey to the same throughput legitimacy requirements imposed internally to activities having similar effects in the EU legal order, in avoidance of a double, presumably lower procedural standard. This premise lies on multiple grounds that find their basis on the legal requirements set by primary law and the effect of these activities.

The extension of openness (in its components, transparency and participation) to the external decision-making of the EU finds multiple legal bases in the Treaties. First of all, the constitutional framework as set by the Treaties creates normative constitutional yardsticks for the totality of EU's governance. Any internal and external rule-making activity in which the EU participates is part of the greater EU governance. Indeed, transparency and participation are constitutional requirements that span EU activities beyond the internal legislative and administrative ones to *"those regulatory activities and institutional practices that shape the EU's "living constitution" outside formalized procedures and that contribute to shaping the EU polity."*[150] Secondly, the administrative work carried out by the EU Commission in the context of Regulatory Cooperation falls under the openness requirements of

---

[146] See Mendes (2011), p. 1849.

[147] Lenaerts (2013), p. 279.

[148] Interinstitutional Agreement Between the European Parliament, the Council of the European Union and the European Commission on Better Law-Making, OJ L 123/1, 12.5.2016, p. 1.

[149] EU Commission (2017), pp. 51ff.

[150] Mendes (2012), p. 1016.

Article 298 TFEU, which is also applicable likewise. Thirdly, the exercise of authority according to the constitutional requirements also externally is in line with the duty of consistency between external action and internal policies of Article 21 (3) TEU.[151] Last but not least, the promotion of good governance and democratic practices in the realm of external relations does not stem only from the fact that the constitutional nature of the rules spans the totality of EU governance, but it is also a requirement on its own, according to Article 21 (1) and 21 (2) (h) TEU.

Seen from a theoretical point of view, the extension of openness to EU's external decision-making is necessary given the interaction of these decisions with and their reception from the EU legal order.[152] Indeed, the 'purifying' legitimation effect that the application of constitutional due process requirements offers, is even more pertinent to decisions taken in the so-called 'black box' of governance, at the international level where the delegation chain is sometimes loosened and the risks not to guarantee procedural standards for the protection of the addressees of the decision are multiplied.[153]

The discussion of glossing international decision-making processes with through-put legitimacy is especially pertinent to international decision-making that entails a certain element. And as such an element has been proposed the exercise of public authority. In a relevant study by von Bogdandy et al. on the need of legitimization of global governance, the authors argued for the need of application of a public law framework to critical international instruments that, although taken into the greater environment of global governance, correspond to or are functionally equivalent to formal exercise of public authority in the classic public law sense of the term, "if it determines individuals, private associations, enterprises, states or other public Institutions".[154] Indeed, not all acts taken at one of the many spheres that form global governance in general can be characterized as acts of public authority.[155]

Regulatory Cooperation activities certainly have a place in the environment of EU's global governance as they govern, without sovereign authority, "relationships that transcend national frontiers".[156] An analysis on whether now its acts also belong to this smaller category of acts entailing exercise of international public authority presupposes a convincing definition of the concept and an application of its components on Regulatory Cooperation activities. As mentioned, the authors consider the exercise of authority as encompassing acts that have the ability to unilaterally determine the legal situations of others, to have a legal effect on others. This capacity takes flesh and bones by various means, including, among others, the legally binding

---

[151] Mendes (2012), p. 1016.

[152] On the rules of reception of international decisions from the EU legal order *see* von Bogdandy et al. (2008).

[153] Curtin and Mendes (2011), p. 105.

[154] von Bogdandy et al. (2008), pp. 1375 and 1381ff.

[155] *See* generally Goldmann (2006).

[156] Finkelstein (1995), p. 369.

force of the instrument.[157] Indeed, the effectiveness of the modification of legal status seems quite independent from the used instrument, as it can also result from non-binding tools, for example ones that set conditions for the realization of a legal situation. Plenty of cases of this kind are only *de lege* non-binding, for the subjects have no choice other than following the imperatives of the instrument, as aligning their actions with them proves more beneficial than ignoring them.[158]

Regulatory Cooperation in establishing mechanisms of discussion and joint examination of possibilities of convergence in the international trade of goods and services presents the ability to alter the legal situation of the market operators that are each time concerned. As it has been pointed in the early days of TTIP, Regulatory Cooperation has a powerful role in determining the conditions of trade, which is also the desired outcome of such activities. In turn, this has then direct consequences on the legal conditions under which trade is carried out, on the legal sphere of the implicated parties in a trade relation, and on the consumers as a whole.[159] The eventual gradual shift of the trade regime realized by the joint cooperation activities will not only create rights and duties for the implicated parties but it will also have indirect distributional effects to different groups, positively and negatively.[160] An example of a cooperation that can have these effects are the MRAs analyzed previously; however, these characteristics are not unique to these agreements. The ability to exercise public authority as in determining the situations of legal others is intrinsic to the nature of Regulatory Cooperation in general and to the potential it can have in the long term.

That being said, the following section will proceed to examine concretely the presence of transparency and participation mechanisms in Regulatory Cooperation activities. Firstly, it will refer to their absence or presence from the FTA provisions. Secondly, it will assess whether the internal EU regimes materializing the principle of openness apply to Regulatory Cooperation activities in the same way they apply to internal decision and rule making, including examples from legislative and non-legislative rule-making activities, which constitute also an exercise of public authority capable of determining the situations of legal others. With regard to transparency, after describing the existing transparency provisions on the FTAs level, we will then examine whether with regard to transparency and access to documents, the same standards of transparency as with internal activities apply. With regard to participation, we will examine whether the structures already provided in the RCF give justice to the level of participation that external parties enjoy with regard to similar internal activities. On the basis of this analysis, we will draw conclusions on the sufficiency of the throughput legitimacy output of Regulatory Cooperation activities.

---

[157] Goldmann (2010), p. 661.

[158] For further considerations on the issue *see* Lipson (1991); Blutman (2010), p. 612.

[159] Mendes (2016), p. 3.

[160] Mendes (2016), p. 4.

5.5.2   The Status of Throughput Legitimacy Mechanisms in Regulatory Cooperation Activities

The openness requirements mentioned above, however are either incomplete or completely absent from the Regulatory Cooperation joint structures. Indeed, neither the institutional structures nor concrete practice give justice to the considerations outlined above, as they do not enforce enhanced transparency nor active participation from the part of the civil society. The next part will proceed on a two-tier analysis with regard to the two components of openness, namely transparency and participation: it will refer both to any presence of such mechanisms on the treaty level, as well as how other tools available in the EU legal order have applied so far. Where relevant, the sections will also make comparisons upon that basis.

5.5.2.1   Transparency in Regulatory Cooperation Activities

As referred above, transparency is now outlined not only as an obligation to report information but also as an active duty of the Institutions according to Article 15 (3) TFEU to ensure the transparency of their proceedings and provide access to all background documents leading to each decision, as per Article 15 (3) alinea d TFEU,[161] exposing also the reasons behind leading to it. As outlined below, neither seems to be the case of Regulatory Cooperation.

Absence of Relevant Passive Transparency Provisions in the FTAs
Regarding the obligation to report information on Regulatory Cooperation activities, CETA and EU-Japan EPA do not provide for a specific provision outlining this duty. For the purposes of the argument, the chapters on 'Transparency' of CETA and EU-Japan EPA do not apply, as they do not refer to the activities of the CETA bodies, but rather outline transparency requirements that parties have to meet internally, with regard to their own regulatory activity.[162] Apart from provisions on transparency and equity regarding measures of general application administrative proceedings, both chapters impose publication requirements on the regulations as such (Article 27.1.1 CETA and Article 17.3.a EU-Japan EPA) on the upcoming plans of the concerned authorities (Article 27.1.2.a CETA), ask for the participation of the public in the proceedings (Article 27.1.2.b CETA and Article 17.2 EU-Japan EPA) and require the efficient administration of the various incoming enquiries (Article 27.2 CETA and Article 17.4 EU-Japan EPA). Also, any regulatory coherence mechanisms within the chapters, part of which are transparency of regulations' requirements, are also referring to the regulatory activity of each party separately (See Chap. 3, Sect. 3.4.1). It is safe to argue that, these requirements mostly have a symbolic functioning or aim to enhance the existing national/regional systems, since

---

[161] Case C-345/06 *Heinrich* [2009] E.C.R. I-1659, paras. 41–47 and 64–66.

[162] Chapter 27 CETA and Chapter 17 EU-Japan EPA.

it would be expected that advanced legal systems do possess such mechanisms, at least from the EU side. We could argue that by including such provisions, the parties recognise their importance as good governance and also democracy enhancing elements. Yet, such principles apply to the individual regulatory activity of each party and at no instance do they apply to the joint Committees on Regulatory Cooperation per se.

Some transparency provisions are included in the CETA Joint Committee's decision on its Rules of Procedure (Decision 1/2018) which also apply to the Specialized Committees as well, hence, also to the RCF.[163] According to provision Rule 8(3) of the said Decision, the parties shall cater for the publication of provisional agendas of the meetings shortly before these take place. After the meeting, according to Article 9(5), parties shall ensure the publication of a summary of the minutes that were taken, which it seems, however are not as detailed as the minutes taken in the first place. With regard to Regulatory Cooperation, the agendas and reports that are to be found under the Commission's registry of documents on the RCF activities, correspond indeed to the ones foreseen in the Rules of Procedure. These are mainly final reports that summarize the discussions that were held and of course, the final versions of the Arrangements reached within the RCF structures. Similarly for the EU-Japan EPA, the EU Commission has disclosed some versions of the minutes of the Regulatory Cooperation Committee.[164]

Interestingly, a similar picture is to be observed internally as well. As far as passive transparency of the relevant documents of the internal decision-making is concerned, there is a mixed picture in the EU area, which only recently started to progress, with the biggest advancement being the transparency regime of delegated acts benefiting from the Interinstitutional Register of delegated acts, which offers, as far as the latter are concerned, access to the meetings agendas and full minutes.[165] On the contrary, with regard to relevant documents for legislative purposes, the Institutions have opted to keep big part of them in the shadows. More specifically, reference is made to the so-called trilogue documents which support the legislative procedure in general. In fact, according to Curtin and Leino, trilogues, as in the informal exchanges between the Parliament, Commission and Council, have come to replace the institutional dialogue that is supposed to take place in the light of the consecutive readings in the ordinary legislative procedure according to Article 294 TFEU.[166] Instead, these trilogues aim to create consensus between the three players, which has led, in the majority of cases, to adoption from the very first

---

[163] Decision 001/2018 of the CETA Joint Committee of 26 September 2018 adopting its Rules of Procedure and of Specialised Committees <https://trade.ec.europa.eu/doclib/docs/2019/february/tradoc_157677.pdf>.

[164] EU Commission, Register of documents of the EU-Japan EPA Committees. <https://circabc.europa.eu/ui/group/09242a36-a438-40fd-a7af-fe32e36cbd0e/library/c9ef4d9b-6ee8-4a5f-aded-e1a0b55374c5?p=1&n=10&sort=modified_DESC>.

[165] EU Commission, Register of delegated and implementing acts https://webgate.ec.europa.eu/regdel/#/home.

[166] Curtin and Leino (2017), p. 1681.

reading.[167] The result of these deliberations is mapped in the known as 'four-column documents', which demonstrate the progress made, as well as the positions taken by the different Institutions. The problem with these informal dialogues, is that, while they do build consensus and facilitate decision-making, they remain largely outside the formal practice and are only explicitly recognized as part of the procedure by the Parliament.[168] This hinders the systematic publication of the four-column documents, as a centralized database and coordination for their publication is missing despite the various calls both by the EU Ombudsman and by the IIA on Better Regulation.[169] The same gap is observed for implementing acts, whereas the EU Parliament has asked for increased transparency of the workings of comitology, without concrete action being taken.

To conclude, although for legislative and implementing acts passive transparency is not as well developed, it is certainly to be observed that this does not correspond to the transparency exigencies of the Treaties and is expected to be changed. Our thesis here is that the same considerations apply to Regulatory Cooperation documents as well. The parallel between these two categories is drawn because preparatory documents of the RCF serve the same purpose for Regulatory Cooperation decision-making as these preparatory documents of legislative do for those purposes: while preparatory documents for legislation support the final proposals, preparatory RCF documents support the decisions that will be taken in the RCF, with regard to the Agreements and its positions.

T-643/21: The Status of the Application of the Access to Documents Regime to Regulatory Cooperation Activities of the RCF

The previous part referred in a general and abstract way to the absence of ad hoc transparency mechanisms, applicable directly to the Regulatory Cooperation activities by virtue of the Treaty provisions. This absence of such concrete mechanisms is rather unfortunate, however, it does not rule out the application of classic transparency mechanisms of the EU legal order. Relying upon the assumption that the concrete Regulatory Cooperation activities fall also under the remit of the EU transparency regime of Access to Documents, subject to the limits, however, (that are set by the participation of a third country that may require greater secrecy) this part turns to analyse some recent developments concerning the application of the Access to Documents Regime to the preparatory documents of the meetings of the Joint Regulatory Cooperation Forum.

On October 5th 2021, an action for annulment arrived before the Tribunal, namely case T-643/21, Foodwatch v. Commission. The action seeks to annul the decision issued by the EU Commission on the 5th of August 2021 pursuant to the Access to Documents Regulation, which rejected the applicant's confirmatory

---

[167] Curtin and Leino (2017), p. 1681.

[168] European Parliament (2016a), point 5.

[169] European Parliament (2016b), Annex I, point 46; European Ombudsman (2016).

application of 6 May 2021 requesting access to the document 'Briefing for the EU RCF co-chair for the Regulatory Cooperation Forum meeting on 3–4 February 2020'.[170]

During that particular meeting various issues were brought on the table of discussions. Progress on existing items, such as pharmaceutical inspections, product safety, cosmetic-like drug products, animal welfare, and cybersecurity was discussed and next steps were elaborated, while new items such as wood pellet boilers, pediatric machines and cooperation mechanisms between the respective standardization bodies were introduced as potential candidates for cooperation.[171] The applicant, NGO Foodwatch, sought access to the Briefing of the co-chair of the EU RCF regarding that particular meeting, a preparatory document which presumably contains the stance and argumentation of the EU Commission with regard to the agenda items. Indeed, while the published report summarizes the main discussion points, it fails to provide with information regarding the intention of each party concerning each action point.

The first plea in law of the applicant, attacking the aforementioned decision informs us of the legal grounds on which full access to the requested document was denied by the services of the EU Commission. In particular, the negative response of the Commission was based on the third indent of Article 4(1)(a) of Regulation No 1049/2001, on the basis of which 'The Institutions shall refuse access to a document where disclosure would undermine the protection of international relations.'[172] The Commission concretised this provision in the specific case by arguing that (a) the disclosure of internal strategic considerations could jeopardise the successful outcome of the ongoing exchanges related to the implementation of the agreement; (b) international relations would be undermined within the meaning of this provision on the basis that the information used could also be used by third countries against the EU and (c) international relations would be undermined within the meaning of this provision on the basis that cooperation with Canada could otherwise be threatened.[173]

Here, it is worth underlining that the Commission insisted on its initial interpretation and provided the applicant with partial access, which was unsatisfactory for the latter. Indeed, before an Access to Documents request seeks the judicial intervention, the Institution has to examine the request twice, firstly on the occasion of the initial application, and, should the applicant require so, on a confirmatory level.[174] The confirmatory application is submitted in case the applicant is not satisfied with the answer received. Only after an unsatisfactory response to a confirmatory

[170]Case T-643/21, *Foodwatch v Commission*, OJ C 481, 29.11.2021, pp. 38–39.

[171]EU Commission (2020a).

[172]Case T-643/21, *Foodwatch v Commission*, OJ C 481, 29.11.2021, pp. 38–39.

[173]Case T-643/21, *Foodwatch v Commission*, OJ C 481, 29.11.2021, pp. 38–39, point 1.

[174]Article 8, Regulation (EC) No 1049/2001 of the European Parliament and of the Council of 30 May 2001 regarding public access to European Parliament, Council and Commission documents, OJ L 145, 31.5.2001, pp. 43–48.

application—and subject to the absence of other internal mechanisms—can an action be brought before the Tribunal. Hence, the Commission was given the opportunity to reconsider the restrictive reading it gave to that particular request, but decided to rather insist on it.

In order to analyse the argumentation of the EU Commission, we shall begin by examining each point against the existing jurisprudence of the Court on the third indent of Article 4(1)(a) of Regulation No 1049/2001.We should begin by admitting that the Court has taken a rather relaxed approach with regard to the specific exception, in a way that could even question the principle according to which exceptions should be interpreted strictly. Generally, the Court has admitted on various instances that with regard to the particular exception 'the Institutions enjoy a wide margin of discretion in determining whether the disclosure of documents relating to the fields covered by those exceptions could undermine the public interest'[175] while admitting that the protection of public interest with regard to international relations in particular covers also the area of international trade,[176] including its implementation phase.[177] Hence, the Commission rightly applied the particular exception in the context of Regulatory Cooperation and used the existing jurisprudence for its own benefit, as long as it allows a wide margin of discretion in the assessment of each situation.

With regard to the first argument specifically, on the basis of which the disclosure of internal strategic considerations could jeopardise the successful outcome of the ongoing exchanges related to the implementation of the agreement, the Court has confirmed indeed that the publication of material relating to ongoing negotiations could damage the confidence between the negotiating parties and weaken the position of the EU.[178]

With regard to the two following arguments, which refer to the risk of the same information being used by other countries and the threat such a disclosure poses to the overall cooperation with Canada respectively, it is standing jurisprudence of the Court that any such threat has to be properly identified and justified. Indeed, the Institutions are bound 'to explain how disclosure of that document could specifically and actually undermine the interest protected by an exception provided for in that provision, and the risk of the interest being undermined must be reasonably fore-seeable and must not be purely hypothetical.'[179] Hence, it is apparent that as long as the Commission does not concretely refer to identification of concrete dangers as well as their likelihood and probability, those claims remain purely hypothetical and cannot be sustained.

From the above, we can primarily infer that the interpretation given by the EU Commission to the specific request does find some support in the jurisprudence, at

[175] Case C-350/12, *Council v in 't Veld*, ECLI:EU:C:2014:2039, par. 63.

[176] Case C-350/12, *Council v in 't Veld*, ECLI:EU:C:2014:2039, par. 42.

[177] Case T-166/19, *Bronckers v European Commission*, ECLI:EU:T:2020:557, par. 70.

[178] Case T-644/16, *ClientEarth v Commission*, ECLI:EU:T:2018:429, par. 47 and 48.

[179] Case T-211/00, Aldo Kuijer v Council, ECLI:EU:T:2002:30, par. 56.

least as far as the invoked exception of Article 4 (1) (a) of Regulation 1049/2001 is concerned. It also looks to be in line with the general practice followed by the EU Institutions regarding access to preparatory documents leading to the adoption of legislation. Indeed, the image that emerges with regard to preparatory documents for legislative purposes, i.e. the so-called four column documents mentioned above, is that they are also not always accessible even by means of a formal request under Regulation 1049/2001. While the Regulations mention this category of documents as a separate case in Article 12 (2), 'real-time' disclosure of such documents, when and if solicited, is left up to each Institution, a practice that varies accordingly from actor to actor and which ultimately ends with the publication of certain parts in the public registries of the Institutions only after the negotiations have ended.[180] Regarding individual access requests, the Institutions are particularly reluctant to share information. The Council, for example, shares positions of other Institutions, the Parliament and the Commission but not its own, and not how its positions were shaped by EU Member States in the COREPER Committees.[181] In recent jurisprudence before the Court of Justice, namely the Access Info Europe case, in which the particular NGO asked for a specific document which included the positions of individual Member States, the EU Council argued that the effectiveness of decision-making would be jeopardized should such a level of transparency be granted to the specific request.[182] The parallels between such lines of argumentation to the ones used by the EU Commission in justifying the restricted access to preparatory RCF documents are visible. While the EU Council relied upon the effectiveness of decision-making to repel the request submitted by Access Info Europe, the Commission relied upon the similar ground of the effectiveness of the negotiations, on the basis of which access to its internal position as depicted in the RCF document was not granted.

On the basis of the above, suffice is to mention at this point that while the disclosure of preparatory documents of the RCF follows to a big extent the restrictive practice of the Institutions for internal legislation, also the Court of Justice jurisprudence has raised the requirements considerably higher. Such suggestions will be made in the last part of this section, after we have also analysed participation.

5.5.2.2   Participation in Regulatory Cooperation

Earlier, participation was referred to as a legitimization factor of the administration's action, according to which it requires the functioning of a certain mechanism that allows interested parties of different backgrounds to contribute to the development and amelioration of regulation. As we will see below, both at the treaty level and on

---

[180] See Curtin Leino (2017), p. 1695.

[181] EU Council (2021), Annex II, Article 11.

[182] Case C-280/11 P Council v Access Info Europe, ECLI:EU:C:2013:671.

the basis of internal EU practices, this is only marginally the case for Regulatory Cooperation activities.

Absence of Participation Mechanisms from the FTA Level

The transparency mechanisms identified above on the treaty level do little, if nothing at all to facilitate external parties' participation. Needless to say, to be able to participate in any formation process presupposes the availability of avenues to do so, which as we shall see, are absent from the Regulatory Cooperation mechanisms.

One could refer to Article 21.8 CETA, entitled 'Consultations with private entities', to constitute such a consultation mechanism. The Article reads:

> In order to gain non-governmental perspectives on matters that relate to the implementation of this Chapter, each Party or the Parties may consult, as appropriate, with stakeholders and interested parties, including representatives from academia, think-tanks, non-governmental organisations, businesses, consumer and other organisations. These consultations may be conducted by any means the Party or Parties deem appropriate.

Still, a careful reading of this vague provision raises several doubts, firstly on the meaning of 'implementation'. Indeed, which stage is considered implementation according to this Article? It is the early phase where parties reach to their stake-holders in order to identify potential areas of cooperation, or it also extends further to the actual decision-making of the cooperation activity? The consultation held in early 2018 by the EU Commission and the relevant Canadian authorities seem to confirm the first speculation. As per the Commission's website:

> With this objective in mind the Commission invites input from all stakeholders and interested parties, including representatives from academia, think-tanks, civil society, non-governmental organisations, trade unions, businesses, consumer and other organisations in identifying sectors/issues where there is a high interest for Regulatory Cooperation with Canada, such as for instance in relation to new technological developments. Another area where the EU and Canada can work together could be to promote common regulatory approaches in international fora.[183]

The repetition of the provision is obvious. The input provided by the online consultation is meant to contribute solely to the identification of cooperation areas. And these limits of this rudimentary online consultation bring us to the conclusion that Regulatory Cooperation lacks an effective participatory mechanism, even one focusing on the early consultations. However, we should admit that even though the capacity of such a mechanism to successfully express the societal concerns and deliver the message to decision-makers is questioned, as it still focuses on early stages,[184] its establishment as separate entity nevertheless constitutes a formal recognition of the legitimising role of societal participation, and adds a certain degree of legitimacy. It needs however to be complemented with more permanent participation mechanisms, which for the moment are not foreseen under the Regulatory Cooperation structures.

---

[183]EU Commission (2018a).

[184]Rioux et al. (2020), p. 55.

This is rather unfortunate, especially given the recognition of the importance of civil society participation, either in various instances within the Agreements, or through the presence of the consulting mechanism set up under Article 22.5 CETA, aiming to increase the participation of interested actors from the civil society to the implementation of the sustainable aspects of the agreement. Today, Regulatory Cooperation of Chapter 21 can only benefit from some borrowed legitimacy from the participatory mechanisms of other chapters only when it treats horizontally subject matters that fall under Chapters 22 on Sustainable Development, 23 on Trade and Labour and 24 on Trade and Environment.[185]

Segments of Participation in Regulatory Cooperation
This part turns to examine more closely other instances of participation of civil society actors which took place independently of the treaty provisions. In this part, we will focus on other instances where societal actors were implicated either in the workings of the RCF and the type of contribution they were asked to provide, or in Canada's input to REFIT evaluation of the pesticides regulation. As mentioned earlier, while transparency internally takes flesh and bones mainly with the regime to the Access to Documents Regulation 1049/2001, participation has not been regulated yet to the same extent, and its operationalization relies upon soft law documents, self-commitment of the Institutions and application of best practices. Hence, with regard to participation, we are currently lacking an established practice against which we could compare to Regulatory Cooperation activities. We will thus limit this part to observing whether any of these internal practices guaranteed an active role for civil society with regard to the Regulatory Cooperation activities or were limited to a passive consultation.

As analyzed in the previous paragraph, civil society is consulted on the basis of Article 21.8 CETA for the purpose of identification of potential candidates for Regulatory Cooperation. However, this provision does not advance participation further. In this regard, it is interesting to see whether the participation of societal actors in the RCF took place by other means after the initiative of the parties. Indeed, about a month before each meeting of the RCF, the EU Commission would publish a call for applications and encourage applicants to participate in the 'Stakeholders Debrief Meeting'.[186] In the relevant call, the Commission would encourage NGOs, consumers associations, workers/trade unions, professional organisations, industry and business associations, companies, regional/local representatives and other stakeholders from either Canada or the EU, to take part in a meeting following the day of the RCF meeting, in order to be informed for the points discussed and the status of progress regarding the relevant discussion items. As its name suggests, the purpose of the meeting is to debrief, to inform the parties on the items discussed, but not to actively seek input from them. Even if some discussion would surely take place in

---

[185]Cross-fertilization between Chapter 21 and chapters on Labour, Environment and Sustainable Development is also possible since they fall under the scope of Article 21, hence the cross-fertilization between the different Committees.

[186]EU Commission (2020d).

that session, the stakeholders lacked the necessary information to be able to actively contribute to the workings. Apart from that, RCF remains largely outside the influence of civil society.

While participation is also rather underdeveloped on the EU level itself, the instances that call for a comprehensive and regulated mechanism to apply thoroughly become more pressing. Its absence is not only fostering ad hoc and patchwork style solutions, it is also depriving policy from a normative benchmark on participation.

5.5.2.3 Throughput Legitimacy Requirements to Regulatory Cooperation Activities

The previous paragraph referred to the concrete throughput legitimacy mechanisms as these have been applied so far to the Regulatory Cooperation activities identified in Chap. 4. This part turns now to discuss in more detail why the practice developed so far is unsatisfactory and what standards of transparency and participation throughput legitimacy requires for the type of Regulatory Cooperation arrangements which are the object of analysis.

Transparency Requirements
The previous parts that discussed transparency arrangements in the context of Regulatory Cooperation revealed certain shortcomings. On the one hand, the absence of transparency mechanisms in the level of the RCF, constitutes an important shortcoming for the institutional duty enshrined in Article 15 TFEU to ensure 'passive' transparency by means of reporting. While the EU Commission does engage in some limited publication of relevant documents, to the extent mandated by the Rules of Procedure 001/2018, these are far from being satisfactory and comprehensive. As we saw, minimum transparency is only met with regard to the communication of the topics that are currently the object of Regulatory Cooperation. On the other hand lies the rudimentary implementation of the active duty to transparency of the Institutions, which, in the EU legal order is regulated by the regime of Access to Documents. The restrictive reading provided by the EU Commission regarding the access to Regulatory Cooperation documents hints that third parties for the moment may have access only to what is being published by the EU Commission in the registry.

However, the bar that is set for transparency requirements by the EU Treaties and the relevant legislation, which as said, covers the whole spectrum of EU activities is much higher. As regards transparency as a passive duty, Article 15 TFEU that requires the Institutions to conduct their work as openly as possible would also pose additional transparency requirements for Regulatory Cooperation activities, with the establishment of a centralized registry being the starting point, similar to the one mandated by Article 12 (1) of Regulation 1049/2001. This registry should include documents informing the public on how the choice of potential cooperation topics takes place, which are the relevant considerations and reasons behind these decisions, which for the moment are not disclosed. Furthermore, the registry should include preparatory documents leading to the final decisions and agreements of the RCF. The same applies to any internal documents received by third parties in the context of Regulatory Cooperation, and how these are used in the formation of internal policies, for example how Regulatory Cooperation has impacted one way or another the revision or adoption of legislation. The purpose of such transparency is to keep the public informed in real time, hence publication should in principle take place shortly after each meeting of the RCF.

As regards transparency as an active duty, suffice is to mention that according to Recital 11 of Regulation 1049/2001, the rule remains that access to documents shall be granted, while non-disclosure is the exception.[187] This statement is supported by the Court of Justice's reading of the Regulation, as confirmed in the case brought up above, Access Info Europe. There, the Court of Justice dismissed the Council's allegation that disclosure of a preparatory document which contained Member States' positions would impede its future decision-making in legislative activity.[188] It recognized the disclosure as part of the democratic legitimacy requirements, on the basis of which Institutions must be held accountable.[189] In that regard, it provided with a different understanding of the balance that needs to be drawn between transparency and effectiveness, by insisting on increased transparency being one of the backbones of EU democracy. Consequently, the Court reminded that according to standing jurisprudence, any particular interest or danger that requires the non-disclosure of a document must be mentioned specifically and not only be speculated or stated as a possibility.[190] This is also the Court's reading of exception 4 (1) (a) of Regulation 1049/2001 as met in various case-law, used by the Commission in order to avoid granting access to the RCF document solicited by Foodwatch.

These considerations of the Court are in principle applicable by analogy to Regulatory Cooperation preparatory documents to the extent they do not interfere with interests of third parties, in that case, the counterpart of Regulatory Cooperation. Increased transparency of the preparatory documents does enhance the democratic implementation of the FTAs by rendering EU Commission more accountable for its positions and decisions. The fundamental principle that sets the bar for invoking the exceptions of Regulation 1049/2001 quite high, still applies. On that basis, the requirement for a satisfactory application of the Access to Documents regime to Regulatory Cooperation should make the use of the exceptions by the EU Commission more demanding. The position here that throughput legitimacy requires that the exceptions provided in Regulation 1049/2001 are to be read restrictively, while recourse to them should be duly justified and grounded.

---

[187] Recital 11, Regulation (EC) No 1049/2001 of the European Parliament and of the Council of 30 May 2001 regarding public access to European Parliament, Council and Commission documents, OJ L 145, 31.5.2001, pp. 43–48.

[188] Case C-280/11 P Council v Access Info Europe, ECLI:EU:C:2013:671, par. 63.

[189] Case C-280/11 P Council v Access Info Europe, ECLI:EU:C:2013:671, par. 32.

[190] Case C-280/11 P Council v Access Info Europe, ECLI:EU:C:2013:671, par. 31.

Apart from this caveat, should such a reading be applied by the EU Commission, it would support the disclosure of a majority of documents, if asked, with only some of them not being allowed in the public sphere. In principle, this balancing exercise should be carried out already for their publication by the EU Commission in the proposed registry. Indeed, a comprehensive registry would definitely lessen the need for such requests.

Participation Requirements
With regard to participation, Sect. 5.5.2.2 demonstrated the presence of limited concrete participation structures. On the one hand, the limited input that stakeholders were asked to provide on the basis of Article 21.8 CETA on the identification of potential candidates for Regulatory Cooperation limits their consultation to the initial phase of the cooperation procedure, leaving them outside of the rest of the negotiations and final outcome. Their 'Debrief' by the RCF after each meeting, which aims to inform them of the status quo of the workings of the RCF is far from being satisfactory in ensuring their concrete input throughout the process. On the other hand, the input received in the context of Regulatory Cooperation which is used for internal purposes, i.e. the revision of a legislation, is also left under the radar of the attention of stakeholders.

Similarly, the normative standard that participation as a constitutional element of EU democracy sets, includes the establishment and functioning of participatory structures during the whole life cycle of Regulatory Cooperation activities. This means that the practice followed by the EU Commission on the basis of Article 21.8 CETA, which included an open call for proposals on potential issues to initiate Regulatory Cooperation should be continued, enhanced and held at regular intervals. Most importantly however, a holistic implementation of the participatory requirement imposes the establishment of permanent consultation structures to support the workings of the RCF and provides input throughout the duration of the negotiations. As we mentioned above, such a mechanism is missing from the treaty level, and has not been implemented internally either.

The previous parts referred separately to transparency and participation, and what throughput legitimacy standards in the EU would require in the operationalization of the undertaken Regulatory Cooperation activities so far. However, these requirements should be read together as they are complementary to each other and should be implemented jointly in a potential new mechanism. Indeed, participation on the early stage of consultations requires that interested parties should be asked to make suggestions on the identification of new subjects for Regulatory Cooperation. Similarly, on this issue throughput legitimacy would require that transparency mechanisms are in place to ensure that the decision-makers communicate on how decisions to begin cooperation on a certain issue are taken and how the input received at that early stage by the stakeholders is used and implemented. As the process of Regulatory Cooperation progresses, throughput legitimacy sets extra requirements for participation and transparency. Stakeholders should be able to have an active say on the RCF workings and to express their view as the negotiations advance. In order for this to happen, transparency mechanisms are necessary to ensure the communication of the relevant preparatory documents that demonstrate progress in the negotiations. This part shall now explore the implementation of these requirements to Regulatory Cooperation activities through the establishment of Domestic Advisory Groups (hereinafter DAGs).

5.5.3   Considerations for Enhancing Throughput Legitimacy on the Implementation Level: Expanding the DAGs to Regulatory Cooperation

This part examines more in detail the institution of DAGs established mainly for the FTA chapters on reconciling trade and sustainability and argues for its potential to be expanded to other issues, in our case, Regulatory Cooperation. The DAGs, along with various other institutional efforts made their apparition in the New Generation FTAs as an effort to include the voice of civil society in the making of trade policy, with a particular focus on the sustainability issues.[191] Inaugurated in the EU-Korea FTA in 2010, DAGs have been since then an integral part of the Trade and Sustainable Development of the concluded FTAs.[192] Their particularity and what makes them interesting for the purpose of our case study is their nature as consultation mechanisms set up by the EU Commission for the implementation stage, an aspect which is missing in Regulatory Cooperation.

As their name suggests, DAGs are domestic, internal groups, consisting of stakeholders of each contracting party. Their composition is supposed to be balanced between the different teams of representation, as the legal basis each time also mandates. Each trading partner has its own DAG, to consult on the issues at hand, while joint DAG to DAG meetings are also foreseen, although with less frequency.[193] The duties of DAGs are mostly of a supportive, consultative and monitoring nature.[194] They may make suggestions on the implementation of the trade and sustainable development issues, they may express their opinions in writing and be informed about the progress made. However, the lack of enforcement mechanisms to ensure accountability from the governmental level is a feature that lessens

---

[191] Westlake (2017), p. 4.

[192] Westlake (2017), p. 4.

[193] With regard to CETA's DAGs, the EU DAGs meet at least twice per year while the EU-Canadian meeting takes place at least once a year. Points 7.1 and 13.1 of the Rules of procedure of the EU Domestic Advisory Group created pursuant to Trade and Labour chapter (Chapter 23 - Article 23.8, paragraphs 4 and 5) and to Trade and Environment chapter (Chapter 24 - Article 24.13, paragraph 5) of the EU-Canada Comprehensive Economic and Trade Agreement (CETA) <https://www.eesc.europa.eu/sites/default/files/files/en_rules_of_procedure_for_eu_dag_for_ceta_0.pdf>.

[194] Orbie et al. (2016b), pp. 30ff.

the potential impact they could have on the process, and has been criticized by the scholars examining civil participation mechanisms in the EU trade relations.[195]

In the context of CETA, DAGs are foreseen by Articles 23.8.4 (for the Trade and Labour chapter), 24.13.5 (for the Trade and Environment chapter). In both cases the requirement for a balanced representation is repeated, and the nature of their duties as purely advisory is also reiterated. In that regard, the CETA DAGs do not differentiate themselves from previous practices in other FTAs. Chapter 22 on Trade and Sustainable Development does not provide for its own DAG, however it is interesting to see to what extent the DAGs differentiate themselves from the Civil Society Forum (hereinafter CSF) of Chapter 22. Indeed the CSF seems to be a high level meeting of wider reach, bringing together representatives from both sides, where DAG and non-DAG members can participate, and the items of discussion of which touch also environmental and labor issues.[196]

Yet, the deliberations of the DAGs as autonomous teams as well as part of CSF, do not extend to issues falling under other chapters, even though when these are of neighboring nature. In the view taken in this thesis, this approach goes against the purpose of their establishment in the first place and for that reason it is proposed that such mechanisms are extended to the working areas of other chapters that need the active participation of civil society in order to legitimize their works from a proce- dural point of view. This opinion is supported by other Institutions, such as the European Economic and Social Committee (hereinafter EESC) and the EU Com- mission. Indeed, the EESC which provides also secretarial support to the existing DAGs, has openly opted for the extension of the scope of DAGs to the implemen- tation of the trade agreements as a whole,[197] while the EU Commission has consid- ered this option as an alternative to enhance the implementation of the agreements at stake.[198]

Regarding Regulatory Cooperation, the establishment of DAGs to be informed and advice on the implementation of the chapter would complement the gap identified in the previous paragraphs. The chapter itself provides the legal basis for the creation of a DAG on Regulatory Cooperation. Indeed, the abovementioned Article 21.8 CETA on Consultations with private entities is as mentioned very vague and allows for a broad reading of the term 'implementation', which could also include consultation with private entities at a more advanced implementation stage. Moreover, *de lege ferenda*, the establishment of a DAG for Regulatory Cooperation is in line with the broad scope of this chapter and the number of subjects that could fall under it, that could include sustainability, labour and envi- ronmental implications, but also serves a number of further objectives equally important, such as consumer protection, health and safety. Indeed, as per the formal opinion of the EESC on the issue, the very purpose of the DAGs is to empower civil

---

[195] Potjomkina et al. (2020), p. 5.

[196] EU Commission (2020c).

[197] European Economic and Social Committee (2019).

[198] EU Commission (2018b).

society actors to look after the EU values, which go beyond sustainability, environment and labour considerations, including, among others social, consumer and environmental standards and cultural diversity.[199]

Of course, there is wide consensus on the fact that the functioning of DAGs has not been optimal until today and there are a number of areas that need to be improved in order for their actions to have an actual impact on the decision-making of the joint Committees. Firstly, as with the selection of participants in the normal consultation procedure of the EU Commission,[200] the DAG membership selection procedure carried out by the EU Commission remains opaque.[201] While the Rules of Procedure give some guiding information on the duration of the membership, they does not mention the concrete criteria along which the Selection by the Commission is made. A rule-based selection system, monitored jointly by the EESC should be set up, which would set on the one hand concrete requirements for a balanced representation not only across the three sectors but also within them, and on the other hand criteria to provide equal access to such mechanisms, for example by means of a rotation system favouring applicants that were not included in future compositions. In that way, transparency will bring fair participation. Secondly, the lack of political and bureaucratic support has further impeded the smooth functioning of the mechanism[202] making necessary a stronger financial support to ensure secretarial functions, the consistent holding of meetings as well the advertisement and promotion of the mechanisms to relevant parties.[203] Last and most importantly, a future reform of these mechanisms should also focus on the establishment of procedures of checks and balances, in other words of reporting mechanisms in order to enhance the accountability of the receiver of the advice. It is argued that the consultative function of the mechanism as provided by the Treaties does not preclude its ability to hold the decision-makers accountable on how they use the advice and to what extent they incorporate them.

To extend this civil-society participation mechanisms to Regulatory Cooperation enhances the throughput legitimacy of the procedures in making them more open. Through the betterment suggestions, we see that transparency and participation are very much interconnected apart from being complementary for guaranteeing openness. Transparency works thus not only as facilitating mechanism for balanced participation but also as a control mechanism for righteous participation, via reason-giving on the handling of different participating interests from the receiver.[204] Indeed, transparency guarantees equal access to participation, clear

---

[199]European Economic and Social Committee, 'Opinion of the European Economic and Social Committee on Trade and sustainable development chapters (TSD) in EU FTAs (FTA)' OJ C 227/27, 28.

[200]Curtin et al. (2013), p. 11.

[201]Potjomkina et al. (2020), p. 5; Also Orbie et al. (2016a), p. 528.

[202]EU Commission (2018b).

[203]Orbie et al. (2016a), p. 528.

[204]Curtin and Mendes (2011), p. 118.

criteria and reason-giving on the selection of input, and its impact to the taken decisions.[205]

DAGs count today more than 10 years of functioning, with their practices not being yet crystallized. However, there are a number of reasons that argue for the need of their regulation. Not only from a semantic point of view, in that they continue to represent a major piece of EU democracy, but also in order to ensure their viability and avoid the so-called 'consultation fatigue' that comes after low satisfaction levels of the participating members.[206] The means by which this could be achieved are explored in the following part.

5.5.4 Inference on Throughput Legitimacy

With this section, the tripartite analysis of legitimacy was concluded with throughput legitimacy being synonymous to the so-called openness requirements, for which much have been written and debated in the EU legal order, but still remains a work in progress. The section pointed to the need to expand such considerations in the field of Regulatory Cooperation due to its intrinsic nature and potential to have a regulatory impact internally. As such, it would be necessary that it is subject to the same transparency and participation requirements as mandated by the EU Treaties for the whole spectrum of its activities.

After examining closely the existence and functioning of transparency and participation mechanisms to Regulatory Cooperation activities of the RCF, it was concluded that the current regime falls short of the expected level of openness as this is mandated by the EU treaties. As regards transparency, the provisions in the FTAs are almost non-existent, while the EU Commission chooses to adopt a quite restrictive reading to the Access to Documents regime for RCF documents. As regards participation, limited arrangements have been implemented so far, with parties asked to propose possible cooperation topics only once back in 2018 (Government of Canada 2018).

However, throughput legitimacy sets the bar much higher, which unfortunately has not been observed so far neither with regard to the activities of the RCF as a whole nor with regard to the adopted Regulatory Cooperation Arrangements. While transparency-wise, the parties need to ensure the timely publication of the activities and outcomes of the RCF meetings, specifying the topics to be considered, how these topics were decided, as well as the progress made after each meeting, the EU Commission has only provided a high level summary, which fails to provide a complete picture to the interested parties. So far, these high-level summaries do not give any background information on any concrete Arrangements that are being negotiated, and do not communicate the position of each party. Indeed, the EU

---

[205] Mendes (2011), p. 1876.
[206] Kube (2019), p. 301.

Commission has failed to publish the documents on the workings of the RCF, the adoption of the Administrative Arrangements as well as the input of the Canadian counterparts in the REFIT process for pesticides. Moreover, the EU Commission has failed to remedy this shortcoming through the Access to Documents mechanism applicable internally, by opting for a broad reading of the applicable exceptions on the basis of which it has denied access to RCF documents. However, transparency exigencies as set by the Treaties and interpreted by the Court call for a more demanding reading of those exceptions, which need to be justified clearly and concretely. Contrary to this, the argumentation provided by the EU Commission in its response to the application of NGO Foodwatch seems to imply the opposite. The inability of the EU Commission to concretely refer to the dangers and risks identified with the disclosure of this document supports the view that the throughput legitimacy requirement has not been met; the recourse to the exception has not been concretised in the specific case and the balancing exercise has not been carried out.

Similarly, the minimum participation requirements have not been observed either in the Regulatory Cooperation activities so far. While throughput legitimacy would require the presence and input from interested parties throughout the whole decision-making process, both the meetings of the RCF, and the adoption of the Administrative Arrangements took place in the shadows, and no concrete input was observed insofar. In fact, we observed that the civil society was asked to make some suggestions back in 2018. Since then however, while we observe that the agenda of the meetings is enriched with additional topics, it is almost 5 years that the civil society has not been asked again.

In view of their limited—if non-existent—application to the Regulatory Cooperation activities, the part finally turned to discuss how the suggested throughput legitimacy improvements could be integrated in the Regulatory Cooperation activities. For this, it suggested the expansion of the DAGs, an institution which is already operational for other CETA chapters. The proposal sees added value to their extension, as DAGs, if properly regulated, could serve as the platform in which these throughput legitimacy requirements would apply. Indeed, a well-functioning mechanism would imply the timely publication of documents, and would include concrete participation of interested parties throughout the circle of Regulatory Cooperation, with a concrete mandate to monitor, intervene and control, when necessary.

5.6 On the Choice of Instruments: Inter-institutional Cooperation and the Idea of an EU Trade Act

While the previous sections commented on the basis of the results which amendments should be considered content-wise, this last section turns to discuss the means by which these could be introduced.

It begins from two major findings. Firstly, according to the legal regime of the FTA as it now stands, a plethora of agreements with political character, if reached within the Regulatory Cooperation Chapter, cannot be successfully concluded. First, the use of an international treaty for each and every agreement, which would provide a gloss of legitimacy especially for political agreements, is not only burdensome but also goes against the need of simplification sought by the negotiators. Secondly, recourse to the procedure of Article 218 par. 9 TFEU cannot be made either. As we proved back in Chap. 3, Sect. 3.5.2, the Regulatory Cooperation Fora lack a decision-making power. As they cannot take decisions on the international level that would need later to be transferred within the internal legal order, the use of 218 par. 9 is excluded as well. Should the RCF acquire a decision-making power, by virtue of a joint decision for example, then 218 par. 9 could be used, although the participation requirements of the Parliament are also absent from that provision. Thirdly, it acknowledges that the use of Administrative Agreements, at least as far as agreements of political character are concerned, are not suitable instruments, as the EU Commission lacks autonomous decision-making power. Moreover, as unregulated instruments, there are no rules as to how they are to be concluded, especially in the novel area of Regulatory Cooperation.

Taking both facts into account, the present section considers two alternatives as to how to codify the proposed legitimacy requirements made in the previous sections: an Inter-Institutional Agreement (hereinafter IIA), targeting mainly the institutional balance to be kept under the various decision-making options that may arise from Regulatory Cooperation activities as described above, and an EU trade act, a formal secondary legislation on the example of the US trade act to include not only the institutional participation criteria, but also the throughput legitimacy enhancing mechanisms.

5.6.1 An Inter-institutional Agreement for Participation Requirements Under Input Legitimacy

Contrary to the possibility of an EU trade act to be discussed below, the solution of an IIA has not been proposed yet by legal literature to remedy legitimacy shortcomings in the international decision-making processes of the Union that partially take place outside the legal framework of the Treaties. The present thesis proposes such a tool, while analysing its pros and cons, based on previous literature on IIAs, both instrument specific but also as autonomous source of institutional law.

Primarily, since the Lisbon Treaty, IIAs find their general permissibility clause in Article 295 TFEU, which in its first alinea provides that the Commission, the Parliament and the Council may reach agreements on their cooperation methods. Moreover, secondary law provisions have occasionally provided an explicit legal basis for the conclusion of ad hoc IIAs,[207] and according to commentators, the

---

[207] Hummer (2007), pp. 53ff.

existence of other IIAs may also rest upon implicit bases. Indicatively, they are said to constitute a direct expression of the obligation of sincere cooperation,[208] an obligation that, according to the Court of Justice extends to the relations of the Institutions between them.[209] Alternatively, they have been grounded to the power of internal organisation of the Institutions, which acquires an external dimension extending to the relations with other Institutions for the sake of facilitation of EU positions.[210] Their legal status as binding or non-binding instruments has been associated on whether they are provided for explicitly or not,[211] although the most correct opinion dissociates the two and relies upon the text of an IIA to judge its legal status.

Despite the ambiguity around their legal basis and status, IIAs are present in the EU legal order and under various combinations. This gives the contracting parties considerable freedom on the way forward and allows the proposition of the instrument for the purposes of the secondary international decision-making. For this purpose, a possible IIA would thus rely on Article 295 TFEU rather than on explicit secondary legal basis. Its legal status would nevertheless depend on the contracting parties. This following part will discuss on the basis of existing findings the pros and cons of the employment of an IIA to encompass the institutional arrangements discussed above.

5.6.1.1   A Pragmatic Answer to the Lack of Concrete Rules

An instrument that could include the suggested repartition of tasks and exigencies of institutional participation could take the form of an IIA. The employment of this instrument is a pragmatic answer to the issue at hand primarily because it is in line with the conditions that demand its presence: institutional power struggle and incomplete constitutional framework, the combination of which leads to the observation that EU Institutions are in fact taking advantage of that incomplete constitutional framework and interpreting it to their own interests in their constant struggle to see their powers grow.[212] As we described above, it is also one of this lacunae that has given rise to the need to control the EU Commission in its autonomous decision-making and regulate in more detailed terms decision-making in the EU external action.

More generally, in the history of EU integration, the practice of IIAs has been born because of the partially uncrystallised and dynamically evolving mandates of the main actors in the decision-making system. Against this backdrop, IIAs are part

---

[208] Bieber (1984), p. 520.

[209] Case 204/86, *Greece v. Council*, [1988], ECR 5323, par. 16 *See* also Case C-65/93 *Parliament/Council* [1995] ECR I-668 par. 23.

[210] See Hummer (2007), p. 56.

[211] Bieber (1984), p. 521.

[212] Monar (1994), p. 695.

of the constitutional evolution, manifested along with seminal rulings of the Court of Justice as well as through intergovernmental conferences of treaty revisions.[213] Of course, IIAs cannot substitute treaty revisions, but they do serve as driving forces of change by creating facts, that may be taken on board at a future revision. This was indeed the case with the failed attempt of the EU Parliament during the negotiations for the IIA on Transparency and Democracy to alter the Treaty of Maastricht by imposing upon the Council the obligation to not adopt a legislative proposal already rejected by the EU Parliament.[214] While introducing a *contra legem* reading at the time, this political demand was incorporated in the next treaty revision, Article 189b (2) (a) of the Amsterdam Treaty, a development that demonstrates the silent power that even failed IIAs may constitute.

Moreover, IIAs form a pragmatic answer to the need to legitimise secondary international decision-making as very often, the institutional dynamics that are formed after IIAs are perceived as legitimacy enhancing. These considerations begin from the position that legitimacy is achieved through parliamentary participation. Indeed, one of the main hypotheses of the scholars studying IIAs is that, by enhancing the powers of the EU Parliament, the solely directly elected organ of the EU, and rebalancing the distortions of representative democracy, they have a positive impact upon the democratic legitimacy of the EU as a whole.[215] This is all the more supported by the fact that IIAs are usually initiated by the EU Parliament in an attempt to stand on an equal footing with the rival Institutions in the decision-making process, the Commission and the Council, an actual proof that the Parliament has evolved as an autonomous institutional actor with its own demands on institutional reform, based on democracy considerations.[216] A characteristic example in that respect is the enhancement of the Parliament's role in the Common Foreign and Security Policy (hereinafter CFSP) for the first time via the 1997 IIA on provisions regarding financing of the Common Foreign and Security Policy.[217]

This leads us to the need to codify the institutional practice, by rendering it also more legitimate in democratic terms, always under the caveat that the enhancement of legitimacy comes through parliamentarisation, which is the thesis that the present work adopts. Indeed, the propositions made above with regard to input legitimacy highlight the absence of parliamentary participation in the current Treaty framework. Hence they argue for its direct implication in informal rule-making should the material legal basis of the informal agreement indicates so.

---

[213] Eiselt and Slominski (2006), p. 209.

[214] Eiselt and Slominski (2006), p. 224.

[215] Puntscher Riekmann (2007), p. 4.

[216] Puntscher Riekmann (2007), p. 14.

[217] Originally in OJ 1997, C 286/80. The IIA later became part of the Inter-institutional Agreement of 6 May 1999 between the European Parliament, the Council and the Commission on budgetary discipline and improvement of the budgetary procedure (OJ 1999, C 172/1).

Being adopted on a consensual basis, a possible IIA shall establish such rules of conduct, which the Institutions will voluntarily agree to follow, an element which will add to their efficiency and abidance, making them eventually more accountable.

Last but not least, such an IIA could also host the provisions of a consultation mechanism, such as the one described above in order to also meet the needs of throughput legitimacy, in the same way as the IIA on better law-making does for legislative and non-legislative decision-making (delegated acts). Consultation in this IIA is not only mentioned abstractly in the preamble as an underpinning value or goal; there are concrete provisions that outline the exigencies on its realisation methods. Indeed, par. 9 of the IIA lists consultation as one of the better law-making tools,[218] while par. 19 outlines the width of the desired consultation, which should be as comprehensive as possible, as well as the publication requirements.[219] Similarly, the Commission is bound on the basis of par. 25 (2) of the IIA to include in the explicative memoranda the issues on which it consulted relevant stakeholders as well as how these have fed the final decisions. It is also worth mentioning that throughout the IIA, the use of 'shall' and 'will' indicate the willingness of the participating Institutions to be bound by the procedural requirements established therein.

5.6.1.2 Possible Reservations on the Use of an IIA

The previous part analysed the reasons why the nature of an IIA could supplement in a pragmatic way the lack of rules to the issue at hand. Surely, while the thesis stands by the considerations above, for which it proposes the use of the IIA as a possible solution, it is for the sake of completeness that it also wishes to analyse possible reservations that could arise. Such reservations relate to the absence of a full legal review of these instruments, their feasibility as well as legitimacy considerations and the limits of their altering power.

The uncertainty around the issue of judicial review of IIAs follows the uncertainty around the legal nature of the instruments as binding or non-legally binding, when it is not clearly provided for. We should mention from the outset that their legal nature is little related to the eventual respect of the rules. Even when they lack directly legal binding force, IIAs do in fact create not only legitimate expectations from the part of the signing parties, but they also reflect the choice made by the Institutions to bind themselves voluntarily.[220] Hence, the choice not to abide by the commitments comes directly with reputation costs, not to mention its high likelihood to go against the primary law provisions of sincere cooperation.

---

[218] Interinstitutional Agreement Between the European Parliament, the Council of the European Union and the European Commission on Better Law-Making, OJ L 123/1, 12.5.2016, p. 1, par. 9.

[219] Interinstitutional Agreement Between the European Parliament, the Council of the European Union and the European Commission on Better Law-Making, OJ L 123/1, 12.5.2016, p. 1, par. 19.

[220] Case 81/72, *Commission v Council* [1973] ECR 575 par. 13.

Review of the commitments by the Court is in fact a legal effect that could arise even from non-binding instruments, however it is a separate issue from compliance. The extent of the review, nevertheless depends as we mentioned on the characterization of the instrument as legally or non-legally binding, on the legal value that the Court chooses each time to give to the IIA at hand, a matter for which it has given very diverging rulings. While in most cases the Court of Justice considers IIAs that arrive before it as political declarations,[221] voluntary coordination frameworks,[222] and in general non-legally binding ones,[223] in some cases it has opted for a different reading by basing its judgements on the legal value of the alleged instrument at stake each time.[224]

Hence, the absence of concrete criteria set by the Court for the characterization of an IIA as legally or non-legally binding does not shed light on which IIAs could be fully reviewed by the Court of Justice. Undoubtedly, they can be the object of an action of annulment, as the Court has widened the scope of eligible acts to any act that could have legal effects. The repartition of competences between the Institutions on a certain area, which would be the object of an IIA is in that respect a legal effect. What depends on the characterization that the Court will choose to give and hence is unclear, is whether they could be used in infringement procedures, as a ground to review the legality of other acts.[225] Some authors have argued that full compliance, while not reviewed on the basis of the IIAs as such, can be grounded to the principle of sincere cooperation and failure to comply with the provisions enshrined therein could constitute a violation of the latter, reviewable by the Court.[226] However, this reasoning, while logical, stretches the limits of law in its effort to legalise a soft instrument, and presumably the Court of Justice would be reluctant to take this legal leap in order to establish the connection between the two. Such an interpretation would constitute law-making from the part of the Court, something that the Court has been reluctant to do, for example on the occasion of the litigation arriving before

---

[221] In its opinion in C-64/80 Giuffrida and Campogrande v Council, the AG argued that the Joint Declaration of the 4th March 1975 on the institution of a conciliation procedure was a political declaration. The Court of Justice however judged differently on the occasion of different circumstances when it gave legally binding force to that same instrument. Case C-211/80, *Advernier v Commission* [1984] ECR 131 par. 23.

[222] The Court of Justice viewed the 'Code of Conduct concerning public access to Council and Commission documents of 6 December 1993' at hand as an expression of the Institutions' will to streamline procedures through a voluntary coordination which lacks legally binding effect. Case C-58/94 *The Netherlands v Council* [1996] I-2195 par. 25–27.

[223] The Court of Justice pointed this out for the first time at Case T-194/94, *Carvel and Guardian Newspapers v Council* [1995] ECR II-2765 par. 62.

[224] *See* for example Case 34/86 *Council v Parliament* [1986] ECR, 2155 para. 50, also Case C-211/80, *Advernier v Commission* [1984] ECR 131 par. 23.

[225] In Case C-25/94 *Commission v Council* [1996] the Court of Justice used an IIA as a legal standard to review the legality of a secondary legislation, basing this on the legally binding character of the IIA at hand. Case C-25/94 *Commission v Council* [1996] ECR I-1469, par. 49–51.

[226] Bieber (1984), p. 522.

it from the independent decision-making activity of the Commission, by failing to establish this constant activity of the Commission.

Apart from the issue of legal review, which normally would arise after the adoption of a future IIA, it is also the feasibility of the agreement on such an instrument that has to be examined. This depends to a great extent on the purpose of their conclusion, namely whether (a) they are employed after explicit reference by primary or secondary law (b) employed on the free will of the Institutions to specify further treaty provisions or (c) to pursue non regulated political interests at a stage where Legalization of undertaken commitments is not an option.[227] The main difference between this categorization is the chances of a successful negotiation and agreement on concrete rules. Indeed, while IIAs already provided for in primary law come in to fill the secondary gaps of a legal regime,[228] this is not the case for the other two categories, and especially for the third one, under which the proposed IIA would fall. As institutional balance to be kept under secondary international decision-making is in fact an issue not mentioned in the Treaties, an IIA on that matter would touch a regulatory area, which has only slightly been addressed in the Framework Agreement on relations between the European Parliament and the European Commission, which strengthened the Parliament's prerogatives in treaty-making. And while the presence of this regulatory area on the one hand asks for concrete rules, on the other hand, the political will might not be so strong as to overcome possibly arising differences on political issues. The issue of institutional balance to be kept with regard to secondary international decision-making is a sensitive issue in this regard as it encompasses theoretical discussions and pre-supposes consensus on the very core of the Institutions' powers.

And in fact, it is exactly on the impact of a possible IIA to the general institutional balance established by the Treaties that a possible reservation could be based. Indeed, it has been argued that the cumulative effect of the numerous IIAs in several areas has pushed the limits set by Treaties by considerably strengthening the position of the EU Parliament contrary to the wish of the Master of the Treaties.[229] Hence, what should be avoided is to alter substantially the institutional balance of EU external decision-making, even as it now stands, in an incomplete form. Whether the propositions made above on the participation of the EU Parliament in the various processes have such a distorting effect, could be a matter of discussion in that regard. However, according to the reasoning outlined above, these concerns can be put at ease. The participation of the EU Parliament to secondary international decision-making that relies upon a material basis bestowing decision rights to the latter is only a natural consequence to mirror the internal repartition of powers and is in line with the institutional balance of Article 218 TFEU. Ensuring the EU Parliament's partic-ipation practically transfers the legitimacy requirements of the latter to an informal decision-making instrument. Moreover, with regard to a possible use of 218 par.

---

[227] Eiselt and Slominski (2006), p. 213.

[228] Eiselt and Slominski (2006), p. 214.

[229] Waelbroeck and Walbroeck (1988), p. 79.

9, the suggestion to include the EU Parliament via a mandatory consultation mechanism or through the imposition of its prior agreement, does not go as far as to alter substantially the institutional balance of the provision, as the main actors remain the same and while the rationale of the need of expediency might need to be somehow compromised. The limit of the compatibility of an IIA with the set institutional balance is drawn on whether the IIA accords new decision-making powers to Institutions or merely accords participatory rights.[230] The propositions we make rather fall under the latter category.

5.6.2 The Added Value of Codifying Secondary Legislation: The Idea of an EU Trade Act

The idea of an EU trade act in the form of a Regulation on Trade and Investment merits reference in the discussion on the available legal instruments for the implementation of the proposed measures. This idea, firstly proposed by Thomas Cottier, is inspired by the US trade act, an instrument used to legally set in a declaratory manner objectives and priorities of the US trade policy as carried out by the President and its administration.[231] As its amendments' history suggests, it sets priorities and objectives in a dynamic way, following the developments of trade policy of the time.[232]

According to the instigator of this proposal, the added value of this instrument lies, among others in creating a benchmark against which the choices of the administration can be judged before the final stages of the international negotiations.[233] This practically means that contentious issues can be set forth and scrutinized by Congress, to ensure alignment with the set trade priorities, and the administrative branch can be controlled as long as it receives its empowerment to engage into trade negotiations from the former. Such a mechanism avoids political controversies after the conclusion of the trade agreement, which are not prevented from happening in the EU context, given its existing international negotiating practices and the limited role of the EU Parliament, that can be merely informed on the progress but in no way formally influence the negotiating directives or the content of the negotiations.

While admitting the structural differences between the EU and the US legal orders, Cottier's proposal envisages to bring best practices to the EU trade policy. On that basis, he submits that an EU trade act under the legal basis of Article 207 (2) TFEU could shape the EU trade policy in a decisive way, providing the means to implement objectives provided for in the Treaties concretely within the

---

[230]Hummer (2007), p. 70.

[231]Cottier (2017), p. 47.

[232]Cottier (2017), pp. 47ff.

[233]Cottier (2017), p. 54.

trade policy with the official support of the EU legislators, as well as national parliaments. The present section builds upon this proposal and argues how it could provide a suitable avenue for the implementation of the measures suggested above.

5.6.2.1   Enhancing the Institutions' Compliance with the Proposed Rules on Secondary International Decision-Making

The two main reservations identified above on the employment of an IIA for the purposes of codifying the decision-making were on the one hand the absence (or limited potential) of judicial review, in light of the legal nature of the IIA, and on the other hand, the feasibility and desirability of its employment as such, given its content.

Regarding the question of judicial review, a legal instrument in the form of a Regulation opens indeed the doors to the Court and the controls it can carry. The added value of the presence of a judicial control is twofold. On the one hand, the access to the Court's chambers increases compliance with the rules, as possible abuses by the Institutions shall be controlled and deemed illegal. Unlike in the case of an IIA, access to the Courts is guaranteed and does not depend on the jurisdictional appetite of the Court on whether to view the instrument as reviewable or not. Hence, even if the implicated actors would have an incentive to follow a non-legally binding instrument, in the case of a Regulation, they are bound to do so. On the other hand, the legality control goes beyond compliance issues, to examine also the constitutionality of the proposed rules. Especially regarding rules that suggest additional decision-making arrangements with regard to specific aspects of the EU external action, as the categorisation made above, which ascribes an active role to the EU Parliament and deviates from Article 218 TFEU, the Court of Justice can examine the coherence of such proposals with the EU's institutional balance and provide a constitutionality seal in that regard.

The direct jurisdictional competence of the Court of Justice granted by the presence of a Regulation has also an additional significance in expanding the role of the Court in the external relations sphere of the EU. While this can be seen by some as an advancement as far as the principle of legality and legal certainty are concerned, others may consider it a compromise. A compromise on the one hand of the flexibility that external negotiations need, as a potential Regulation sets in stone certain requirements to be followed at all times and guides the negotiations. On the other hand, a compromise of the certainty that an international agreement requires, which should not be challenged at a later stage, as an EU trade Regulation provides an additional ground of contestation. This is in direct relation to the question of desirability and feasibility of a legislative instrument in general for the purposes of regulating further secondary external decision-making, which can be addressed by adjusting the regulatory density of such a piece of legislation to the existing political appetite as well as the practical reality of international negotiations and decision-making.

5.6.2.2 Establishing a Regulatory Yardstick for the Functioning of Civil Society Mechanisms

The institutionalisation of lobbying that was observed in the previous sections, namely the dominance of certain interest groups because of their power and the amount of pressure they exert towards one direction in the decision-making processes was documented to be exacerbated by the absence of civil society participation mechanisms embedded in the RCF with a controlling function. The problem, however, is not only on the international level. The absence of concrete provisions in secondary legislation to implement the primary law requirement on participation for internal decision-making has been long criticized in the legal literature. Similarly, the functioning of the DAGs is ad hoc, only for the FTA chapters they are provided for, and their regulation depends on the Rules of Procedure adopted each time.

The added value that a reviewable Regulation could bring in that regard is twofold and as mentioned above, mainly relies upon its presumed binding nature. Hence, on the one hand, it would regulate their functioning (membership, level of intervention) in a mandatory way, and any decision taken in breach of the rules could be challenged and reviewed. On the other hand though, its addition into an act that is trade act brings the extra value that its functioning could be inserted horizontally and be sector specific, as a precondition to any secondary international decision-making in FTA joint Committees generally. That would give a concrete legal basis for the mandate of such mechanisms to the various international trade fora when it comes to international decision making activities. In addition, the present thesis posits that an IIA would not be as a suitable instrument to include these issues, even though it recognises that consultation mechanisms have been included in the past in the IIA on Better Law-Making, as analysed above. The thesis supports that an IIA by its nature is used to regulate the relations between the Institutions, crystallise their obligations as indicated by the Treaties. In a secondary international decision-making context, the functioning of such a mechanism should be autonomous to the action of the Institutions, which should only have a coordinating role in the process.

Hence, even though it accepts as possible the inclusion of such a mechanism in an IIA, the thesis argues that its inclusion in potential instrument like the EU trade act would render the functioning of the mechanisms less dependent on the actions of a specific Institution and more autonomous as a self-standing requirement. This approach was also adopted in the US. In fact, one of the primary objectives of the US trade act of 2015 is to 'collaborate with the private sector through direct engagement'.[234] In that respect, along with other civil society initiatives, it has established the Commercial Customs Operations Advisory Committee (COAC) to advice on the Custom and Borders' Protection regulations, policies, and practices.[235]

---

[234] Section 310 (3) (B), Trade Facilitation and Trade Enforcement Act of 2015, Public Law 114–125—Feb. 24, 2016.

[235] Section 109, Trade Facilitation and Trade Enforcement Act of 2015, Public Law 114–125—Feb. 24, 2016.

The act has set not only its establishment, but also its purpose, structure and formal role, being in that respect, suitable instrument for similar purposes also on the EU side.

Admittedly, a future EU trade act could accommodate to regulate and enhance all three aspects of legitimacy identified in the previous sections, input legitimacy through detailed decision-making provisions for the Commission's arrangements, input legitimacy through the inclusion of rules for autonomous but legitimate secondary international decision-making; output legitimacy by highlighting how regulatory principles must be balanced against liberalisation objectives and guide the said decision-making processes; and throughput legitimacy through the mandatory involvement of civil society mechanisms and their adherence to certain rules. Not only does the judicial review that comes hand in hand with a legislative instrument enhance the formal character of the rules, it also highlights the significance of the subject matters to be included within it. Such an act could fundamentally increase the legitimacy of Institutions acting in the external arena, through the formalization of processes that adhere to the fundamental Treaties, and by avoiding the patchwork application of unwritten rules that rely mostly on unanimous actions by each individual institution. In that way, the external action of the EU would be enhanced, not hindered, as it would apply within a certain legal environment that is on the one hand flexible enough to accommodate changes, but on the other hand rigid enough to control its function within certain limits. That is why the exploration of this possibility is not only worth exploring but also necessary in the current web of the EU's external relations.

5.7 Conclusion

The legal analysis to which this chapter proceeded aimed to point to the constitutional shortcomings that the Regulatory Cooperation results have presented and could present in the EU legal order and propose solutions to address these shortcomings. To the extent that the shortcomings were found to be in direct relation to the elements of democracy as proclaimed in the EU Treaties, the chapter was built upon the three categories of democratic legitimacy present in academic literature, input, output and throughput.

With regard to input legitimacy, which corresponds to the identification of the decision-makers, as in who formally adopts the outcomes, it was found that the current practice of the EU Commission, according to which the outcomes entered the EU legal order as informal administrative arrangements by the Commission departments and the Canadian counterparts on an administrative level, could be held with regard only to a limited category of agreements, which are of technical or administrative nature, pertaining to the EU Commission's own operation or possibly complementing existing political commitments; however this avenue cannot be employed for agreements that introduce for the first time political choices. Section 5.3 drew the line on what could be signed by the EU Commission solely exactly on the political or administrative character of the agreements and analysed what commitments each category could entail. For example, the formal recognition of third country regulatory standards from possible MRAs that could be decided as a form of a more intensive Regulatory Cooperation would involve a transfer of regulatory authority to third parties. This is because these regulatory standards draw from the MRA a formal equivalent status to the standards in force in the EU legal order. Moreover, commitments that relate to policy-making, that may interfere with human rights and may underpin legislative choices were also found to be outside the scope of the EU Commission's autonomous decision-making power. On the basis of this categorisation, the chapter put the Administrative Arrangements already signed under the Regulatory Cooperation Chapter under this test and concluded that while the Administrative Arrangement on Pharmaceuticals was rightly signed by the EU Commission solely, the Administrative Arrangement on the exchange of non-food information could implicate unauthorised data transfers and hence have an impact on human rights. Apart from proposing the drawn categorisation as a criterion to assess the input legitimacy of future potential agreements, Sect. 5.3 also highlighted some avenues to enhance the role of the Commission in international secondary decision-making, which would require the participation and input of other Institutions.

As regards the results of regulatory dialogue upon output legitimacy, namely the reflection of fundamental regulatory values in the decision-making results, it was demonstrated that its impact can be both substantial and decisive. The example of the non-application of the precautionary principle on a substantive piece of legislation for chemicals, the MRLs Regulation (Regulation (EC) No 396/20054) along with the omission to change this inconsistency on the occasion of the REFIT programme, indicates that this decision, which is otherwise incompatible with the precautionary principle has been influenced by the Canadian counterparts and the industry actors that participated in the consultation and had an interest for the regime to stay as it is.

Of course, since such intrusive intentions and potential threats to fundamental regulatory values are inherent to the Regulatory dialogue, strong accountability mechanisms are needed in order to control how the input received by the trading partners in the context of bilateral dialogues impacts internal decision-making. It is there that the issue of throughput legitimacy, as in the 'procedural legitimisation' comes to play. This procedural legitimisation in the EU legal order can take place through the operationalisation of transparency and participatory mechanisms on the level of specialised Committees. While transparency and participation form an additional leg of the EU idea of democracy and they form a governance standard for the EU actions in general, the findings suggested that they have not found their place on the level of specialised Committees yet. To that end, Sect. 5.5 suggests the extension of existing participation structures of other chapters to the Regulatory Cooperation one, also commenting upon their enhancement in order to better operationalise the purpose of these throughout legitimacy mechanisms.

The chapter concludes by discussing the legal means by which these proposals could be introduced in the EU legal order. Two options were identified. The first one, an inter-institutional agreement, was suggested as a second best solution, however mostly to regulate the participation of each Institution in the decision-making on Regulatory Cooperation matters, addressing thus mainly, the input legitimacy question. As an alternative, the thesis builds upon the idea of an EU trade act, by analysing the added value that it could bring, namely, on the one hand its ability to address the shortcomings deriving from the legal nature of an IIA, and on the other hand, its ability to regulate the proposals for throughput legitimacy as well.

References

Abazi V, Adriaensen J (2007) Allies in transparency? Parliamentary, judicial and administrative interplays in the EU's international negotiations. EU Inst Polit Secrecy Transparency Foreign Aff 5:75–86

Bartl M (2017) Regulatory convergence through the backdoor: TTIP's regulatory cooperation and the future of precaution in Europe. German Law J 18:969–992

Bartl M, Irion K (2017) The Japan, EU Economic Partnership Agreement: flows of personal data to the land of the rising sun. DaRE Project, University of Amsterdam. https://www.ivir.nl/publicaties/download/Transfer-of-personal-data-to-the-land-of-the-rising-sun-FINAL.pdf

Bieber R (1984) The settlement of institutional conflicts on the basis of Article 4 of the EEC Treaty. Common Mark Law Rev 21:505–523

Blumann C (2005) Article I-23- Le Conseil des Ministeres. In: Burgorgue-Larsen L, Levade A, Picod F (eds) Traité établissant une Constitution pour l'Europe: commentaire article par article. Bruylant, Belgium, pp 310–318

Blutman L (2010) In the trap of a legal metaphor: international soft law. Int Comp Law Q 59:605–624

Borchardt E (1944) Shall the executive agreement replace the Treaty? Yale Law J 53:664–683

Burdeau G (1981) Les Accords Conclus entre Autorités Administratives ou Organismes Public de Pays Différents. In: Mélanges offerts à Paul Reuter: le droit international, unité et diversité. A. Pedone Editions, Paris, pp 103–126

Chamon M, Demedts V (2017) The Commission back on the leash: no autonomy to sign non-binding agreements on behalf of the EU: Council v. Commission. Common Mark Law Rev 54:245–261

Chamon M, Demedts V (2019) Constitutional limits to the EU agencies' external relations. In: Hofmann H, Vos E, Chamon M (eds) The external dimension of EU agencies and bodies. Edward Elgar, Cheltenham, pp 12–33

Cottier T (2017) Front-loading trade policy-making in the European Union: towards a trade act. In: Bungenberg M, Krajewski M, Tams C, Terhechte J, Ziegler A (eds) European yearbook of international economic law 2017. Springer, Cham, pp 35–39

Council of the European Union (2013) Procedure to be followed for the conclusion by the EU of Memoranda of Understanding, Joint Statements and other texts containing policy commitments, with third countries and international organisations. https://data.consilium.europa.eu/doc/document/ST-5707-2013-INIT/en/pdf

Cremona M (2013) Expanding the internal market: an external regulatory policy for the EU. In: Vooren V, Blockmans W (eds) The EU's role in global governance. Oxford University Press, Oxford, pp 162–177

Curtin D, Leino P (2017) In search of transparency for EU law-making: trilogues on the cusp of dawn

Curtin D, Mendes J (2011) Transparence et Participation: Des Principes démocratiques pour l'administration de l'Union Européenne. Revue française d'administration publique 137/138: 101–121

Curtin D, Hoffmann H, Mendes J (2013) Constitutionalising EU executive rule-making procedures: a research agenda. Eur Law J 19:1–21

Dashwood A, Dougan M, Rodger B, Spaventa E, Wyatt D (2011) Wyatt and Dashwood's European Union law. Hart Publishing, Oxford

d'Aspremont J, de Brabandere E (2001) The complementary faces of legitimacy in international law: the legitimacy of origin and the legitimacy of exercise. Fordham Int Law J 34:190–235

de Sadeleer N (2001) Le Statut Juridique du Principe de Précaution du Droit Communautaire: Du Slogan à la Règle. Cahiers de droit européen 1:79–120

de Sadeleer N (2006) The precautionary principle in EC health and environmental law. Eur Law J 12:139–172

Dogan M (1992) Conceptions of legitimacy. In: Howkesworth M, Kogan M (eds) Encyclopedia of government and politics, vol 1. Routledge, London, pp 116–128

Dyzenhaus D, Hunt M, Taggart M (2001) The principle of legality in administrative law: internationalisation as constitutionalisation. Oxf Univ Commonwealth Law J 1:5–34

Edjaharian V (2013) Article 16 '[The Council]'. In: Blanke H, Mangiameli S (eds) The Treaty on the European Union: a commentary. Springer, Heidelberg, pp 645–680

Eeckhout P (2011) EU external relations law. Oxford University Press, Oxford

Eiselt I, Slominski P (2006) Sub-constitutional engineering: negotiation, content, and legal value of interinstitutional agreements in the EU. Eur Law J 12:209–225

EU Commission (1993) Communication from the Commission "An open and structured dialogue between the Commission and special interest groups". https://op.europa.eu/en/publication-detail/-/publication/a9e0a8b1-5fa4-42bb-a7d7-c77640d81f78/language-en

EU Commission (2000) Communication from the Commission on the precautionary principle. https://eur-lex.europa.eu/legal-content/EN/TXT/?uri=celex%3A52000DC0001

EU Commission (2001) Communication from the Commission of 25 July 2001 "European governance - A white paper". https://eur-lex.europa.eu/legal-content/EN/TXT/HTML/?uri=LEGISSUM:l10109&from=EN

EU Commission (2002) Communication from the Commission "Towards a reinforced culture of consultation and dialogue - General principles and minimum standards for consultation of interested parties by the Commission." https://ec.europa.eu/governance/docs/comm_standards_en.pdf

EU Commission (2017) Commission Staff Working Document: better regulation guidelines. https://www.europarl.europa.eu/RegData/docs_autres_institutions/commission_europeenne/swd/2017/0350/COM_SWD(2017)0350_EN.pdf

EU Commission (2018a) Call for proposals for Regulatory Cooperation activities in the Regulatory Cooperation Forum (RCF) under CETA. http://www.sice.oas.org/TPD/CAN_EU/Committees/CETA_RCF_Call_02_2018_e.pdf

EU Commission (2018b) Feedback and way forward on improving the implementation and enforcement of Trade and Sustainable Development Chapters in EU FTAs. https://trade.ec.europa.eu/doclib/docs/2018/february/tra

EU Commission (2020a) 2nd Meeting of the CETA Regulatory Cooperation Forum 3-4 February 2020, Ottawa and by videoconference. https://circabc.europa.eu/ui/group/09242a36-a438-40fd-a7af-fe32e36cbd0e/library/972e6f0e-5f4b-4be6-aed0-657a04720ba7/details. Accessed 27 Dec 2021

EU Commission (2020b) REPORT FROM THE COMMISSION TO THE EUROPEAN PARLIAMENT AND THE COUNCIL: evaluation of Regulation (EC) No 1107/2009 on the placing of plant protection products on the market and of Regulation (EC) No 396/2005 on maximum residue levels of pesticides. https://eur-lex.europa.eu/legal-content/EN/TXT/PDF/?uri=CELEX:52020DC0208&from=EN

EU Commission (2020c) Joint Report of the Comprehensive Economic and Trade Agreement (CETA) Meeting of the Civil Society Forum. https://trade.ec.europa.eu/doclib/docs/2020/march/tradoc_158679.pdf

EU Commission (2020d) CETA Regulatory Cooperation Forum of 3-4 February 2020, Stakeholder Debrief Meeting

EU Commission (2021) Better regulation guidelines. https://commission.europa.eu/system/files/2021-11/swd2021_305_en.pdf

European Economic and Social Committee (2019) The role of Domestic Advisory Groups in monitoring the implementation of FTAs. https://www.eesc.europa.eu/en/our-work/opinions-information-reports/opinions/role-domestic-advisory-groups-monitoring-implementation-free-trade-agreements

European Ombudsman (2016) Decision of the European Ombudsman setting out proposals following her strategic inquiry OI/8/2015/JAS concerning the transparency of Trilogues. https://www.ombudsman.europa.eu/en/decision/en/

European Parliament (2016a) Rules of procedure, 8th Parliamentary Term, September 2016. https://www.europarl.europa.eu/doceo/document/RULES-8-2016-09-15-ANN-20_EN.html?redirect

European Parliament (2016b) Activity report on Codecision and Conciliation 14 July 2009 – 30 June 2014, 7th Parliamentary term. https://www.europarl.europa.eu/cmsdata/198144/activity_report_2009_2014_en.pdf

Finkelstein L (1995) What is global governance. Glob Gov 1:367–372

Garcia Andrade P (2018) The role of the European Parliament in the adoption of non-legally binding agreements with third countries. In: Santos J, Sanchez-Tabernero S (eds) The democratisation of EU international relations through EU law. Routledge, Oxon, pp 115–131

Garcia Anrade P (2016) Who is in charge? The external representation of the EU on dialogues on immigration and asylum with third countries. EU Migration Blog. https://eumigrationlawblog.eu/who-is-in-charge-the-external-representation-of-the-eu-on-dialogues-on-immigration-and-asylum-with-third-countries/

Goldmann M (2006) A matter of perspective: global governance and the distinction between public and private authority (and not law). Glob Constitutionalism 5:48–84

Goldmann M (2010) Inside relative normativity: from sources to standard instruments for the exercise of international public authority. In: von Bogdandy A, Wolfrum R, von Bernstorff J, Dann P, Goldmann M (eds) The exercise of public authority by international institutions: advancing international institutional law. Springer, Heidelberg, pp 661–712

Gosalbo-Bono R, Naert F (2016) The reluctant (Lisbon) Treaty and its implementation in the practice of the Council. In: Eeckhout P, Lopez Escudero M (eds) The European Union's external action in times of crisis. Hart Publishing, Oxford, pp 13–84

Government of Canada (2018) First Meeting of the Committee on Regulatory Cooperation. https://www.international.gc.ca/trade-commerce/trade-agreements-accords-commerciaux/agr-acc/ceta-aecg/2018-12-14_rcf_report-rapport_fcr.aspx?lang=eng

Greven M (2007) Some considerations on participation in participatory governance. In: Kohler-Koch B, Rittberger B (eds) Debating the democratic legitimacy of the European Union. Rowan and Littlefield, Maryland, pp 233–248

Hamzeh F (1968) Agreements in simplified form - modern perspective. Br Yearb Int Law 43:179–189

Hillion C (2018) Conferral, cooperation and balance in the institutional framework of EU external action. In: Cremona M (ed) Structural principles in EU external relations law. Hart Publishing, Oxford, pp 117–174

Hummer W (2007) From "Interinstitutional Agreements" to "Interinstitutional Agencies/Offices"? Eur Law J 13:47–74

Kube V (2019) EU human rights, international investment law and participation. Springer, Cham

Lejeune Y (1984) Le Statut International des Collectivités Federées à la lumière de l'expérience suisse. LGDJ Thèses

Lenaerts K (2013) The principle of democracy in the case law of the CJEU. Int Comp Law Q 62:271–315

Lipson C (1991) Why are some international agreements informal? Int Organ 45:495–538

Manners I (2002) Normative power Europe: a contradiction in terms? J Common Mark Stud 40: 235–258

McNair A (1960) The law of the treaties. Oxford University Press, Oxford

Mendes J (2009) Participation and participation rights in EU law and governance. In: Hofmann H, Türk A (eds) Legal challenges in EU administrative law: towards an integrated administration. Edward Elgar, Cheltenham, pp 257–288

Mendes J (2011) Participation and the role of law after Lisbon: a legal view on Article 11 TEU. Common Mark Law Rev 48:1849–1877

Mendes J (2012) EU law and global regulatory regimes: hollowing out procedural standards? Int J Constitutional Law 10:988–1022

Mendes J (2016) Participation in a new regulatory paradigm: collaboration and constraint in TTIP's Regulatory Cooperation. IILJ working paper 2016/5 (MegaReg Series). https://www.iilj.org/publications/participation-in-a-new-regulatory-paradigm-collaboration-and-constraint-in-ttips-regulatory-cooperation/

Monar J (1994) Interinstitutional agreements: the phenomenon and its new dynamics after Maastricht. Common Mark Law Rev 31:693–719

Morrison F (2007) Executive agreements. In: Wolfrum R (ed) Max Planck Encyclopedia of Public International Law. https://opil.ouplaw.com/view/10.1093/law:epil/9780199231690/law-9780199231690-e1403

Nikolaides K, Schaffer G (2005) Transnational mutual recognition regimes: governance without global government. Law Contemp Probl 68:263–317

Noel E (1973) The Commission's power of initiative. Common Mark Law Rev 10:123–136

Oliver P, Martenczuk B (2018) The Commission. In: Schütze R, Tridimas T (eds) Oxford principles of European Union law, The European Union legal order, vol 1. Oxford University Press, Oxford, pp 549–580

Orbie J, Martens D, Oehri M, van den Putte L (2016a) Promoting sustainable development or legitimising free trade? Civil society mechanisms in EU trade agreements. Third World Thematics: A TWQ J 1:526–546

Orbie J, Martens D, van den Putte L (2016b) Civil society meetings in European Union trade agreements: features, purposes, and evaluation. CLEER papers 2016/3. https://www.asser.nl/media/3044/cleer16-3_web.pdf

Ott A (2020) Informalisation of EU bilateral instruments. Yearb Eur Law 39:569–601

Paul J (2001) Implementing Regulatory Cooperation through executive agreements and the problem of democratic accountability. In: Bermann G, Herdegen M, Lindseth P (eds) Transatlantic Regulatory Cooperation: legal problems and political aspects. Oxford University Press, Oxford, pp 385–403

Potjomkina D, Orbie J, Shahin J (2020) Forging their path in the Brussels bubble? Civil society resistance within the domestic advisory groups created under the EU trade agreements. Camb Rev Int Aff 36:352–371

Prechal S, de Leeuw M (2008) Transparency. In: Bernitz U, Nergelius J, Cardner C (eds) General principles of EC law. Kluwer, Alphen aan den Rijn, pp 201–242

Puntscher Riekmann S (2007) The cocoon of power: democratic implications of interinstitutional agreements. Eur Law J 13:4–19

Rasmussen A (2007) Challenging the Commission's right of initiative? Conditions for institutional change and stability. West Eur Polit 30:244–264

Reuter P (1985) Introduction au Droit des Traités. Graduate Institute Publications, Geneva

Rioux M, Deblock C, Wells G (2020) CETA, an innovative agreement with many unsettled trajectories. Open J Polit Sci 10:50–60

Rosas A (2017) Recent case law of the Court of Justice relating to Article 218 TFEU. In: Czuczai J, Naert F (eds) The EU as a global actor - bridging legal theory and practice: Liber Amicorum in Honour of Ricardo Gosalbo Bono. Brill, Leiden, pp 363–379

Röttger-Wirtz S (2021) The interplay of global standards and EU pharmaceutical regulation. Hart Publishing, Oxford

Rousseau C (1970) Droit International Public: Tome 1, Introduction et Sources. Éditions Sirey, Paris

Scharpf F (1970) Demokratietheorie zwischen Utopie und Anpassung. Universitätsverlag, Konstanz

Scharpf F (2003) Problem-solving effectiveness and democratic accountability in the EU. MPIfG working paper 03/1. http://apps.eui.eu/Personal/Researchers/pblokker/Week%206_Scharpf.pdf

Schmidt V (2006) Democracy in Europe. Oxford University Press, Oxford

Schmidt V (2013) Democracy and legitimacy in the European Union revisited: input, output and 'throughput'. Polit Stud 61:2–22

Seerden R (1992) The public international law character of trans frontier agreements between decentralized authorities. Leiden J Int Law 5:187–213

Spencer M (1970) Weber on legitimate norms and authority. Br J Sociol 21:123–134

Templeman S (1991) Treaty-making and the British Parliament. Chic-Kent Law Rev 67:459–484

Van der Mei AP (2016) EU external relations and internal inter-institutional conflicts: the battlefield of Article 218 TFEU. Maastricht J 23:1051–1076

Verellen T (2016) On conferral, institutional balance and non-binding international agreements: the Swiss MoU case. European papers. https://www.europeanpapers.eu/en/europeanforum/conferral-institutional-balance-and-non-binding-international-agreements

Vierdag E (1989) De Praktijk van de Zogenoemde Internationale Administratieve Akkoorden. Recht en Praktijk in het Verdragenrecht. Mededelingen van de Nederlandse Vereniging voor Internationaal Recht 99

von Bernstorff J (2010) Procedures of decision-making and the role of law in international organizations. In: von Bogdandy A, Wolfrum R, von Bernstorff J, Dann P, Goldmann M (eds) The exercise of public authority by international institutions: advancing international institutional law. Springer, Heidelberg, pp 777–806

von Bogdandy A, Dann P, Goldmann M (2008) Developing the publicness of public international law: towards a legal framework for global governance activities: an introduction: the project in a nutshell. German Law J 9:1375–1400

Waelbroeck M, Walbroeck D (1988) Les 'declarations communes' en tant qu'instruments d'un accroissement des compétences du Parlement européen. In: Louis J, Waelbroeck M (eds) Le Parlement européen dans l'évolution institutionelle. Editions de l'Université de Bruxelles, Bruxelles

Warin C, Zhekova Z (2017) The Joint Way Forward on migration issues between Afghanistan and the EU: EU external policy and the recourse to non-binding law. Camb Int Law J 6:143–158

Weiss W (2018) Delegation to treaty bodies in EU agreements: constitutional constraints and proposals for strengthening the European Parliament. Eur Constitutional Law Rev 14:532–566

Wessel R (2021) Normative transformations in EU external relations: the phenomenon of 'soft' international agreements. West Eur Polit 44:72–92

Westlake M (2017) Asymmetrical institutional responses to civil society clauses in EU international agreements: pragmatic flexibility or inadvertent inconsistency? Bruges political research papers 66/2017. https://www.coleurope.eu/sites/default/files/research-paper/wp66_westlake_0.pdf

Wildhaber L (1971) Treaty-making power and constitution: an international and comparative study. Helbing & Lichtenhahn, Duitsland

Wolf K (2006) Private actors and the legitimacy of governance beyond the state: conceptual outlines and empirical explorations. In: Benz A, Papadopoulos Y (eds) Governance and democracy: comparing national, European and international experiences. Routledge, Oxon, pp 200–228

Chapter 6
Conclusion

The thesis deals with the Chapters on Regulatory Cooperation in the newest FTAs and engages in the presentation and legal analysis of their content, legal nature and possible interaction in the EU legal order. As the Introduction (Chap. 1) of the thesis establishes, the Regulatory Cooperation Chapters as included in the so-called new generation FTAs were at the epicentre of the trade negotiations starting from TTIP, for two distinct reasons, namely the failure of advancement on such issues on the WTO level and the changing nature of the exigencies of contemporary trade relations, the liberalisation of which depends more on the behind- the-border regulatory barriers, rather than on the abolishment of tariffs. The stubbornness with which these trade nuisances have established themselves, has led to the extensive regulation of Regulatory Cooperation Chapters in the respective parts of the new generation FTAs, which however are separate from the advancement of TBT and SPS issues. Indeed, certain new generation FTAs go beyond that, in introducing Regulatory Cooperation on a more general basis, extending it thus to plethora of possible 'candidate' subjects. Accordingly, such a horizontal Regulatory Cooperation, in the forms it holds today, has gained academic interest, regarding its manifestation and application, as well as its application in the EU legal order. The thesis in particular provides answers to the legitimacy concerns that were raised by part of the legal scholarship, i.e. the threat that Regulatory Cooperation can present to the democratic accountability, the upholding of high standards and the regulatory sovereignty.

The thesis chooses to analyse the Regulatory Cooperation Chapters of the CETA and the EU-Japan EPA. The choice to focus on these two despite the plethora of FTAs and to limit the analysis only on the Regulatory Cooperation Chapters, thus leaving outside TBT and SPS, is done consciously, and relies on two reasons that substantiate the originality of the thesis. Firstly, the respective provisions on Regulatory Cooperation in CETA and EU-Japan EPA include the most advanced version of these commitments so far, in comparison to the other FTAs. Secondly, the choice to dedicate the thesis on this particular issue reflects its importance, its upcoming

K. Pipidi-Kalogirou, *Regulatory Cooperation Chapters in the new Generation FTAS*, EYIEL Monographs - Studies in European and International Economic Law 36, https://doi.org/10.1007/978-3-031-71900-4_6

potential but also its differentiations with the TBT and SPS Chapters. Indeed, based on the nature of these Chapters and the economic ties of the EU with the countries concerned, the thesis can be used to draw some parallels in case of inclusion of advanced Regulatory Cooperation Chapters in future FTAs with countries of similar ties and values. Hence, the thesis aspires to prove useful not only for the application of the existing Chapters so far, but also in indicating their future potential in FTAs beyond the ones under analysis.

The political circumstances, the negotiation standstill and the limited potential of legal provisions on WTO level that led to the existing trade landscape are further explained and analysed in Chap. 2. Such an analysis is not carried out for storytelling purposes. On the contrary, it serves a very specific purpose. It aims to highlight the reasons that guided this trade re-orientation. In other words, the thesis aims to support with facts what the Introduction had previously described as existing landscape. In that regard, it bestows upon the Regulatory Cooperation as described in the thesis the concept of 'characteristics'. Regulatory Cooperation as analysed through the relevant Chapters of the FTAs is bilateral and legalized. While the 'bilateral' part is self-explanatory, as in implicating two parts in the trade relation-ship, the reason behind the bilateral regulatory model is twofold. It follows, of course, the general trade strategy of the EU, which faced an unavoidable turn after multiple unsuccessful efforts on reviving the WTO negotiations' advancement. The lack of willingness to include modern disciplines to address regulatory barriers and to enhance Regulatory Cooperation was the main point of hesitance among partic-ipating states. More specifically, the existing rules on non-tariff barriers as enshrined in the WTO TBT and WTO SPS Agreements proved to bring limited results, especially because of the fact that they relied on outdated for the issue principles, such as the non-discrimination principle and certain rationality requirements. Given the above, the regulation of more intensive cooperation seemed more appropriate and manageable on a bilateral basis.

And while one might contend that certain Regulatory Cooperation efforts pre-existed the new FTA Chapters, the thesis uses this argument to refer to the second characteristic of the FTA Regulatory Cooperation, that of the inclusion in a legally binding treaty. It is true that especially on the transatlantic level (EU-US) various schemes tried to initiate Regulatory Cooperation activities between the two economies in pressing pending issues, either through the establishment of joint fora or the opening of thematic transatlantic parliamentary and industry dialogues. However, these schemes successively led to unsatisfactory results, especially because of the absence of enforcement and monitoring mechanisms. Indeed, the commitments only reached the political level; after that, however, they were of limited importance. The shortcomings in this area revealed the importance of the law, as an element that fosters compliance, even in the absence of enforcement mechanisms, solely through its normative importance. The thesis argues that the inclusion of the commitments as part of a legally binding treaty has now completed this legal gap.

Hence, a glance to the past explains the current framework, but also gives to the reader a holistic view of the events that preceded the current ones. The approach taken at Chap. 2 contributes in a twofold manner to the existing literature: Firstly, it combines the reading of existing events, namely of the general turn to bilateralism, the limited effects of the WTO structures and the failure of informal bilateral efforts, in order to explain the recent inclusion of Regulatory Cooperation Chapters in FTAs. In other words, it highlights further consequences of the otherwise well-known events. Secondly, the analysis uses the element of 'law' in order to provide explanations and make connections. While many studies that explain the turn to bilateralism consider the use and power of law less important than the course of political and historical events, this Chapter presents the normative power of law as equal, if not more important to that of events.

Building on that argumentation, Chap. 3 turns to analyse further the emerging Chapters on Regulatory Cooperation in order to demonstrate the changes observed in relation to the previous Regulatory Cooperation efforts and to reflect on the consequences of that turn. In order to capture the various aspects of the process, the thesis uses the concept of 'Legalization' as developed by leading scholars in the discipline of international relations. This approach applies this concept to Regulatory Cooperation and as such offers an interdisciplinary perspective to the analysis.

After the Regulatory Cooperation Chapters were introduced, various scholars doubted the normative value because of their soft language and absence of enforcement mechanisms. The application of the concept of 'Legalization' on the Regulatory Cooperation Chapters demonstrates the opposite. As a concept, Legalization relies upon three pillars, namely obligation, precision and delegation. In the analysis carried out in Chap. 3, these three anchors proved to be quite developed, thus pointing towards increased Legalization of the current regime.

Obligation refers to the legal value of the commitments. As far as it is concerned, the thesis relies upon doctrinal literature on hard and soft law in order to establish the difference between soft law and 'soft treaty law', namely legal obligations that are framed in less strict terms and that are not necessarily accompanied by an enforcement mechanism. This distinction is crucial, as upon it relies the normative nature of the provisions. Undoubtedly, talking about soft law for provisions enshrined in a legally treaty would be a legal paradox, which nevertheless needed to be disputed for the sake of legal completeness. Regarding precision, the provisions of the Chapters, especially of CETA proved to be quite developed, using clear languages and setting clear objectives, while precision in EU-Japan EPA proved to be quite limited in terms of the foreseen activities. As far as the element of delegation is concerned, this is viewed either as the presence of an adjudicating body or a decision-making body. Also here, the results were also quite different with respect to the two FTAs. Type A delegation, which indicates the presence of an adjudicating body was foreseen for Regulatory Cooperation in CETA, through the inclusion of Chapter 21 under the adjudicating capacity of the DSM; this was not the case for EU-Japan EPA, where Regulatory Cooperation was explicitly excluded from the respective mechanism on the basis of Article 18.19 EU-Japan EPA. However, in both Regulatory Cooperation Chapters, Type B delegation, namely the decision-making capacity of the bodies was absent. Indeed, a careful analysis of the provisions demonstrates that the specialised committees created for the purposes of the Chapters, as well as TBT and SPS specialised committees, do not enjoy a decision-making capacity for issues that fall under their scope; hence, they are deprived of the 'living' character that a secondary decision-making capacity bestows to an international agreement.

This exercise, apart from confirming the hypothesis made in Chap. 2 on the Legalization of Regulatory Cooperation through their inclusion in a treaty, serves also further objectives, aiming to complete the existing literature on the subject. Firstly, it confirms the legally binding nature of the provisions in doctrinal terms. Secondly, the description of the relevant commitments for the sake of precision allows exploring in detail of the Chapters and building a categorisation of commitments. Finally yet importantly, the analysis carried out for the element of delegation disproves with accuracy and explicit reference to the legal provisions of the treaties why decision-making in the specialised committees is absent, a statement that was employed quite frequently in various contributions. This observation paves the way to alternative forms of decision- making of those Chapters, with which the thesis engages extensively.

In that regard, Chap. 4 uses the available sources in order to map the regulatory priorities and explores the actions that have been taken in that regard. It looks for Regulatory Cooperation activities in the document repository of the EU Commission dedicated to the two FTAs under analysis. And indeed, it reaches the conclusion that until the time of the writing, the CETA Joint Structures are not used for regulatory making purposes per se, but rather as dialogue fora, that support the decision-making taking place autonomously elsewhere. Based on the available documents, it leads to the finding that Regulatory Cooperation is manifested through administrative rule-making but also through dialogue channels between the several services of the EU Commission with the Canadian administration.

Although the thesis actually followed the developments that took place each semester and the progress made on the CETA Regulatory Cooperation files, hence, it worked on the issues before they were crystallized, it is able to reach for the first time conclusions on the form of Regulatory Cooperation and its manifestation in the EU legal order. So far, the first manifestation mechanisms consists of autonomous administrative rule-making between the two administrations. Examples to this constitute the various Administrative Arrangements signed on the Mutual Recognition of the Compliance and Enforcement Programme regarding GMPS for Pharmaceutical Products and on the Exchange of Information on the Safety of Non-food Consumer Products. The second manifestation mechanism concerns the role of the regulatory dialogue in the internal rule-making process in general. The review of the legislation on Pesticides and of the Market Access Regulation showed that the channels that the Regulatory Cooperation Chapters have established and the commitment of the parties to keep them open can influence the course that an internal legislative revision may take. Although not written in paper as the Administrative Arrangements, regulatory dialogue also interacts and manifests its results in the EU legal order. For this reason, the thesis puts both manifestation mechanisms on an equal footing.

As mentioned, the research and demonstration of the manifestation mechanisms followed the developments the moment they took place. Hence, since it is up to date with the most relevant developments, it also gives a taste of what future activities might look like. However, by doing so the thesis does not suggest that the framework for their manifestation is neither clear nor legitimate. With the manifestation mechanisms only taking place in real time, and the Regulatory Cooperation being so active as it currently is, it was difficult to predict what would follow in order to frame the activities in a legitimate environment. Hence, the analysis of Chap. 4 was indispensable for the discussion of Chap. 5, which focuses, among others on the legal constitutional constraints that the EU legal order places on the said manifestation mechanisms.

Indeed, Chap. 5 aims to discuss the legitimacy of the said manifestation mechanisms by adopting a tripartite distinction of the notion, namely its categorisation as input, output and throughput legitimacy.

As far as input legitimacy is concerned, which refers to the question 'who is competent to take which decision, hence raising the question of the competent decision-maker for the Administrative Arrangements, the thesis proceeds with an analysis of the role of the EU Commission in international decision-making. While in principle the EU Commission does not have such a role for classic treaty making of Article 218 TFEU, the thesis relies upon emerging literature that analyses the rise of informal instruments concluded by the EU Commission in order to reach a conclusion on the scope of its autonomous decision-making, in both political and technical/administrative issues. In that regard, it proposes a clear framework that delineates the contours of the Commission's autonomous decision-making capacity on the basis of Article 335 par. 3 TFEU. Indeed, the latter remains quite limited, including either agreements that pertain to the Commission's operation or agreements that complement political commitments made elsewhere. Other types of agreements, such as ones that entail political choices, that interfere with fundamental rights, that implicate a transfer of regulatory authority or that may underpin legislative choices, fall out of the scope. On the basis of this categorisation it assesses the concrete Administrative Agreements. While it finds the Administrative Arrangement to be an implementing instrument mandated by the CETA Protocol on the mutual recognition of the compliance and enforcement programme regarding good manufacturing practices for pharmaceutical products, the conclusion is not as clear for the Administrative Arrangement on the exchange of information on non-consumer products.

On the basis of the above, ultimate aim of the section on input legitimacy is not only to comment upon the legality of adoption of the aforementioned Administrative Agreements by the EU Commission, but also to propose a delineation of the autonomous decision-making capacity of the EU Commission as such. Such an enumeration on the one hand sheds light upon the unclear area of autonomous decision-making of the EU Commission, recently discussed in the legal literature and on the other hand in practical terms serves as a benchmark to judge the legality of the autonomous decision-making of the EU Commission at hand, but also more generally.

Acknowledging the limited scope of the EU Commission's autonomous capacities, additional avenues to broaden the scope of the Commission's action through some alternatives to international decision-making are also proposed. The thesis proposes the use of non-binding political agreements as preparatory instruments to formal decision-making and the consideration to advance decision-making within the structures of the FTAs. Of course, the thesis acknowledges the limitations they pose, especially the requirements for extended institutional participation. These alternatives do not broaden the autonomous scope of action of the EU Commission, as they require the participation of the EU Council and the EU Parliament, but can elevate the role of the EU Commission in international negotiations and decision-making while respecting the institutional balance and delineation of institutional competences as defined by the Treaties. This inclusion hence proposes a revised use of existing practices, as is for example the use of political non-binding agreements, for which the Commission is not competent but which it can conclude with the participation of other actors.

Output legitimacy is used as a concept to map the quality of a result, in terms of its adherence to fundamental principles and values. In the EU legal order, the relevant policies must not only adhere to the common values of Article 2 TEU but also to sector-specific principles outlined in the respective Chapters of the TFEU. The thesis argues that these values and principles of constitutional value are to be upheld and not circumvented in the context of Regulatory Cooperation activities. In that respect, it examines the role of the Regulatory Cooperation dialogue in the revision of the pesticides legislation and concludes that the impact it presented was considerable, insofar the EU Commission decided to abstain from revising the legislation according to a reading that respects the precautionary principle. This study brings additional value to the existing literature, as it examines legitimacy from a different angle and sheds light upon a cooperation exercise that is more easily kept in the shadows in the absence of transparency mechanisms.

Regarding the last category of legitimacy, namely throughput legitimacy, while political science literature on the types of legitimacy usually discusses only the previous two types of legitimacy, the thesis on-boards the notion of throughput legitimacy as developed by a strand of the literature in order to discuss the presence or absence of procedural legitimacy requirements, which in the EU legal order form part of openness and participatory democracy. The analysis of the interactions between the EU Commission as part of the RCF and the civil society proved to be limited. In terms of transparency, the limited publishing activity was found to bring limited information to the civil society, while Access to Documents requests for RCF documents were treated and interpreted in a restrictive manner. In terms of participation, the reach-out to civil society remained also limited in the absence of concrete participation structures. The decision to add this additional legitimacy dimension is innovative as much as it is relevant. Indeed, by mentioning the shortcomings in terms of procedural legitimacy, this part complements the considerations on output legitimacy by explaining how, in the absence of proper transparency and participation mechanisms, possible output legitimacy threats could stay unnoticed. The thesis proposes the expansion of Domestic Advisory Groups to the Regulatory Cooperation Chapters, present already for other Chapters in the FTAs as a possible solution to remedy this gap. Of course, this comes with many caveats, as this institution needs enhancement and strict regulatory requirements.

Hence, the categorisation of legitimacy and the examination of each specific angle under this Chapter offers a new perspective in the study of the phenomenon of Regulatory Cooperation. First of all, the part on input legitimacy proposes a framework of the decision-making capacity of the EU Commission that can be used for the future assessment of legitimacy of Regulatory Cooperation activities carried out by the latter. Secondly, the output legitimacy part brings to the attention of the reader aspects of legitimacy which could go otherwise unnoticed since they do not take place in the context of Regulatory Cooperation Fora, as for example the input to internal revision procedures of the legislation. Thirdly, the part on throughput legitimacy highlights an important part of the idea of EU democracy and proposes solutions in order to include it in the Regulatory Cooperation activities. Lastly, it proposes the inclusion of these frameworks to either an IIA or a legislative instrument to enhance the visibility of the legitimacy considerations so that they can be part of the assessment of the EU Institutions during the Regulatory Cooperation.

Overall, the findings of the thesis give answers to the legal constitutional considerations raised by scholars during the early days of the inclusion of Regulatory Cooperation in FTAs. Input legitimacy confirmed that democratic accountability can be threatened insofar the EU Commission acts outside the scope of its mandate, assumes decision-making for which it lacks competence and disturbs as such the institutional balance. Output legitimacy demonstrated that the race to the bottom and the threat to the regulatory sovereignty during the various stages of a legislative cycle and beyond can occur, while they should be contained. Throughput legitimacy highlighted the absence of openness of the procedure, lacking both transparency and balanced participation of stakeholders. Hence, the journey to which the thesis embarked proved to be of direct relevance to the existing literature, which it supplemented accordingly.

Most importantly, these findings of the thesis are of direct relevance to the ever changing landscape of EU action in trade, with a recent addition being the EU-UK Trade and Cooperation Agreement. Not surprisingly, the agreement includes specific provisions on Regulatory Cooperation from Articles 340 and onwards, very similar to the ones included in the FTAs under analysis. Indeed, it encompasses commitments on regulatory coherence as well as envisaging the possibility for Regulatory Cooperation to be initiated, to be coordinated and supervised by the Trade Committee on Regulatory Cooperation. Indeed, the implementation of this Chapter in the specific agreement does present a particular interest, given the former membership of the UK in the EU, which entailed regulatory harmonisation to the greatest extent. It is exactly because of this, that more intense forms of Regulatory Cooperation are more likely to take place in this bilateral trade relation. The regulatory approximation which nevertheless remains, can act as a facilitating actor in that regard. Here, the findings in Chap. 5 that consider legitimised potential Regulatory Cooperation through forms of approximation also in issues beyond mere technicalities could be of direct application.

Beyond the relevance of the findings to the FTAs that include joint structures on Regulatory Cooperation as such, the thesis works upon the creation of new avenues for secondary law-making in the EU external relations and brainstorms on how different regulatory outcomes can fit in legal tools and under which conditions. This of course applies to several other joint structures with eventual aim to engage in joint decision-making. A simple look in the new generation FTA provisions confirms the plethora of such structures, the mandates of some might even mention joint decision-making explicitly. Hence, the results are transferrable and can be applied by analogy to any given subject.

Most importantly, however, the legal puzzle that lied in the heart of the thesis pinpoints to a pressing issue in the constitutional literature of EU External Relations, which is exactly the absence of legal tools to encompass the variety of regulatory relations of the EU in its external action. This respectively has resulted in legal inventions, such as the creation of a myriad tools of soft nature to be employed when necessary. These solutions, while always welcomed in the spirit of the advancement of EU law, can nevertheless endanger the rule of law themselves. By hiding in the shadows, outside the normative frameworks of the Treaties, it is not the advancement of law that is promoted, but rather its disregard. On the light of the above, the update of the available options for the EU external action is more than necessary. In the end, the law is, to a certain extent, a dynamic element. It sets the foundations, but should always follow the needs of reality, and accommodate it to its fundamental values and norms.

Printed by Printforce, the Netherlands